Elizabeth Cady Stanton, Feminist as Thinker

Elizabeth Cady Stanton, Feminist as Thinker

A Reader in Documents and Essays

EDITED BY

*Ellen Carol DuBois and
Richard Cándida Smith*

New York University Press

NEW YORK AND LONDON

NEW YORK UNIVERSITY PRESS
New York and London
www.nyupress.org

Library of Congress Cataloging-in-Publication Data
Elizabeth Cady Stanton, feminist as thinker : a reader in
documents and essays / edited by Ellen Carol DuBois and
Richard Cándida Smith.
p.   cm.
Includes bibliographical references and index.
ISBN-13: 978-0-8147-1981-7 (cloth : alk. paper)
ISBN-10: 0-8147-1981-3 (cloth : alk. paper)
ISBN-13: 978-0-8147-1982-4 (pbk. : alk. paper)
ISBN-10: 0-8147-1982-1 (pbk. : alk. paper)
1. Stanton, Elizabeth Cady, 1815–1902. 2. Suffragists—United States—
Biography. 3. Feminists—United States—Biography. 4. Women's rights—
United States—History—19th century. I. DuBois, Ellen Carol, 1947–
II. Cándida Smith, Richard.
HQ1413.S67E55 2007
305.42092—dc22
[B]
2006035505

New York University Press books are printed on acid-free paper,
and their binding materials are chosen for strength and durability.

Manufactured in the United States of America
c 10 9 8 7 6 5 4 3 2 1
p 10 9 8 7 6 5 4 3 2 1

Contents

Acknowledgments

The editors' collaboration on this project began at the University of Michigan, where the Program in American Culture sponsored a course on The Thought of Elizabeth Cady Stanton that we taught together in the fall of 1999. We brought the idea for a conference honoring the centennial of Stanton's death to Robert Ritchie, Director of Research at the Huntington Library, San Marino, California. Ritchie responded with the personal and intellectual enthusiasm and generosity that everyone who has worked with him knows. The Huntington Library organized and sponsored the May 2002 conference, "The Social Theory of Elizabeth Cady Stanton: Exploring the Roots of U.S. Feminist Intellectual History," with additional support from the Center for the Study of Women at UCLA. Our great thanks to the Huntington Library and its staff, especially Ritchie and Carolyn Powell, whose efficiency and good cheer made it a real joy for us to be co-organizers of this conference. Scholars in addition to those represented in this volume made important contributions to the conference. Carroll Smith Rosenberg, University of Michigan, Rosalyn Terborg-Penn, Morgan State University, and Fusako Ogato of Tezukayama University presented illuminating papers that contributed substantially to the conference. Joyce Appleby, Brenda Stevenson, Carole Pateman, all of UCLA, and Richard Wightman Fox, of the University of Southern California, chaired sessions and offered insightful commentary. The great success of the conference encouraged us to take the next step and we presented a proposal for the present volume to Eric Zinner of New York University Press who responded with whole hearted enthusiasm. In the three years which it has taken us to revise and edit the volume, we had considerable help from Ellen Broidy, of the UCLA Young Research Library, without whose expert assistance we would have taken even longer. Help also came from the staff of the Regional Oral History Office at UC Berkeley.

We want to thank Coline Jenkins Sahlin, Stanton's great-granddaughter, for reaching into the family's treasure of Stanton photographs and providing the illustrations for this volume's cover.

Finally, we dedicate this volume to the memory of our common friend, the late, dear Eric Monkkonen, who brought us together for this project and with whom we were fortunate enough to share the good news that we had pulled it off.

Introduction

Ellen Carol DuBois and Richard Cándida Smith

Although Elizabeth Cady Stanton (1815–1902) was a prolific writer who produced far-ranging explorations of the political, social, historical, and religious dimensions of women's subordinate status, little of her writing has been easily available. She is an important figure in the development of intellectual life in the United States but known today for only a handful of pieces, most prominently "The Declaration of Sentiments" drafted for the 1848 Seneca Falls women's rights convention and her 1892 address, "Solitude of Self."[1] Historians of women's rights have concentrated on Stanton's role as activist and agitator in the earliest woman's suffrage organizations,[2] but her lifelong contributions as a movement leader are at times overshadowed by those of Susan B. Anthony, her more politically disciplined partner. Even though much of Stanton's writing pointed toward subsequent feminist theories of social and personal development, her place in either U.S. or feminist intellectual history remains largely unexplored.[3] This volume is intended to remedy this problem by drawing attention to Stanton's contribution as an original thinker with insights— and contradictions—relevant for contemporary feminism. It combines a selection of Stanton's diverse writings with analytical essays by contemporary scholars taking a variety of perspectives on her important and understudied oeuvre.

The editorial collaboration underlying this book brings together two sets of historical expertise. From the perspective of U.S. intellectual history, this volume seeks to place Stanton more prominently in the framework of nineteenth-century liberal political theory, with particular attention to the role that her concerns with women's condition played in the emergence of modern conceptions of social organization. Stanton's half-century struggle to understand the factors holding back the development of female self-sovereignty challenges us to rethink the relationship of nineteenth-century feminism and liberalism. Instead of seeing liberalism as an overarching, autonomous ideology that imprinted itself on the nine-teenth-century women's rights movement, we find it more useful to treat it as a dynamic set of ideas developing over time, as all sorts of people played an active, creative role, prominent among them Elizabeth Cady Stanton struggling with the problem of women's place in modern society.

At the same time, from the perspective of the history of feminist thought, this volume explores the importance of Stanton for intellectual genealogies of Anglo-American feminism. Systematic analysis of Stanton's numerous and complex writings on women's condition have not yet risen to the level paid to figures such as Catharine Beecher, Margaret Fuller, Charlotte Perkins Gilman, and Jane Addams.[4] On the broader historical stage, we seek to demonstrate that Stanton's body of writing deserves a place alongside Mary Wollstonecraft's passionate *A Vindication of the Rights of Woman* (1792) and John Stuart Mill's Olympian *The Subjection of Women* (1867) as documents essential for the intellectual history of fem-inism. The fact that Stanton did not produce an equivalent single sus-tained work on the status of women appears to pose an obstacle to such a project, but it also provides an opportunity. One of her strengths as a thinker was her refusal to write another set of formalized but vague ab-stractions of the type so prevalent during the nineteenth century. Stan-ton's restraint was especially admirable given that so little was known in her time of the social and psychological conditions of women's lives.

Instead, Stanton's insights grew out of a lifelong project to define and correct the problems women faced. Her numerous articles, speeches, and pamphlets most typically emerged as responses to immediate situations or as contributions to campaigns for an immediate goal. Stanton's engage-ment with the real-life issues of her day offers the opportunity to see a mind continuously rethinking the problem of women's subordination across a wide variety of situations. The specific issues that inspired her to take up her pen are today often obscure, but they kept pushing Stanton forward to understand why women fared so poorly from liberal, demo-cratic revolutions. In her acceptance of progress as an inherent feature of modern life, Stanton might have accepted liberal ideas as she inherited them but for her persistent question: Why was it that the social condition of women had grown relatively worse even as the material gains of mod-ern society became more evident. In her search for answers to this ques-tion, certain themes remain consistent. Three institutions lay at the center of her analysis of the sources of women's continuing inferior status: citizenship, marriage, and religion. Over the long period of her career, her emphasis shifted back and forth across the structures of gender inequality these institutions created and enforced, as did her understanding of the methods needed to undo women's inferiority.

She understood from the start of her career as a women's rights advocate that the status of women was a product of laws serving the privileged to the detriment of the weak. Because the law was human made, she knew it could be changed through dedication and the exercise of free will. After the Civil War, she increasingly embraced the notion of progress as an impersonal process that emerged from social dynamics rather than from the exercise of individual free will. She accepted the idea that societies were governed not only by formal legal codes but by natural laws that reformers had to understand before they could secure full democratic rights. Change beneath and beyond legal reform drew her attention.

The overlay of positivist conceptions of natural law on top of her still strong belief in individual rights led Stanton increasingly to foreground "woman" as a distinct subject who had to become an autonomous voice within modern society. She moved from an emphasis on the alikeness of the sexes to a focus on their differences. We wish to emphasize, however, that Stanton never embraced a thoroughly essentialist view of women's potential, though she accepted on a commonsense basis that women's reproductive functions gave them a distinctive vantage point from which they viewed every political and social question. To the degree that she remained a natural-rights liberal, however, she understood gender difference as historically situated and flowing out of the legal and customary limits put on women's freedom of action rather than as the unalterable condition of female life. Remove social restrictions, she believed, and women would explore as many paths to personhood as did men. Through all of this, she continued to insist that the emancipation of woman had to be first and foremost a political movement that demanded the full integration of women into the governance of the nation. From that difficult but simple change, other, more profound transformations would occur in every aspect of personal and collective life.

After the Civil War, as Stanton focused on the gendered foundation of social difference, her sensitivity to other forms of social inequality, particularly racial, waned. Embittered by the failure of constitutional change to include women's rights, she employed with increasing frequency crude stereotypes of African Americans and immigrants to express her outrage that she, a cultured, educated woman, would still be denied the vote while men she considered her social and intellectual inferiors were enshrined in the Constitution as her legitimate political masters. With what she called "an aristocracy of sex" incorporated into the highest law of the land by the postwar constitutional amendments, the government of the United States, she insisted, had moved away from the republican ideal for which so many had died.

Given her clear commitment to revolutionary republicanism, how to understand Stanton's use of racial stereotypes, particularly during her campaign to challenge the exclusion of women's rights from the Reconstruction amendments, has provoked considerable debate among contemporary feminists. She readily shifted between expansive statements about equal rights for all citizens to brutal dramatizations of the plight of native-born white American women that belittled black and immigrant men. Why did she fail to see beyond her personal limitations or remain apparently so disinterested in the lives of black, poor, and immigrant women who faced much greater restrictions on what they could do than women of her class? Her contradictory positions might be related to her parents having been wealthy slave owners, a painful truth that she never fully confronted and, indeed, as Kathi Kern has argued, concealed in her memoirs. She was, in several senses of the word, a daughter of the American Revolution whose personal contradictions reflected the young republic's difficulty in deciding what groups of people were fully entitled to "liberty and justice for all."

The problem posed by Stanton's racism leads to a broader set of questions concerning the limitations built into the liberal, individualist feminism of which she is such a fine exemplar: Is the assertion of every woman's fundamental right to individual agency the sine qua non of the feminist project, or does such a privileging of individualism inevitably reinscribe privilege and social hierarchy among women? Can we historically contextualize the racism evident in Stanton's work in order to clarify the conditions that have limited the ability of all groups to secure recognition of their rights to equal protection under the law and equal participation in the life of the nation? How can recognition of the racism marking almost all early white feminists contribute to refounding a contemporary multiracial alliance for women's rights? These questions are not easily answered, but each of the essays in this volume explores how Stanton's career and thought illuminates issues of vital importance for contemporary feminists.

In the end, it is difficult to separate Stanton's understandings of racial and cultural difference and inequality from her conceptions of democracy precisely because the commitment to democracy is not a state of personal grace that descends on each person as she or he joins the struggle to make society truly just. Democratic faith is necessarily flawed, indeed imbued with the very inequalities against which it protests. It grows from a desire for change that addresses the conflicts inherent to each person's place in society. It is one's own deficiencies, one's own failings, one's own sometimes invidious discontents, rooted in a deep connection to a society that is profoundly unjust, that makes an individual see the imperative for change.

The degree to which Stanton held to ideas of racial difference and inequality shows how one radical thinker was held back by the very structures of thought and feeling that stimulated her to reject the conventional ideas of her time in the first place. In the gap between her rejection of and her insistent participation in American society is the space where her most provocative ideas formed, important precisely because they emerged out of the conflict of having to work with the ideas that were ready at hand but were not truly capable of supporting her quest for self-sovereignty. But to what other ideas did she have access for thinking about the contradictions of her life except those available to her living in a society where the patriarchal institutions she opposed secured the limited but real privileges she enjoyed?

The Essays

The first section of the book consists of eight interpretive essays grouped into four pairs. The essays aim to situate Stanton within her own historical context while assessing what she has bequeathed to the modern feminist imagination. We begin with the contributions of Vivian Gornick and Christine Stansell. They provide contrasting overviews of Stanton's legacy for contemporary feminism. Gornick finds Stanton a powerful inspiration for women who claim the right to think, speak, and argue an opinion. As such, Gornick contends, Stanton provides the foundation for a genuine, lasting individuality among women. Whether Stanton was right or wrong on specific issues is of less importance than her having been a woman engaged in the life of the mind.

By contrast, Stansell sees Stanton as a leader who permanently weakened the U.S. women's rights movement by breaking the ties that had allowed black and white women to work together. Stansell proposes the lifelong antiracist Sarah Grimké as an alternative founding figure for American feminism. Both essays are provocative in the broadness of their claims. Together, they set out the terms of a basic debate over how to assess Stanton and the liberal roots of feminism in the United States.

The essays by Barbara Caine and Richard Cándida Smith place Stanton in the major Anglo-American intellectual currents of her day. Caine juxtaposes Stanton's writings against John Stuart Mill's world-famous tract on women's rights, *The Subjection of Women* (1867), the single most influential nineteenth-century book defining the contours of liberal feminist thought. Comparing Stanton with Mill, Caine finds Stanton the more satisfying successor to their eighteenth-century predecessor, Mary Wollstonecraft. Stanton acknowledged Mill's influence, but went beyond his arguments to explore the complexities of women's existence. She insisted on the multiple fronts along which the campaign for expanded freedom of action for women had to proceed.

Moving to the last decade of the nineteenth century, Richard Cándida Smith's essay interprets Stanton's single most famous piece of writing, "Solitude of Self" (1892), in the context of emergent ideas about the self. "Solitude of Self" is properly understood as a manifesto for the recognition and cultivation of female individuality. Nevertheless, Cándida Smith demonstrates that Stanton assumes that a community of robust dialogue and collective inquiry is required for the cultivation of strong individuals. Influenced by ideas ranging from transcendentalism to positivism, she pointedly challenged the authority of theological institutions to define or limit women's spiritual experience.

The essays by Ellen Carol DuBois and Kathi Kern focus on Stanton's analysis of the institutional anchors of women's subordination. DuBois concentrates on Stanton's examination of marriage in the decade before the Civil War. Stanton crafted her critique of women's conjugal subordination by combining elements of the temperance and socialist traditions. The contradiction built into liberal feminism, between regarding women as individuals entitled to full, equal rights and as members of a social class with distinct interests, was already evident in her earliest sustained efforts to delineate a feminist approach to marriage reform.

After the Civil War, Stanton shifted her attention to religion as the institutional mainstay of women's subordination, and this is the subject of Kathi Kern's paper. Kern examines Stanton's controversial critique of Christian misogyny in terms of a growing interest in free thought and positivism. Stanton's positions remain interesting because, unlike many nineteenth-century utopians, she did not simply reject marriage and religion as inescapably oppressive institutions. After demonstrating how marriage and Christianity limited women, Stanton proposed strategies for reorganizing these institutions so they might foster and expand women's capacities.

Finally, Ann D. Gordon's and Michelle Mitchell's chapters consider how Stanton's adherence to then-current ideas of inherent racial difference interacted with her strong democratic and natural rights commitments. Gordon demonstrates that Stanton's positions on race were fluid and contradictory. Speeches and essays containing demeaning racial and ethnic stereotypes also include passages defending the vote as a right of genuinely universal citizenship. Gordon shows that Stanton never abandoned her commitment to universal citizenship rights.

Nonetheless, Michele Mitchell documents the clear influence that scientific racism exercised on Stanton after the Civil War. Stanton's racializing comments were not simply momentary lapses uttered in the heat of rough-and-tumble argument. The racial science to which she subscribed was part of her faith in modernity and scientific rationality even though it was at war with the egalitarian republican values that originally motivated her. These two essays suggest how deeply intertwined Stanton's racism was with the sturdy republicanism of her politics and the questioning modern tenor of her mind. This synthesis of egalitarian and hierarchical perspectives goes a long way to explaining why Stanton's racism, even if shared with most other educated white Americans of her time, is particularly disturbing to contemporary students of the history of feminism.[5]

The Documents

The second section in the book presents some of Stanton's most important writing on the subordination and emancipation of women. They are organized to show major developments over a half-century of writing in her analysis of the sources of woman's oppression and of possibilities for emancipation.

As a young woman, Stanton had read widely in her father's law library and discussed cases with him. Selections 1 through 3 make clear that her legal training allowed Stanton to bring to the early women's rights movement a keen sense of the role of law in creating inequality between the sexes. In the initial selection, her first major speech, presented in 1854 to the New York state legislature, Stanton argued that laws depriving women of the right to control their own property or income tutored men that women lacked authority to define their own needs. In the second selection, Stanton's analysis of contract and property law extended her earlier argument that law shaped everyday life to explain why marriage within U.S. legal principles resulted inevitably in female subordination. The third selection, a speech from 1860 on divorce, is a particularly fine analysis of interaction of state and family, in which she justifies full female participation in governance on the grounds that even the most intimate of personal relationships are shaped by law.

The antislavery movement fundamentally shaped the understanding Stanton had as a young woman of American law as a system for producing inequality. Like slaves, the wives and daughters of free male citizens were dispossessed of property and without control over the product of their own labor. Like slaves, they were legally subordinate to a patriarchal master whose absolute power corrupted him. Yet, as evident in her 1860 speech delivered just as Southern secessionists prepared to plunge the nation into civil war, Stanton's dedication to women's emancipation was her primary allegiance. She argued, even at that moment, that the prejudice against sex is more deeply rooted than that against color because only a minority of men directly profited from their control of slave labor, while the great majority of them exercised control over their wives' bodies and earnings.

Stanton welcomed the Civil War as a chance to complete the unfinished republican revolution of 1776. She hoped that a Union victory would sweep away the most powerful and entrenched opposition to the emancipation and enfranchisement of all Americans, especially including African Americans and women. But the promise of national Reconstruction began to give way earlier for women's rights advocates than for other radical reformers. By 1870 the Fourteenth and Fifteenth Amendments to the Constitution were ratified, and not only were women's demands for recognition of their citizenship rights ignored, but the exclusion of women from the national electorate was now made explicit in the new language added to the Constitution.

Nonetheless, into the 1870s the temporary reinvigoration of republican thought in the wake of emancipation continued to find expression in many of Stanton's speeches on behalf of political rights for women. She enthusiastically embraced the constitutional and philosophical argument that the natural, inherent rights of all citizens embraced the right to vote. She took the position that the federal constitution required no further modification to sustain voting rights regardless of sex. As Susan B. Anthony and other suffragists put this theory, known as the "new departure," to the test by presenting themselves at polling places as fully enfranchised citizens, Stanton turned her pen to elaborating a radical natural rights argument for woman suffrage.[6] At this point, however, Stanton embraced, indeed celebrated, the power of the national state. Reversing many of the precepts of classical liberalism, Stanton argued in "National Protection for National Citizens" (1877) that the federal government was the essential guarantor of equal rights for all, regardless of race or gender.

For Stanton the failure of post–Civil War politics to secure a full democracy meant that the revolutionary phase of American life had come to an end. Privilege, custom, and habit had prevailed over the logic of ideals. Universal personhood faded as a practical goal, though the ideal continued to motivate her. Political emancipation for women would be a longer, harder battle than she had expected, but it was clear to her that any battle for democracy had to center firmly on the status of women.

In the aftermath of Reconstruction, Stanton explored new theoretical frameworks that helped her grapple with the contradictions of woman's position in modern life. Surely the family was the foundation of collective life, and even more certainly woman was the anchor of the family. Why then did liberal society with its rhetoric of universal self-sovereignty make it so difficult for women to resist their status as dependents of the families built around them? Darwin's theories, positivism, free thought, socialism, anthropology, and higher biblical criticism all provided raw material for her ongoing effort to explain why women's status remained so stubbornly degraded.

She wrestled with these difficult questions in essays that are stunning for their wide variety of starting points. In "The Subjection of Women" (1875), Stanton located the opposition of her contemporaries to women's rights in a historical context extending back from English common law to the ancient Hebrews and Greeks. In claiming their rights, women would have to redeem humanity's religious and civil legacies by stripping away overlays that Stanton considered vile superstition. Feminists would develop an alternative historical interpretation that supported modern demands for justice and equality. Stanton expressed in clear terms a conclusion that grew in importance as she aged: transforming women's status required transforming religion, law and education all at the same time.

She understood that feminists had to be vigilant to prevent modern science as well from being made into a tool serving the enemies of women's rights. In "The Other Side of the Woman Question" (1879), Stanton intervened in the debates over evolutionary theory among well-known male scientists and physicians such as Edward H. Clarke of Harvard University that natural and sexual selection led to women being both intellectually and physically inferior to men. [7] She inverted their use of Darwin so that she could suggest that continued inequality between the sexes would eventually weaken the republic and endanger the future of the human race. In an argument redolent with eugenic overtones, Stanton saw that legislated inequality threatened the species by biologically "selecting" for female weakness, a position pointing forward to the more fully Darwinian argument that Charlotte Perkins Gilman made in 1898 in her book *Women and Economics.*[8]

In these and other writings, Stanton had come to understand that emancipation was not a single moment but an extended process of reform occurring simultaneously in the personal, the civic, and the legal realms. She regarded legal reform as essential for women to be able to discover their capabilities, but as still only one step in a much bigger struggle. Her focus had shifted from recognizing the inherent, natural rights of all women and men to creating a society that actively fostered individuality for all, an argument that found its most eloquent expression in "Solitude of Self," the farewell address she delivered when she retired from the presidency of the National American Woman Suffrage Association in 1892. In "Solitude of Self," Stanton proposed to women that they must never surrender the truth they learned from sharing experience, and this has remained a fundamental postulate of feminism throughout the twentieth century.[9]

In addition to constituting a mature restatement of the political philosophy that had led her to press for women's civil and political rights, Stanton's defense of individual rights has a powerful personal dimension: her sober confrontation with her own mortality. She was seventy-six years old, still vibrant intellectually, but facing the increasing physical limitations of old age, By the last decade of her life, Stanton had lost the cheery optimism of her early writings. She recognized that every aspect of human society assumed the subordination of women. The process of unraveling millennia of gender inequality involved every aspect of women's lives. Every time a woman decides to do something new, she changes the institutions within which she lives, as she encounters and challenges the resistance built into their very warp and woof to the idea that all humans are equal.

As Stanton surveyed the forces holding back the development of women's potential, she insisted with new conviction that Christianity was the most insidious and powerful foe of women's emancipation and as such of the republic. Her frank opinions on American religion made Stanton a scandalous figure during the last decade of her life. Even the woman suffrage organization she had founded officially condemned her because she sought to alert women to the damage that the nation's religious traditions/beliefs did to them. As examples of her writing on the role of religion in repressing women's self-sovereignty, we include "Has Christianity Benefited Woman?" (1885), "Worship of God in Man" (1893), and selections from *The Woman's Bible* that present her radical rereading of Genesis (1895) as well as an interpretation of the parable of the wise and foolish virgins in the Gospel according to Matthew. Her critique of religion became bolder in part because of what she was learning from new anthropological research on ancient societies. Her short article "The Matriarchate, or Mother-Age" (1891) reveals Stanton's effort to understand the contemporary implications of theories that patriarchy was a relatively recent historical phenomenon that had violently overthrown an earlier era of woman-rule.[10]

In the 1890s, Stanton confronted the development of a women's movement that was growing large and powerful but yet diverged in many essentials from her vision of human freedom. What she had proclaimed in 1848 at Seneca Falls was not a movement for votes for women but for self-sovereignty. The final selections from Stanton's writing reflect this difficult evaluation of a movement that was at once fifty years old yet only just beginning. "Divorce versus Domestic Warfare" (1890), "Significance and History of the Ballot" (1898), "Progress of the American Woman" (1900), and "Degradation of Disenfranchisement" (1901) recapitulate long-standing themes in variations that incorporate Stanton's newfound appreciation for the long battle that remains before all women can take for granted their rights to make the basic choices affecting their life, liberty, and happiness.

We hope that the issues raised by the analytical essays and primary documents in this collection help to make clear that the dilemmas Stanton confronted are inherent to any struggle to define democracy in the United States. To grasp the complexity and variety of her thought, Stanton's insights and contradictions need to be understood in their specific historical context precisely because her effort to develop a critical understanding of women's subordination reveal the conflicts within the American thrust toward expanded democracy and social reform. Stanton articulated with clarity the desperate longing to be included fully in a world where equality has been an inspiring notion but not yet the firm basis for how people of different backgrounds, talents, and perspectives live together.

NOTES

1. We have not included either "The Declaration of Sentiments" or "Solitude of Self" in the selection of documents included in this volume because of space limitations. These important works can be easily located on the Web at the site for *Not for Ourselves Alone: The Story of Elizabeth Cady Stanton and Susan B. Anthony* (PBS–WETA), http://www.pbs.org/stantonanthony/resources/index.html?body= resources.html, http://www.pbs.org/stantonanthony/resources/index.html?body= solitude_self.html. See also Web site for Gifts of Speech, http://gos.sbc.edu/s/ stantoncady4.html and http://gos.sbc.edu/s/stantoncady1.html; the Women's History Web site, http://womenshistory.about.com/library/misc/blsolitudeself.htm; or the site for Votes for Women, Selections from the National American Woman Suffrage Association Collection, 1848–1921 (Library of Congress: American Memory, Historical Collections for the National Digital Library), http://lcweb2.10c.gov/ cgi-bin/query/D?nawbib:2:./temp/~ammem_5zgO::. The most complete source of Stanton's writings remains *The Papers of Elizabeth Cady Stanton* (Washington: Library of Congress, 1979), for which a guide has been prepared by Patricia G. Holland and Ann D. Gordon, eds. (Wilmington: Scholarly Resources, 1992); for the most comprehensive selection of Stanton's most important writings on all subjects, see Ann D. Gordon, ed., *The Selected Papers of Elizabeth Cady Stanton and Susan B. Anthony* (New Brunswick: Rutgers University Press, 1997–2006), four volumes published, and more planned. See also Ellen Carol DuBois, ed., *The Elizabeth Cady Stanton–Susan B. Anthony Reader: Correspondence, Writings, Speeches* (Boston: Northeastern University Press, 1992); Stanton's *Eighty Years and More: Reminiscences, 1815–1897*, republished with an introduction by Ellen Carol DuBois by Northeastern University Press in 1993, and *The Woman's Bible*, reprinted in 1988 by Ayer Press and in 1999 by Prometheus Books.

2. See Lois W. Banner, *Elizabeth Cady Stanton: A Radical for Women's Rights* (Boston: Little, Brown, 1980); Elisabeth Griffith, *In Her Own Right: The Life of Elizabeth Cady Stanton* (New York: Oxford University Press, 1984).

3. Recent books that have addressed aspects of Stanton's contribution to intellectual life include Mary Beth Waggenspack, *The Search for Self-Sovereignty: The Oratory of Elizabeth Cady Stanton* (New York: Greenwood Press, 1989); Mary D. Pellauer, *Toward a Tradition of Feminist Theology: The Religious Social Thought of*

Elizabeth Cady Stanton, Susan B. Anthony, and Anna Howard Shaw (Brooklyn: Carlson, 1991); Kathi Kern, *Mrs. Stanton's Bible* (Ithaca, N.Y.: Cornell University Press, 2001); Judith Wellman, *The Road to Seneca Falls: Elizabeth Cady Stanton and the First Woman's Rights Convention* (Urbana: University of Illinois Press, 2004).

4. See Kathryn Kish Sklar, *Catharine Beecher: A Study in American Domesticity* (New Haven: Yale University Press, 1973); Dolores Hayden, *Catharine Beecher and the Politics of Housework* (New York: Whitney Library of Design, 1977); Jeanne Boydston, *The Limits of Sisterhood: The Beecher Sisters on Women's Rights and Woman's Sphere* (Chapel Hill: University of North Carolina Press, 1988); Nicole Toncovich, *Domesticity with a Difference: The Nonfiction of Catharine Beecher, Sarah J. Hale, Fanny Fern, and Margaret Fuller* (Jackson: University of Mississippi Press, 1997); Barbara Anne White, *The Beecher Sisters* (New Haven: Yale University Press, 2003); David Watson, *Margaret Fuller: An American Romantic* (New York: St. Martin's Press, 1988); Charles Capper, *Margaret Fuller: An American Romantic Life* (New York: Oxford University Press, 1992); Fritz Fleischmann, ed., *Margaret Fuller's Cultural Critique: Her Age and Legacy* (New York: Peter Lang, 2000); Belle Gale Chevigny, ed., *Margaret Fuller's Life and Writings: The Woman and the Myth* (Boston: Northeastern University Press, 1994, revised edition); Jean Bethke Elshtain, *Jane Addams and the Dream of American Democracy: A Life* (New York: Basic Books, 2002); Louise Knight, *Citizen: Jane Addams and the Struggle for Democracy* (Chicago: University of Chicago Press, 2005); Victoria Bissell Brown, *The Education of Jane Addams* (Philadelphia: University of Pennsylvania Press, 2003); Ann J. Lane, *To Herland and Beyond: The Life and Work of Charlotte Perkins Gilman* (Charlottesville: University Press of Virginia, 1990); Louise Michele Newman, *White Women's Rights: The Racial Origins of Feminism in the United States* (New York: Oxford University Press, 1999); Gail Bederman, *Manliness and Civilization: A Cultural History of Gender and Race in the United States, 1880–1917* (Chicago: University of Chicago Press, 1996).

5. "My Stanton, Myself," Kathi Kern, Berkshire Conference on the History of Women, Storrs, Connecticut, June 2002.

6. For more on the new departure, see Ellen DuBois, "Taking the Law into Our Own Hands: Women's Direct Action Voting in the 1870s," in *Visible Women: New Essays on American Activism*, ed. Nancy Hewitt and Suzanne Lebsock (Champaign: University of Illinois Press, 1994).

7. Edward H. Clarke was a prominent professor of medicine at Harvard University who in 1873 published his book *Sex in Education; or, A Fair Chance for the Girls*. Long known for his advocacy of equal rights, Clarke stunned the women's rights movement when he reversed course to argue that scientific evidence had demonstrated that intellectual stimulation was harmful to young women. As a trustee of Harvard College, he voted against opening the school to female students. For a discussion of Clarke's argument and the challenge it posed to nineteenth-century feminists, see Michele Mitchell's chapter in this volume; Rosalind

Rosenberg, *Beyond Separate Spheres: Intellectual Roots of Modern Feminism* (New Haven: Yale University Press, 1982), 1–27; Louise Michele Newman, *White Women's Rights: The Racial Origins of Feminism in the United States* (Oxford: Oxford University Press, 1999), 86–106.

8. See Charlotte Perkins Stetson (later Gilman), *Women and Economics: A Study of the Economic Relation between Men and Women as a Factor in Social Evolution* (Boston: Small, Maynard, 1899).

9. The argument in "Solitude of Self" seems to look forward to existentialism, but its language and argument clearly reflect the classically Lockean and Scottish Common Sense philosophies that Stanton learned in her youth. The only thing I know for certain, Locke had insisted, is my own existence and the immediate sensations I experience. Stanton added to these simple sense impressions her own experience of both discrimination and inequality. Stanton claimed for her own individual experience a higher standard of truth than the assertions of male experts that women were necessarily, inherently, inescapably, empirically men's inferiors.

10. In 1861, Johann Jakob Bachofen's *Das Mutterrecht* (The Matriarchy) argued that the vestiges of matrilineal descent found in aspects of Greek, Roman, and Near Eastern culture were evidence of a lost matriarchal stage, in which women had ruled society. His conclusions were supported by Henry Sumner Maine's *Ancient Law* (also published in 1861), Fustel de Coulanges' *The Ancient City* (1864), John Ferguson McLennan's *Primitive Marriage* (1865), and the American Lewis Henry Morgan's *Systems of Consanguinity and Affinity of the Human Family* (1871) and *Ancient Society* (1877). All these scholars argued that matriarchy had been a phase of simple democracy and communal ownership of property. With the subjugation of women came the establishment of military-based monarchies, private property, and the enslavement of conquered peoples. More recent scholarship on nineteenth-century theories of an earlier matriarchal stage in social development can be found in Cynthia Eller, *The Myth of Matriarchal Prehistory* (Boston: Beacon Press, 2000); Matriarchy Study Group, *Politics of Matriarchy* (London: The Group, 1979); Philippe Borgeaud, *La Mythologie du matriarcat: L'Atelier de Johann Jakob Bachofen* (Geneva: Droz, 1999); Deborah Gewertz, ed., *Myths of Matriarchy Reconsidered* (Sydney: University of Sydney Press, 1988).

Part I

The Essays

Chapter 1

Elizabeth Cady Stanton, the Long View

Vivian Gornick

Elizabeth Stanton once wrote of Susan Anthony: "In ancient Greece she would have been a Stoic; in the era of the Reformation, a Calvinist; in King Charles' time, a Puritan; but in this nineteenth century, by the very laws of her being, she is a Reformer." ·

"And you?" I remember thinking when I read these words. "What about you? Is that how you are to be summed up? As an essence of an Age of Reform?"

Just to ask the question was to hear it answered. The description was insufficient. If anything, it made her reader (this reader, at least) more aware than ever of the difference between Stanton and her great comrade-in-arms; between Stanton and the mass of vibrant, eloquent women who stood shoulder to shoulder with her, if it came to that.

Elizabeth Cady Stanton is the American visionary thinker equal in intellectual stature to the two feminist greats who preceded and followed her: Mary Wollstonecraft and Simone de Beauvoir. Like them, she had the philosophic cast of mind large enough to see the thing whole, to grasp with radical speed the immensity that women's rights addressed. Each of these women—Wollstonecraft, Beauvoir, Stanton—had been an ardent partisan of a powerful social movement connected with a great war (the Enlightenment, the antislavery movement, existentialism) and the contribution that each made to feminist understanding turned, appropriately enough, on an application of the central insight of the movement to which she had been devoted. Wollstonecraft urged passionately that women become rational beings; Stanton that every woman exercise governance over her own inviolable self; Beauvoir that women cease to be "other" (that is, become the central actor in their own lives).

Stanton differed from the other two in that each of them wrote a single famous-making book at white heat in a comparatively short time—*Vindication of the Rights of Women* over a period of a few weeks, *The Second Sex* over a few years—while she, Stanton, lived within the embrace of feminist thought for half a century, thinking the matter out decade by decade, provocation by provocation, through a series of speeches, letters, and essays that demonstrate an ever deepening, ever more encompassing worldview. Had she written "the book," we would be reading her today instead of John Stuart Mill on the subjection of women. As it is, she left political life with a final public address—"Solitude of Self"—written by a woman possessed of a vital piece of understanding tempered by fifty years of political struggle that had made what she knew cast long shadows back to Plato, forward to the moderns. Hers was the American contribution, and it makes clear why feminism as a liberation movement has flourished here as nowhere else in the Western world.

She was the brilliant relative of brilliant people—daughter of a distinguished jurist, cousin and wife to abolitionists of reputation. As a girl she had read law in her father's office and had as many thoughts as his students on the nature of political liberty. As a young woman she was a constant visitor to her cousin Gerrit Smith's home—a stop on the Underground Railway—and took part in the impassioned conversation going on there. Then, she and her husband went to the 1840 antislavery meeting in England, but the conference refused to seat her: a meeting called in the name of equality for all would not seat women. Henry Stanton was disturbed, but not that disturbed: he took his place in the hall; William Lloyd Garrison, on the other hand, would not. The great zealot had crossed an ocean to appear at this convention—all within were waiting for the words of the famous American—but his politics ran deep and true. Garrison meant it when he said equality for all. If the women couldn't speak, neither would he. Elizabeth was twenty-five, not long married. Lucretia Mott —patient, intelligent, twenty years older, also not seated at the conference —walked her around London and explained the reality of the larger world in which she lived, the one that she had until now not actually experienced. With all the thinking Elizabeth had done about slavery, liberty, and the American idea, it had never dawned on her until this moment: when the democracy was conceived, *she* was not what was had in mind.

She never got over that flash of plain sight. It was a stunning moment of conversion—the moment when she realized that in the eyes of the world she was not what she was in her own eyes; she was "only a woman." In her writing, the memory of it returns repeatedly to galvanize mind and spirit. One can almost see her picking up the pen to make the moment live again. And each time she puts it down there is Susan Anthony nodding at her side; and always, behind Anthony, a few hundred more. In this country we have produced no one in feminist thought who surpasses Stanton, but many who are grouped around her. Wollstonecraft and Beauvoir could not say the same. They wrote their books and then, in their own countries, the response among their countrywomen—while often painfully acute— remained insufficient. But in 1848 Elizabeth Stanton called a meeting, made a speech, and nineteenth-century American feminism was launched.

It's the promise of the democracy outraged that is working in her, flaring as brightly at the end as at the beginning. That is what makes her important. Behind that enduring slow burn lies the whole strength of American liberationist movements. It's what makes them American.

I remember once, in the early 1970s, deep into feminist protest myself —with the democracy continuously on my mind—walking down the street in New York and, to my surprise, found myself suddenly thinking, "Hey, here I am, making my bid for my part of the body politic." And for the first time in my life I, the daughter of Russian-Jewish immigrants, was feeling American. It was the idea of making the bid that had done it. This, it now occurred to me, is what the populists must have felt a hundred years ago, farmers out on the Nebraska plain suddenly realizing that they'd have to fight for what they'd grown up thinking was theirs by right of birth; it was *this* that had put iron in their souls. It flashed on me then that, in that moment, when they had understood that they'd have to *take possession* of those famous inalienable rights, that the populists had actually become Americans. I thought this because that is what *I* was now feeling. Feminism was making me an American. I went home, and started reading Elizabeth Cady Stanton all over again.

That unyielding sense of outrage—the one that's experienced when one realizes the democracy is being withheld by virtue of class, race, or sex —is serious in this country, serious and lasting. It is responsible for the great civil rights movements of our time. Certainly, it is responsible for the fact that modern feminism has repeatedly taken root here and not elsewhere, even though its intellectual beginnings can be traced to the work of brilliant Europeans. Much as the Europeans burned over their second-class status, it was impossible for them—from Wollstonecraft to Beauvoir —to give up their longing for inclusion in the world as men had made it: too lonely a prospect. This longing—immense in its power to compel— bound them to a dividedness of will that was politically crippling. The

Americans, on the other hand, staring into democratic inequality, hardened their hearts against the romantic pull of the world as it is, and eroticized feminism: they could do it, they had enough company. Women's rights—in the name of Republic with a capital R—became their single-minded passion. This made them undivided in their pursuit of equality, and incomparably more revolutionary.

Elizabeth Stanton's life encompasses all of these influences and equations. In her is gathered an essence of Americanism informing this particular movement. She is fiercely concentrated on the denial of what is promised her by right of birth—not birth into the world, birth into the American democracy. That concentration is the poetry of her political existence: it multiplies her insight, deepens her thought, clarifies her spirit. It infuses everything she wrote and said for the fifty years between Seneca Falls and death.

Her temperament was extreme: simple actually, but extreme. To all who ever knew her, the self-confidence was extraordinary. She might have taken Flaubert's dictum "Dress like a bourgeois, think like a revolutionary" for her motto. She always observed the social amenities—good manners and proper dress—but nothing could make her temper her thought. While her personality was vivid, fun loving, and cheerful, it was also caustic, headlong, and autocratic. She hardly ever spoke before she thought, but she *always* spoke without consultation or strategic consideration. Beneath the grandmotherly image that overwhelmed her body in early middle age and lasted throughout her long years, was a strong-willed, high-tempered young woman who faced all comers until she was eighty-five with her hands on her hips, her head tilted back, and her eyes narrowed skeptically against the boring, the stupid, the uneducated.

Her intellectual independence was seen by many as high-handedness: it broke party ranks, alienated radicals and reformers alike, and drove Lucy Stone wild—as well as Garrison, Abby and Stephen Foster, Wendell Phillips, and countless others whose good will she could have used. But what she needed was to speak truth, as she saw it, at any given moment. This is what she *needed*. She needed it more than she needed the approval of family or steady comradeship or even political success. The need often made her recklessly insensitive.

In her memoir she tells of how after she'd written her obituary of Lucretia Mott, she received a letter from a man who accused her of using an anecdote of his without attribution. "I laughed him to scorn," she writes, "that he should have thought it was my duty to have done so. I told him plainly that he belonged to a class of citizens who had robbed me of all civil and political rights . . . and now it ill became him to call me to account for using one of his little anecdotes that, ten to one, he had cribbed from some woman. I told him that I considered his whole class as fair game for literary pilfering. That women had been taxed to build colleges to educate men, and if we could pick up a literary crumb that had fallen from their feasts, we surely had a right to it. . . . Moreover, I told him that . . . he should feel highly complimented, instead of complaining, that he had written something I thought worth using." .

In Nebraska in 1875, out on the circuit, she is baited by a man in the audience: "My wife has presented me with eight beautiful children," he announces. "Is not this a better life work than that of exercising the right of suffrage?" Stanton looks him up and down and says, "I have met few men worth repeating eight times."

On a Sunday afternoon—also in the 1870s—sitting in a railroad hotel, she writes to her daughter Margaret, who has written to ask if it's not lonely traveling as she does, "It is indeed, and I should have enjoyed above all things having Hattie with me." Sensitive mother! Hattie is Margaret's sister Harriot, Stanton's favorite child.

When all New York was buzzing with the Beecher-Tilton scandal in 1872 (the most famous preacher in America stood accused of sleeping with a married parishioner), Susan Anthony, the soul of rectitude who knew all the principals intimately, would speak not a word on the subject. Stanton, on the other hand, ran around town, both talking and writing freely on the case, advocating divorce in hot, sweeping terms, thereby prompting a woman in Chicago to write in the *Tribune:* "Of course, Mrs. Stanton has a right to her opinions, but I question her prerogative to load the Woman Suffrage Movement with the[ir] dead weight. . . . Any right-minded person who can believe that the enfranchisement of woman would bring such philosophy as Mrs. Stanton teaches . . . into popular favor, must pray and labor to prevent that catastrophe."

Even Wendell Phillips, that lifelong friend of women's rights, was appalled. In a letter to Susan Anthony, Stanton reveals that he has berated her publicly for her views on divorce, and she responds hotly, "With all his excellence and nobility Wendell Phillips is a man. His words, tone, and manner came down on me like a clap of thunder. We are right, however. My reason, my experience, my soul proclaims it."

She had a sharp tongue—ironic, mocking, challenging—and her brains were unrelenting. She was not as loved as Susan Anthony because she was feared intellectually—and her voice must often have not sounded "loving." I think, in fact, that she got more and more on people's nerves as time went by.

"To many thoughtful people," she wrote years later, "it seemed captious and unreasonable for women to complain of injustice in this free land, amidst such universal rejoicings. When the majority of women are seemingly happy, it is natural to suppose that the discontent of the minority is the result of their unfortunate individual idiosyncrasies. . . . But the history of the world shows that the vast majority, in every generation, passively accept the conditions into which they are born, while those who demand larger liberties are ever a small, ostracized minority, whose claims are ridiculed and ignored. . . . That a majority of the women of the U.S. accept, without protest, the disabilities which grow out of their disenfranchisement is simply an evidence of their ignorance and cowardice, while the minority who demand a higher political status clearly prove their superior intelligence and wisdom."

It galled her—as it has many others after her—that the majority of women in her country did not see clearly on the matter of their own rights, and this grievance held her attention year after year after year.

In 1848 at Seneca Falls, New York, she wrote: "Resolved, that the women of this country ought to be enlightened in regard to the laws under which they live, that they may no longer publish their degradation, by declaring themselves satisfied with their present position, nor their ignorance, by asserting that they have all the rights they want."

In 1855 she wrote: "Go watch the daily life of fortune's most favored woman. . . . Who that has mingled with this class, is ignorant of the senseless round, the utter vacuity of such an existence. The woman who has no fixed purpose in her life is like a traveler at the depot, waiting hour after hour for the cars to come in—listless, uneasy, expectant—with this difference, the traveler has a definite object to look for, whereas the woman is simply waiting for something to 'turn up.' . . . She may write books, but they are popular only so far as they echo back man's thunder, hence our literary women instead of dealing stout blows . . . are all trimming their sails to the popular breeze. . . . Had [they] 'all the rights they want,' we should have better books from them on subjects which they understand and feel most deeply."

In 1867: "Sometimes when I sit alone, and all the bearings of this question [of suffrage] loom up before me, I am filled with wonder at the apathy and indifference of our women. . . . When [they] come to see that ideas as well as babies need the mother soul for their growth and perfection, that there is sex in mind and spirit, as well as body, they will appreciate the necessity of a full recognition of womanhood in every department of life."

What is amazing is how *fast* her mind went to work once she had something serious to think about.

In 1841, just home from England, Stanton writes a letter to Elizabeth Neall (there must have been a thousand Elizabeths, every other correspondent is a Lizzie) filled, typically—and this for years on end—with what amounts to chitchat and gossip. She and Henry are undecided as to what they'll do or where they'll live; they're going to Peterboro in the morning; cousin Gerrit is making a match between Mr. Birney and Nancy's sister, Elizabeth Fitzhue; she spent two weeks in New York but didn't see Angelina Grimké because she was "on the eve of her confinement" but got a letter from her assuring her that her views on the woman question are *un*changed and *un*changeable; and "Oh Lizzy what a voyage we had from Liverpool to Boston, head winds & storms all the time."

In 1849, practically the day after Seneca Falls—and this is just an extract from a very long letter—she writes briskly to Mary Anne Johnson (an early feminist comrade):

> Dear Mary Anne, How rejoiced I am to hear that the women of Ohio have called a Convention preparatory to the remodeling of their State Constitution. . . . It is important now that a change is proposed that [women] speak, and loudly too. Having decided to petition for a redress of grievances, the question is *for what shall you first petition?* For the exercise of your right to the elective franchise—nothing short of this. The grant to you of this right will secure all others, and the granting of every other right, whilst this is denied, is a mockery. For instance: What is the right to property, without the right to protect it? The enjoyment of that right today is no security that it will be continued tomorrow, so long as it is granted to us as a favor, and not claimed by us as a right. . . . Depend upon it, this is the point to attack, the stronghold of the fortress—*the one* woman will find most difficult to take —*the one* man will most reluctantly give up.

And *this* letter went on for forty years.

Stanton had discovered that the exercise of her intelligence was what most compelled her. The passion for women's rights was the catalyst, but in the end it was the use of her own mind that was the driving force.

Absorbed as she was by every new thing that ever came her way, for the first years of marriage she was taken up by the business of making a home, and having babies. A supremely healthy animal—and in this she gloried—by her own account, she gave birth like a peasant in the field: labor would begin, she'd push out the baby, clean herself up, and be up and about in twenty-four hours. In the end, she had seven of them, and she was most tenderhearted toward the little creatures who had come out of her body. Raising them up to be human beings set her a problem that she embraced wholeheartedly for quite a long time. Then, suddenly, she'd had it. "I now fully understood" she wrote, looking back on this time, "the practical difficulties most women had to contend with in the isolated household and the impossibility of woman's development if in contact, the chief part of her life, with servants and children." For years she cared assiduously for her children. But, then, while her affections remained strong, they also became absent-minded. The children quickly became people, most of whom did not hold her real interest, nor could they take center stage on the field of a mental landscape that required continual stimulus to fill itself in.

Then there was husband Henry, who had, after all, turned out not to be a soulmate. As Lois Banner discreetly puts it in her Stanton biography: "He did not interfere in her reform activities, no small gesture from a man of his era. . . . Yet there were tensions all during these years. [Before the war] he was a spokesman for political antislavery; [whereas] she became a Garrisonian. [After the war] he supported the Republican stand on Reconstruction, while she mounted a campaign against the antifeminist 14th and 15th Amendments. [Then] he supported Horace Greeley [while she came to] loathe Horace Greeley." The connection remained amiable. She once wrote that she and Henry continued to laugh together and to enjoy reading the morning paper together throughout their shared life—but I think it is safe to say that fifteen years into the forty that they more or less spent together, the marriage no longer engaged her. As Emerson wrote in 1840, the very year the Stantons were married, "*Do you love me?* means at last *Do you see the same truth I see?* If you do, we are happy together; but when presently one of us passes into the perception of a new truth, we are divorced and the force of all nature cannot hold us to each other." In time, I think, the conflict bored her.

But most important was her open break with men like Garrison and Gerrit Smith. It must have been wrenching to break with them, as the antislavery movement had been a huge part of her life. But when the abolitionists made clear after the Civil War that they would support only the bid for manhood, not universal suffrage, her heart, along with that of many others, raged with grief and betrayal. Everyone was disappointed, everyone suffered; yet for some feminists—people like Lucy Stone, Angelina Grimké, Abby Foster—it was unbearable to go against the men beside whom they had labored so long in service to the Great Cause. For Stanton, however, it meant checking her brains at the door, an act against which she narrowed her rebel's eyes and hardened her feminist heart. Either we all go through the door, she said, or no one goes through the door.

She spoke and she wrote fully, freely, directly, without tact or political caution, engrossed only by where the argument was going, where her thought would come out. She did this because life on the intellectual barricades was, for her, the only real exhilaration. Yes, family was delicious, and politics were exciting. But it was only when she was thinking—on her feet or on paper—that she felt clarified: brave, generous, unequivocal, alive, and whole. She knew this about herself, she'd always known it, from the first moment, in 1848, when her husband had said, "You ask for suffrage, and I'm leaving town," and Lucretia Mott had said, "Lizzie, thou wilt make us ridiculous"—and neither of them could make a dent in her. Once the idea of suffrage had occurred and she'd seen it in all its brilliant, dazzling rightness, nothing and no one could make her back down. To go forward *into* her thought was her only compulsion. *This* was where she now lived. This is what harnessed the resentment over inequality, made ever more penetrating the question that women's rights had raised of what it actually means to be a human being; this was what made her arrive finally at definitions of independence that would speak intimately to all women alive more than a century later, even though it spoke to only a fraction of those alive in her own time.

Irving Howe once wrote of Emerson what could have been written of Stanton—that what distinguished him from the hordes of reformers around him was that he understood instinctively the division then alive inside most Americans over religious faith—and his work helped them move to where they wanted to go: into "an enlightened commonality of vision justifying pride in the republic." Stanton, too, articulated a profound inner conflict alive in society. But for Emerson, to name the thing was to receive immediate and universal acclaim; for Stanton, of course, it was otherwise.

At eighty she wrote:

> I was always courageous in saying what I saw to be true, for the simple rea-
> son that I never dreamed of opposition. What seemed to me true I thought
> must be equally plain to all other rational beings. Hence I had no dread of
> denunciation. I was only surprised when I encountered it, and no number
> of experiences have, as yet, taught me to fear public opinion. What I said on
> divorce thirty-seven years ago seems quite in line with what many say now.
> The trouble was not in what I said, but that I said it too soon, and before
> the people were ready to hear it. It may be, however, that I helped them to
> get ready: who knows?

Here we have the very definition of a radical: the one who sees clearly just a little in advance of what others will see tomorrow—and will give no quarter on what she sees. It's the giving no quarter that makes Stanton what she is. Imagine speaking as she did during abolition, when to do so was to become a social pariah not in the eyes of her conservative family but in the eyes of her radical comrades. Everyone she knew and cared for —men and women who had worked their guts out for years, risking death and imprisonment, loss of status, and the comfort of respectable society— were saying, "Not now. This is the Negro's hour. Your turn will come next." And she looked at them, eyes and words blazing, and replied, "No. It's now or never." We are where we are today because for her it was always "Now or never."

Which leads us to her famous racism. Namely, that in a number of places, both publicly and privately, she used the word "Sambo" when referring to blacks. In particular, when she realized that the Fourteenth Amendment was going to give black men the vote but not women, she wrote, in a rage, that she couldn't believe that Sambo was going to walk through the door before her.

In her own time, the radicals were scandalized that Stanton would not give on "this is the Negro's hour," but no one really held her accountable for the epithet, as none of them held themselves responsible for all the epithets then commonly in use. The zealots of the nineteenth century were willing to give their lives for the democratic principle of equality, but they thought nothing of the casual vilification inherent in "ignorant Irish," "Chinese heathen," "those of the Hebrew persuasion." These references are shocking to contemporary ears because we have moved past such crudities but, in fact, it would not be difficult to catalogue the many ways in which

Emerson's plea to "treat all people as if they are real, because who knows, perhaps they are" still applies. Regardless of whatever social progress is made, it is remarkably easy, in every age, to see the resistance to according full, unstinting reality to all those "not like ourselves." This incapacity is endemic—in "us" as well as in "them"—historic and endemic.

That black hole of human failure is the bitterness of all our lives. The sheer, breathtaking void of the soul that is experienced when you wake up one day to realize that you yourself are not as real to the people with whom you live as they are to themselves. That moment feels profoundly humanizing, but, as it turns out, it has only opened a can of worms. We do not wake up to such a realization as saints, we wake up as wounded animals. The awakening does not humanize us—on the contrary, more often than not, "they" are more "they" than ever; it is, actually, only the beginning of a long, painfully slow process of self-rehabilitation. As Chekhov so memorably put it, "Others made me a slave, but I must squeeze the slave out of myself, drop by drop."

The unreality of those not like ourselves is *the* great, often dismissed or unacknowledged, presence in American history. And it has been from the very beginning. The founders of the Republic are remarkable for this, and this only: they *declared* equality before the law a natural right of all; but most of them never really grasped what that extraordinary sentiment required to become operative. They had, in fact, a tiger by the tail. The declaration could not legislate out of the legislators themselves the psychological need to believe otherwise. At one and the same time, they could sustain "equality for all" *and* the unpuzzled conviction that blacks, women, and Native Americans are, by nature, children who neither need nor want political freedom, much less equality. Deep within ourselves, regardless of the universal passion for equality, some psychological hierarchy of value persists in preventing us from truly seeing ourselves in all others. It was this terrible contradiction that drove William Lloyd Garrison to cry out recklessly that the Constitution was a compact with the devil, an agreement made in hell. Yet, the abolitionists themselves—including Garrison—were unwilling to go the whole length on behalf of women's rights, and radical feminists like Stanton could not contain their own bias when it came to suffrage. Emancipation for the blacks was one thing, but suffrage was another. It wasn't that she didn't want blacks to have the vote—not at all; she wanted everyone to have the vote—but the thought that *they,* ignorant black men, would get it while she did *not* filled Stanton's head with blood; and the ingrained emotional prejudice that resists color or sex blindness kicked in. If we live long enough—as Stanton did, and as we ourselves are doing—we come to understand how persistent a human necessity it is: to *not* let go of the unreality of a class of beings other than ourselves.

It was Garrison above all others who was the radical of Elizabeth Stanton's radical heart. It was through him that she learned who she was. She never forgot that he had refused to take his seat at the 1840 antislavery meeting in London because women weren't being seated. It wasn't so much that he was a partisan of her cause as that he had taken a principled position. This action of his spoke deeply to her, showed her that politics, properly experienced, should reach right down to the center of a human being.

Garrison's evangelical zeal either thrilled or repelled. Stanton was thrilled. As she grew into herself and discovered that it was always the principled position that made her think better, made her remember where she was, why she was, who she was, she saw that it was Garrison who was ever her model. As he stood up and said anywhere, everywhere, without a thought to strategy, "Better the world should perish than that slavery should continue another day," so she too came to think it better to stand up and demand suffrage, divorce, an end to church influence *now, right now,* than to consider the strategic consequence.

In the early 1850s she tried temperance reform in order to join her new friend, Susan Anthony, in political work, but very quickly found the association distasteful, and the experience taught her one of the great lessons of her political life. In a letter to Anthony, she cautions her to not let the conservative element in temperance take control. "For instance," she writes, "you must take Mrs. Bloomer's suggestions with great caution, for she has not the spirit of the true reformer. . . . [S]he will not speak against the Fugitive Slave Law, nor . . . will she criticize the equivocal position of the Church. She trusts to numbers to build up a cause rather than to principles, to the truth and the right. Fatal error!"

And in later years, remembering these times, she concluded: "A multitude of timid, undeveloped men and women, afraid of priests and politicians are a hindrance rather than a help in any reform." She had learned from Garrison, who had forced national recognition of the need to end slavery with, as she said, a "thoroughly sifted" group of "picked men and women."

The key to antislavery lay in changing public consciousness, and so it was to be with women's rights. Only when the shared sensibility of the nation changed would the internal self-description of what it was to be a woman or a man change. And only then would women and men recognize and understand that all people need to be living under the same fundamental conditions in order to feel themselves free and equal beings. To make this point, one had to take the visionary high road. If negotiation, accommodation, amelioration were words not in Elizabeth Stanton's vocabulary, it was because she honestly believed that only by sticking to the clear, simple, moral definition of what a human being needed to feel human could the cause of women's rights be won.

The Civil War was, of course—as it was for all sorts of Americans—her philosophic watershed. Like many radicals—abolitionists, utopians, republicans with a small *r*—she, too, could see that the war had released into the open air social issues that were as profound as such issues would ever be. What was at stake here was not just slavery, but the whole question of the American idea of building a world free of inherited privilege and inherited disadvantage. She (a daughter of the Revolution, as she said repeatedly) saw this war in the most elemental of terms. Now, at last, America could begin to make the reality square with its own ideal. The insight made her burn, as Garrison had burned, with the same evangelical zeal. "This," she said, "is our opportunity to retrieve the errors of the past"—the *errors* of the past—and "build a true republic. . . . This war is music in my ears . . . every nation that has ever fought for liberty on her own soil is now represented in our army." Then she announced recklessly that she'd be proud to have her sons die for the cause that was so dear to her heart.

Like many other radicals, she thought Lincoln a detriment rather than a partisan—a deal maker, a negotiator with the enemy, a politician through and through—and she worked to unseat him from the presidency. Late in life, she wrote, "I see now the wisdom of his course. . . . My conscience pricks me when I recall how I worked and prayed in 1864 for the defeat of [his] re-election."

But at the time she could do no other. Her devotion was to individuation, not to the preservation of nationhood, and, as always, she called the shot as she saw it. One afternoon in January 1892, in a packed convention hall in Washington, D.C., the seventy-six-year-old Elizabeth Stanton rose from her seat to address the annual meeting of the National American Woman Suffrage Association of which she was president. She looked out at the few thousand faces gathered before her, many belonging to people she'd been gazing at for more than forty years. She was the oldest living radical feminist among them—the first to demand suffrage, the first to denounce the laws regarding marriage and divorce, the first to claim organized religion as the sworn enemy of equality for women. Now she was stepping down from the presidency. This would be her last public address as head of the woman suffrage movement.

The speech Stanton delivered, "Solitude of Self," was to become famous the world over. She asked the audience to consider that while the idea of human individuality was a declaration of proud independence, it was also a recognition that we are, in fact, a world of Robinson Crusoes, each of us alone on the island of life.

"No matter how much women prefer to lean," she began,

> to be protected and supported, nor how much men desire to have them do so, they must make the voyage of life alone, and for safety in an emergency, they must know something of the laws of navigation. To guide our own craft, we must be captain, pilot, engineer; with chart and compass to stand at the wheel; to watch the winds and waves, and know when to take in the sail, and to read the signs in the firmament over all. It matters not whether the solitary voyager is man or woman; nature, having endowed them equally, leaves them to their own skill and judgment in the hour of danger; and, if not equal to the occasion, alike they perish.

The strongest reason that she, Stanton, knew for giving women every means of enlarging their sphere of action was because we are, each of us, indeed alone:

> The talk of sheltering woman from the fierce storms of life is the sheerest mockery, for they beat on her from every point of the compass, just as they do on man, and with more fatal results, for he has been trained to protect himself, to resist, and to conquer. Such are the facts in human experience ... rich and poor, intelligent and ignorant, wise and foolish, virtuous and vicious, man and woman; it is ever the same, each soul must depend wholly on itself. . . . [I]n the long, weary march, each one walks alone.

Therefore, she insists, it is necessary to fit "every human soul for independent action." The "immeasurable solitude of self"—"this solitude which each and every one of us has always carried with him, more inaccessible than the ice-cold mountains, more profound than the midnight sea"—demands it. To deny *any*one the tools of survival—that is, the power to act—is criminal. "Who, I ask you, can take, dare take on himself the rights, the duties, the responsibilities of another human soul?"

I read these words for the first time eighty years after they were written, as I myself was climbing the newly reconstructed barricades of radical feminism, and I still remember thinking, with excitement and gratitude, "We are beginning where she left off."

Reading Elizabeth Stanton in the 1970s made me feel on my skin the shock of realizing how slowly (how grudgingly!) politics in the modern world has actually moved, over these past hundreds of years, to include unwanted classes of being in the much vaunted devotion to egalitarianism. I had known that the kaleidoscope of my experience was being shaken; that all the same pieces would still be there, only now surrounded by a new space, forming a new design—one I thought had not been seen before. Now I saw that my new design was *old*. So old! Elizabeth Stanton had looked at it more than a hundred years before me, and had described it in the same words that I was now speaking, using the same examples, staring into the same historical void, feeling the same thin air thicken with the same anger and, more important, the same scared wonder. I realized how repeatedly, throughout modern history, this stunned awakening had taken place among women, and in how absolutely *similar* a set of words and phrases it had been experienced, from the Enlightenment to this late twentieth-century moment. I didn't know whether to laugh or cry, feel energized or depleted, sprout wings of hope or curl up in terminal depression. In truth, I remember thinking, it isn't over till it's over—and until it *is* over, each time around, *things look pretty much the same*. I knew that Stanton had stood where I was now standing, and I knew what she had done when she had seen that *she* was standing where others had stood before. It was through her fifty-year devotion to the Cause that I began to develop an altogether new appreciation (familiar from a left-wing childhood) of taking "the long view."

Chapter 2

Missed Connections

Abolitionist Feminism in the
Nineteenth Century

Christine Stansell

The sweep of the feminist tradition in the United States, arguably the locale of its most radical innovations, throws up both enormous achievements and dispiriting failures. Of the failures, none has been more noticed, more pronounced than feminism's difficulties in making an enduring common cause with democratic race politics. Facing the blockages, historians have searched for a logic that explains the inadequacies of a women's politics which, some have argued, were indelibly marked from the very beginning by racism and a fixation on race-privilege: all the perfidies conjured up by the category "whiteness." In the 1960s, scholars exaggerated the egalitarianism of early white abolitionist-feminists; now a new generation focuses on their dubious motives.

Central to these arguments has been Elizabeth Cady Stanton, whose episodic outbursts after the Civil War of xenophobic and racial language still disturb, exasperate, and anger. Why was Stanton, a one-time abolitionist and America's greatest theorist of women's freedom, so startlingly inured to the postwar cause of the freedpeople, including the freedwomen? Stanton spent the last half of her immensely productive life thinking about and working for women's "liberty," as she termed it. But her distance from a parallel African American politics of freedom, from the struggles of Reconstruction through the nadir of the 1890s, was vast.

Acknowledging Stanton's racism, though, has had the deleterious effect of conflating her own political development with that of the entirety of nineteenth-century women's rights—and beyond. Stanton's racism appears the mark of original sin. I propose we leave behind the old question of "was she or wasn't she?" to ask instead: In the history of racism and antiracism, how does Elizabeth Stanton figure? As Glenda Gilmore has argued about white women in another context, racism is not a timeless and ahistorical property. "It waxes and wanes in response to a larger social context, sometimes perniciously defining the contours of daily life, sometimes receding as behavior and speech challenge the boundaries of racial constructs."[1] The approach can yield much more in terms of comprehending both Stanton and the post–Civil War movement—segregated, with black and white women on different tracks—in which she was so prominent. Why did Stanton embrace racist tenets of thought and political practice? And how did she come by them?

Historians Consider the Problem

Stanton's invention of a fierce separatist, women-only militancy after the war coincided with her break with abolitionist colleagues over the issues of black manhood suffrage raised by the Fourteenth and Fifteenth Amendments, which effectively made full citizenship and voting rights male, enfolding the freedmen into universal manhood suffrage. Ellen DuBois, in her groundbreaking *Feminism and Suffrage* (1978), a study otherwise admiring of Stanton, faced the problem head-on with an honest and still admirably judicious assessment. Writing of Stanton and Susan B. Anthony's break with the Republican Party and the resulting alliance in a Kansas suffrage referendum campaign with the flamboyant, wealthy Copperhead mischief-maker George Frances Train—an in-your-face provocation for radical old friends—DuBois judged that "at this point their racism was opportunist and superficial, an artifact of their anti-Republicanism and their alienation from abolitionists." But there was a deeper problem that went beyond the bitterness of that particular moment: their racism, she proposed, also "drew on and strengthened a much deeper strain within their feminism, a tendency to envision women's emancipation in exclusively white terms. They learned from Train how to transform white women's racism into a kind of sex pride."[2] Writing at the very beginning of the second wave of scholarship on feminism, DuBois didn't specify what that "deeper strain" of racism was, but the phrase suggests some essence of racial identification, what some historians later called "whiteness."

Stanton objected to the enfranchisement of black men, along with immigrants and uneducated (so she depicted them) workingmen as an outrageous injustice to a white female population she called, in the racial parlance of the times, "Saxon." The denunciations of manhood suffrage need to be put in context. She was not a demagogue, and the outbursts were periodic rather than endemic. There were no swoons of outraged Saxon womanhood, for instance, in the major speeches: "Subjection of Woman," crafted in 1873 as a major statement of her thought and a bid to take a place alongside John Stuart Mill on the woman question; and "Home Life," a staple of her lecture offerings. Nor are there any racist overtures in her proposal to form a third party, which she advanced in 1872, a moment when the effects of the Reconstruction amendments still rankled.[3] But when she was on the road her stump speeches did call forth with some predictability a line-up of caricatures of vulgar ignoramuses unjustly granted citizenship before noble Saxon women—the so-called Sambos, Han Yungs, Patricks, and Hanses.[4] Kathi Kern, in her recent look at Stanton in the 1880s and 1890s, *Mrs. Stanton's Bible,* argues that Stanton's racism congealed with prevailing white attitudes of the Gilded Age, the coalescent being her near-religious faith that gender rather than any other social situation—race, poverty, class—was the signal source of all oppression. Stanton's blindered views, Kern suggests, instituted a feminist habit of seeing black women as "incomplete," "insufficient," or "unqualified" feminists: race prejudice became endemic to the feminist tradition. Louise Newman has gone very far with this line of interpretation: in her 1999 book she portrays Stanton as an aggressively racist figure whose politics—along with the movement she represented—were actively deleterious to the cause of democracy, biracial and otherwise.[5]

Kern did raise a new issue: Stanton's inconsistency. There were limits to sticking a label on Stanton and letting the matter rest at that: "It seems only fair . . . to point out that Stanton's racism was inconsistent and contradictory. Certainly she did not consider herself prejudiced along racial and ethnic lines, and she frequently lamented the mistreatment of racial, ethnic and religious groups." She provided two examples as counterpoints to Stanton's racist remarks. From 1881: "I never look a colored man, woman, or child in the face that my soul does not glow with an intense desire . . . to give them some sign of my recognition of their equal humanity." And during the 1890s, at the nadir of American racism: "I am much worked up over the infamous Geary bill against admission of the Chinese. . . . How my blood boils over these persecutions of the Africans, the Jew, the Indians, and the Chinese. . . . I wonder if these fanatical Christians think that Christ died for these people, or confined his self-sacrifice to Saxons, French, Germans, Italians, etc."[6] These were not laments of a con-

ventional liberal bleeding heart. They represent extrapolations from Stanton's much-vaunted (by herself) belief in universal democracy.

But the moments of egalitarianism and open-mindedness, which we
have seen as a legacy of Stanton's abolitionist days, were only occasional.
Why did Stanton's early education in the "school of antislavery," as she
later called her abolitionist years, not lead to stronger demurrals or dissent
from rising postwar tendencies to criticize universal democracy? Her faith
in equal rights did not foster any second thoughts about "Saxonism"—a
prelude to the "Anglo-Saxonism" of the 1890s—as a political value. Perhaps we have taken Stanton's own account of her abolitionism too much
at face value. In truth, Stanton's experience of abolition was more muted
than she let on. She came into the movement after radical experimenta-
tion with the race issue among women had stopped. Her early education
in race relations, in contrast to her education in womanhood, never took
her outside the conventions of her class.

Stanton in the School of Antislavery

In the 1830s, when Stanton was still living in her parents' household in upstate New York, a milieu of women's politics across the color line flowered
briefly in Philadelphia and Boston. It was a political culture, which gave
rise to the woman's rights thought, which gathered into a coherent defense
of women's right to participate fully in the movement, culminating with
the Grimké sisters' controversial lecture tour and Sarah Grimké's great
Letters on the Equality of the Sexes (1839). Stanton was too young and far
away to enter into these urban exchanges. This meant that unlike the first
generation of women reformers—a group that included Lucretia Mott,
Angelina and Sarah Grimké, Lucy Stone, and Abby Kelley Foster—she
never worked politically with black women. Her most sustained contact
with a black person was in fact with a slave.

Although the fact did not enter her public representations until she
published her autobiography in 1898, Stanton was the child of a slaveholder. In the little town of Johnstown, New York, where she grew up, her
father owned, before the final New York State emancipation of 1827 (a
wave of de facto self-emancipation occurred in and around New York City
earlier in the 1820s), at least one slave, a house servant named Peter
Tiebout. Peter Tiebout, we learn from Stanton's *Eighty Years and More*, was
the adored caretaker of the Cady children.[7] The autobiography begins

with a portrait of a benign black nursemaid, gifted and gruff with children, patient with and provoked by his rambunctious charges. It is a set piece from the Southern literature of the Lost Cause—those happy days of slavery, with the loyal servants and their appreciative white folks—which was gaining ground in the 1890s.[8]

Peter—Stanton only calls him by his given name—is rendered with broad strokes. He is "black as coal." He follows and fetches the girls, tells them marvelous stories, and saves them from disastrous pranks. He cooks flapjacks, plays a banjo, sings, and tells them marvelous stories. He gives Stanton a felicitous early experience of antiracist principle when she and the others insist on sitting with him in the Negro pew in their Episcopalian church. Stanton does slightly broaden the stereotype: Peter never becomes the buffoonish naïf of moonlight-and-magnolias tales but rather remains prepossessing, a grand "specimen of manhood," handsome and smart. Still, the banjos keep strumming. Of Peter's fate she alludes, coyly, to a minstrel song: he is "at rest now with 'Old Uncle Ned in the place where the good niggers go.'" This is the racism of domestic intimacy, the sensibility that thrived among white female employers of black domestic servants at the time Stanton was writing but which surely existed, too, in the antebellum Northern slave-owning household of her youth.[9]

The one place where the young Stanton could have met African Americans on different terms was Peterboro, the nearby estate of her cousin Gerrit Smith. Smith was a Garrisonian abolitionist later implicated in the "Secret Seven" who funded John Brown's raid in 1859. Smith established a multiracial community of freed slaves in the small village near the huge estate he inherited; he chipped away at the remains of the family fortune in order to give land grants to newcomers. The Smith house was a hotbed of radical practice, bringing together many reformers of different races. But Stanton recorded no memories of meetings there with black villagers or visiting activists. Rather, she wrote about her encounter with a fugitive slave, importing into the autobiography another racial set piece, this one lifted from the evolving romance of the Underground Railroad. At Peterboro, Stanton meets "a beautiful quadroon girl"—another stock black character—who tells her story to Stanton as they huddle in her hiding place in the attic. From her vantage point fifty years later, Stanton drapes the episode in intimations of sexual abuse, the prism through which, perhaps, she could most readily represent slave women's experiences.[10]

Intellectually, Stanton gained everything from female antislavery. The abolitionists, with their insistence on the genderless conscience and universal moral duty, gave the young woman a sense of a bedrock stratum of social and moral humanity that lay below and beyond sexual identity. Once Sarah Grimké declared that whatever was right for men to do was right for women too, a daring thinker like the young Stanton could see that being a woman was secondary rather than primary, that the accoutrements of sex were an afterthought, not first principle. But she was never educated in the other radical enterprise of urban female antislavery: its defiance of the color line. That defiance was fleeting and, in the long run, politically unproductive. But it is important to acknowledge and understand if we are to imagine alternative paths of historical development. Envisioning what might have been for Stanton allows us to comprehend properly what actually *was*.

Action along the Color Line, across the Color Line

Women's rights within abolition were much more involved in cross-racial alliances than has been allowed. Indeed, abolition cannot be understood aside from African Americans, since until the 1830s the demand for the immediate abolition of slavery came only from free black people in the Northern cities; white antislavery sentiment was essentially confined to support for colonization. So when William Lloyd Garrison formed the American Anti-Slavery Society in Boston in 1833, he drew upon black politics and black leaders to push and educate his white recruits.

With the exception of a few books, female abolition continues to be treated as a white affair, but free black women were instrumental in the societies.[11] They formed the first women's society in Salem, Massachusetts, in 1833. By 1838 there were eleven female societies, with some 6,400 members, stretching from the Northeast into Pennsylvania, Ohio, and Indiana. African American women's numbers were not insignificant. In Philadelphia, for which the best documentation exists, at least nine of the twenty-nine women who signed the constitution of the Pennsylvania Female Anti-Slavery Society were African American; at the first national female convention in New York in 1837, at least 10 percent of the two hundred delegates—a bloc of about twenty women—were black. The numbers are tiny, but then, so were the totals.[12]

In Philadelphia and Boston, black and white women worked together. In other places—Rochester, for instance, closer to Stanton's home—there were parallel organizations with sporadic contact; in others, like New York

City and Worcester, Massachusetts, strict segregation. But while black and white women did not always work together, race mixing defined the political character of female antislavery, in the eyes of both adherents and opponents. At the time, detractors called this "amalgamation"—referring not only to marriage or sex between whites and blacks, but to any social encounter between the two groups: sitting in the same pew in church, for example. In eighteenth-century Anglo-America, amalgamation was a morally neutral word, which denoted any cultural contact between different peoples. In the 1830s, under the political pressure of abolition and the growing assertiveness of Northern free black city dwellers, it became a derogatory term connoting polluting contacts between blacks and whites. ("Miscegenation," with its overtly sexual meaning, was not used until 1864, when Democrats coined it for the presidential campaign to cast aspersions on Lincoln's presidency.)[13]

In this overwhelmingly segregated society, the mixed circles of abolition, with their sprinkling of African Americans, were statistically insignificant and by no stretch of the imagination typical of the general urban population, or even of moral reformers. But while tiny, they were intellectually fructifying and politically explosive. After Nat Turner's failed insurrection in 1831, fears of Negro rebellion had grown among even antislavery Quakers; everywhere, white moderates backpedaled. In this context, women's radical societies were strikingly heterodox. Among Philadelphia and Boston abolitionists, all respectable sorts, mixing was a point of Christian conduct for some, a matter of intimacy and the daily crawl of life for others. These were more mundane companionships than the Romantic friendships of leading men like Gerrit Smith and Frederick Douglass described in John Stauffer's *The Black Hearts of Men:* there were no gestures of defiance, no antiracist postures. But perhaps the connections were all the more significant for the dailiness and lack of self-dramatizing.

The evidence is sparse but worth considering because it emerges in context as unremarkable rather than singular. In Boston, the Ball sisters were so intimately involved in African American life that they have been mistakenly identified as black. In Philadelphia, the eminent Quaker preacher Lucretia Mott worked habitually with women from leading African American families—the Fortens, Purvises, and Douglasses. People went to one another's houses and argued politics, and white and African American women spoke of each other as "friends." The Purvises and the Motts lived in a lifelong concourse, the large kinship networks knit together by births, deaths, illnesses, and shared battles. The Grimké sisters' friendship with

Sarah Mapps Douglass, a teacher, was similarly long-lived and intellectually and politically transformative. It was Sarah Douglass who took the naive Southerners under her wing in Philadelphia. They were timid renegades from a great South Carolina slave-owning family and novices to Quakerism. She argued them out of their support of colonization and converted them to immediate abolition. To Sarah Grimké, in turn, Sarah Douglass spoke of the humiliation of urban race prejudice.[14]

The female societies addressed the "sin" of race prejudice as well as that of slavery. They consistently linked both to the situation of women and, as feminist perceptions deepened through the 1830s, to women's rights. The Grimkés, in particular, but other white women as well, struck a note of identification with black women—both their fellow political workers and slaves—that would later drop out of the discourse. Early on, for example, Philadelphia agitator Elizabeth Chandler insisted, "We would have the name of *Woman*, a security for the *rights* of the sex. Those rights are withheld from the female slave: and as we value and would demand them for ourselves, must we not ask them for her?"[15] The Philadelphia society saw education and action against race discrimination as a major task, always in a necessary relationship to the battle against slavery and at times equivalent. In Massachusetts, women in Lynn and Boston joined a 1837–1839 petition campaign against state laws forbidding intermarriage and preventing blacks and Indians from serving in the militia. Women in the countryside gathered signatures, drawing sexual taunts as they went from door to door.[16]

This is not to sentimentalize women's political work as happily mutual and egalitarian, free of racial discord. The mixed societies encompassed many white women and few black women. White women would have called the shots and controlled the resources; black women would have endured slights and doubtless insults. Yet it is possible to acknowledge the problematics of the case and still see it as testimony to the fluid, experimental, and daring elements of 1830s abolition—elements that defined the movement, moreover, at precisely the moment when the woman question first agitated the ranks and the political imagery of "sisterhood" gained credence.

Agitation over the woman question conjoined with and strengthened the politics of race mixture, provoking violent reaction. The years 1837–1839 were a turning point. Through the thirties, violence against abolitionist speakers and meetings mounted: mobs nearly lynched Garrison in Boston, attacked black neighborhoods in New York and Philadelphia, murdered the antislavery newspaper editor Elijah Lovejoy in Illinois, and routinely threatened gatherings and violently disrupted meetings. In Philadelphia in 1838, popular anger surged when private amalgamation flowed into public; the violence turned against women. Furor over the mixed crowd at the wedding of well-known abolitionist speakers Theodore Weld and Angelina Grimké fueled popular outrage at the national women's convention held downtown a few days later. Threatened by an enraged crowd of men, the meeting disbanded: black and white women linked arms and made their way through a howling mob which, the next night, burned down the hall. The next year, there was another convention, but the pressure and threats devastated the female societies. Throughout the Northeast the societies folded or became all-white. African American women withdrew into working in black communities.[17]

White female antislavery lecturers for a time kept alive the connections of social mixing, racial egalitarianism, and women's rights. A handful of agitators, embodying women's rights in their mobile persons as well as their lecture topics, spoke before mixed African American and white audiences, and traveled in company with male lecturers, white and black. Indeed, the development of women's rights looks different, more intimately bound up with racial issues, from what we have thought if we follow the paths taken by these women and men rather than adhere to the narrative that has treated abolition as a chance for Elizabeth Cady Stanton to jump into prominence with a purer sexual politics at Seneca Falls in 1848. The traveling speakers expanded their sphere and popularized a rich repertoire of versatile metaphors—of "bondage" and "mastery"—that could serve for both slave and woman. Abby Kelly Foster, who became a tough and seasoned speaker in the field, raised women's rights constantly in her talks in the New York and New England countryside, provoking charges of amalgamation in terms that were so sexual that they anticipated what was to come after the Civil War.

Indeed, Abby Kelly stirred the upstate town of Seneca Falls, New York, "to its deepest foundations," speaking there six times in 1843. The tumult of Kelly's sojourn increased when a female church member chastised her minister for refusing to announce the meetings from his pulpit. He chastised her for un-Christian conduct and the case turned into a two-month-long church trial during which the rights of women to bear witness against slavery were matters of contention. The reverberations probably account for the instantaneous and widespread response to the 1848 call for a meeting at Seneca Falls, rather than the notion that some mysterious feminist impulse had been quiescent for years, called forth by the wizardry of Elizabeth Stanton.[18]

In general, though, the violence shut down a particular line of development for the women's movement and had enduring consequences for the next generation of reformers, including Elizabeth Stanton. The result of African American women's withdrawal was an altered texture to women's politics. Race mixing continued, but in private; in public, it was African American men who carried on abolitionist work and represented black politics. Garrisonian abolition had comprised a tiny racial avant-garde with influence that outstripped its numbers, comparable in some ways to the transcendentalist avant-garde in Boston during the same years. Stanton missed out on both. Understanding this fact places her within a different generational experience and intellectual development.

Stanton's Distance from Abolition

Black women were a cipher for Stanton. She knew virtually no African American women. She missed some possible connections. She knew Frederick Douglass slightly (we know he supported her call for the vote at Seneca Falls); but if she visited him in Rochester after 1848, when she lived nearby, she would not have spoken to his wife Anna, a one-time activist who had withdrawn into a servant's role, appearing in her own parlor only to serve her husband's guests but not to sit and converse. There is no evidence Stanton crossed paths with the writer and fugitive Harriet Jacobs, who also lived in Rochester for eighteen months beginning in 1848 while she worked for Douglass at his newspaper and became close to the leading white antislavery activist, Amy Post. After the war, Stanton once entertained Sojourner Truth.[19] But she had no acquaintances beyond these. Neither she nor other antislavery women of her generation worked for the abandoned principle of racial amalgamation.

Politically, however, Stanton did encounter distinguished African American men like Douglass, Robert Purvis, and Charles Lenox Remond. In national antislavery politics, these black men still *mattered;* they provoked, inspired, and indeed demanded political recognition of their collective presence. Their prominence as spokesmen and (despite the pressures of marginalization) political actors may explain the ease with which Stanton flipped between adhering to the stereotypes of degraded "Sambos" and giving respectful tribute to the social gravitas of black men. This tendency became apparent right after the war, when in a letter to the editor of the *Anti-Slavery Standard* in 1865, she disparaged "Sambo," the newly freed slave, in one paragraph and paid tribute in the next to the African American soldier (whom she imagined, most likely, as a Northern freed black). Respect could turn into overwrought assessments of the power accruing to black men, tinged with the sarcasm and ridicule she always included in her charges of male privilege. In 1858, for example, she angrily and enviously contrasted the plight of abolitionist women to that of Douglass and Remond, remembering how long ago Wendell Phillips had pontificated on "woman's place" when he sided with the British in refusing to seat the women delegates at the World Anti-Slavery Convention in London in 1840. Would Mr. Phillips have made such a remark, she demanded, had it been a matter of the fitness of seating black men of the stature of Douglass and Remond? "Think you, had they listened through one entire day, to debates on their peculiar fitness for plantation life, and unfitness for public assemblies and the forum," would they have been content? Of course not: no one ever directed that kind of prejudice at them![20] That serious black leaders were accorded the stature and dignity that was theirs by right was, for her, an article of faith. In 1869, in the midst of the break with the Republicans, she wrote for *The Revolution* (the journal she and Susan Anthony edited) a description of Robert Purvis in the ennobling language that had long draped African American men in the abolition movement: "[He] rose, and, with the loftiest sense of justice, with a true Roman grandeur, ignored his race and sex . . . and demanded for his daughter all he asked for his son or himself."[21] Purvis had supported her side of the argument at a convention, and on this occasion she could join in the chorus of admiration with plaudits of her own.

The predominance of influential African American men in her political milieu and her distance from black women increased her difficulties in imagining a significant black female political persona. Like others of her generation, she usually thought of the slave as a "he." Black women were almost always absent from her thoughts. She was blind to women's leadership in Northern free black communities. With African American women appearing only as a collective abstraction, she could attribute to free black men wildly exaggerated privileges of their sex. In doing so she mapped her beloved male/female opposition onto the other duality at the core of her thought, slave/free, and collapsed black and white men's "mastery" over their women into the monolith of a deplorable "aristocracy of sex."

Before the war, one can find in her collected papers two exceptions to her habit of characterizing the slave as male. Both are remarkable, evoking old connections of the politics of race and sex that were once vibrant but had become highly attenuated by the time she conjured them up. The first instance was a rip-roaring speech she gave in 1860 to 1,500 Garrisonian abolitionists which she ended with an eloquent tribute to enslaved womanhood. Building to a climax, Stanton queried rhetorically, "Are not nearly two millions of native-born American women, at this very hour, doomed to the foulest slavery. . . . Are they not doubly damned as immortal beasts of burden in the field, and sad mothers of a most accursed race?" In answering, she moved into a reverie in an older key of female abolitionist empathy, shifting into a first-person singular that channeled the voice of the slave woman—Yes! yes! all this is true, and more.

> I have asked the everlasting hills, that in their upward yearnings seem to touch the heavens, if I, an immortal being, though clothed in womanhood, was made for the vile purposes to which proud Saxon man has doomed me. . . . I have asked this bleeding heart, so full of love to God and man . . . if this graceful form, this soft and tender flesh was made but to crawl and shiver in the cold, foul embrace of Southern tyrants.[22]

But by 1860, the oratorical melodrama was so familiar as to be hackneyed. The language was worn out, the empathy emptied out of whatever substantive political content it once held. And in any case, the country was about to go to war, and such talk at the moment did not stand out from the rest of the abolitionist chorus.

That same year, Stanton scandalized the National Woman's Rights Convention by calling for freedom to divorce. Given her interest in the marriage question, she might have gone on to flesh out the connection between the sexual brutality of slavery and the forced dependencies of marriage—"mastery" being the key term linking the two situations. There was a long history of using the word both ways, analogizing the slaveholders' power to husbands' rights by law and custom: the intellectual doubling went back to Sarah Grimké in the 1830s and to the British Owenite William Thompson, in the 1820s, influenced by British abolition. Although Stanton would go on to milk the melodramatic allusions to slave masters when she conjured up tyrannical husbands, she never did tie her increasingly daring ruminations on marriage to the situation of the freedwomen.

It is interesting to speculate about the reasons for her disinterest. After the war, if she had been more curious about the fate of the once-enslaved women, she might have sought out those Northern women, black and white (Sojourner Truth, Charlotte Forten, Josephine Griffing, Frances Ellen Watkins Harper, Frances Gage), who were returning home from working with the freedpeople. She might have learned that some of the freedwomen were mulling over the meaning of bodily self-ownership and freedom from their husbands' mastery in ways she would have found congenial; some took freedom to mean the freedom to self-divorce when conjugal arrangements did not suit them. Northern reformers noticed (usually with dismay) some women's reluctance to marry—even when encouraged by the Freedmen's Bureau—and their stubborn conviction that women do not need to stay with men who abused them. Surely Stanton would have liked to hear about the North Carolina freedwoman who, when her husband hauled her into court for adultery, stated for the record, "I am my own woman and will do as I please."[23]

Why did she not inquire? Here we encounter the particular liabilities of the break in women's politics across the color line that Stanton signified and sealed. She knew no African American women well. For all her brilliance, she was not an empirical thinker, drawn to the particularities of other women's lives; and indeed, in an age when social science and investigative journalism had yet to take shape, there were few examples to follow, except some novels that represented with exactitude and precision any women's milieu. Despite her claims that women poured out their stories to her, the narratives of real life she employed in her speeches were melodramas and allegories, taken from newspaper reportage, peopled with villains and victims, and always ended with a moral or political point.

Stanton lived in a mental universe of abstract principles—we now call this "theory"—that at times had tenuous relations to the realities of historical time and place. Like many abolitionists, she saw the postwar South as a reclaimed region of despicable traitors and tyrants and pitiable ex-slaves, best left to the magical properties of freedom that would, sooner or later, empower the victims. In her extensive travels around the country, she never ventured south of Washington, D.C. Slavery would remain with Stanton her whole life as a fundamental trope through which she understood social relations, but it had lost all the historical reality with which she had endowed it. After 1870 slavery shifted, for her, into a metaphor and floated away from the pitched battle the freedpeople were fighting on the ground.[24]

The second time that she mentioned Southern black women was in 1865. As she gathered her intellectual and political arguments to oppose universal manhood suffrage, she furiously assaulted the flawed logic of protecting the freedpeople by pretending that the freedwomen did not exist. "May I ask just one question based on the apparent opposition in which you place the negro and the woman?" she wrote with cutting sarcasm in a letter to Wendell Phillips, once a supporter of women's suffrage, now a defector from the cause. "My question is this: do you believe the African race is composed entirely of males?" Stanton was pointing out the connection Phillips and his allies had missed—between the freedpeople's rights and the demand for universal suffrage, including the vote for all women, white and black. Later that year, she fleetingly touched upon the real dilemmas of the freedwomen (in the same letter in which she derided Sambo): "If the two millions of Southern black women are not to be secured in their rights of person, property, wages, and children, their emancipation is but another form of slavery."[25]

The freedwomen were far away—geographically, politically, and imaginatively. There were women closer at hand who provided a link, but Stanton's connections to Northern African American female reformers were only secondhand. The tragedy is that she was never able to evoke in her own mind, as had an earlier generation of women, either the difficulties or the achievements of Anna Murray Douglass, Frances Watkins Harper, Sojourner Truth, or her friend Charles Remond's sister Sarah, who had cut a swath through England as an antislavery lecturer. These women never interested her; or to put a finer point on it, they did not bear political significance. Her indifference in this regard was more surprising and more revealing than we have allowed. Surprising , because Stanton understood so much about the lives of women and men, and because she was so brave and uncompromising in working out the implications of her ideas. Also surprising, because her commitments to democracy were keen. Revealing, because it grew out of Stanton's remove from a particular women's politics and a particular historical moment.

Stanton was not alone among either old friends or old adversaries in her indifference toward the freedwomen. She was also not the worst. The prize for racist activism of a former abolitionist would have to go to Henry Blackwell. Blackwell, and his wife Lucy Stone, stayed loyal to the Reconstruction amendments and the Republican line after the war. The two headed the American Woman Suffrage Association, a Boston suffragist group. But as early as 1867, even as he ostensibly followed the Republican dictum to "remember the Negro," Blackwell came up with the idea that white women's votes could solve the South's looming "Negro problem" by creating a solid white majority of voters. For years Blackwell campaigned for what eventually turned into the "Southern strategy" adopted by white suffragists in the 1890s, whereby they kept black women out of mainstream suffragism, in return (they thought) for winning the support of the Southern states.[26]

Stanton was not unusual in her support of education as a basis for suffrage. Across the board, Northern white reformers fell prey to the white Southern account of the depredations that universal democracy and black men's votes were inflicting on the South. By the 1890s, during the highwater mark of the tide of *revanchiste* sentiment and disenfranchisement campaigns, attacks on voters' "ignorance" and susceptibility to corruption were so deeply engraved into politics both in the North and the South that African American reformers, too, were driven back to claiming the vote for the "educated" of their race: the platform of the National Association of Colored Women, for example, with Mary Church Terrell at its head, included votes for educated women.

Even in 1869, when women's rights advocates split, the sides did not line up neatly in terms of race or abolitionist bona fides. Not all African Americans went with the Republicans: Sojourner Truth moved back and forth between the two positions; and Charles Lenox Remond, Harriet Purvis, Robert Purvis, and Mary Ann Shadd Cary (probably the most independent woman in the African American leadership) sided with Stanton and Anthony. Abby Kelly Foster sided with the Republican Party for the first time in her life, but acknowledged that she might be making the wrong decision.[27] The irony is that no one in either wing sought to repair the missed connection Stanton had pointed out so cogently in 1865; no one reminded their audiences that the "colored race" consisted of women as well as men. African American women carried on their political struggles on their own, invisible to the vast majority of the women's rights movement.

To the end of her days, Stanton was oblivious to the costs of her towering disregard for black women. In later years, the most straightforward connection she made between racism and her own preoccupations came during the fracas that Frederick Douglass kicked up among reformers in 1883 by defying the color line to marry a white woman. Anthony, always loath to touch the marriage question in any form, counseled discretion, but Stanton dived in with a letter of solidarity to her old colleague and sometime antagonist. "In defense of the right to . . . marry whom we please . . . we might quote some of the basic principles of our government. In some things individual rights to taste should control."[28]

NOTES

1. See Glenda Gilmore, *Gender and Jim Crow: Women and the Politics of White Supremacy in North Carolina, 1896–1920* (Chapel Hill, N.C.: University of North Carolina Press, 1996).

2. Ellen Carol DuBois, *Feminism and Suffrage: The Emergence of an Independent Women's Movement in America* (Ithaca, N.Y.: Cornell University Press, 1978), 96.

3. *The Selected Papers of Elizabeth Cady Stanton and Susan B. Anthony,* vol. 2: *Against an Aristocracy of Sex,* ed. Ann D. Gordon (New Brunswick, N.J.: Rutgers University Press, 2000), 621–39; *Elizabeth Cady Stanton/Susan B. Anthony: Correspondence, Writings, Speeches,* ed. with commentary by Ellen Carol DuBois (New York: Schocken Books, 1981), 121–38, 166–69.

4. The familiar examples come from *Elizabeth Cady Stanton/Susan B. Anthony,* ed. DuBois.

5. Kathi Kern, *Mrs. Stanton's Bible* (Ithaca, N.Y.: Cornell University Press, 2000), 112–13; Louise Newman, *White Women's Rights: The Racial Origins of Feminism in the United States* (New York: Oxford University Press, 1999), 184.

6. Kern, *Mrs. Stanton's Bible,* note 63 on p. 251.

7. On Tiebout, see Kern, *Mrs. Stanton's Bible,* 22–29.

8. David W. Blight, *Race and Reunion: The Civil War in American Memory* (Cambridge, Mass.: Harvard University Press, 2001), Chapter 7.

9. Stanton, *Eighty Years and More* (1898; Boston: Northeastern University Press, 1993),14–19, 5–6. The point about domestic intimacy comes from Gilmore, *Gender and Jim Crow.*

10. Stanton, *Eighty Years and More,* Chapter 4. On Peterboro, see John Stauffer, *The Black Hearts of Men: Radical Abolitionists and the Transformation of Race* (Cambridge, Mass.: Harvard University Press, 2002). On the emerging narrative of the Underground Railroad, see Blight, *Race and Reunion,* 231–37.

11. The important exception is Shirley Yee, *Black Women Abolitionists: A Study in Activism, 1828–1860* (Knoxville, Tenn.: University of Tennessee Press, 1992).

12. Paul Goodman, *Of One Blood: Abolitionism and the Origins of Racial Equality* (Berkeley: University of California Press, 1998), Chapters 13–14; Deborah Gold Hansen, *Strained Sisterhood: Gender and Class in the Boston Female Anti-Slavery Society* (Amherst, Mass.: University of Massachusetts Press, 1993); Nancy A. Hewitt, *Women's Activism and Social Change: Rochester, New York, 1822–1872* (Ithaca, N.Y.: Cornell University Press, 1984); Carolyn Williams, "The Female Anti-Slavery Movement: Fighting against Racial Prejudice and Promoting Women's Rights in

Antebellum America," in *The Abolitionist Sisterhood,* ed. Jean Fagan Yellin and John C. Van Horne (Ithaca, N.Y.: Cornell University Press, 1994), 159–78; Kathryn Kish Sklar, *Women's Rights Emerges within the Anti-Slavery Movement, 1830–1870: A Brief History with Documents* (Boston: Bedford, 2000).

13. Leslie M. Harris, "From Abolitionist Amalgamators to 'Rulers of the Five Points': The Discourse of Interracial Sex and Reform in Antebellum New York City," in *Sex, Love, Race: Crossing Boundaries in North American History,* ed. Martha Hodes (New York: New York University Press, 1999).

14. See my "Sisterhood and the Abolitionists," in *Sisterhood and Slavery,* ed. Kathryn Kish Sklar and James Stewart (Yale University Press, forthcoming), for an extended argument of these points.

15. Quoted in Goodman, *Of One Blood,* 184–90.

16. Louis Ruchames, "Race, Marriage, and Abolition in Massachusetts," *Journal of Negro History* 40 (1955): 250–73; Dorothy Sterling, *Ahead of Her Time: Abby Kelly and the Politics of Antislavery* (New York: Norton, 1991).

17. Leonard L. Richards, *"Gentlemen of Property and Standing": Anti-Abolition Mobs in Jacksonian America* (New York: Oxford University Press, 1970); Otelia Cromwell, *Lucretia Mott* (Cambridge, Mass.: Harvard University Press, 1958), 56–60; Hansen, *Strained Sisterhood,* passim. This was the second time violence had threatened. Abolitionist women's first experience of near-lethal violence was the vendetta carried on in 1834 against Prudence Crandall's school for Negro girls in Connecticut.

18. For an account of the controversy and ensuing church trial, see Judith Wellman, "How Abby Kelly Turned Seneca Falls on Its Ear," speech at the Women's Rights Historical Park, May 2004, http://www.wwhp.org/Resources/akfoster.html.

19. On Anna Douglass, see *Love across Color Lines: Ottilie Assing and Frederick Douglass* (New York: Hill and Wang, 1999); on Jacobs, see Jean Fagan Yellin's introduction to the reissued edition, Harriet A. Jacobs, *Incidents in the Life of a Slave Girl: Written by Herself* (Cambridge, Mass.: Harvard University Press, 1987); on Truth, see Nell Irvin Painter, *Sojourner Truth: A Life, a Symbol* (New York: Norton, 1996), 225–26.

20. *The Selected Papers of Elizabeth Cady Stanton and Susan B. Anthony,* vol. 1: *In the School of Anti-Slavery, 1840–1866,* ed. Ann D. Gordon (New Brunswick, N.J.: Rutgers University Press, 1977), 367 ("Address to the Eighth National Woman's Rights Convention, New York City, May 13, 1858").

21. *Selected Papers,* 1:564 (*Anti-Slavery Standard,* December 26, 1865); ibid., 2:205 (January 22, 1869).

22. *Selected Papers,* 1:415 (speech, May 8, 1860).

23. On links between women's rights in South and North, see Amy Dru Stanley, *From Bondage to Contract* (Cambridge: Cambridge University Press, 1998), Chapter 1. The Southern situation is analyzed in Laura F. Edwards, "'The Marriage Covenant Is the Foundation of All Our Rights': The Politics of Slave Marriages in

North Carolina after Emancipation," *Law and History Review* (Spring 1996). For the freedwoman's assertion, see p. 109.

24. Elizabeth B. Clark, "Self-Ownership and the Political Theory of Elizabeth Cady Stanton," *Connecticut Law Review* 21 (1989): 905–41.

25. DuBois, *Feminism and Suffrage,* 206; *Selected Papers,* 1:564.

26. Marjorie Spruill Wheeler, *New Women of the New South: The Leaders of the Woman Suffrage Movement in the Southern States* (New York: Oxford University Press, 1993), 113–16.

27. Painter, *Sojourner Truth,* 225–33; *Selected Papers,* 2:205; Roslyn Terborg-Penn, "Black Women and Woman Suffrage," *Potomac Review* 7 (1977): 15–17.

28. William McFeely, *Frederick Douglass* (New York: Norton, 1990), 321; *The Life and Writings of Frederick Douglass,* vol. 4: *Reconstruction and After,* ed. Philip S. Foner (New York: International Publishers, 1955), 410–11.

Chapter 3

Elizabeth Cady Stanton, John Stuart Mill, and the Nature of Feminist Thought

Barbara Caine

In what was ostensibly a letter of praise, the English writer H. G. Wells once wrote to Dora Russell (Bertrand Russell's first wife) how much he admired her energy and initiative. "Bertie thinks," he wrote, "and I write but you *do.*"[1] As she was well aware, this praise contained a sting. Like Bertrand Russell, Wells often made clear his sense of women's intellectual inadequacies—and he rarely went so far as to suggest that a capacity for action was to be rated more highly than writing or thought. Indeed, this letter illustrates very neatly the gendered division between thought and action as respectively masculine and feminine spheres of activity that has long bedeviled the history of feminism, making it hard to claim attention for women's ideas, and even harder to assert their importance as feminist intellectuals and theorists. This point can be seen very clearly in relation to nineteenth-century feminism in the way in which Elizabeth Cady Stanton, like her leading British contemporaries Josephine Butler or Millicent Garrett Fawcett, is regarded as an important activist in movements for women's rights, while John Stuart Mill continues not only to be seen as the most important and influential theorist of feminism both in Britain and the United States, but also as one who makes the ideas of women seem superfluous.

Mill's general eminence as a philosopher made his advocacy of women's rights very welcome in both countries, and there were few nineteenth-century feminists who did not accord him almost heroic status. Millicent Garrett Fawcett in Britain and Elizabeth Cady Stanton in the United States both played a part here, insisting on his central importance for their cause. Cady Stanton was fulsome in her praise both of Mill's ideas and of his personal conduct, particularly in his approach to marriage. In recent years, however, several feminist scholars have argued that Mill's analysis of the oppression of women was considerably narrower in range and more limited in its extent than was that of a number of contemporary women.[2] This case has been made strongly in relation to several nineteenth-century British feminists, but it can be made even more strongly in relation to Elizabeth Cady Stanton. Her sense of the problems and dilemmas that faced Mill as well as her feminist vision were considerably more comprehensive and radical than his. Drawing on personal experience, on the one hand, and seeking to explore the ways in which women's subordination was reinforced by almost every social, cultural, and religious institution, on the other, Cady Stanton encompassed within her feminist framework a range of discussions about sexual, moral, and religious questions that Mill rarely addressed—and indeed sought rather to avoid. In the process, she demonstrated her sense of the need for a feminist agenda that went far beyond the political and legal changes that Mill advocated as the most effective way to improve the situation of women. In this essay I want both to outline her ideas about Mill—and to contrast her approach to the question of women's rights with his. I want also to look at the connection between her ideas and those of earlier women writers, especially Mary Wollstonecraft, who shares with her a primary place in any Anglo-American feminist tradition.

Even before the publication of his essay, *The Subjection of Women,* John Stuart Mill was widely admired and respected by advocates of women's rights both in Britain and the United States. His support for women's suffrage, both in his earlier writing and during his term as a member of Parliament, ensured that this would be the case. Indeed, in Britain, it was Mill's speeches in the House of Commons and the petition in favor of women's suffrage he presented in 1866 that provided the first step in the women's suffrage campaign. The publication of *The Subjection of Women* three years later made his position as the women's champion and as the foremost philosopher to support the cause absolutely unequivocal. This work was warmly welcomed by advocates of women's rights throughout Europe and the United States. Many women wrote to him to express their pleasure and gratitude on reading it. Bertrand Russell's mother, Viscountess Kate Amberley, was one of them. She was thrilled with the book, she wrote to Mill, and planned to study it well so "that I may get all the arguments in my head and have them ready for any scoffers."[3]

While many recent feminists have been critical of Mill, one cannot sufficiently emphasize the extent to which most nineteenth-century feminists accepted his intellectual and theoretical preeminence willingly and without question. Indeed, the British suffrage leader Millicent Garrett Fawcett suggested that Mill had created the intellectual framework that made the women's movement possible.

> There can be no dispute that Mr. Mill's influence marks an epoch in the women's movement. He was a master and formed a school of thought. Just as in art, a master forms a school and influences his successors for generations, so the present leaders and champions of the women's movement have been influenced and to a great extent formed by Mr. Mill.[4]

Feminist leaders in the United States generally concurred. Elizabeth Cady Stanton, while not going quite as far as Fawcett, would not have expressed any serious disagreement. She was deeply impressed by his essay on *The Subjection of Women* and suggested that "every women's suffrage association in America and Europe should pass a resolution thanking him."[5]

Mill was extremely pleased with the response his work met from women. Indeed, one cannot help thinking that responses like that of Kate Amberley demonstrated that *The Subjection of Women* served, as he intended it to, not only as the application of his own liberal economic and political theory to women, but also to provide contemporary feminists with the arguments and the intellectual framework they needed in such a way as to obviate the need for them to bother with any further intellectual or theoretical endeavor. As a result of this, it is hard not to see Mill's role and importance in the women's movement as serving both to silence women and to limit their claims to making a distinctive intellectual or theoretical contribution to the cause. His international eminence as a philosopher completely overshadowed the writing and the ideas of his women contemporaries—and Mill himself never sought to alter or remedy this in any way. He extolled the intellectual merits of his partner and wife, Harriet Taylor, but he rarely had a good word for any other women, and he certainly did not grant women any special claim in articulating or elucidating the wrongs of their sex. On the contrary, his emphasis in *The Subjection of Women* on the artificiality of women in the present state of society made him reject the idea that women had provided or could provide any particular insight into their own immediate situation or into that of women more generally. Literary women, he conceded, "were becoming more free spoken, and more willing to express their real sentiments." Unfortunately, however, especially in Britain "they are themselves such artificial products, that their sentiments are compounded of a small element of individual observation and consciousness and a very large one of acquired associations."[6] Moreover, while strongly supporting fundamental change in political and legal rights, Mill seemed to feel no compunction to encourage women's intellectual development in his own particular world, and he certainly did not accept the idea that some women might perhaps benefit from access to the specialized intellectual circles to which he belonged. This was made evident particularly in regard to Millicent Fawcett, one of the major leaders of the British movement for women's suffrage. Before she emerged as a suffrage leader in the 1880s, Fawcett had written and published quite extensively on the subject of political economy. She had been taught this discipline by her husband, Henry Fawcett, and she published articles written jointly with him and by her. She was accorded quite significant recognition among political economists and accepted as the most able woman economist in Britain. She was writing at the same time as Harriet Martineau and several other prominent women—so the claim was not a negligible one. While acknowledging Fawcett's claims as an eminent female political economist, Mill nonetheless opposed her admission to the Political Economy Club, a forum in which he met with other specialists in the field, including Fawcett's husband, Henry, to debate questions about economics.[7]

Just as many nineteenth-century feminists accepted Mill's intellectual preeminence, so too many of them followed him in a tendency to disregard the writings or ideas on the subjection of women from other women. Elizabeth Cady Stanton illustrates this point very clearly. While recognizing her own capacity, as she said, "to philosophize," she rarely seems to have thought of her women contemporaries in similar terms, or to acknowledge their ideas or intellectual contribution. This was particularly evident in her response to her British counterparts. Cady Stanton took great pride in the extent of her acquaintanceship among British feminists and in the closeness of her relationships with some of them. But although she mentions her enjoyment in meeting the women about whom she had read when she went to England, her comments and discussions of them focus entirely on their activities and campaigns, and rarely, if ever, on their ideas or published works. She described with pleasure her meetings with Josephine Butler and Millicent Fawcett, for example, but at no point did she engage with their ideas or even refer to the ways in which both Butler and Fawcett were critiquing the contemporary liberal political thought they supported in general, but saw as failing the needs of women.[8] Even

Frances Cobbe, who was probably the most eminent feminist writer of the nineteenth century, is represented in Cady Stanton's autobiography not through her well-known and extensive writings on theology or feminism, but rather in terms of an argument that Harriot Stanton Blatch had with her over vivisection and in which Elizabeth Cady Stanton felt that her daughter had triumphed.[9] This is the more notable as Cobbe was in some ways closer to Stanton than any other British feminist in terms of her admiration of Theodore Parker, whose works she edited, and her critical approach to Christianity and to the role of Christian theology in reinforcing the subordination of women. But Cady Stanton had nothing to say of this, and while she noted the writings of some contemporary British women, she saved her admiration for Mill's *Subjection of Women*.

While Cady Stanton herself did not ever discuss the ideas of her British contemporaries, or the extent to which she shared or disagreed with their views and assumptions, such a discussion is important in establishing her place in nineteenth-century feminist thought. The expansive, even protean nature of her interests and ideas means that there are few significant nineteenth-century British feminists whose interests Cady Stanton did not address and with whom she does not bear some kind of comparison. The scope of her writings and ideas encompasses them all. Clearly her writings on the suffrage and its potential impact on personal and social life, and her insistence on the connection between women's political nonexistence and their marital degradation is strongly reminiscent of the ideas of John Stuart Mill. However her ideas about the distinctive nature of women's citizenship, and of its meaning and importance, reflect matters of particular concern to Millicent Garrett Fawcett, while her sense of the connection between enforced and unhappy marriage and prostitution is strongly reminiscent of Josephine Butler. Stanton was politically more radical than either of these women, and her insistence in the 1880s and 1890s that political rights be demanded for all women and not allowed to be limited by the doctrine of coverture to single women only connected her closely, as Sandra Holton has shown, with Wolstenholme Elmy and the radical British women of the Bright Mclaren Circle.[10] Stanton's classic and best known speech, "Solitude of Self," however, points not to any of these people but rather to Frances Power Cobbe, the self-proclaimed moralist of the English women's movement, the one who argued most strongly for the need to recognize women's responsibilities and duties to themselves.[11] But none of these women, in Cady Stanton's view, bore comparison with Mill, whose *Subjection of Women* she continued to see as unquestionably the most important feminist statement of the nineteenth century. She singled out his ideas on marriage for particular mention. "No thinker," she argued, "has yet so calmly, truthfully, logically revealed the causes and hidden depths of women's degradation, and so clearly pointed out the secret springs of the surveillance and sycophancy of the most fortunate woman to man."[12] And his ideas on marriage were ones she referred to often. The speech on marriage and divorce, entitled "Home Life," which she delivered on lecture tours throughout the 1870s, for example, takes as its starting point Mill's insistence that "the generality of the male sex cannot yet tolerate the idea of living with an equal at the fireside."[13] Two decades later, in the 1890s, in the midst of the furor created by the publication of her *Woman's Bible,* she compared her selection of the provocative title for this work with Mill's *Subjection of Women,* insisting that "the title in both cases brought attention to the book."[14]

Cady Stanton's admiration of Mill is not really surprising. He wrote with great logic and clarity, and many of the views he espoused were ones she shared. Mill's completely secular outlook and his insistence that women's emancipation was necessary, not to enable them better to exercise moral suasion, but rather to ensure their own freedom, to enable them fully to develop their own capacities and to live their own individual lives as they wished, fitted very well with Cady Stanton's views—and differed markedly from those of many women who supported the idea of women's rights. Mill's searing indictment of the marriage laws that gave men control over the person and property of their wives, moreover, bore a close resemblance to her own views. Cady Stanton agreed even with some aspects of Mill's thought that have been subject to very critical comment by recent feminist scholars. Although accepting that nothing can really be known about women's intellectual qualities in their present subordinate state, Mill nonetheless assumed that there were likely always to be intellectual differences between men and women, with men being more inclined to abstract ideas and the promulgation of general rules, while women were likely to be quicker to perceive "present fact" and particular points of detail. From the 1870s onwards, Cady Stanton had come increasingly to believe that there were intellectual differences between the sexes, and she commented on the differences between her views on this question and those of English feminists such as Lydia Becker, who rejected the idea that there was sex in mind.

For all these similarities, however, there were marked differences between her approach and that of Mill, which was evident even in the em-
phases they placed on matters where they appeared to be in agreement.
This is particularly clear in their approach to marriage. While both agreed
about the urgent need for reform of the laws pertaining to marriage, Cady
Stanton went much farther than Mill in her demands for the legal reforms
that were necessary to end the oppression of women, while at the same
time arguing that legal reform was but one part of the problem. Thus, in
her speech on "Home Life," she argued strongly for liberal divorce laws on
the grounds that "marriage as an indissoluble tie is slavery for women,"
while Mill, although clearly moving in that direction, remained equivocal.[15] He addressed the question briefly in *The Subjection,* but regarded it
as not one he needed to address:

> Surely, if a woman is denied any lot in life but that of being the personal
> body-servant of a despot, and is dependent for everything upon the chance
> of finding one who may be disposed to make a favourite of her instead of
> merely a drudge, it is a very cruel aggravation of her fate that she should be
> allowed to try this chance only once. The natural sequel and corollary from
> this state of things would be, that since her all in life depends upon obtain-
> ing a good master, she should be allowed to change again and again until
> she finds one. I am not saying that she ought to be allowed this privilege.
> That is a totally different consideration. The question of divorce, in the
> sense involving liberty of remarriage, is one into which it is foreign to my
> purpose to enter. All I now say is, that to those to whom nothing but servi-
> tude is allowed, the free choice of servitude is the only, though a most insuf-
> ficient, alleviation.[16]

For Cady Stanton, by contrast, the question of marriage and divorce was
crucial. The suffrage and the public issue of women's rights were already
widely acknowledged, she argued in the 1870s, but what remained to be
addressed were "the social problems," particularly the fundamental issue
of the need for women's equality within the home.

The marriage question, in her view, was far more complex than it was
for Mill. As a married woman herself, strongly imbued both with a sense
of the importance of motherhood and maternal duty and also with a passionate desire for independence and a public life, she felt strongly the difficulties and dilemmas that faced married women in the course of their

daily life, in terms not only of their legal and social position, but also the demands on their time and energy that prevented their engagement in public life and activity. Insofar as Mill was even aware of this aspect of the question, he showed little interest in it. Marriage, in his view, was effectively a career choice for the women who entered into it. "Like a man when he chooses a profession," he argued, "so, when a woman marries, it may in general be understood that she makes choice of the management of a household and the bringing up of a family as the first call upon her exertions, during as many years of her life as may be required for the purpose; and that she renounces, not all other objects and occupations, but all of which are not consistent with the requirement of this."[17] Mill was careful to insist on the need to recognize that this generalization was not a law and that "utmost latitude ought to exist for the adaptation of general rules to individual suitabilities [*sic*]." Mill's wife, Harriet Taylor, had not accepted this position, and it certainly was not the view held by Cady Stanton. Her capacity in both letters and speeches to evoke the pressing nature of immediate demands, needs, frustrations, and anxieties of women, concerned both to do the best for their children and to live fully and follow their own imperative inclinations, makes very clear how distant and bland Mill's proposed remedies were.

In a similar way, Cady Stanton was both more forthright and more explicit in her approach to women and citizenship than either Mill or his British female contemporaries. Both Mill and Cady Stanton were concerned fundamentally to argue the case for the removal of women's legal and political disabilities. Mill was often at his best and most interesting in explaining the impact of these disabilities on women themselves and on society. As Martha Nussbaum has argued, his discussion of the eroticization of women's dependence and its importance throughout nineteenth-century society is one of the particularly memorable sections of his *Subjection of Women*.[18] On the other hand, Mill was considerably less willing than Cady Stanton to explain precisely what the removal of these disabilities entailed, or what the citizenship of women might mean. For the most part, he saw enfranchisement as the major way to ensure the removal of women's disabilities. He believed clearly in the need for reform of the property laws pertaining to women, something of extreme importance in Britain in the 1860s when women had no rights either to their inheritance nor to their earnings. But his primary concern was the vote, a measure he believed capable not only of bringing women's voice into the public arena, but also of transforming the private sphere by raising the status of women in the estimation of their husbands and by expanding their range of public and political interests.

While Cady Stanton shared Mill's sense of the importance of the vote both politically and symbolically, her demand for "the full recognition of all our rights as citizens" was more extensive than this.[19] She sought for women not only the suffrage, but also immediately the right to sit on juries, in addition to reform of the marriage laws as regards not only property but also custody and divorce. Mill did not press these other matters, and, indeed, particularly in regard to the question of jury rights, it is not clear that he would have done so. His insistence that married women would normally accept, as their primary responsibility, the care of household and family was for him sufficient reason to assume that most women would not, and should not, engage in paid work, and presumably the same held good for other activities in the public sphere.

Cady Stanton never attempted to articulate her differences from Mill, and it is not clear that she noticed or cared about them. Her admiration for him was too great. She approached him, moreover, as something more than just a thinker, but as an ideal husband whose own marriage offered a model of what that relationship could mean. Thus her admiration for Mill was greatly enhanced by her appreciation of his relationship with Harriet Taylor. This point was made clear in her first major discussion of Mill's *Subjection of Women*. Mill's emphasis on the importance of Harriet Taylor's intellectual influence appealed particularly to Cady Stanton. Mill, she wrote, "enters into the very life and experience of a proud true womanhood, and nobly uses the freedom of mankind . . . to say what few women dare to say for themselves. This work is in fact subjectively written for that true soul's wife, near whose grave he longs to linger, speaks through every page."[20] Mill's feelings for Harriet and his understanding of women made him appear to Cady Stanton also as a complete human being who contained within himself the finer qualities of both men and women. "In his writings," she noted, "Mill unites the consciousness and strength of the man with the tenderness and inspiration of the woman, and whether speaking of trade, science, philosophy or law. A deep abiding love for humanity breathes in every line."[21]

It is hard not to see Cady Stanton's enthusiasm for Mill and for his marriage as being all the more significant because of its contrast with her own. Her comments on Mill's marriage and on his adulation of Harriet Taylor stand in marked contrast to her descriptions of her own marriage.

Still, her domestic relations were far happier than those of 99 percent of married people, she assured her friend, Isabella Beecher Hooker, in 1869:

> Mr. Stanton is a highly cultivated liberal man; hence we are one in our literary tastes, he is a very cheerful, sunny, genial man, hence we can laugh together. His health is perfect hence we can walk and eat together, he loves music so do I, he loves oratory so do I, he is interested in all political questions so am I, but our theology is as wide apart as the north and south pole so we never talk on those points where we both feel most. My views trouble him. I accept his philosophically, knowing that certain organizations and education must produce certain results. If he could do the same, we should be nearer and dearer.[22]

Her letter came to a rather abrupt end at that point, as if the truth of what she was saying had become rather painful to her.

This picture of her own marriage was absolutely different from the "true marriage" of Mill and Harriet Taylor: "He and his glorified wife were one in all their studies, interests, and ambitions . . . this is marriage, a true union of the soul and intellect which leads, exalts and sanctifies the physical consummation."[23] Mill scholars and biographers are in general agreement that his relationship with Harriet Taylor was never consummated, and Cady Stanton's picture testifies far more to her own desires than it does to Mill's life.

Cady Stanton's admiration of Mill, and her sense of common endeavor with him, points to a strong central core of shared belief, one that is made very evident indeed in what many regard as her most significant statement of her beliefs, "Solitude of Self." In this speech, she insisted that every woman had self-sovereignty as a birthright and that ultimately, as an individual, she had to rely on herself. Both in her idea of society as made up of isolated individuals, in her stress on the importance of education for the full development of human faculties, and throughout in her insistence on the need to separate the rights and freedoms of the person from the accidental duties that arose through particular familial and social relationships, Cady Stanton was laying down ideas that accord closely with the views Mill has stated in his essay "On Liberty." Nor would he have disputed her application of these ideas to women. His only possible questioning of her views would have come from her insistence that the women of her day were now fully developed as intellectual and moral beings and that it was this that entitled them to exercise political rights.[24]

Nonetheless, despite the areas of agreement between them, and even despite Cady Stanton's sense of Mill's appreciation and understanding of women, it is unlikely that he would ever have accorded her any of the respect and admiration she offered him. Mill and Cady Stanton never actually met. Mill was invited to send a letter a women's suffrage convention in 1869, but declined the invitation on the grounds that "the cause, in America, has advanced beyond the stage at which it could need a recommendation from me, or from any man."[25] He died a few years later. Mill never mentioned Cady Stanton in his writing. His many critical comments on her English women contemporaries suggest strongly that he would often have disapproved of her ideas, her statements, and her activities. In particular, it seems likely that he would have deplored the breadth of her approach and her characteristic attempts to expand the basis for thinking about what women's emancipation entailed.

Although Mill's analysis of women's subordination was a broad and fairly comprehensive one, he did not accept the view that the women's movement should be similarly broad in its campaigns or objectives. On the contrary, he used all his influence in Britain in the late 1860s to insist that feminists focus their activities entirely on the suffrage question. The vote was to him the crucial measure. All else, he insisted, would follow from it—and any suggestion that energy be devoted to causes other than the suffrage course was to be strongly discouraged. Thus Mill strongly opposed the agitation to end the Contagious Diseases Acts that regulated prostitution in British naval ports and garrisons. He certainly accepted that the Contagious Diseases Acts were wrong in principle and socially damaging. But he feared that by becoming involved in an agitation that directly addressed the sexual double standard and the question of prostitution, women would bring opprobrium on themselves and thus damage the suffrage cause.[26] Cady Stanton's tendency to speak on many public and private matters, and to ignore strategic considerations, would have appalled him.

Nor would Mill have accepted all of Cady Stanton's ideas either on the kind of freedom that women needed, or on the wider social implications of their emancipation. Just as he raised doubts about the wisdom of Josephine Butler and indeed of Millicent Fawcett and about their suitability to lead campaigns, he would have raised them about Stanton. He would have deplored some of her more radical statements and seen her as unreliable in the extreme. Her speech on "Free Love" delivered in New York in 1869 is a case in point. In this speech, Cady Stanton insisted that what was needed to reform the position of women and society more broadly was not merely equality between women and men "in all the sense in which it is possible," but also something more expansive that she termed "free love." What is wanted, she insisted,

> is not merely suffrage and civic rights, and not merely in the second place the social recognition of the equal rank of the sexes, though both of these must be had, but Freedom, freedom from all unnecessary entanglement and concessions, freedom from all binding obligations involving impossibilities, freedom to repair mistakes; to express the manifoldness of our own natures, and to progress or to advance to higher planes of social development.[27]

Even freedom was not quite enough, for what was wanted was a new approach to virtue in which love is incorporated almost as the basis of a new religion. Men and women, Cady Stanton argued in a highly utopian moment, "must fall in love, not so much with each other as contributors to their own selfish wants as with each other's well being, in love with the truth, in love with goodness, in love with true harmonious relations, with the best possible conditions of culture and embodiment for all." It is this exalted feeling that Cady Stanton terms "free love" because of its lack of connection with any existing institutions, on the one hand, and its close connection with the highest forms of freedom, on the other. Mill would have found these views impossible to accept, if he was even able to grasp what she meant, and Cady Stanton made no mention of him in expounding them.

Although she rarely referred to the ideas of contemporary British women in her writing, in this as in several other speeches and essays Cady Stanton acknowledged both a debt and a sense of connection with Mary Wollstonecraft. "If I mistake not," she wrote toward the end of her speech on free love,

> the true lovers are among the most progressive and the most virtuous of women and men. The true nobility and virtue of Mary Wollstonecraft compelled her admission into the most aristocratic and the most moral circles in England . . . while she rejected all allegiance to the marriage institution and lived or had lived as the mistress of the man of her choice. Freedom is demanded at this day by the most enlightened and the most virtuous and not by the vicious.[28]

The importance of Wollstonecraft's influence on nineteenth-century American advocates of women's rights has recently been stressed by Eileen Hunt Botting and Christine Carey.[29] Insisting that the controversies surrounding her life after the publication of William Godwin's memoir of her had little effect on the importance attributed to her ideas, they trace both agreement with her ideas and knowledge of her expressed in the lives and letters of a number of prominent nineteenth-century feminists.[30] Botting and Carey trace Cady Stanton's early reading of Wollstonecraft (in the 1840s) and the important discussions about her work with another Wollstonecraft devotee, Lucretia Mott. It was in a letter to Mott that Cady Stanton made her most passionate statement of her hostility toward those who had condemned Wollstonecraft, as they did other radical women who rejected conventional sexual morality. "We have had women enough sacrificed to this sentimental, hypocritical prating about purity," she wrote.

> This is one of man's most effective engines for our division, & subjugation. he creates the public sentiment, builds the gallows, & then makes us hangmen for our sex. Women have crucified the Mary Wolsencrafts [sic], the Fanny Wrights, the Georges Sands, the Fanny Kembles, the Lucretia Motts of all ages, & now men mock us with the fact and say we are ever cruel to each other. Let us end this ignoble record and henceforth stand by womanhood.[31]

Cady Stanton had a particularly strong sense of Wollstonecraft as having been in some way a martyr to her views and to her belief in women's rights. In her view, Godwin, far from creating the opprobrium around Wollstonecraft that recent scholars have pointed to, was seeking rather to address the hostile response that arose as a result of her book. *The Vindication*

> examined the position of woman in the light of existing civilizations, and demanded for her the widest opportunities of education, industry, political knowledge and the right of representation. Although her work is filled with maxims of the highest morality and purest wisdom, it called forth such violent abuse, that her husband appealed for her from the judgement of contemporaries to that of mankind.[32]

But while Cady Stanton was clearly engrossed by the romance surrounding the life and death of Wollstonecraft, it is clear that her approach points to a strong intellectual affinity with her. One of the aspects of Wollstonecraft's thought that has been stressed most in recent scholarship centers on her insistence on the need to combine reason and emotion in thinking about both domestic and political systems. Wollstonecraft's Enlightenment heritage and her close reading of Rousseau provided the background for this, and her distinctive contribution was to demand an understanding of the ways in which they came together in thinking about the situation of women within both the family and the wider social and political world.[33] It is thus appropriate that Cady Stanton referred to her in her speech on "free love" because it was precisely this combination of reason and emotion that she herself was demanding, as she did later in her emphasis on the importance of feeling in "Solitude of Self." In the former work in which Cady Stanton allowed herself to move beyond the question of legal and social reform and to engage in a utopian dream of a complete transformation of sexual relations, it was Wollstonecraft, who had had similar dreams a century earlier, rather than Mill who came to mind. In the course of the twentieth century, Wollstonecraft has been rehabilitated and come to be recognized by many as the founding figure in Anglo-American feminism. Like Cady Stanton, she combined a strong belief in natural rights and in individualism with a sense of the need to understand the complex webs in which women were subordinated and bound by social, familial, and cultural ties and attitudes. Rarely are Cady Stanton's references to Wollstonecraft as fulsome as are those to John Stuart Mill. And yet the points at which she is mentioned are precisely those at which the focus is on the sexual oppression of women, on the one hand, or in which there is a utopian vision of a possible future in which there is a quite new relationship between the sexes, on the other. Cady Stanton's sense of affinity with Wollstonecraft emphasizes their shared radicalism, evident most clearly in their demand for a quite new kind of relationship between men and women.

NOTES

1. Dora Russell, *The Tamarisk Tree*, vol. 1: *My Quest for Liberty and Love* (London: Virago, 1977).

2. See Zillah Eisenstein, *The Radical Future of Liberal Feminism* (New York: Longman, 1981), 14–15; Barbara Caine, *Victorian Feminists* (Oxford: Oxford University Press, 1992), 34–37.

3. Kate Amberley to John Stuart Mill, 9 June 1869, Mill–Taylor Papers, British Library of Political and Economic Science.

4. Millicent Garrett Fawcett, "The Woman's Suffrage Movement," in *The Woman Question in Europe,* ed. Theodore Stanton (London: Low, Marston, Searle, and Rivington, 1888), 4.

5. Elizabeth Cady Stanton, "John Stuart Mill," 26 August 1869, in *Selected Papers of Elizabeth Cady Stanton,* ed. Ann D. Gordon (New Brunswick, N.J.: Rutgers University Press, 2000), 2:260.

6. John Stuart Mill, *The Subjection of Women* (1869); reprinted in John Stuart Mill and Harriet Taylor Mill, *Essays on Sex Equality* (Chicago: University of Chicago Press, 1970), 71.

7. David Rubinstein, *A Different World for Women: The Life of Millicent Garrett Fawcett* (New York: Harvester Wheatsheaf, 1991).

8. Elizabeth Cady Stanton, *Eighty Years and More Reminiscences, 1815–1897* (1898; reprinted, New York: Schocken Books,1971), 352–53, 371. For a discussion of their critiques, see Barbara Caine, *Victorian Feminists.*

9. *Eighty Years and More,* 363.

10. Sandra Stanley Holton, " 'To Educate Women into Rebellion': Elizabeth Cady Stanton and the Creation of a Transatlantic Network of Radical Suffragists," *American Historical Review,* October 1994, 1112–34.

11. See Sally Mitchell, *Frances Power Cobbe: Victorian Feminist, Journalist, Reformer* (Charlottesville: University of Virginia Press, 2004).

12. Cady Stanton, "John Stuart Mill."

13. Elizabeth Cady Stanton, "Home Life," in *Elizabeth Cady Stanton/Susan B. Anthony: Correspondence, Writing, Speeches,* ed. Ellen Carol DuBois (New York: Schocken Books, 1981), 131–38.

14. Lisa S. Strange, "Elizabeth Cady Stanton's *Woman's Bible* and the Roots of Feminist Theology," *Gender Issues,* Fall 1999, 29.

15. Cady Stanton, "Home Life," 133.

16. Mill, *Subjection of Women,* 86.

17. Ibid., 88.

18. Martha Nussbaum, *Sex and Social Justice* (New York: Oxford University Press, 2000).

19. *Elizabeth Cady Stanton/Susan B. Anthony: Correspondence, Writings, Speeches,* 45.

20. Cady Stanton, "John Stuart Mill," 260.

21. Ibid.

22. Elizabeth Cady Stanton to Isabella Beecher Hooker, 8 September 1869, Gordon, 2:263–64.

23. Cady Stanton, "John Stuart Mill."

24. Elizabeth Cady Stanton, "Solitude of Self" (1892), reprinted in *Elizabeth Cady Stanton/Susan B. Anthony: Correspondence, Writings, Speeches,* 246–54.

25. John Stuart Mill to Elizabeth Cady Stanton, 25 April 1869, in *The Later Letters of John Stuart Mill, 1849–1873*, ed. Francis E. Mineka, *Collected Works of John Stuart Mill* (Toronto: University of Toronto Press, 1972), 14:1594.

26. Barbara Caine, "John Stuart Mill and the English Women's Movement," *Historical Studies* 18 (1978), 52–67.

27. Elizabeth Cady Stanton, "Speech on Free Love," delivered in New York in 1869, in *Selected Papers of Elizabeth Cady Stanton and Susan B. Anthony*, 2:394.

28. Ibid., 396.

29. Eileen Hunt Botting and Christine Carey, "Wollstonecraft's Philosophical Impact on Nineteenth-Century American Women's Rights Advocates," *American Journal of Political Science* 48 (2004), 707–30.

30. William Godwin, *Memoirs of the Author of* "A Vindication of the Rights of Woman" (1796).

31. Cited in Botting and Carey, "Wollstonecraft's Philosophical Impact," 722.

32. Elizabeth Cady Stanton, Susan B. Anthony, and Mathilda Joslyn Gage, *The History of Woman Suffrage* (New York: Fowler and Wells, 1881), 1:34.

33. See particularly Virginia Sapiro, *A Vindication of Political Virtue: The Political Theory of Mary Wollstonecraft* (Chicago: University of Chicago Press, 1992), and Barbara Taylor, *Mary Wollstonecraft and the Feminist Imagination* (Cambridge: Cambridge University Press, 2003).

Chapter 4

Stanton on Self and Community

Richard Cándida Smith

Elizabeth Cady Stanton's apparently absolute defense of individual rights in her talk from 1892, "Solitude of Self," rests on a sober confrontation with mortality. She was seventy-six years old, still vibrant intellectually but facing the increasing physical limitations of old age. The feminist movement she had piloted since the 1840s was shifting away from a broad natural rights defense of women's equality in all areas of life into a narrower, more respectable campaign for the vote. Without question, she understood the importance of suffrage, for without the vote no person could participate in the great decisions of the day, in the decisions that affected the course of all lives. Stanton knew from years of experience that war and peace, slavery, immigration policy, definitions of moral and immoral behavior, or the course of economic development were not men's issues. The life of every woman was bound to the fate of her community. Suffering and success were inevitably shared. Stanton's defense of individual rights assumed the connections that tied people together. The work of her last decade presupposed the inextricability of self and community as she reasserted the simple proposition that every person needed to share responsibility for the fate of the world.

In "Solitude of Self," mortality is no longer knocking at Stanton's door. It walks with her wherever she goes. It challenges her with the question, What have you wrought? Was the life you shaped for yourself worth the sacrifice? The immediate response to the second question is yes!, but the first question is harder to answer when freedom, equality, and justice remain works in progress. Her image of the soul as pilot of a vessel heading into uncharted waters summarizes deftly the dilemma of all revolutionaries. A leap of faith is required to support the conviction that the future one intuits will overturn the evils of the present. Yet in "Solitude of Self" Stanton did not dwell on the bright world her daughters and granddaughters might inherit. She insisted instead on the uncertainty of the future. She based her claim for individual rights on the inescapable fact of ignorance. Her figure of the soul moving into uncharted waters symbolizes with crystal clarity the dilemma of free will. Why were humans blessed with the gifts of inquiry and choice if they can never know with certainty anything about their place in the structure of the world?

The question Stanton raised with its Calvinist overtones harking back to the religious education of her childhood must have resonated with all her listeners, the pious Christians as well as freethinking radicals. Stanton's answers, however, located the origins of free will in language that was aggressively positivist and social Darwinian. The struggle for survival stimulates intelligence and the acquisition of skill. Without the capacity for self-support, the individual is vulnerable to extinction. The finitude of individual existence does not support conservative religious instruction that a good Christian woman tames her will and submits to authority. Such passivity contradicted the laws driving biological and social development. The logic Stanton deployed insisted instead that survival required self-development, which in turn required self-sovereignty. The spiritual development of each person rested on freedom to exercise free will and to learn from the consequences of choices made.

This eclectic synthesis of liberal theology with increasingly popular scientific notions provided a rhetorical basis for long-standing arguments Stanton had made for the full extension of civil and political rights to women. Nonetheless, the word "self" used in the title of the talk presents a problem for contemporary readers. In the twentieth century, the self and self-actualization were such commonplaces for speaking of individuality that it is difficult to read the term independently of the psychological theories that did not yet exist when Stanton wrote "Solitude of Self." Indeed in 1892, "self" was still a new, indeed peculiar, term for signifying individuality. Stanton was part of a new movement that dates largely from the 1880s to talk about individuality in terms of self rather than character or will.

There were precursors to this development in transcendentalist thought, and certainly the word "self" existed in the English language long before the 1880s, but as a referential grammatical form rather than as a proper noun standing on its own and indicating an active agent. Stanton participated in this transformation of the subjective repertoires available to middle-class Americans. In this she was part of a movement that jettisoned religious ideas of personhood to develop new concepts of identity that were secular and scientific. Still, Stanton's talk relied as much on the concept of the soul as of the self. She refused a fully psychological conception of the subject. Throughout her adult life, Stanton stood with modernity against dogma. She was a skeptic freethinker in all matters of religion. At the end of the nineteenth century, however, both established religion and modern science provided justification for the restrictions society placed on women's lives. The rising star of Darwinian thought led to a decline of the natural rights philosophy that had guided her understanding of politics since her youth. She was not about to reject modern science when it provided a powerful explanation for the universality of free will, but she could not accept the new theories that explained female inferiority in terms of their role in sexual reproduction.

She engaged in a delicate, difficult balancing act during the last decade of her life. She turned to religious ideas as needed to rebuke modernist misogyny but relied on the conceptual tools provided by modern science and higher criticism to battle religious orthodoxy. Her defense of self-sovereignty in "Solitude of Self" required a more complicated conception of inner life than the much later theories of self-actualization that most twentieth-century readers brought to the interpretation of Stanton's argument.

In the very first sentence of the talk, Stanton speaks of the "individuality of each human soul" as the basis for Protestant and republican ideals of conscience and citizenship. *Soul* presents a conception of individuality that rests on a relation with the eternal. Soul as a reflection of the divine transcends history and social relations. *Self* appears in the essay in contexts of action and agency. Self is thought that leads to action. Self summarizes learned abilities, but soul points toward the uniqueness of each individual.

Every woman must develop the capacity for independent judgment, Stanton asserted, but, despite references to the struggle for survival that every biological entity faces, the goal is intellectual independence. It is this focus on spiritual gains that undercuts the atomistic aspects of liberal individualism in Stanton's work despite the powerful rhetorical flourishes that make "Solitude of Self" appear to be relentlessly suspicious of community. Each life is led alone, Stanton told her readers, a voyage in which each person is navigator, captain, and engineer. The deepest personal feelings, hopes, ambitions, disappointments "are known only to ourselves," meaning that no matter how hard we try they can never be fully shared. Every individual ultimately is isolated as she faces the most fundamental facts of her existence.

Nonetheless, community and public engagement remain defining conditions for realized individuality. Stanton identified books, interests in the "vital questions of the hour," "watching the consummation of reforms" as her own personal antidotes to the looming threat of senility. Engagement keeps the faculties of mind developed and in use. These engagements "mitigate the solitude that at times must come to everyone." Stanton established a dichotomy that is central to her argument: each soul is absolutely and inherently independent, but vitality is measured by activity, engagement, concern, by self moving out into the world.

Social engagement notwithstanding, inner life contains a center, the solitude of self, that remains independent from social demands because it has another, more powerful interlocutor. "Solitude of Self" presents a dichotomy within each individual's mental life that we can compare with William James's relatively simultaneous idea of consciousness alternating between active and reflective modes. The active self, James wrote, is unaware of what it is doing or even who it is. The reflective self examines but cannot act without stumbling. Its inward glance prepares the individual for the next burst of activity, but the fully self-conscious being is incapable of doing anything.[1] What Stanton called the soul is the equivalent of James's reflective self. An active, socially engaged self surrounds the soul, which stands forever apart from the social because it is connected to what she called the "the immeasurable and the eternal," one of her terms for God. While James was ready to describe the innermost workings of spirit as natural processes, simultaneously social and biological, Stanton found "omniscience"—a term most of her audience would have heard as a synonym for God—entering into the innermost recesses of the self.

William James was one of the writers who introduced the conception of the self as an agency into the English language. In 1884 in an essay for the journal *Mind*, James enunciated one of his most central themes: the soul, the self, consciousness, *whatever* one might call mental states, are not things, but only words giving substantive form to activities. The self was simply a cultural construct, a process of reflection upon past activity, a definition inaugurating new approaches to subjectivity that in effect translated inner life out of a religious, theocentric realm into one of cultural and social interaction.

In 1890 John Dewey wrote "On Some Current Conceptions of the Term 'Self,'" an essay appearing in *Mind* as part of an ongoing series of articles about the relation of "self," "self-consciousness," "soul," and "mind" as categories for understanding mental action.[2] Dewey saw a growing interest in phenomenology as the source of this new discourse of the "self" appearing in the 1880s. At the beginning of the essay, Dewey carefully noted that his argument did not deal with the actual nature of the "self," an empirical problem he left to others. He proposed only to consider its formal attributes within the Kantian and Hegelian theories of knowledge, which he assumed had provided the source for the new terminology. This proved to be more than a methodological position, for his argument hinged on an assumption that for both philosophers, although for quite distinct reasons, the self was a contentless category, unknowable and lacking inherent character.

The category of the self as most widely used in late nineteenth century Europe and America derived from Kant's definition of the transcendental self as the knower, as "the notion of knowledge in general." It is a container or form for thought-in-general, a principle of unity and connection. Dewey demonstrated that Kant's deduction of the self was an analytic proposition solely, a term using the law of identity to posit and discuss a personal consciousness of knowledge. Each individual consciousness was distinguished by its unique awareness of knowledge. The contents of consciousness were irrelevant, for "the identity of self-consciousness cannot be derived from knowledge of [its contents], for this knowledge presupposes that identity."[3]

The self was an atemporal, logical term covering the proposition that an individual (however constituted) knows only the contents of its own consciousness.[4] The self is a name "for the incident in which our knowledge occurs."[5] It cannot have a content beyond the "I think . . ." that the Cartesian turn had posited as the first condition of intelligent being. The self was not sensation, it was not reason, it was not will. Its contents comprised experience, but the self as such was only the possibility for reflecting upon events and transforming sensations into experience. The self is "an ideal which serves at once to organize and to reveal the incompleteness of experience."[6] While pointing to real processes, it must be without content. At most, we can say the self is a potentiality for making representations, and recedes once an image has formed.

As writers in the late nineteenth century, including Stanton, increasingly engaged the concept of self, a historical question raises itself starkly: Why this need for a category that did not have a content? The turn to the self involved a turn away from prior conceptions of character, will, and soul that more adequately conveyed spiritual unity, prescriptive values, continuity, and substantiality. The answer cannot lie in a greater explanatory power of the "self" concept since a definitional proposition that individual consciousness knows individually was simply, as Kant had bluntly accepted, a tautology that allowed him to proceed to analysis of the categories inherent to pure thought irrespective of who or what the thinker was.

Stanton held tight to the category *soul,* but her comments in her memoir *Eighty Years and More* (1898) about her adolescent conflict with Charles Finney may help explain her motivations for adopting *self* as a useful concept. Finney, like most other early nineteenth century revivalists, put great emphasis on the development of what he called "character." For Stanton, Finney's understanding of character was rooted in a conception of natural depravity. Finney and his followers manipulated their listeners' fears by insisting that sinful impulses would define them if they did not follow a narrow set of proper behaviors. In the aftermath of her encounter with Finney, Stanton embraced instead the very different assumption that the basic impulses of the soul were healthy and aimed toward growth. The concept of character was not needed as a stimulus for personal development. Indeed, it was negative because its power derived from fear of natural instincts, arbitrarily and falsely classified as depraved. "Good character" meant accepting uncritically the inevitability and the permanence of the social situation into which a person was born. The result of an emphasis on developing a "character" was persistent psychological depression, a malady that Stanton briefly but painfully experienced as a result of her efforts to be converted. She forcefully repudiated religious conformity for the rest of her life in part because it shut down interaction with the world and stunted personal development.[7]

The self provided an attractive alternative to character because it foregrounded curiosity, imagination, inquiry, creativity, and critical collaboration rather than restraint, discipline, fear, and obedience. After her brief exposure at school to Finney's evangelical movement, Stanton's appetite for knowledge and critical self-development was stimulated through reading and long discussions with friends and family. Social interaction restored her mind, she recalled, to "its normal condition." The self began to emerge through questioning the social realities that the category of character led to accepting as absolute goods.

Stanton gave credit especially to her eldest sister, Tryphena, and her husband, Edward Bayard, for providing her an intellectual environment that encouraged her as a young woman to develop her own feelings and articulate them into opinions. Stanton also stressed the importance of conversation with Lucretia Mott for learning how to express her doubts about politics, religion, and family. The self emerges in this contradictory picture through what her generation understood as the Socratic method, learning through questioning, dialogue, and identification of contradictions in arguments put forward. The process is neither individual nor even necessarily self-directed.[8]

While embracing the new concept of the self as a principle postulating active agency and engagement with the world, Stanton nonetheless resisted subordinating spiritual processes to social realities—even if the relationships were liberatory. The self is a function of community formation. Its inherent social character draws it back to existing social relations and hence to the bastions of the enemy—family, church, state, and finally science, all institutions that in Stanton's lifetime largely supported conceptions of female intellectual inferiority. She retained and indeed favored the term "soul" to indicate the importance of an inner life that transcended historical relationships and which took form in the individual conscience. Her concept of experience develops in the dialectic between social engagement and the "chamber of Eleusinian mystery" where the soul is infused with the sublime and otherworldly. As with "omniscience," Stanton's language is careful to avoid an anthropomorphic figure of God. The encounter of soul and eternity allows an intuited but ultimately unknowable divine presence to erupt into social life as a transformative force, thanks to the ability of the soul to take on the transient form of a self whenever it enters into dialogue with other human beings.

In *Eighty Years and More,* Stanton presented her life-experience in disarmingly simple, direct terms. She started with the everyday activities that defined the lives of women of her class and race—education, courtship, marriage, motherhood, household management. Maternity in particular unites the deeply social with the most permanent aspects of existence. Having raised seven children, Stanton had the opportunity to develop a well-tested set of experiences on child rearing. She wrote with verve and confidence, stating simply that motherhood was a "department of knowledge on which I particularly pride myself."[9] She emphasized the curiosity she brought to the task and a determination to get beneath appearances and find out the causes of problems. This was the self-image Stanton wanted to introduce to her readers.

"I never hear a child cry that I do not feel I am bound to find out the reason," she wrote in a statement that uses child rearing as a pattern applicable to other social relations where conflict and difficulties have arisen.

"A child's cry is telling you something hurts it," she continued, "—do not rest till you find what it is. Neither spanking, shaking, or scolding can relieve pain."[10] She followed this general statement with several accounts of how, while traveling on the train between speaking engagements, she helped many inexperienced young parents learn how to uncover the reasons their children were unhappy and take the necessary steps to restore family harmony. Experience in and of itself does not lead to understanding. Critical engagement that gets beneath superficial semblance is required.

In another anecdote, Stanton recalled how she intervened to stop drunken husbands in an Irish community near her home in Seneca Falls from beating their wives and children. Her account of relations with troublesome neighbors is rife with nativist assumptions about poor immigrants, suggesting the limitations of Stanton's ideas for how best to develop ties of community between old and new Americans. Nonetheless, Stanton starts with the assumption that human life is a struggle against ignorance. The challenge for revolutionaries is to spark a desire to know more. Rather than imposing her will on people who she recognizes might well be suspicious of her because of the social and ethnic inequalities dividing her world from theirs, she hoped to cultivate good feelings by sharing the knowledge she had gained. She lent reading materials that might provide a glimpse of the broader world. She gave her children's old toys to their children. She provided medical care and shared medicines she had made. As she described the relation, it was her willingness to share her critical engagement with everyday experience that turned her into a respected authority figure for her neighbors.

Her account certainly transforms the social capital she possessed as the daughter of a prominent jurist and landowner and the wife of a lawyer and political organizer into packets of knowledge that she could convey to the less fortunate. Expertise is operating in this account as unabashed social control. She was oblivious to the lessons she might learn from her neighbors, nor did she recognize the wealth and property of her family or her formal education as the bases for the deference exhibited to her, much less any traditions of patron-client relations transferred to Seneca Falls from rural Ireland or the Hudson River Valley. She described the key to her authority simply as her learned ability to synthesize from a broad range of experience lessons that could be applied to new situations.[11] The foundation for this ability was the "healthy discontent" that blessed her, an inner conviction that whatever confronted her was deficient in some form, as well as a "sympathy and imagination" that could embrace the sorrows of others and "learn all the hard lessons of life from the experience of others."[12]

Stanton provided a clue for understanding this productive relation of self and conscience in her highlighting in *Eighty Years and More* the powerful impact that Theodore Parker's sermon, "The Permanent and the Transient in Religion," had on her philosophy of life when she heard him deliver it in Boston in 1842. So impressed was she, she reported, that she traveled to another city simply to hear the sermon a second time. She noted that on reading it years later after Parker's work was published, his ideas no longer struck her as radical. They were simply good common sense whose truth any inquisitive person could recognize.[13]

Parker's sermon argued that Christianity had developed a fluctuating set of institutions and rites that had swallowed a permanent core of principles provided by Jesus' own words. Ideas and practices bearing the same relation to Jesus' teachings as "the phenomena of outward nature, such as sunshine and cloud, growth, decay, and reproduction, bear to the great law of nature, which underlies and supports them all" had corrupted Christianity.[14] The parables provide a demonstration of how to arrive at the truths to be learned through engagement. They describe the most familiar aspects of life in ways that encourage the truly faithful to feel a connection to the most permanent aspects of the universe. Parker questioned why the truths of Christianity should rest on the personal authority of Jesus, "more than the axioms of geometry rest on the personal authority of Euclid or Archimedes. The authority of Jesus, as of all teachers . . . must rest on the truth of his words, and not their truth on his authority."[15] The truth is to be tried by "the oracle God places in the breast," "the perpetual presence of him who made us and the stars over our head."[16] "We never are *Christians* as he was the *Christ,* until we worship, as Jesus did, with no mediator, with nothing between us and the Father of all."[17] In this direct communication, that which always is—the contact of God with the soul—reappears. The challenge is to cultivate the soul so that a person is ready to feel the divine presence.

The question implicit in Parker's sermon posed one of the most important problems Stanton faced as a late nineteenth century, religiously skeptical social reformer who nonetheless needed to maintain the role of the eternal soul in opposition to the historically situated self. At the same time, she needed to adopt the dynamic and interactive concept of the self to oppose the passive conception of character. Actually, existing individuals are deficient, indeed to the point of having forfeited their individuality. Habit, custom, institutional prerogatives prevail over selfhood.

"Statecraft, priestcraft, the cupidity of moneyed interests, and the ignorance of the masses," she stated, were all forces for evil separating human beings from divine and natural law and entrapping them in institutions that served the interests of one set of the population instead of all.[18] Precisely because all institutions governing everyday life are flawed, people are prevented from learning from experience even though they have the natural ability to engage their environment critically.

The process of constituting oneself as an individual begins with direct engagement with other persons who work together to develop critical detachment from all given institutions. They form a community of learning whose goal is the strengthening of each individual's capacity to think critically about every aspect of the world. Civic and political rights are necessary for this unfolding, but rights are insufficient for they are constituted through engagement with the transient. The challenge for social activists is to create an environment where the individual is trained to trust her inner voice, where she is pushed along toward self-reliance.

Cooperative structures were needed to support the development of a person able to think for herself. Otherwise, she would be so confused by the vertigo of free thought or victimized by the conflicting demands made on her that she might return to the security of dogma. In the most practical terms, women needed to transform family life with cooperative households that would free them from the tasks that occupied all their time, without, however, divorcing them from the direct human contact, especially with children, which gave them a distinctive perspective on existence. Women cannot develop as independent thinkers within the family unless the state helps to ensure the conditions for their children's growth.[19] To provide these resources, the system of economic competition that had developed through the nineteenth century needed to give way to socialism, which Stanton defined as the systematic organization of social resources along cooperative, scientific lines. Indeed, by 1898 suffrage had taken second place in her hierarchy of goals for the women's movement. The chief goal had become replacing competition with cooperation as the principle guiding "industrial economics."[20]

Stanton's vision described in *Eighty Years and More* of the collective conditions for individual growth provides a stark contrast to the unshareable core of individual existence presented in "Solitude of Self." To foreground either the individualist or the cooperative side of Stanton's thought is to ignore the dialectic principles embedded in her conception of self-development. Conscience served as a test of community for it provided the starting point for mutual evaluation of shared problems, which nonetheless were inevitably apprehended from distinct standpoints.

In her address delivered at Seneca Falls in 1848, Stanton insisted, in the course of arguing, that natural rights philosophy extended to women: "Man cannot speak for [woman], because he has been educated to believe that she differs from him so materially, that he cannot judge of thoughts, feelings, and opinions by his own. . . . The moment [moral beings] assume a different nature for any of their own kind, they utterly fail."[21] Men are unable to represent the needs of women because those needs have been defined as different, not because they actually are that way inherently or absolutely. Individuals who work to share moral standpoints can share their judgments and in the process grow as moral beings. This is not the same thing as interior life, however. Sharing does not eliminate difference but it creates a new form of social life through a process of reasoning, response, and negotiation. Conscience leads to comparison of findings, not to the withdrawal of each individual into his or her own private universe. In her 1875 essay, "Home Life," Stanton wrote, "The right of individual judgment in the family must of necessity involve discussion, dissension, division." Struggle within the family provides the dialectic conditions through which the family evolves as a group and the individuals within it continue to develop their distinctive capabilities.[22]

Stanton was clearest about the need to incorporate sexual difference into collective decision making, but her argument rested on a broader conception of dialogue. The encounter between any two people generates a continual puzzle of thinking through and learning from another person's experience. One has to work hard to make the lessons of the other meaningful, and this process of engagement keeps alive the process of growth that constitutes the self.[23] This position keeps Stanton in continuing communication with contemporary feminists who work on the intersection of gender with race, class, sexuality, and other social categories such as disability that combine into a complex hierarchy directly affecting each person's ability to contribute to a common life. Even though Stanton's ontology postulates an absolute differentiation of individuals before God, her epistemology of learning through engagement, dialogue, and working through the puzzle of difference puts a tension at the core of her thought that resists simple conclusions.

Difference may be inescapable but can be bridged if social organization is based on sharing perspectives. Social life gains its authenticity from a process of testing and retesting both personal and collective assumptions. This was not mere tolerance, for "experience has fully proved, that sympathy as a civil agent is vague and powerless until caught and chained in logical propositions and coined into law."[24] But the other side of Stanton's perspective is awareness that law as an institution must remain in dialogue with the thoughts and dreams of those for whom it provides rules. Stanton did not believe that virtue could be based on fear of punishment and spoke of freedom and social harmony growing out of "unwritten law and public sentiment" in contrast to the horrors of the inflexible legal and theological systems.[25]

The lessons that a person draws from her experience are relevant to others only as a person becomes critical and self-conscious. Without that awakening, a person simply repeats what she has learned from the institutions that demean her. Stanton's linkage of difference to self-development provides an important perspective on her frequent racist statements and reflects her own unexamined ethnocentrism. Stanton was scathingly critical of *all* community traditions and the resources they offered for change, those of her own class as well as those from other backgrounds. Women did not usually oppose their oppression because raw experience could not transform into positive lessons unless there was critical detachment from the dogma that united families into a community and provided a sense of personal identity.[26] Feminism became possible because modern thought allowed individuals to form new communities based on skeptical assessment of experience.

If tradition, whether popular or elitist, reinforces dominant ideologies rather than providing a bulwark for opposition, then the salience of difference changes. The critical thinker determines which differences are inherent to natural law and which have been falsely imposed by society. To the degree that differences are based in nature, social organization improves as those differences are recognized and incorporated into structure and function. Gender differences are a permanent feature of human life even though the interpretation of those differences varies, but class and race differences can be discounted as purely historical products of inequities that can be addressed only through a persistent emphasis on education and the encouragement of all to see what they have not yet experienced.

Stanton's strategies for sharing experience were consistent with her ideas about critical dialogue as the foundation of self-development. The lack of systematic theory in her work is notable and inevitably leads to

depreciation of her contribution to the understanding of social organization, a devaluation that occurs before her ideas are analyzed. Lack of theory does not mean absence of abstraction, but lessons appear in a stream
of charming anecdotes. Their casual form masks the ways in which they
function as parables, that is, as redacted experience linking the everyday to
conceptions of natural development. In her memoirs, we find the parable
of the daughter who takes up the study of Greek and horseback riding to
assuage her father's grief at the loss of his only son. Having won a prize for
her scholarship, she rushes home with one thought alone:

> "Now," said I, "my father will be satisfied with me." . . . I ran down the hill,
> rushed breathless into his office, laid the new Greek Testament, which was
> my prize, on his table and exclaimed: "here, I got it!" He took up the book,
> asked me some questions about the class, the teachers, the spectators, and
> evidently pleased, handed it back to me. Then, while I stood looking and
> waiting for him to say something which would show that he recognized the
> equality of the daughter with the son, he kissed me on the forehead and ex-
> claimed, with a sigh, "Ah, you should have been a boy!"[27]

This deeply moving and personal account sums up neatly the emotionally
self-destructive effects of gender conventions on both men and women. If
we take this as a purely personal story, we miss the craft and concision that
went into the telling of an *experience,* a welding together of ethical and social values into a single image that conveys a grounded judgment.[28]

This lesson was drawn from Stanton's own experience, but she found
useful lessons for her readers in the lives of people she met during her
many years of campaigning for women's rights. In the humorous parable
of the congressman's wife who bought a stove for her house without waiting for her husband's approval, Stanton tells of a woman who in a simple
act faced the fears that had long stymied her self-development. She
learned a new mode of thinking and, in reward, deepened the love her
husband felt for her. In both stories, the parable form allowed Stanton to
present abstract conclusions through concrete examples that to be interpreted must be taken into the heart. *Eighty Years and More* is full of these
anecdotes, but so are her writings throughout her career, including the
multivolume *History of Woman Suffrage.* The trail of anecdotes leads readers past many stopping points for thinking and judging. The effort to
abstract knowledge took the form of a dialogue shifting back and forth
from community with other transient social beings to communion with

the divine and permanent. By emphasizing this form of communication, Stanton affirmed her conviction in the irreducibility of difference in the formation of community. Without different perspectives, there would be no need for language and communication. Parables showed paths to self-autonomy within a community that need not be engulfed by institution, privilege, and habit.

One may wish that Stanton had augmented her parables with a theorized model of gender, individuality, community, but she offered instead a pragmatic, narrative knowledge. "Concordance" is the word that Paul Ricoeur uses to characterize the results of narrative understanding. Stories provide a sense of harmony. Those who participate in events become who they are through their role in the action, or as Ricoeur puts it, "The composition of the action governs the ethical quality of the characters."[29] There are no a prioris, but there are finite and unchangeable conclusions that determine everything that must be confronted if a change of heart is to take place. Stories provide an "intelligibility" of praxis by providing a moral standard for evaluating the outcomes of social relations. The knowledge provided leads one to grapple with the contradictions and inconsistencies of active social life. Community is revealed as common action not despite but because of difference.

This part of her thought is still lively and provocative and needs recovery as we reconsider the legacy of the twentieth century's often deadly wars of theoretical systems. Stanton wrote with a strong belief in the ultimate triumph of knowledge. Eternity, she said in 1895 in "My Creed," was a "continual progress of development." In commenting on Bjorn Bjornson's novel *In God's Way*, Stanton was puzzled by Bjornson's title because the characters all come to sad ends, which was not consistent with her understanding of the divine promise made to the soul. People's treatment of one another, yes, that was usually awful. Social relations typically extinguished people's spontaneous spiritual aspirations. That was why the soul remained for her an inner reality that stood with the divine against the limitations of society and biology, but not against the limitations of law. The observance of laws, both physical and psychic, she wrote in *The Woman's Bible*, is essential to health. This may be why, while authority was an important word for her, will was not. The self that she envisioned was never a law unto itself imposing its fantasy upon its environment, but an intelligence that sought happiness by learning and obeying the laws of life that the soul could discern always in conjunction with others who are equally inquisitive.[30]

NOTES

1. William James, *Principles of Psychology* (Cambridge, Mass.: Harvard University Press, 1983; originally published 1890), 1:271.

2. John Dewey, "On Some Current Conceptions of the Term 'Self,'" *Mind* 15 (1890), 2–18.

3. Ibid., 8.

4. The term "person" covered unity of consciousness across time.

5. Dewey, "Current Conceptions," 10.

6. Ibid., 17.

7. An influential mid-nineteenth century writer on character was Thomas C. Upham. In his essay "Immutability of Moral Distinctions" (*Biblical Repository and Quarterly Observer* 5 [July 1835], 117–36), Upham defined "character" as a sentiment that emerges in reaction to an "immutable standard of right and wrong . . . when any particular right or wrong comes to our notice" (125). Character changed through the development of fixed habits.

8. Stanton, *Eighty Years and More: Reminiscences, 1815–1897* (Boston: Northeastern University Press, 1993; originally published 1898), 41–44, 48, 82–84.

9. Ibid., 124.

10. Ibid., 122–23.

11. Ibid., 148.

12. Ibid., 189.

13. Ibid., 134.

14. Theodore Parker, "The Transient and the Permanent in Religion," in *Theodore Parker: An Anthology* (Boston: Beacon Press, 1960), 41.

15. Ibid., 49.

16. Ibid., 51, 56.

17. Ibid., 57.

18. Stanton, *Eighty Years and More*, 132.

19. Ibid., 429.

20. Stanton to Susan B. Anthony, 27 April 1898; in Ellen DuBois, ed., *The Elizabeth Cady Stanton–Susan B. Anthony Reader: Correspondence, Writings, Speeches* (Boston: Northeastern University Press, 1992), 288.

21. Stanton, address to the Seneca Falls Women's Rights Convention, 19 July 1848, in DuBois, *Stanton–Anthony Reader*, 28.

22. Stanton, "Home Life," in DuBois, *Stanton-Anthony Reader*, 133.

23. Stanton, *Eighty Years and More*, 36.

24. Stanton "Address of Welcome to the International Council of Women" (1888), in DuBois, *Stanton–Anthony Reader*, 211.

25. Stanton, *Eighty Years and More*, 8, 33.

26. In this, she held a perspective shared by Marx and Lenin, who both argued that "spontaneity" only reinforced exploitation and oppression.

27. Stanton, *Eighty Years and More,* 23.

28. Ann Gordon's epilogue to the republication of *Eighty Years and More* carefully traces Stanton's craft in congealing her political points into well-honed vignettes.

29. Paul Ricoeur, *Time and Narrative* (Chicago: University of Chicago Press, 1984); see vol. 1, ch. 2.

30. *The Woman's Bible* (Edinburgh: Polygon, 1985), 31.

Chapter 5

"The Pivot of the Marriage Relation"
Stanton's Analysis of Women's Subordination in Marriage

Ellen Carol DuBois

Soon after they first met, Elizabeth Stanton wrote to her new friend Susan B. Anthony, "It is vain to look for the elevation of woman so long as she is degraded in marriage. . . . I feel as never before that this whole question of woman's rights turns on the pivot of the marriage relation."[1] Six years later, Stanton elaborated her conviction that the subordination of women had its roots in the institution of marriage:

> In the review of woman's position—of her profitless labor—of her crippling, dwarfing dress—of her civic and legal disabilities—of her religious bondage—of her social degradation—we have by turns believed that in regulating any one of these abuses, we should reach all the rest. But those who in their own bodies and souls have borne the yoke of womanhood, . . . now clearly see that the most fatal step a woman can take, the *most false* of all earthly relations, is that under our present legal marriage institution . . . marriage is the question before us: the women's movement has brought us to that point."[2]

To appreciate Stanton's pioneering women's rights leadership, more sustained attention needs to be paid to her unrelenting search to understand the roots of women's subordination. Throughout her long career, two basic objects of these investigations into the roots of the degraded female condition stand out: marriage and religion. The first, the subject of this chapter, marked her early career, into the 1870s. The second, which characterized her later years, grew out of the first. Together, these long, creative inquiries into the sources of women's oppression alert us to the fact that Stanton's vision of women's emancipation, while rights based and rights focused, was fundamentally about something much deeper than legal status: the creation of a female self and the deepening of women's subjectivity. Understanding the ideas of Elizabeth Stanton in all their complex richness can be a way to reassert the deepest and most visionary strains in the feminist tradition, the elevation of women to full personhood.

The disabilities of women within marriage inspired Stanton's first foray into women's rights activism. She had been one of three women who had lobbied the New York legislature for a law allowing wives to retain the right to contract for real property.[3] For Stanton, the passage in the spring of 1848 of New York's first—and very limited—married women's property act was of great significance, opening up the larger project of reforming marriage. The inauguration of a women's movement for women's rights, declared in Seneca Falls a few weeks later, was meant to take advantage of this opening, so that legal alterations in the institution of marriage would lead to fundamental changes in the condition and character of women.

Carefully read, the 1848 Declaration of Sentiments points to Stanton's convictions about the fundamental role of marriage in explaining the "history of repeated injuries and usurpations on the part of man toward woman." "Government," which the Preamble condemns for "becoming destructive" of women's rights to "life, liberty and the pursuit of happiness," should be understood to be private as well as public, intimate as well as grand, the little commonwealth on which the greater one is premised. In the family, especially in the marital relation, man's aspiration to establish "an absolute tyranny" over woman had its clearest expression, perhaps even its source. The declaration's enumerated deprivations flowing from disfranchisement emphasize the disabilities of marriage: "Without representation, he has made her, if married, civilly dead"; and "in the covenant of marriage she is compelled to promise obedience to her husband, he becoming to all intents and purposes her master."

Stanton's feminist critique of marriage was preceded and perhaps influenced by Ernestine Rose, the Polish Jewish immigrant and British Owenite who was the first woman to lobby for the 1848 married women's property act. The Owenite critique of marriage was fundamentally economic. It targeted the privatization of property as organized through the family and condemned the economic dependence of women as enforced in it. Speaking before the 1851 national women's rights convention, Rose passionately declared: "I wish I had the power to make every one fully realize the degradation contained in the idea [of the husband's economic protection of the wife]. . . . He keeps her, and so does he a favorite horse, [for] by law they are both considered his property."[4] From Rose, Stanton may have learned to see that marriage as a social institution overpowered and shaped marriage as a personal relationship. "We did not . . . assemble to go into the detail of social life alone," explained Stanton soon after Seneca Falls, "we did not propose to petition the legislature to make our Husbands just, generous and courteous."[5]

Stanton's analysis of the institution of marriage, while shaped by the socialist critique, was not identical with it, nor limited to its essentially economic objections. One of the hallmarks of the socialist critique of marriage was that it was voiced as much in the name of men as of women; indeed, to the degree that men had more personal liberty to lose by entering into marriage, they were the major objectors to it. Historically, the socialist critique of marriage has been tainted by the suspicion that it increased men's privilege and power over women. For an aspiring women's rights movement, this was a problematic basis for proceeding. "[M]an, too, suffers in a false marriage relation," Stanton granted in a 1857 letter to Anthony, "yet what can his suffering be compared with what every woman experiences whether happy or unhappy? A man in marrying gives up no right, but a woman, every right, even the most sacred of all, the right to her own person."[6] For feminists to overcome this suspicion, they needed to develop a critique of marriage that took account of the distinctive subordination of women in marriage and tried to overcome rather than exacerbate it. They had to develop a convincing alternative to women's commonsense inclination to regard marriage as a protection from male irresponsibility and depredation.

Stanton found this more woman-focused critique of marriage in the temperance movement, to which she turned soon after Seneca Falls. As historians have pointed out, women were especially drawn to temperance reform because by indicting men's drinking, they were also able to protest the domestic vulnerability of women, which it exposed and intensified. In retrospect, we can see women's protests against men's drinking as thinly veiled condemnations of domestic abuse and marital rape. To the socialist economic critique of marriage and women's dependence in it, the female temperance tradition thus added a compelling condemnation of the sexual dimension of women's conjugal subordination.

The slogan used by Stanton to draw out the feminist implications of the temperance critique of women's sexual subordination in marriage was "legalized prostitution." Stanton may have learned the term from Wollstonecraft's *Vindication of the Rights of Women*, which she read at Lucretia

Mott's direction. "So long as our present false marriage relation continues, which in most cases is nothing more nor less than legalized prostitution," Stanton argued, referring to husbands' sexual rights over their wives, "woman can have no self respect, and of course man will have none for her. . . . There will be no response among women to our demands until we have first aroused in them a sense of personal dignity and independence," she wrote to Anthony.[7]

As Amy Dru Stanley argues, antebellum women's rights charges of marriage as legalized prostitution were meant to go beyond particular incidents of forced conjugal sexuality to indict the unfree quality of marital sexuality for women in general.[8] Until they had the right to refuse their husbands sexually, wives could never truly consent. Given the cultural importance of distinguishing the virtuous from the vicious, good women from bad, this rhetorical tactic was very effective in disrupting social complacency about marriage and calling the institution into question. The charge that marriage sheltered endemic sexual corruption challenged the crucial nineteenth-century moral distinction between legitimate and illegitimate heterosexuality by associating the former with the taint of the latter. In skilled feminist hands such as Stanton's, the slogan intimated that immoral sexuality began in marriage and from there moved into the streets, rather than the other way around.

Other women activists responded with relief and excitement to Stanton's forthright articulation of the widespread discontent of women with marriage. Lucy Stone, whose famous 1855 marriage under protest to Henry Blackwell may have been encouraged by Stanton's boldness, urged Stanton to go farther. The sexual corruption of marriage, she believed, "is a great, serious subject that only a few intuitive souls dimly understand, while a thousand aching and uncompanioned hearts and minds, wedded only in name, wait for the first ray of light to lead out of their abyss of sorrow. . . . I very much wish that a wife's right to her own body should be pushed at our next convention. It does seem to me that you are the one to do it."[9]

The high point of the antebellum women's rights marriage campaign was the Albany convention of 1854. The convention resolved that coverture, "the preposterous fiction that in the eye of the law husband and wife are one person, that person being the husband," was "the fundamental error of the whole structure of legislation and custom whereby women are practically sustained." The erosion of women's selfhood in marriage was not only economic but also moral and psychological. Marriage "impaired women's self respect and men's respect for them." Furthermore, the convention resolved, the structures of marriage reached beyond the conjugal couple to subordinate even unmarried wage-earning women via "that system of tutelage miscalled protection by which the industry of women is kept on half-pay, their affections trifled with, their energies crippled, and even their noblest aspirations wasted away in vain efforts, ennui and regret."[10]

Stanton was the convention's president. Her case for marital reform was so boldly put that it caused a near break with her father, even though he was an advocate of modernizing the New York legal code. In an elaborate analysis addressed to the New York legislature, Stanton asked, what kind of relationship was marriage? And what authorizes its claims? It was, she concluded, an unsatisfactory hybrid, a "kind of half-human, half-divine institution . . . which you may build up but not regulate," a compact that could be freely entered but never left. When it came to the implications of marriage for women, she was especially forceful: it was "instant civil death," turning "she who gave to the world a Saviour," into an "ignoble servile cringing slave" for whom "there is no higher law than the will of man."[11]

Marriage needed to be reorganized to make it like any other voluntary relationship, by which separate parties undertaking common ends "retain their identity and all the power and independence they had before contracting, with the full right to dissolve" the partnership at any time. Stanton's insistence that marriage should be fully and normatively contractual was a powerful approach. In a society based on private property, the only alternative to being a property holder, with rights to make contracts, was to be property itself, which is what she believed marriage made of women. "The sanctity of contract competed, perhaps on equal terms, with the sanctity of marriage," observes legal historian Hendrik Hartog; he therefore contends that Stanton's mobilization of contract theory on behalf of marital reform was "a necessary transgression," the emancipatory effect of which was the exact opposite of the creeping reification that classical Marxism predicted for the wage contract. As in the abolitionist movement, the women's rights intent was to shield the individual, the person, the self—not just legally, but morally and psychologically—from the full force of "commodity relations."[12]

Reaction to the 1854 meeting was predictably hostile. The legislature rejected women's rights petitions for further marital law reform, refusing, in the words of one assemblyman, "to put the stamp of truth upon the libel here set forth, that men and women in the matrimonial relation are to be equal."[13] Marriage and the social harmony it was meant to create, he contended, necessitated exactly "those inherent inequalities" which the petitioners sought to overthrow. The legislative committee charged with examining the petitions refused to "regard marriage as a mere contract," an idea the committee regarded as "a fatal error."[14] The committee was willing to recommend a few reforms in the more flagrant abuses of male marital privilege, but only so long as they were separated from the petitioners' objectionable anti-marriage "theory."[15]

But while Stanton's critique of marriage seemed to clarify the women's rights path and purpose, it also threatened to plunge feminism into the threatening waters of what was already being called "free love." Ever since the days of Frances Wright, "free love" had been an epithet thrown at freethinking female reformers, but by the 1850s an assorted crew of individualist radicals had embraced the term to designate a philosophy that called for the abolition of all government and church regulation of marriage. Beyond what marriage should *not* be (a state regulated institution), even self-acknowledged free lovers could not agree on what marriage *was,* on what form human affection might take when left to its own devices to develop naturally. Among the overwhelming majority appalled by this threat, however, there was consensus: free love meant sexual chaos, multiple partners, and infidelity.

Women's rights activists were drawn to and appalled by free love notions in equal portion. They agreed that normal conjugal sexuality was unfree and involuntary for women. But they feared that marital deconstruction alone would expose women to oppression of a worse sort, to the even greater economic dependency and sexual exploitation that awaited them if unmarried. "I am not one bit afraid of the censure which a discussion of this thing will bring," Lucy Stone wrote to Stanton, soon after undertaking her own marriage to Henry Blackwell. "If I were only sure what was the right. . . ."[16] Anthony, single herself though not by nature a social radical, responded to Stone with a powerful defense of Stanton's position: "Lucy, . . . we have played on the surface of things quite long enough. Getting the right to hold property, to vote, to wear what we please &c &c are all good—but Social Freedom, after all, lies at the bottom of all—& until woman gets that, she must continue the slave of man in all things."[17]

These tensions are clear in Stanton's writings and speeches on marriage in the 1850s. On the one hand, she was less afraid of (indeed more influenced by) free love than virtually any other women's rights leader of the time. She corresponded with the most prominent woman in the free love movement, Mary Gove Nichols, from whom she may have borrowed the term that she eventually came to use for women's right to full control of their reproductive and sexual capacities, "self sovereignty." Nichols wrote to her in 1852, "Every article you write hits the nail on the head. I like you vastly. I was complimented by being asked . . . by my own husband if I wrote that article of yours in *The Tribune*."[18] Speaking before the Progressive Friends of Rochester in 1857, Stanton came close to outright advocacy of the free love movement. "The Spiritual Union," she proclaimed, needs "no force to make it enduring; no cement but that which love and friendship ever produce." Adhering to a radical version of the anti-institutional convictions nourished in Garrisonianism, she declared, "let us cast [marriage] aside with other false institutions of the past. Let it fall with thrones and altars, with kings and priests. . . . In a republican government, man claims to stand above all institutions. Whatever is in the way of his development must be removed."[19]

Yet even in this 1857 speech, which reflected the hyperindividualist side of her thought, Stanton never called for the complete deregulation of sexual intimacy between women and men. She knew that women and men came to the reform of marriage with different, indeed conflicting, interests. "In the best condition of marriage as we now have it," she insisted, "to woman comes all the penalties and sacrifices . . . in marriage woman gives up all."[20] In addition, she was a convinced maternalist, who believed that women's mothering shaped the character of a society, for good or for ill. Indeed, her desire to empower motherhood socially and politically was one of the sources of her conviction about the importance of enfranchisement. Thus, when it came to marriage, she was not a "no government" person. She wanted government policy, formulated on women's behalf and under women's control, to oversee and regulate the family. She looked forward to a sort of female dictatorship over family relations.

All this might have remained elusive and abstract had it not been for the very concrete issue of divorce law reform. On the one hand, the necessity of allowing women a way of escape from bad marriages led to the very threshold of divorce. On the other hand, the power relations of men and women made easier divorce seem much more a threat than a promise to women's well-being. Resolving this contradiction was the dilemma that faced the nineteenth-century women's rights movement.

Liberalization of divorce law had long been a staple of the utopian socialist program, and in the 1850s it was beginning to be discussed in New York and other state legislatures. Stanton included the way that divorce laws favored men over women in the list of grievances presented at Seneca

Falls. Encouraged by the sentimental trope of the suffering drunkard's wife imploring heaven for relief, she and Anthony attempted to bring the case for divorce reform onto the women's temperance platform. "Shall the [drunkards' wives and children] be introduced but . . . as pathetic touches for the speakers' eloquence?" Stanton challenged. "Or shall we take active steps to relieve them of their suffering?"[21] But the churchly women of the temperance movement objected, and advocacy of divorce law liberalization cost Stanton and Anthony their temperance leadership.

Even among women's rights radicals, divorce was controversial. At the 1860 convention, it was the subject of a major debate, the first serious disagreement in the pre–Civil War movement. In the wake of the passage through the New York legislature of a much more comprehensive married women's property act, Stanton identified divorce law reform as the next step in dismantling women's marital subjection. She wanted the women's rights movement to support additional grounds for divorce, in particular drunkenness and abandonment, but more fundamentally, her goal was to decriminalize divorce. "An unfortunate or ill-assorted marriage is ever a calamity," Stanton insisted, "but . . . never, a crime."[22]

Antoinette Brown Blackwell, the first ordained woman minister, made the anti-divorce argument. Blackwell's understanding of marriage, while attentive to women's suffering, was far more conventional than Stanton's, and her efforts to deal with the corruptions of marriage were more tortured. "Marriage . . . with its possible incidents of children . . . must be from the nature of things as permanent as the life of the parties," she declared. Conceding "that women had a first and inviolable right to themselves, physically, mentally and morally," she offered unhappy wives a difficult prescription: "to go to some State where she can be legally divorced; and then . . . to return again . . . to work for [her husband's] redemption." Divorce or not, she must remember "that in the sight of God and her own soul, she is his wife, and that she owes to [her husband] the wife's loyalty." Ernestine Rose, implying that Blackwell's position was theologically rooted, caustically remarked, "The Rev. Mrs. Blackwell gave us . . . an excellent sermon in its proper place, but . . . she treats woman as some ethereal being. It is . . . quite requisite to be a little material also."[23]

Even in this debate, where Stanton's fierce individualism was on full display, she hesitated at the brink of a thorough deregulation of marriage. In the end, she too conceded that society as well as individuals had an interest in marriage, an interest she redefined in a feminist way as protecting women against men's abuse. This is the stirring point on which she concluded her pro-divorce remarks: "Thus far," she concluded, "we have had the man-marriage and nothing more . . . if in marriage either party claims the right to stand supreme, to woman, the mother of the race, belongs the scepter and the crown."[24] I still remain divided as to whether this tension between rights and protectionism represents an inconsistency in Stanton's analysis, or is the core of her perspective.

Where Stanton would have gone with her explorations into marriage is impossible to know because the debate was halted as soon as it had begun by outbreak of the Civil War. When the women's rights movement returned to the issue of marriage and divorce in the late 1860s, the terms had changed. The presence of the notorious Victoria Woodhull and her involvement with the Beecher adultery scandal moved the debate to the more abstract and incendiary territory of who did and did not support free love and who, by so doing, threatened the very fabric of family and thus of national order. The Woodhull episode contributed to the closing down of political and social debate on marriage, to the sexual and domestic stasis of American Victorianism.[25] In the aftermath of the Woodhull affair, Stanton switched her exploration of the sources of women's subordination from "marriage" to "religion," although she often linked the two subjects.

Even so, gains had been made. By 1870, even the most conservative of spokeswomen, Antoinette Brown Blackwell's sister-in-law, Dr. Elizabeth Blackwell, believed in the necessity of tackling women's marital subordination. And much of the credit must be given to Stanton. "To her lectures is due a healthier tone of public sentiment on the marriage question," Paulina Wright Davis wrote in 1871. "It is slowly beginning to be felt that in that relation there is a vast amount of legalized prostitution, bearing the semblance of virtue, which is rotten below the fair exterior."[26]

It is striking how very little interest the most recent wave of feminism has had in exploring marriage. To be sure, the seminormalization of lesbianism has provided a functional alternative to marriage, and no-fault divorce has made it easier to leave a bad marriage. Perhaps feminists agree with most other modern liberals that marriage has become, finally, a thoroughly personal option, an essentially private relationship. But recent political developments, from the Defense of Marriage Act to the hysterical reaction against the specter of gay marriage to the Bush administration's program of "encouraging marriage" among the poor, suggest otherwise. In her new history of marriage, Nancy Cott writes, "The whole system of attribution and meaning that we call gender relies on and to a great extent derives from the structuring provided by marriage."[27] In an essay I wrote some time ago, I made a companion claim about feminism and marriage: "Within the history of feminism . . . the battle against coverture . . . can be traced into the twentieth century and through to our contemporary concerns . . . [there are still] radical possibilities to be found in protesting the institution of marriage as the root of women's subordination."[28] Stanton's project, of locating the sources of women's subordination in the institutional structures of marriage, remains incomplete. Exploring her provocative writings on this matter holds more than antiquarian interest.

NOTES

1. Stanton to Anthony, 1 March 1853, *The Elizabeth Cady Stanton–Susan B. Anthony Reader: Correspondence, Writings, Speeches,* ed. Ellen Carol DuBois (Boston: Northeastern University Press, 1992), 48. Of the letters that remain between them, this is only the second.

2. "Paper by Elizabeth Cady Stanton for the Yearly Meeting of the Friends of Human Progress, 1857," *The Selected Papers of Elizabeth Cady Stanton and Susan B. Anthony,* ed. Ann D. Gordon (New Brunswick, N.J.: Rutgers University Press, 1997), 1:342.

3. The other two were Ernestine Rose and the physical and moral reformer Paulina Wright Davis.

4. Yuri Suhl, *Ernestine Rose and the Battle for Human Rights* (New York: Reynal, 1959), 282.

5. "Address by Elizabeth Cady Stanton on Women's Rights, 1848," in *Selected Papers,* 1:103.

6. Stanton to Anthony, 20 July 1857, in *Elizabeth Cady Stanton as Revealed in Her Letters,* ed. Theodore Stanton and Harriot Stanton Blatch (New York: Harper and Brothers, 1922), 69.

7. Ibid.

8. Amy Dru Stanley, "Conjugal Bonds and Wage Labor: Rights of Contract in the Age of Emancipation," *Journal of American History* 75 (1988), 471–500.

9. Stone to Stanton, 22 October 1856, in *Elizabeth Cady Stanton as Revealed in Her Letters,* 67.

10. *History of Woman Suffrage,* ed. Elizabeth Cady Stanton, Susan B. Anthony, and Matilda Joslyn Gage (Rochester, N.Y.: Susan B. Anthony, 1889), 1:594.

11. *Selected Papers,* 1:246–47.

12. Hendrik Hartog, "Marital Exits and Marital Expectations in Nineteenth-Century America," *Georgetown Law Review* 80 (1991), 107–8. Amy Dru Stanley

argues the same in *From Bondage to Contract: Wage Labor, Marriage and the Market in the Age of Slave Emancipation* (Cambridge: Cambridge University Press, 1998), 254.

13. *History of Woman Suffrage,* 1:613.

14. Ibid., 1:616–17.

15. Specifically, that a wife with a profligate, drunken, or deserting husband could keep her own earnings, and that a mother must agree to the apprenticeship of her children.

16. Stone to Stanton, 22 October 1856, *Elizabeth Cady Stanton as Revealed in Her Letters,* 67.

17. Anthony to Stone, 16 June 1857, *Selected Papers,* 1:345. Anthony was personally uncomfortable with remarriage even in the cases of widowhood.

18. Nichols to Stanton, 21 August 1852, *Elizabeth Cady Stanton as Revealed in Her Letters,* 44.

19. "Paper by Elizabeth Cady Stanton for the Yearly Meeting of the Friends of Human Progress, 1857," *Selected Papers,* 1:344.

20. "Speech to Tenth National Women's Rights Convention, May 11, 1860," *Selected Papers,* 423.

21. *History of Woman Suffrage,* 1:496.

22. *Selected Papers,* 1:116.

23. *History of Woman Suffrage,* 1:729.

24. *Selected Papers,* 1:427.

25. This was William O'Neill's contention in *Everyone Was Brave: A History of Feminism in America* (New York: Quadrangle, 1971), with which I now agree.

26. Quoted in *Stanton–Anthony Reader,* 97.

27. Nancy Cott, *Public Vows: A History of Marriage and the Nation* (Cambridge, Mass.: Harvard University Press, 2000), 3.

28. "A Vindication of Women's Rights," in Ellen DuBois, *Woman Suffrage, Women's Rights* (New York: New York University Press, 1998), 284.

Chapter 6

"Free Woman Is a Divine Being, the Savior of Mankind"

Stanton's Exploration of Religion and Gender

Kathi Kern

In 1896 the National American Woman Suffrage Association repudiated Elizabeth Cady Stanton's recently published book, *The Woman's Bible*. In a debate that was widely publicized in the national press, suffragists weighed and measured the extent to which Stanton's controversial work had damaged their movement. Stanton was devastated. But she was also convinced that her critique of religion was more timely than ever. [1] The very integrity of the republic was at stake. "Much as I desire the suffrage," she wrote, I would rather never vote than to see the policies of our government at the mercy of the religious bigotry of [such] women. My heart's desire is to lift women out of all these dangerous, degrading superstitions & to this end will I labor my remaining days on earth."[2] Stanton wrote with a sense of urgency, instructing the editor of the paper, "Squeeze in this week if possible." But the editor in question, Clara Colby of the *Woman's Tribune*, was reluctant to offend her suffrage readers, many of whom were deeply religious, with Mrs. Stanton's latest pronouncement. Colby had defended Stanton vigorously in the Bible debates just two months earlier, but now she hesitated. Disappointed, Stanton responded, "In view of what you say I will consider my article a little further before publishing. Return it to me, I will weigh your suggestions. Something must be said to show women their dangerous tendency to bigotry & how fatal it would be to a liberal government."[3]

The question that concerns me is how did Elizabeth Cady Stanton come to embrace this position? Was she truly willing to sacrifice her own right to suffrage in order to protect the government from the influence of other women? While the conflict over *The Woman's Bible* may provide the immediate context for Stanton's remarks, her ambivalence toward collective female agency did not emerge suddenly out of the bitterness of the Bible debates. Rather, it grew out of her lifelong negotiation with religious ideas.

In recovering Stanton as a historical subject, we need to pay close attention to the place of religious discourse in her arguments for women's equality. Stanton firmly believed that women's emancipation could only be achieved through what she called "religious liberty," freedom from "the old theological superstitions." In championing women's religious liberty, Stanton rejected outright one article of faith in the nineteenth-century woman's movement: that Christian piety was the starting point for women's political agency. Her efforts to emancipate women from traditional Protestantism drew heavily upon the intellectual traditions of her time, particularly the broad reconstruction of theology inspired by positivism.[4] Stanton's early and passionate attachment to positivism remained an anchor in her intellectual voyage. But she also steered in the direction of free thought and agnosticism. The tension in these intellectual frameworks pulled Stanton's thinking about women's emancipation in conflicting directions. Positivism allowed Stanton greater latitude to rework religious traditions and to maintain a pivotal role for women's collective agency in the broader transformation of the society. Free thought, an essential tool in Stanton's efforts to challenge clerical and biblical authority, undercut her commitment to collective female agency.

Stanton's Theological Project

A nearly lifelong interest, the religion question preoccupied Stanton especially for the last two decades of her life. Despite Susan B. Anthony's plea that Stanton abandon her attack on St. Paul and "let 'Jimmy Grind' out against colorphobia & sexphobia [of] men & women to day," Stanton kept her unwavering eye on the Bible and the church.[5] It is worth pausing on this point because Stanton is routinely identified as a "secularist" for whom religion was presumably a vestige of the past, an obstacle in the path toward modernity. But as her prolific religious writings—lyceum lectures, pamphlets, journal articles, and manuscript writings—attest, Stanton was deeply immersed in theological ideas. She acknowledged the fundamental importance of religion to women and to American society of the nineteenth century. And she hoped to use her skills to refashion Christianity into a creed that was true to its radical potential. Stanton's intellectual engagement with religion and gender centered on four interrelated questions: What can be preserved, what needs to be purged, what can be substituted, and what will the next step be?

What Can Be Preserved?

Although Stanton did not see herself as part of a larger religious movement, she nevertheless engaged in the same intellectual quest that occupied many Protestant theologians of the nineteenth century: the reconstruction of theology.[6] Stanton frequently acknowledged aspects of organized Christianity that were worth preserving. She departed from the rather prevalent anti-Catholicism that undermined the women's rights movement in this era and heaped praise upon the feminized aspects of the Catholic Church: the convents and Catholic sisterhoods, as well as the Catholic veneration of the Virgin Mary—evidence, she thought, of the recognition of a feminine aspect of God.[7]

She also believed that Jesus and his teachings were worth preserving, that is, if you could access them in an uncontaminated form. Stanton was no doubt influenced by the radical Quaker women who shaped her outlook as a young woman. Lucretia Mott wrote to her not long after the two had met in London at the World Antislavery Convention of 1840:

> And my dear, what is the result of all the enquiries of they open, generous confiding spirit? Art thou settled on the sure foundation, of the revealed will of God to the inner sense? Or is thy mind still perplexed with the schemes of salvation, and plans of redemption which are taught in the schools of Theology? It is lamentable, that the simple & benign religion of Jesus should be so encumbered with the creeds & dogmas of sects—Its primitive beauty obscured by these gloomy appendages of man.[8]

Stanton carefully preserved that legacy from Lucretia Mott and continued to modify it, to assert its relevance to the culture of the late nineteenth century. Fifty years after she first encountered Mott, Stanton echoed Mott's point about the power of that "simple and benign" message:

> The life and teachings of Jesus, all pointing to the complete equality of the human family, were too far in advance of his age to mould public opinion.

We must distinguish between the teachings attributed to Jesus and those of the Christian Church. One represents the ideal the race is destined to attain; the other, the popular sentiment of its time. Had Jesus lived in Russia in the nineteenth century, he would have been exiled as a Nihilist for his protests against tyranny and his sympathy with the suffering masses. He would have been driven from Germany as a socialist, from France as a Communist, and imprisoned as a blasphemer in England and America, had he taught in London and New York the radical ideas he proclaimed in Palestine.[9]

The Messiah of the religion Stanton decried was actually a sympathetic figure. Reincarnated in the nineteenth century, Jesus would have been persecuted anew for his radicalism. Stanton hoped to rescue Jesus from the corruption of organized religion; she embarked on a similar mission with the idea of God. Within her theology, Stanton assigned a pivotal role to "Intelligence, or Supreme Law, Nature, God or whatever one may choose to call the eternal forces that set all this in motion." God, for Stanton, was benevolent, never angry or vengeful. Nor did her theology accommodate the devil. "Our sorrows in life are not caused by the direct fiat of a malevolent Being," she asserted, "but by our own ignorance or indifference to the laws of our being."[10]

Stanton's belief in God reflected her commitment to positivism. She drew upon scientific analogies to comprehend the spiritual world. "God only is positive," she explained, "evil a negation, just as light is positive [and] darkness a negation." The contrasting view promulgated by the Church had brought devastating consequences: "Man has been so sedulously educated with the belief of evil as a supreme force the total depravity of the race, a stern God punishing us by direct fiat for our violations of law that justice love mercy & happiness have been eliminated in large measure from this life & the life to come." As humanity ignored the "unchangeable" law of God, the law of "tender emotions, of love friendship sympathy & charity," the people suffered accordingly. "If we defy the law of gravitation," Stanton explained by way of analogy, "a broken neck or leg will be the penalty." The moral world worked in a similar fashion.[11]

Christianity, then, offered Stanton a versatile set of raw materials to rework into a viable faith for women's emancipation. With a little excavation, both Jesus and God could be released from the traditions that had captured them and muted their emancipatory potential. Even prayer was worth preserving. The problem with prayer, according to Stanton, lay in the common assumption that God answered prayer through divine intervention. She saw no evidence of that. She believed, however, that the value of prayer lay in its ability to motivate the seeker. Prayer "may culminate in action & enable us to assume responsibility we lay on the Spirit of Good or Evil. We must understand that we hold our destiny in our own hands, whether for weal or woe are wholly responsible."[12] Like prayer, the Christian concept of immortality resonated with possibility for Stanton. Immortality reflected her foundational belief in the eternal progress of civilization. While she could not know for certain, Stanton believed "we may logically infer that the same laws will govern the eternity & that the next life will be a continual progression and development."[13] But of all the articles of Christian faith that Stanton refurbished—Jesus, God, prayer, immortality—none was more valuable to her theology than the Protestant notion of conversion.

Stanton, always regarded as a raconteur, was fond of telling her own conversion story. In her autobiography, she artfully narrates the plot of her failed conversion to evangelical Christianity, but her real conversion comes a bit later. At Niagara Falls—not coincidentally a site that signified the "Religion of Nature" to nineteenth-century readers—Stanton was converted to rationalism. "My religious superstitions gave place to rational ideas based on scientific facts, and in proportion, as I looked at everything from a new standpoint, I grew more and more happy, day by day."[14] Once converted, Stanton made the conversion of other women her sacred duty: "I have endeavored to dissipate these religious superstitions from the minds of women and base their faith on science and reason, where I found for myself at last that peace and comfort I could never find in the Bible and church."[15]

Conversion hinged on the premise of the individual conscience and, without a doubt, this was the most crucial aspect of traditional Christianity worth preserving. In her legendary speech, "Solitude of Self," Stanton fused "our Protestant idea, the right of individual conscience" with "our republican idea—individual citizenship."[16] Stanton argued that the isolation and self-reliance of every human soul necessitated its political autonomy, the fulfillment of its "birthright to self-sovereignty." The tragic life of Jesus illustrated her point: "In the highways of Palestine; in prayer and fasting on the solitary mountain top; in the Gardens of Gethsemane; before the judgment seat of Pilate; betrayed by one of His trusted disciples at His last supper; in the agonies on the cross, even Jesus of Nazareth, in those last sad days on earth, felt the awful solitude of self."[17] Jesus' teachings were a valuable artifact in Stanton's preservation project, but perhaps his life story held even more potential as it illustrated the harmony of Protestantism and republicanism, the individual conscience with the individual citizen.

What Needs to Be Purged?

The individual human soul—the right of individual conscience—this was the potentially good news of Christianity, despite the stark destiny of isolation that awaited each individual soul. But in Stanton's mind this universal truth of Protestantism had been corrupted. Instead of teaching the doctrine of individual conscience, Protestants had taught the subjection of one class of individuals to another and undercut the radical potential of Christianity. Much of Stanton's work on religion needs to be understood as an intervention: she desperately wanted to rescue the individual conscience from the grasp of Christianity. Stanton firmly believed that change in the social order began at the level of the individual conscience; hence it became crucial to her to "save" women from religion, from the perversion of their individual consciences by false superstitions. "When woman discards the church," she wrote, "she will be free & free woman is a divine being, the savior of mankind. Would you have man deify & worship a slave?"[18]

"My convictions from year to year have been growing stronger," Stanton wrote in 1901, "that before we can secure woman's emancipation from the slavery and superstitions of the past, we have an important work to do in the Church."[19] Although many of Christianity's central features were worthy of maintaining in some form, several required serious tweaking, including the idea of a personal God. Stanton stressed her belief in a higher power—"Intelligence, or Supreme Law, Nature, God"—the evidence was all about her in the physical, material world. God was the author of "law everywhere—the sun moon & stars the constellations the days & nights, the seasons, at regular intervals all come & go."[20] While she did not doubt the existence of God, she did question how people conceptualized God. "Sometimes, yes often, I think the best thing that could be done for woman & hence for humanity would be to destroy the present false idea of a personal God in the skies or elsewhere, that we might see & worship the divine in humanity."[21] The idea of a personal God only served to create a barrier between people. "A loving human fellowship is the real divine communion."[22]

Christians' anthropomorphic notions of God limited their potential for divine communion. The Bible only encouraged such behavior. The center of Stanton's theological work was her call for an "expurgated Bible." Her own Bible had been published and in circulation for six years, but Stanton continued to agitate for a Bible censored for misogyny, one that would be appropriate for use in the public schools, one that would not humiliate women when they heard it read in their churches. In the months preceding her death, Stanton continued to publish articles calling for an international convention of liberal men and women to review the Bible and edit a version "in harmony with science and philosophy, worthy the reverence and belief of intelligent human beings."[23] The traditional focus on the Bible and its literal interpretation was too static for Stanton; it did not allow for an evolving, progressive society. "The new religion," Stanton explained "will teach the dignity of human nature, and its infinite possibilities for development."[24]

What Can Be Substituted?

Even as Stanton persisted in her public critique of the Bible, she never questioned the ultimate value of faith itself. "My dream of the future is cooperation," she wrote in 1882. "But is there any other foundation outside of religion on which it can be based? Can a belief grounded on science, common sense, and love of humanity sway the human soul as fears of the torments of hell and promises of the joys of heaven have done?"[25] Stanton frequently wondered aloud: what could be substituted for traditional religious faith? Her answers varied over time: A heavenly mother? Education? The love of humanity? Reason? A new religion? Socialism?

Stanton's notion of religious liberty evolved in dialogue with some of the major concepts of social theory in the nineteenth century. As Ellen DuBois has noted, Stanton's particular contribution was to push male-dominated movements to a more radical stance on gender issues as she simultaneously worked at translating and applying their critiques to woman's condition.[26] On the issue of religious faith, Stanton applied the insights she gained from positivism and free thought to woman's condition. Within these two intellectual traditions, Stanton found support for her views. But as analytical frameworks, these theories offered very different visions of women's agency. With her engagement in positivism and free thought, Stanton's position on the place of "woman" as a potential agent of change shifted and mutated.

Like many a nineteenth-century reformer, Stanton was inspired by the work of the French positivist, Auguste Comte. Basing his theories on the "immutable laws" of science that controlled the physical, material world, Comte argued that immutable laws similarly governed the moral world of human affairs. In understanding Stanton's positivism, we are dragged back into a murky nineteenth-century world of immutable laws and verbal dichotomies: mind and matter, feminine and masculine elements, centripetal and centrifugal forces, moral force and brute force. As the historian William Leach has argued, these paired dichotomies underscored a model of symmetry that was rooted in the body and reflected reformers' notions of health and well-being. Every healthy body balanced its masculine and feminine elements in a perfect equilibrium. Social organization should ideally magnify the model of the body. This symmetry within was projected outward and served to bind individuals into the harmonious action of a balanced social order.[27]

Comte particularly privileged the role of the "feminine element" in bringing about the new world order. Not long after her own conversion to positivism in the 1860s, Stanton informed the readers of the *Revolution* that Comte made woman "primal to the reconstruction of the state, the church, and the home."[28] Stanton was particularly persuaded by Comte's notion of the "Religion of Humanity."[29] While she was never formally a practitioner herself, she nevertheless championed this theological innovation. "As I read the signs of the times," she wrote to the World Parliament of Religions in 1893, "I think the next form of religion will be the 'Religion of Humanity,' in which men and women will worship what they see of the divine in each other."[30] This was an appealing, hopeful message for American women. "To change the position of woman in dogmatic theology, where she is represented as the central figure in Paradise Lost . . . is to revolutionize the system; hence all those who believe in progress within the Church should hail the present movement for woman's emancipation, as that brings us to the next onward step in the new religion."[31] From her earliest embrace of positivism to her late-in-life conversion to socialism, Stanton had an eye on the future. She frequently asked, "What will the next step be?" Her focus on purging Christianity of its problematic features kept her thinking a great deal about the past, much to the chagrin of Susan B. Anthony. She lectured Stanton: "The trouble is in ourselves to day—not in men or books thousands of years ago."[32] But Stanton was every bit as interested in imagining a future: a true republic, a true religion, and "woman" as the causal agent who brings that imagined future to fruition. Positivism provided a compelling strategy, particularly at this moment of social and political crisis:

> As we look around us to day & see the vice pauperism & crime, the misery in our jails& prisons, the wretched hovels in which those who are doing the work of the world are crowded, the degradation & ignorance of the despairing masses, & listen to the low threatening thunders of discontent, nihilism in Russia, socialism in Germany, Communism in France, mob strikes & dynamite in England and American, the mothers of nations are warned, that they must bestir themselves to avert if they would save their children [from] the coming dangers of the gathering storm.[33]

Woman was the moral force whose proper inclusion in the Church and state could restore balance and, perhaps, avert the gathering storm.

Positivist ideas had great currency among nineteenth-century American reformers and clergy. Yet it is curious that Stanton, who was always on the lookout for would-be colleagues who shared her views, did not connect more substantively with Comte's other American followers. One suspects that Stanton's primary political commitments to women's equality and to republicanism may have kept her at a principled distance from some of the leading male proponents of the Religion of Humanity.[34]

In the 1880s and 1890s, Stanton experimented with a variety of new religions in search of a viable faith for woman's equality. Her confrontation with theosophy serves as a case in point. In 1890 during an extended stay with her daughter Harriot Stanton Blatch in England, Stanton—after "many appealing epistles"—successfully lured Annie Besant to Harriot's home for a visit. Besant was a disciple of the famed Madame Blavatsky and a leading theosophist in her own right. She was one of the most well known women in Great Britain. Stanton was charmed by Besant and very impressed with her "unselfish devotion to the public good."[35] She was also intrigued by the regimen deemed necessary for the study of the occult— "early rising, abundant exercise, a vegetarian & fruit diet." Throughout the visit, Harriot and Mrs. Stanton accommodated Besant's vegetarianism. Stanton did register a small victory when she convinced Besant to show her "special respect for republican institutions" by eating some of their delicious American "angel food" cake—"a cake fit not only for the Gods but the Theosophists."

Here we find Stanton, allegedly at the height of her agnostic convictions, thoroughly engrossed in Annie Besant, and not just her diet, but also her metaphysical ideas. Spending most of their visit in "high discourse," Besant introduced Stanton to the doctrine of reincarnation, which, Stanton explained: "I particularly enjoyed. It satisfies my sense of justice." Reincarnation might be just the thing to "purge us of selfishness, egotism & pride & cultivate in us the love of justice mercy & equal rights to all. I do hope the doctrine of reincarnation is true," she continued. "In this case all those wicked Democrats in Congress who have opposed woman suffrage will return to earth as women to taste . . . disfranchisement, while women reincarnated as Senators & Congressmen will sit in their places at the Capitol . . . and listen to [men's] eloquent pleadings for enfranchisement."[36] Delighted by Besant's company, Stanton was intrigued by the radical possibilities inherent in her doctrine of reincarnation. Overcoming her own materialist tendencies, Stanton immediately went to work applying Besant's theory of reincarnation to women's political needs in a republic. She fired off an article for her women readers at home, lauding the promises of reincarnation for the women's cause, and claiming the superiority of American cake.[37]

As it turned out, Stanton's fondness for angel food cake outlasted both her appreciation of Besant and her faith in the potential of theosophy to liberate women and to bring men to justice. Privately, Stanton lamented that theosophy had distracted Besant from Fabian socialism, "which can do more for the amelioration of humanity than the Theosophical Society."[38] Still, the story underscores a central truth for Stanton. It was a worthy cause to search for a true religion, one that could be harnessed in the service of justice. As she frequently reminded her readers: "The law of life and growth is liberty, justice, equality; and whatever spirit robs woman of her natural rights,—to think, to know, to be all of which she is capable . . . cannot be the spirit of a true religion."[39]

Although Stanton endeavored to locate a "true" religion, one that made woman an equal partner, one that served the higher purpose of a democratic society, she was invariably disappointed. She never relinquished her hope for a new religion, but increasingly, Stanton allied herself with agnostics who made up the free thought movement. Freethinkers were engaged in a number of projects that drew Stanton in: they evaluated the intellectual challenges to religious beliefs; they actively sought out alternatives that could take the place of religion; and finally, they launched a critique of the declining morality of Christian societies.[40]

It would be difficult to overestimate the importance of the free thought movement to Stanton personally, politically, and intellectually. Personally, freethinkers like Sara and Benjamin Underwood, Matilda Joslyn Gage, as well as Robert Ingersoll, proved to be her most liberal correspondents. They provided for her a community of like-minded colleagues who eased the isolation of her later years. Politically, freethinkers in the suffrage movement were her staunchest allies. And the free thought press and its editors, particularly Horace L. Green of the *Free Thought Magazine,* offered her shelter from the torrent of abuse she endured for publishing *The Woman's Bible.*[41] Intellectually, the free thought movement lent her the necessary analytical tools to further her critique of the Church and Bible. But in terms of its theoretical potential, explanatory power, and particularly its ability to inspire a vision of women's agency, free thought was limited in ways that would constrain Stanton as well.

While the free thought movement paid lip service to women's rights, it offered a very narrow conception of womanhood. Tied too closely to social Darwinism, the free thought movement made little space for "woman" as an agent for change. As the historian Beryl Satter has demonstrated, social Darwinists privileged Anglo-Saxon male competition (and not a divine feminine element) as the "force" that would bring about evolutionary progress. Women were conceptualized as passive mothers of the race. Woman's primary responsibility in evolution was simply that: to give birth to a new generation.[42] This formulation appealed to some nineteenth-century women reformers, according to Judith Walkowitz, because, "it placed women, at least in their reproductive capacity, at the center of history."[43] But would science prove to be a friend to women's progress? Consider, for example, a book Stanton enthusiastically recommended, *The Ethic of Free Thought* by Karl Pearson, a British intellectual, who was a proponent of both socialism and Darwinism.[44]

In his extended discussion on "The Woman's Question," Pearson repeatedly qualified his support for women's rights: "We have first to settle what is the physical capacity of woman, what would be the effect of her emancipation on her function of race-reproduction, before we can talk about her 'rights.'" Higher education, a cardinal virtue as far as Stanton was concerned, raised some anxiety for Pearson, as it may "connote a general intellectual progress for the community, or, on the other hand, a physical degradation of the race, owing to prolonged study having ill effects on woman's child-bearing efficiency." Women's intellectual inferiority to men, her "less fully developed mental organ," was also natural, Pearson explained. Still, these disabilities should not necessarily limit women's rights, as Pearson pointed out: "Nowadays neither intellectual nor physical inferiority excludes [some men] from the franchise—possibly they ought to do so." Pearson concluded: "If child-bearing women must be intellectually handicapped, then the penalty to be paid for race-predominance is the subjection of women."[45]

Pearson's analysis, while militantly anti-Christian, offered a vision of evolution that necessitated women's subordination for the larger goal of Anglo-Saxon "race-predominance."[46] In fact, feminist freethinkers (including Stanton) rejected these "scientific" views of women's capacity. At the International Council of Women in 1888, freethinker Helen Gardener addressed this very issue of "woman's capacity" and called upon Stanton, Anthony, and others to join her in donating their brains to Cornell University. This was a peculiar turning point for Stanton. Rather than championing a universal "feminine element," Stanton seized this opportunity to assert the superiority of certain educated white women whose donated brains could set science straight.[47]

Proponents of free thought similarly conceptualized "woman" as a dangerous threat to democratic institutions. An educated womanhood would result in race suicide; and a female electorate would threaten the separation of Church and state. Women were a liability, according to freethinkers, because the Church and clergy controlled them. Stanton repeatedly warned her readers in the 1880s, "The liberals in religion are afraid of us." Free thought, then, essentially painted Stanton into a theoretical corner. And much as she deftly maneuvered—by employing its critique of Christianity but challenging its position on women—Stanton still was left in a peculiar bind. The satisfaction she derived from "turning her guns on the church" was deep. She reveled in it. Yet it forced her to temporarily jettison a central component of her faith: the power of the feminine element.

What Will the Next Step Be?

So which was it then? Was "woman" the missing element whose mere inclusion in the republic, the Church, and the Godhead, would bring about the "next step"? Or was "woman" a deciding factor in current political and religious stalemate, the conservative element whose very participation in the state would threaten its secular nature? Were women destined to revolutionize the state? Or did the state need to be protected from women?

Despite Stanton's alliance with free thought, she never completely relinquished the concept of the feminine element and a specific role for emancipated "woman" to play in the transformation of society. In the 1890s she sometimes fused these two views: woman as moral force and woman as inert conservative. Stanton offered a synthesis of her two seemingly incompatible positions: "In her education hereafter substitute reason for blind faith, science for theological superstitions; then will our most liberal men, our scientists, scholars and statesmen, find in the women of their households a reserve force for building a higher, purer civilization."[48] Woman was still a potential force, but she needed to be retooled and held in reserve. But in other moments, the resurgence of the feminine element in Stanton's argument was uncomplicated by free thought reservations about women. In fact, in the last years of her life Stanton increasingly resuscitated an inspiring message from her past. Women do have a vital, pivotal role to play, she wrote in 1899: "Owing to the slowly growing influence of the feminine element in humanity, brute force is dying out, and more humane sentiments are moulding our religion, government, industrial and social life."[49] As this passage suggests, Stanton's return to the feminine element accommodated an evolutionary perspective—just not the social Darwinist insistence that Anglo-Saxon male competition and survival of the fittest would bring about the elusive higher civilization.

Stanton's conviction that the feminine element and not masculine brute force would evolve the race shaped her adaptation to socialism:

> Before we can realize the dream of socialism we must establish the equilibrium of the masculine and feminine elements in humanity. In talking with my socialistic confreres I find they do not realize that the fully developed independent woman is the great factor in the new civilization we propose. What the centripetal and centrifugal forces, the positive and negative electricity in equilibrium are in the material world, the masculine and feminine elements are in humanity, in the world of morals. To suspend the equilibrium of these material forces one half hour would result in chaos—the destruction of the planet. We have chaos in the moral world to-day, because the two great ruling forces are out of equilibrium. . . . Those who have eyes to see, behold the race making ready for the next step in civilization, the Amphiarchate, in which man and woman will be equal, the masculine and feminine forces in perfect equilibrium; then the dream of socialism will be realized.[50]

This passage bears no obvious resemblance to socialism. Missing are the telltale elements we have come to expect: class struggle, the ownership of the means of production, etc. Yet this text, like many others written in her final years, demonstrates that Stanton saw socialism as the next step whose onward progress was thwarted by the suppression of the feminine element. Stanton joined her more spiritually oriented colleagues in offering a moral challenge to industrial capitalism. Ultimately it was woman's moral force, the unleashing of the feminine element, that would reverse the present trend toward ever-increasing, male-driven competition. "The first step to this end," she wrote, "is to educate the people into the idea that such a moral revolution is possible."[51] In embracing socialism and fusing it with her positivist faith, Stanton returned to a familiar stance: she could be optimistic about the imagined future and "woman's" prophetic role in it.

Ultimately, what are we to make of Stanton's embrace of the feminine element? For that matter, how did a materialist like Stanton understand such a concept? Its use made more sense for some of her more spiritually inclined colleagues, thinkers for whom the connection between what is seen and unseen was a vital part of the theoretical premise they operated by. But did it make sense for Stanton, who claimed to have tried "faithfully" to be spiritualized, but to no avail, held back by her "too solid flesh"?[52] Yet, as Stanton wrote to the World Parliament of Religions in 1893, "What could sustain mortal man in this awful 'solitude of self' but the fact that the great moral forces of the universe are bound up in his organization?"[53] Stanton routinely invoked the feminine element: as having power; as having been repressed; whose very existence—proven through the laws of centripetal forces and positive and negative electricity—offered scientific and divine proof of woman's equality. The scientific analogy allowed Stanton to continue to believe in an entity she could not see. Neither could she see positive and negative electricity (or the law of gravity), but she understood and believed in the principle and could see the result of those laws in the physical, material world.

In the world of morals, Stanton could likewise see the chaos that resulted from the violation of an immutable law every bit as valid as the law of gravity: the repression of the feminine element. "True" science had been corrupted by the "hereditary bias" of its male practitioners. A "true" republic has eluded the country as well. And a "true" religion—and the accompanying moral revolution it would spawn—was similarly thwarted. Moreover, Christianity, which claimed to be a true religion, only perpetuated the conditions of women's mental and spiritual bondage. Stanton's persistence in championing the feminine element persuades me that this was both her foundational belief and her greatest hope: that the equilibrium of the sexes was the natural, immutable law—unseen, resisted, repressed—but a law that would eventually triumph as sure as the law of gravity.

NOTES

The author would like to thank Ann D. Gordon, Ellen DuBois, and Richard Cándida Smith for their sage advice on this essay.

1. For a discussion of the Bible debates of 1896, see Kathi Kern, *Mrs. Stanton's Bible* (Ithaca, N.Y.: Cornell University Press, 2001), 181–98.

2. Unidentified writing about religious bigotry of women, Elizabeth Cady Stanton Papers, Library of Congress (hereafter ECS, DLC). This manuscript is undated but references to Robert Ingersoll (and other events) within this text, as well as the marginalia, suggest that it was the article Stanton and Colby debated in their correspondence in March 1896. See Elizabeth Cady Stanton to Clara Colby, 25 March 1896, State Historical Society of Wisconsin, Madison (hereafter WHi).

3. Stanton to Colby, 25 March 1896, WHi. Of particular issue was Stanton's praise of Ingersoll, the famous agnostic.

4. See Charles Cashdollar, *The Transformation of Theology, 1830–1890* (Princeton, N.J.: Princeton University Press, 1989), 46. Cashdollar writes that nineteenth-century clergy tended to have one of two reactions to Comte. Either they saw him as threatening to Christianity and therefore studied him carefully in order to contain the threat; or they saw Comte and positivism as an opportunity for the renewal of theology. In either case, Comte had a broad impact that has not always been appreciated by historians.

5. Susan B. Anthony to Elizabeth Cady Stanton, 2 December 1898, Anthony Family Papers 24 (5), Henry E. Huntington Library, San Marino, Calif.

6. See Cashdollar, *Transformation of Theology,* 443, particularly his argument about the vast accommodation of positivism that Protestants made by the end of the nineteenth century. This "reconstruction" was evident in various ways, including an increased interest in empirical evidence and a greater concern for a social gospel.

7. Stanton's relatively benign attitude toward Catholicism may have been influenced by her interest in the writings of Auguste Comte. Comte was frequently criticized by clergy for his attachment to medieval Catholicism. See Cashdollar, *Transformation of Theology,* 52. In any case, her praise of Catholicism stands in stark contrast to her anti-Semitism expressed in *The Woman's Bible.* See Kern, *Mrs. Stanton's Bible,* 209, 217–19.

8. Lucretia Coffin Mott to Stanton, 23 March 1841, *The Selected Papers of Elizabeth Cady Stanton and Susan B. Anthony,* vol. 1: *In the School of Anti-Slavery, 1840–1866,* ed. Ann D. Gordon (New Brunswick, N.J.: Rutgers University Press, 1997), 21–22.

9. Stanton, *Bible and Church Degrade Woman* (Chicago: H.L. Green, [1898?]), 11.

10. Stanton, "My Creed," undated manuscript, ECS, DLC.

11. Ibid.

12. Ibid.

13. Ibid.

14. Stanton, *Eighty Years and More: Reminiscences, 1815–1897* (1898; reprinted, Boston: Northeastern University Press, 1993), 44; Kern, *Mrs. Stanton's Bible,* 40–45.

15. Stanton, "Bible and Church Degrade Woman," 6.

16. Stanton, "Solitude of Self," *Woman's Tribune,* 23 January 1892. Stanton delivered this speech to the House Committee on the Judiciary on 18 January 1892.

17. Stanton, "Solitude of Self."

18. Stanton, "Why Has Woman Been Degraded in All Forms of Religion?" Undated manuscript, ECS, DLC. Much of the text of this manuscript appeared in her speech written for the Parliament of Religions in 1893, variously titled "The Ultimate Religion" and "The Worship of God in Man."

19. Stanton, "Elevation of Womanhood: The Duty of the Church at This Hour," *Torch of Reason* 5 (3 October 1901): 1.

20. Stanton, "My Creed."

21. Stanton, "Why Has Woman Been Degraded in All Forms of Religion?"

22. Stanton, "Worship of God in Man," *Open Court* 7 (26 Oct 1893): 3851.

23. Stanton, "Woman's Position in the Bible," *Boston Investigator,* 5 July 1902.

24. Stanton, "Worship of God in Man," 3851.

25. Stanton, *Elizabeth Cady Stanton as Revealed in Her Letters, Diary, and Reminiscences,* ed. Theodore Stanton and Harriot Stanton Blatch, 2 vols. (New York: Harper, 1922), 2:195.

26. See Ellen DuBois, "The Limitations of Sisterhood: Elizabeth Cady Stanton and Division in the American Woman Suffrage Movement, 1875–1902," in *Woman Suffrage and Women's Rights* (New York: New York University Press, 1998), 163.

27. William Leach, *True Love and Perfect Union* (New York: Basic Books, 1980), 136.

28. Stanton, "Rev. Henry Edgar [sic.]," *Revolution,* 10 June 1869. This was Stanton's reading of Comte and one that was rejected by some male positivists. But Stanton's use and, perhaps, selective application of Comte was a fairly standard practice. See Cashdollar, *Transformation of Theology,* 47.

29. The Religion of Humanity had few actual adherents. Charles Cashdollar explains that Comte elaborated a highly structured, hierarchical faith, complete with priests, rituals, prayers, a calendar of saints, and a "host of other Roman embellishments." Even some of Comte's most loyal disciples did not accept the details of Comte's religion. See Cashdollar, *Transformation of Theology,* 12, 63.

30. Stanton, "Worship of God in Man."

31. Stanton, "Elevation of Womanhood."

32. Anthony to Stanton, 2 December 1898.

33. Stanton, "Why Has Woman Been Degraded," 40.

34. Stanton's experience with male positivists was mixed. She publicly feuded with Henry Edger and struggled as well with Octavius Brooks Frothingham. On the other hand, she had very positive connections with Theodore Parker and Moncure Conway. See Leach, *True Love and Perfect Union*, 138, 154; Kern, *Mrs. Stanton's Bible*, 56–57; and *The Selected Papers of Elizabeth Cady Stanton and Susan B. Anthony*, vol. 2: *Against an Aristocracy of Sex*, ed. Ann D. Gordon (New Brunswick, N.J.: Rutgers University Press, 2000), 621–23.

35. Stanton, "Mrs. Annie Besant. Theosophy. English Schools. American Cake," [27 December 1890] incomplete manuscript, ECS, DLC.

36. Ibid.

37. Stanton, "Mrs. Annie Besant,—Theosophy.—English Schools.—American Cake," *Woman's Tribune*, 27 December 1890.

38. Stanton, *Elizabeth Cady Stanton as Revealed*, 2:264

39. Stanton, "Has Christianity Benefited Woman?" *Index*, 23 July 1885.

40. These themes are developed more fully in James Turner, *Without God, without Creed: The Origins of Unbelief in America* (Baltimore: Johns Hopkins University Press, 1985), 172.

41. Kern, *Mrs. Stanton's Bible*, 63–68, 196–98.

42. Beryl Satter, *Each Mind a Kingdom: American Women, Sexual Purity, and the New Thought Movement, 1875–1920* (Berkeley: University of California Press, 1999), 10–13.

43. Judith Walkowitz, *City of Dreadful Delight: Narratives of Sexual Danger in Late-Victorian London* (Chicago: University of Chicago Press, 1992), 142.

44. Stanton endorsed Pearson's book publicly in interviews as well as in her private correspondence. See, for example, "Mrs. Elizabeth Cady Stanton," *Women's Penny Paper* (London) 3 (1 November 1890): 17; and Stanton to Elizabeth Smith Miller, 3 January 1891, Elizabeth Cady Stanton Papers, Rutgers University Library, New Brunswick, N.J. Stanton probably encountered Pearson's work through several of her British friends and correspondents. Annie Besant, Henrietta Muller, and Mond Caird all debated women's place in evolution with Pearson. See Walkowitz, *City of Dreadful Delight*, 135–67.

45. Karl Pearson, *The Ethic of Free Thought* (London: T. Fisher Unwin, 1888), 371, 376, 377, 389.

46. The appeal of Pearson's work to Stanton may well have rested in the robust discussion his essays generated among women and men. Some of Pearson's conclusions were challenged by feminists in his sphere, but in general, he was perceived as progressive. See Walkowitz, *City of Dreadful Delight*, 154.

47. Kern, *Mrs. Stanton's Bible*, 106–16. Stanton continued on this path on issues such as "educated" suffrage and immigration restriction, arguing that only petty distinctions of sex separated white women from their white male peers.

48. Stanton, "Bible and Church Degrade Woman," 4.

49. Stanton, "Moral Power, or Brute Force," *Boston Investigator,* 25 February 1899, from Papers of Elizabeth Cady Stanton, Scrapbook 3, Vassar College Library.

50. Stanton, "The Equilibrium of Sex," *Commonwealth* 6 (June 24, 1899): 12–13.

51. Stanton, "The Worship of God in Man," in *The World's Parliament of Religions . . . Held in Chicago in Connection with the Columbian Exhibition of 1893,* ed. John Henry Barrows (Chicago, 1893), 2:236.

52. Stanton to Elizabeth Smith Miller, 31 October 1886, Theodore Stanton Collection, Elizabeth Cady Stanton Papers, Rutgers University Library.

53. Stanton, "Worship of God in Man," in *Parliament of Religions,* 2:235.

Chapter 7

Stanton and the Right to Vote
On Account of Race or Sex

Ann D. Gordon

Elizabeth Cady Stanton's luster as an advocate of women's voting rights is dimming under the close scrutiny of intellectual and cultural historians focused on her racial constructions. These writers would have us believe (a) that Stanton was motivated principally by humiliation that black men voted before she did; (b) that she pursued the interests of her social class and the white race, while speaking in terms of universal rights; and (c) that she changed little, if at all, between her opposition to the Fifteenth Amendment in 1869 and her advocacy of literacy as a qualification to vote in the mid-1890s.[1] To reach such conclusions, historians must ignore Stanton's core convictions and oversimplify complex problems in her thinking and in American history.

Stanton's insistence that voting rights mattered, both to the quality of public life and to the well-being of individuals, distinguished her among advocates of women's rights at the moment she entered politics in 1848, and she never let go of that faith in the remaining fifty-four years of her life. When she crafted women's demand for suffrage in the antebellum period, she relied on the Declaration of Independence as her standard: "It is the duty of the women of this country," she wrote into the resolutions adopted at Seneca Falls, "to secure to themselves their sacred right to the elective franchise."[2] The notion that individuals "were endowed by their Creator" with rights which just governments are bound to respect provided reformers with a recognizable ideal in arguing for wider participation in republican government.

Stanton's reference point changed during the Civil War, when she joined a larger discussion about how to make citizens of the former slaves and empower them to protect their new status. Attention turned to the

Constitution and its potential, in its existing form and through amendments, to guarantee equal citizenship. Like abolitionists and Radical Republicans, Stanton weighed the Constitution's promise of republican governments in all the states and its inchoate ideas about the privileges and immunities of citizenship in the United States. "This is the hour to settle what are the rights of a citizen of the Republic," she told audiences in 1867; "and upon the right settlement of that question depends the life of this nation."[3] The time had arrived, she said, "to bury the black man and the woman in the citizen,"[4] and build "a genuine republic" on the foundation of universal suffrage.

Both before and after the Civil War, Stanton's mission was to establish that the rights of the Jeffersonian individual, or the rights of a citizen of the United States, belonged equally to women and men. On the one hand, she joined reformers of many stripes to push government toward its egalitarian ideal. On the other hand, she committed herself to a particular battle over the rights of women, a battle that set her apart from, and sometimes at odds with, her putative allies. How one understands Stanton's (sometimes inept) negotiation of these roles depends to a considerable degree on how seriously one takes the need for woman suffrage.

Stanton took that need very seriously. Like American colonists protesting British rule, she had no use for the idea of "virtual representation." In 1854, while instructing legislators about which laws of New York usurped women's rights, she anticipated the thoughts of her audience: "But, say you, are not all women sufficiently represented by their fathers, husbands and brothers? Let your statute books answer the question."[5] Laws governing marriage, custody, inheritance, criminal justice, and contracts imposed disabilities on women of every age and class, she demonstrated. Women's disfranchisement reflected the belief that the sexes were unequal, and it produced a society governed by laws that treated women at a disadvantage. Nearly two decades later, she returned to this formulation in a private tirade about the impact of manhood suffrage after the Civil War. In her mind, the Fifteenth Amendment reaffirmed female subordination, and "swift on the heels" of its passage, legislators attempted to regulate prostitution for the better protection of men from disease, and courts acquitted men charged with murder in cases where they killed to assert ownership of their wives.[6] Suffrage for women promised both an abstract recognition of a common humanity shared by men and women and a tool in the hands of women to overcome the everyday consequences of male dominance. Stanton sought to vote, she explained, "because it is my right, and all women need this power for their protection, dignity and moral influence."[7]

Stanton knew well that the fate of her demand for woman suffrage depended as much upon Americans' willingness to extend voting rights to new groups as it did upon their views of women's fitness for the right. As prevailing opinion on both scores changed during the postwar decades, so too did her mission. Stanton arrived on the national stage at a unique moment, when, in the words of historian Alexander Keyssar, "the mid-nineteenth-century wave of prodemocratic sentiment" crested immediately after the war in the Fifteenth Amendment. In a long career advocating women suffrage, Stanton came closest to winning at that moment. But the war, Keyssar explains, "provided only a temporary check against the current of antidemocratic sentiments."[8] Thereafter, Stanton worked for woman suffrage in a political environment distinguished by its distrust of voters and efforts to contract their numbers. In her lifetime, this tendency culminated when southern states reversed Reconstruction with the acquiescence of northern states. Stanton also arrived on the national stage at the moment when leaders in Congress decided to exclude women from Reconstruction. Under continued pressure for woman suffrage, Congress and the federal courts resisted the change; they aimed narrow readings of the new amendments and arguments for limited suffrage at women but ultimately used them too against black men. In the decades after Reconstruction, resistance to woman suffrage spread out, penetrating local levels of government and sanctioning countless decisions against sharing political power with women. In her last years, Stanton faced a political community in which popular opposition to woman suffrage provided a socially acceptable and politically safe way to reject the importance of any suffrage.

By her relentless push for woman suffrage under these unfavorable conditions, Stanton established herself as a rare voice of resistance to the devaluation of voting rights and of commitment to an ideal of equal rights, guaranteed to American citizens. Without a doubt, Stanton can be heard to stray from an ideal of universal rights and lapse into the language of social and racial hierarchies, usually at moments when her vision of a genuine republic had lost public support. But at those same moments, her convictions about the importance of achieving equal citizenship in a republican government also shine through.

Elizabeth Cady Stanton's most infamous moment as a manipulator of racist stereotypes and propagandist for social hierarchies in politics occurred in the early months of 1869, when she campaigned against ratification of the Fifteenth Amendment. It is difficult but necessary to comprehend that she pursued this tactic in defense of universal suffrage. To her, it was consistent with a larger critique that had occupied her since 1865 about how to guarantee black suffrage. Two key elements were lacking in the amendment: voting rights were not guaranteed by the Constitution, and citizens were not assured of political rights. Her conviction that women should be enfranchised, rather than carrying within it the negation of black suffrage, positioned her to be critical of the legal and constitutional compromises made to achieve manhood suffrage. That the two causes were interconnected she never doubted.

The key to Stanton's actions in this period lies not in Wendell Phillips and his somewhat disingenuous declaration that this was the Negro's hour, when he meant men.[9] Phillips stood relatively close to Stanton, seeing the attainment of universal suffrage as a series of steps, the first step to be for black men. The key lies in Congress and its cautious measures toward Reconstruction. Proposals for the Fourteenth Amendment, made as soon as Congress convened after the war in December 1865, spurred Stanton and others into action. Insofar as the eventual text of the amendment addressed voting rights at all, it adopted an indirect method of extending voting rights to former slaves by threatening the self-interest of each state. Section 2 apportions representation in Congress based on a state's total population, but promises to reduce representation if *male* inhabitants of the state are denied their voting rights. If a southern state refused to enfranchise its African American men, that state's power in Congress would diminish.[10] The amendment fell far short of what reformers had hoped to achieve in Reconstruction. It offered no new federal protection over voting rights, and for the first time, it placed in the Constitution an acknowledgment that states could legitimately disfranchise potential voters.

Stanton, with the *Congressional Globe* arriving daily, watched in horror as Congress crafted the amendment around the language of "male inhabitants" and "male citizens." Appealing for action in December 1865, she wrote: "As this would be to turn the wheels of legislation backward, let the Women of the Nation now unitedly protest against such a desecration of the Constitution, and petition for that right which is at the foundation of all Government—the right of representation."[11] While debate continued in Congress, women petitioned that the ballot be placed in the hand of every citizen to realize the constitutional guarantee of "a Republican form of Government" in every state. The word "male" entered congressional debate about the amendment as soon debate began: the first item introduced for the consideration of the House of Representatives, House Resolution No. 1, recommended the language that became, months later, section 2. Without the specification about male inhabitants, there would be new problems. Since disfranchised women were counted in the basis of representation for all the states, language about reducing a state's representation for failure to admit adult citizens to the electorate would affect all states. Of particular importance in Congress, such language would hit especially hard in powerful northeastern states like Massachusetts, Pennsylvania, and New York, where women outnumbered men in the population. After many attempts to find another formula, Congress agreed to draw a constitutional distinction between disfranchised males and disfranchised females. The maleness of this decision was even more pronounced in regard to the amendment's intended beneficiaries: freedwomen outnumbered freedmen in every state of the Confederacy.[12] They would be counted in the population of southern states, but their disfranchisement would not subject the states to punishment. Twenty years later Stanton characterized the congressional enterprise of 1865 and 1866 as "wasting reams of paper and an immense amount of brain force in drawing up the fourteenth amendment expressly to keep this class [of freedwomen] out of the body politic."[13]

The fact that Congress began its cautious steps toward black suffrage by first codifying an exclusive, male right to the vote changed a political debate about citizenship and suffrage into one also about gendered privilege. The offending section of the Fourteenth Amendment had no positive effect on black suffrage. In the short run, recognition of its weakness led Congress to craft the Fifteenth. In the long run, Congress did not use its provisions to punish the South, not even when black men formally lost their voting rights. Its greatest impact was its codification of women's disfranchisement. Every congressional committee and judicial opinion that sustained women's disfranchisement in the next decade cited the language in section 2.

Passage of the Fourteenth Amendment activated a large, grassroots movement for equal rights across the North. Its participants were men and women who shared Stanton's view that suffrage should be made universal at that moment. With little central direction, local groups showed remarkable power in their efforts to achieve the goal in the states and territories. State-based demands for universal suffrage came within a few votes of passage in places like Connecticut, Wisconsin, and Nevada, and tied up Michigan's constitutional convention for most of a summer. The movement ran strong, racially mixed campaigns in New York and the District of Columbia.[14]

Their congressional allies tried to make universal suffrage a national strategy too. Among dozens of drafts for a Fifteenth Amendment submitted by congressmen in December 1868, at least two proposed that voting rights be tied to U.S. citizenship. In the House of Representatives, George Julian sought to enact that "the right of suffrage shall be based upon citizenship" and all citizens "shall enjoy this right equally, without any distinction or discrimination whatever founded on race, color, or sex." In the Senate, Samuel Pomeroy used a different text to the same effect: suffrage based on citizenship and all citizens to "enjoy the same rights and privileges of the elective franchise."[15] In that interval between the Fourteenth and Fifteenth Amendments, Stanton summed up the aims of the equal rights movement: to offer the nation "a broader platform than 'State Rights' or a 'white man's government.'" She went on to say that if states could deprive citizens of political rights, it would be "a virtual surrender of all the freedman has gained by the war."[16]

The Fifteenth Amendment adopted by Congress in 1869 fell far short of those goals, meeting only one of Stanton's three criteria. It too recognized the right of states to disfranchise their citizens and then limited the grounds states could use: "on account of race, color, or previous condition of servitude."[17] Reinforced by the Fourteenth Amendment, the language could not even be used to win suffrage for African American women. All the advocates of universal suffrage in associations for equal rights and universal franchise faced a serious predicament. None doubted the pressing need for the freedmen to secure political rights. But to support the amendment was to forsake their goals. For the women in these associations, the predicament was still more complex: could a woman suffragist endorse newly fortified and constitutionally mandated manhood suffrage? The fights on these questions within the various associations are well-known stories; their lingering effects shaped the history of the woman suffrage movement for decades. Frederick Douglass, the movement's reliable ally since 1848, struck harsh blows, insisting that white women did not need suffrage as they were well represented by their fathers, husbands, and brothers. Silent on the rights of black women, he implicitly offered them the virtual representation that the movement had always challenged.[18]

Stanton spoke out against the Fifteenth Amendment and tried to turn public opinion against it on a tour through the Midwest. No one has tried to assess how dangerous that may have been, whether she in fact could have jeopardized the amendment's ratification. She insisted she never doubted it would pass. "But as it was the great national act on which all eyes were centered," she wrote, "there was the point for us to make men feel."[19] Her language of opposition is abhorrent. The amendment threatened to degrade "mothers, wives and daughters, in their political status, below unwashed and unlettered ditch-diggers, boot-blacks, hostlers, butchers, and barbers."[20] Or, in a rallying cry for the troops: "[I]f you do not wish the lower orders of Chinese, Africans, Germans and Irish, with their low ideas of womanhood to make laws for you and your daughters . . . demand that woman, too, shall be represented in the government."[21] Stanton, however, did not always sound this way. In the same few months she also wrote: "When we contrast the condition of the most fortunate women at the North with the living death colored men endure everywhere, there seems to be a selfishness in our present position. But remember we speak not for ourselves alone, but for all womankind, . . . for the women of this oppressed race too, who, in slavery, have known a depth of misery and degradation that no man can ever appreciate."[22] Quoting selectively from Elizabeth Cady Stanton is a risky business.

By the time the Fifteenth Amendment was ratified in March 1870, Stanton had ceased her opposition and turned in a new direction to seek woman suffrage. With the help in particular of Francis and Virginia Minor of St. Louis and later of Victoria Woodhull and Congressman Benjamin Butler, Stanton and the national movement she now led pursued the broadest possible interpretations of the amendments. Historian Ellen DuBois has traced some of that story; some of it is in the *Papers of Stanton and Anthony*.[23] Although their immediate aim was to gain woman suffrage under the terms of the amendments, it was also an attempt to secure voting rights on a federal basis. This New Departure, as it became known, revived the ideals and constitutional thought of universal suffrage and also tried to exploit inconsistent language in the amendments themselves. At this moment, Stanton was *aligned* with, though hardly *allied* with, the pressing needs of African Americans. The legal and constitutional standing of the rights of women and black men intersected repeatedly. In this period, with their advocacy of constitutional guarantees for voting rights, Stanton's woman suffrage movement mounted resistance to the narrow interpretations and to the political backpedaling that characterized the early years of Reconstruction, regressive actions that stymied women and unraveled the basis on which more than a million black men had gained the chance to vote.[24]

An important measure of how far the nation had retreated from federal protection for voting rights came in a decision not about black suffrage but about woman. Although the Supreme Court's decision in *Minor* v. *Happersett* in the spring of 1875 immediately closed off the route to woman suffrage through existing provisions of the Constitution, ending the New Departure, it also signaled how little protection the amendments provided for anyone. With clear purpose and system, the Court dismissed all the arguments dating back to the Radical Republican, African American, and white abolitionist push for black suffrage. In a unanimous opinion by Chief Justice Morrison Waite, the Court insisted that the "United States has no voters in the States of its own creation,"[25] that the Constitution as amended did not add "the right of suffrage to the privileges and immunities of citizenship," and that "the Constitution of the United States does not confer the right of suffrage upon anyone."

Stanton knew what that meant. Within weeks of the Court's decision, she attacked the Court in a speech called "Self-Government," delivered to the National Woman Suffrage Association's annual meeting. "Chief Justice Waite," she protested,

> tells us that these three principles, universal freedom, universal suffrage, universal citizenship are not inscribed in the constitution. . . . [The Court's decisions] have all been decidedly retrogressive in their tendency, so much so, that in this strenuous effort, to prove that woman has no new guarantees of liberty by the amendments, there is danger lest the rights of the black man be imperilled also. Even Chief Justice Taney in his decision in the Dred Scott case gave more scope, power dignity to the term "citizen" than Chief Justice Waite now does.[26]

Better than most Americans, she foresaw the price the nation would pay for its rejection of universal suffrage tied to citizenship.

Stanton never opposed universal suffrage, even when that ideal lost its political and intellectual support. However, like many other Americans, including African Americans, she, at specific times, favored restricted suffrage—like literacy requirements—as a way to open the door and break down the male monopoly on voting. She suffered a bout of educated suffragism in 1877, within months of launching the campaign for a sixteenth amendment. In apparent contradiction to the federal strategy, she endorsed a resolution passed at the National Woman Suffrage Association meeting in January 1877: "We should have education compulsory in every State of the Union," she wrote after the meeting, "and make it the basis of suffrage, a national law, requiring that those who vote, after 1880, must read and write the English language."[27]

It was not a cause of her own creation at this moment, and who influenced her is hard to fathom. From Susan B. Anthony one learns that members of Congress were considering that winter a federal literacy requirement combined with federal funding for education, hoping to stem violence and racial hostilities in the South.[28] Strange to tell, Charles Purvis, the son of black abolitionists and a professor at Howard University, was on the National's committee that wrote the resolution. Whatever the reason or influences for this tactic, it echoed changes evident among white abolitionists and black leaders, similarly concerned about how to break down prejudice in the South as violence and disfranchisement spread.[29]

In part, Stanton's endorsement of the proposal expressed a hope that if the federal government returned to the question of voting rights—even of restricted rights—women would be included in their action. But there's another issue in this incident. Stanton's critics as well as many other historians assume that educated suffrage existed in American history only as a concept propounded by elites or partisan politicians to enhance their control or majorities. But in fact it arose also among the disfranchised in the nineteenth century, when there was little hope for winning on the grand principle. In and of itself, advocacy of educated suffrage under such circumstances did not necessarily mean abandoning the fundamentals of universal rights. When Stanton reiterated her support for the National Woman Suffrage Association resolution in May 1877, she spoke to this ambiguity by explaining that it did not, in her mind, conflict with "the popular theory that suffrage is a natural right," because "the condition is one with which all may comply," and the lengths of time allowed could vary.[30] Not necessarily a wise choice, it was one made by Stanton and by many black leaders from the early 1870s through the crisis of the 1890s.[31]

Like other moments when Stanton gave priority to educated suffrage, this one coexisted with her convictions about a genuine republic based on universal suffrage. The evidence lies in her sudden and passionate return to her fundamental values in 1878. Pulled up short by the mounting national crisis over voting that followed the withdrawal of federal troops from the South by President Rutherford B. Hayes, Stanton redefined the demand for woman suffrage as "National Protection for National Citizens."[32]

Stanton arrived in Washington in January 1878 to speak to the National Woman Suffrage Association and to the Senate Committee on Privileges and Elections. She planned, she told Isabella Beecher Hooker in November, to speak on taxation, but she somehow changed her mind.[33] She relied on at least three bundles of paper to write "National Protection": she literally recycled pages from the manuscript of her first speech to Congress, delivered in 1870, on the subject of suffrage in the District of Columbia; pages and paragraphs came out of her speech to the National association in 1873, at the peak of the New Departure; and she pasted a dozen clippings onto her sheets, almost all of them dating from the spring and summer of 1877. Out of this motley collage, she crafted a stunning attack on the collapse of Reconstruction.[34]

The Fourteenth and Fifteenth Amendments were, she told the senators, "steps in the right direction," but their interpretation was seriously flawed. The United States, she insisted, would be locked into an "imperfect development of our own nationality" until the nation "protect[ed] the humblest citizen in the exercise of all his rights." Although Stanton revived the ideas of the New Departure, as Ellen DuBois noted years ago,[35] she used them on this occasion to underscore for her audience that there were alternatives in American constitutional thought to the Supreme Court's narrow interpretations of rights and citizenship, alternatives that would not only incorporate women into the electorate but better protect black voters. "National Protection for National Citizens" meant that voting rights be guaranteed and protected by the federal government, not left to the states, and that voting rights be joined to citizenship, putting an end to the separation imposed by courts in the early 1870s. Her own text of a sixteenth amendment, incorporated into her speech, reinforced these larger points: "The right of suffrage in the United States shall be based on citizenship, . . . and all citizens of the United States, whether native or naturalized, shall enjoy this right equally, without any distinction or discrimination whatever founded on sex." It focused on the distinction of sex, but if adopted, it contained the language to reverse *Minor* v. *Happersett* and similar decisions about the right of suffrage.

Stanton added one more argument: that federalism was not in the disrepute that Republicans thought it to be. From her pile of clippings, she detected both a retreat from protecting citizens' rights and a surge in federal power wielded for other—in her mind lesser—purposes. Her examples included willingness to use federal troops against the strikers who halted the railroads in 1877 but not to exercise federal authority against the criminals who murdered black voters in Ellenville, South Carolina, that same year. Or in another contrast: to send federal troops into Mexico to chase back marauders but not to implement federal protection of voters. She recognized that by 1878, political will mattered at least as much as disputed readings of the Constitution.[36]

"National Protection for National Citizens" bears comparison with what other outspoken proponents of black suffrage were saying at the same time. Many people expressed outrage over the violence against voters more directly than Stanton did. But her critique of Reconstruction made her more realistic than some prominent champions of African American rights, who placed their hopes on the amendments and the political will to enforce them. In the spring of 1879, Senator James G. Blaine, a man known for waving the bloody shirt with his eye on the presidential nomination in 1880, wrote in the *North American Review's* symposium on negro suffrage: "There will be no step backward, but under the provision which specifically confers on Congress the power to enforce each amendment by 'appropriate legislation,' there will be applied . . . the restraining and correcting edict of national authority."[37] A few months later, Frederick Douglass expressed the same faith: "[The Negro] has a standing in the supreme law of the land, in the Constitution of the United States, not to be changed or affected by any conjunction of circumstances likely to occur in the immediate or remote future. The Fourteenth Amendment makes him a citizen, and the Fifteenth Amendment makes him a voter. . . . The permanent powers of the Government are all on his side."[38] Only one year later the Republican Party would soften the language of its platform, promising only to protect "all our citizens in the enjoyment of all privileges and immunities guaranteed by the Constitution," a category the Supreme Court had already ruled did not include political rights.[39]

The campaign for "National Protection for National Citizens" grew over the next few years into a remarkable force opposing not only the end of Reconstruction but also the antidemocratic shift in political thought that made the end of Reconstruction possible. Wendell Phillips, writing to the Third Decade Celebration in 1878 (the event marking thirty years since the conventions of 1848), noted the importance of what Stanton and the National Woman Suffrage Association were doing. "Woman's claim to the ballot," he wrote, "has had a much wider influence than merely to protect woman. Universal suffrage is itself in danger. Scholars dread it; social science and journalists attack it. The discussion of woman's claim has done much to reveal this danger, and rally patriotic and thoughtful men [*sic*] in defence."[40]

Another measure of how people understood the National's role at the time can be taken by the "return" of African Americans to the National Woman Suffrage Association, where they were a stronger presence at the end of the 1870s than at any time since 1869.[41] Frederick Douglass, a regular participant in the conventions since his move to the capital in 1872, journeyed to Rochester in 1878 to be a part of the Third Decade Celebration. There he was joined by Sojourner Truth, not seen in this crowd since the equal rights campaign of 1867 and 1868. Two generations of the Purvis family attended meetings. The presence of Robert Purvis, the father, was no surprise: he stood with Stanton against the Fifteenth Amendment; but his son Charles, one of the most vocal opponents of seeking woman suffrage before the Fifteenth Amendment was ratified, served on committees and spoke to the audience. His sister Harriet joined the National's executive committee in 1877. She was not alone as an African American officer: Mary Ann Shadd Cary served on the powerful Resident Congressional Committee in 1877 and moved to the executive committee in 1878 for three years.

From the early years of Reconstruction, Stanton took away the lesson that no one's voting rights had been well secured. At Reconstruction's end, when that lack of security endangered the political rights of black men, she mustered a very large political constituency to press for federal guarantees of voting rights. An increasingly Democratic and southern Congress had little interest in her cause, and in 1887 the Senate rejected the suffragists' proposed Sixteenth Amendment. By the 1890s, her dim view of the compromises and evasions of Reconstruction was proving to be terribly right. Voting rights had sunk lower and lower in the political sky by the last decade of the century: the North stood idle while the South implemented formal disfranchisement of black men, beginning with Mississippi's new constitution in 1890; the Republican majority in Congress could not be bothered to pass the Federal Elections Bill to reinvigorate enforcement of the amendments; and by the middle of the decade, the Fourteenth and Fifteenth Amendments were dead letters.[42]

At the same time, northern states implemented their own limits on voting rights.[43] Notions of voting *rights* were in disrepute. In New York's constitutional convention of 1894, the majority agreed, while rejecting woman suffrage, that an ideal of universal suffrage was a myth: "Suffrage is not a right," intoned one delegate in the majority. "It is an obligation; it is a trust; it is a duty, which the State, when it thinks it wise, imposes upon its citizens; . . . [the question to be decided is] whether or not it will be for the best interest of the State to grant that suffrage."[44] A fellow delegate added that suffrage "is conferred . . . not for the benefit, or to gratify the wish, of the recipient, but solely for the benefit of the State."[45] These views of voting rights differed little from those of southerners intent on disfranchisement.

Delegates to that same convention were so confident in their privileges that they dismissed the largest ever state campaign for woman suffrage with the explanation that if women voted, prostitutes would vote, and people willing to sell their bodies would surely sell their votes.[46] To paraphrase Frederick Douglass, woman suffrage had been redefined as the question: whether woman could with safety be free.[47]

At this historical moment, no one concerned about voting rights knew what to do. The opposition was enormous; the ideological leverage was gone; a faint light hinted that capitulating on class and quality might point the way out. Advocates of educated suffrage in the 1890s included many prominent African Americans, W. E. B. Du Bois among them. "We must remember," Du Bois was quoted as saying, "that a good many of our people . . . are not fit for the responsibility of republican government."[48] Congressman John Mercer Langston, described by one historian as "that weathervane of public opinion" among African Americans, endorsed literacy qualifications if applied to both races equally.[49] Booker T. Washington made his famous Atlanta speech in 1895, diverting African Americans from the contest for rights in favor of self-improvement. Elizabeth Cady Stanton swung like a pendulum through the decade, hopeful and infuriated, expansive about rights and narrowly class centered. For many of the same reasons that black leaders were willing to compromise, Stanton revived her interest in educated suffrage. Educated suffrage would be more than either black men or any woman could look forward to.

When Wyoming squeaked into the Union as a state in 1890 with its woman suffrage intact, over the objections of southern Democrats, Stanton was ecstatic. "This is the first genuine republic the world has ever seen," she wrote, "the first recognition in government of the great principle of equal rights for all."[50] She was also very optimistic that Wyoming might open the gates to more woman suffrage. Four years later, shortly after the conclusion of New York's constitutional convention, Stanton wrote the oft-cited essays about educated suffrage for the *Woman's Journal.* They are riddled with nativism and elitism: "For our own safety and for their education," she wrote, "the ignorant and impecunious from the Old World landing on our shores by hundreds every day" should learn to read and write English before going to the polls.[51] But even in these essays Stanton repeatedly reaffirmed the ideal of universal suffrage. In the last of the series, Stanton began: "It is not the principle of universal suffrage that I oppose, but ignorant, impecunious, immoral, 'mankind suffrage,' while sex is made a disqualification for all women. I am opposed to the domination of one sex over the other."[52] It is a jarring pronouncement—"universal" at odds with a geyser of disdainful adjectives. At best she retained faith in—though not much hope for—universal suffrage. Most poignant is the final sentence about the domination of one sex over the other: at eighty years of age she had lost all patience with men's obfuscating rationales for their privileges.

Speaking about the sole black delegate to Mississippi's constitutional convention of 1890, Frederick Douglass condemned him for his treachery in acceding to the disfranchisement of black voters, but he also described Isaiah Montgomery with some empathy: the man uttered "a groan of bitter anguish," Douglass said, "born of oppression and despair. It is the voice of a soul from which all hope has vanished . . . his condition awakens pity."[53]

Perhaps some of the same empathy might be extended to Elizabeth Cady Stanton. The point of reviving her impressive record as a critic of all disfranchisement and champion of guaranteed and equal political rights is not to urge forgetfulness of Stanton's inability to build alliances or to talk about the disabilities of gender without fragmenting society into competitive units of race, nativity, and class. Those failures are now well established. Her racial constructions, imperial presumptions, and evolutionary elitism are not unimportant signs. Nonetheless, the exploration of *what* they signify needs better tools and maps than are currently in use. In *their* acknowledgment, it is equally important to keep in sight—and in the nation's sight—the struggle that engaged her and the opposition she met.

Stanton was in conflict over equality—not because she knew better about her privileges and whiteness, but because she stayed wedded to republican ideals and the self-sovereignty of individuals. Can anyone find that mysterious place in her psyche where two, seemingly contradictory strains of thought coexisted? Probably not ever. But in the political world, those contradictions are often overpowered by context. W. E. B. Du Bois, a decade after Stanton's death, when he had changed his mind about the importance of political rights, urged his readers to recognize that woman suffragists and black suffragists occupied common space outside the political system and shared a common goal, based simply on the will to enlarge the electorate and to reassert the centrality of voting rights to the American system. "[B]oth are great movements in democracy," he added in 1915.[54]

NOTES

1. Histories of suffrage underlie the examination of Stanton and race in Louise Michele Newman, *White Women's Rights: The Racial Origins of Feminism in the United States* (New York: Oxford University Press, 1999), throughout; and Kathi Kern, *Mrs. Stanton's Bible* (Ithaca, N.Y.: Cornell University Press, 2001), especially 109–15. The history of suffrage is more detailed in Barbara Hilkert Andolsen, *"Daughters of Jefferson, Daughters of Bootblacks": Racism and American Feminism* (Macon, Ga.: Mercer University Press, 1986).

2. Resolutions, Woman's Rights Convention at Seneca Falls, 19 July 1848, in *Selected Papers of Elizabeth Cady Stanton and Susan B. Anthony*, ed. Ann D. Gordon (New Brunswick, N.J.: Rutgers University Press, 1997), 1:77. Hereafter *Papers*.

3. "Reconstruction," 19 February 1867, *Papers*, 2:28.

4. Eleventh National Woman's Rights Convention, 10 May 1866, *Papers*, 1:587.

5. Address to Legislature of New York, 14 February 1854, *Papers*, 1:243.

6. To Isabella Beecher Hooker, 3 February 1871, *Papers*, 2:413.

7. "The Subjection of Woman," 1873, *Papers*, 2:629.

8. Alexander Keyssar, *The Right to Vote: The Contested History of Democracy in the United States* (New York: Basic Books, 2000), 183, 119.

9. Ellen Carol DuBois, *Feminism and Suffrage: The Emergence of an Independent Women's Movement in America, 1848–1869* (Ithaca, N.Y.: Cornell University Press, 1978), 59–60.

10. For examples of the debates over introducing "male" into the Constitution, see *Congressional Globe*, 39th Cong., 1st sess., 25 January 1866, 433–34; and Charles Sumner, "Political Equality without Distinction of Color. No Compromise of Human Rights," 7 March 1866, in *The Works of Charles Sumner* (Boston: Lee and Shepard, 1874), 10:316–21.

11. Appeal and Petition, 26 December 1865, in *Papers*, 1:566.

12. Bureau of the Census, *A Compendium of the Ninth Census (June 1, 1870)*, comp. Francis A. Walker (Washington, D.C.: Government Printing Office, 1872), 547, 549.

13. Senate Committee on Woman Suffrage, *Hearing before the Committee on Woman Suffrage, United States Senate, April 2, 1888*, Sen. Misc. Doc. 114, 50th Cong., 1st sess., Serial 2517.

14. The history of the equal rights movement needs to be written. DuBois, *Feminism and Suffrage,* 78–104, treats the Kansas campaign of 1867. Events in many other states are noted in *Papers,* vol. 2.

15. *Congressional Globe,* 40th Cong., 3d sess., 6, 21; 40th Cong., 3d sess., Joint Resolution, S.R. 180, and Joint Resolution, H.R. 371.

16. "State Rights," 25 June 1868, *Papers,* 2:147–48.

17. For an account of the amendment in Congress, see Keyssar, *Right to Vote,* 93–104.

18. Speeches of 19 November and 11 December 1868, in *The Frederick Douglass Papers. Series One: Speeches, Debates, and Interviews,* ed. John W. Blassingame and John R. McKivigan (New Haven, Conn.: Yale University Press, 1991), 4:180–86. Hereafter Douglass, *Speeches.*

19. To Paulina Wright Davis, 12 August 1869, *Papers,* 2:257–58.

20. "Manhood Suffrage," 24 December 1868, *Papers,* 2:196.

21. "The Sixteenth Amendment," 29 April 1869, *Papers,* 2:237.

22. "Editorial Correspondence," 22 January 1869, *Papers,* 2:205.

23. Ellen Carol DuBois, "Taking the Law into Our Own Hands: Bradwell, Minor, and Suffrage Militance in the 1870s," in Ellen Carol DuBois, *Woman Suffrage and Women's Rights* (New York: New York University Press, 1993), 114–38.

24. An excellent window on the conflict over interpreting the amendments is provided by Wisconsin's senator Matt Carpenter, chair of the Committee on the Judiciary in 1871 and 1872. See his letter to Theodore Tilton and Tilton's reply in *Golden Age,* 30 September 1871, and Carpenter's Senate report on woman suffrage: U.S. Senate, Committee on the Judiciary, *Report,* 25 January 1872, 42d Cong., 2d sess., S. Rept. 21, Serial 1483.

25. *Minor v. Happersett* 21 Wallace 162 (1875). The quotations appear on pages 170, 171, and 178.

26. "Self-Government," 11 May 1875, *Papers,* 3:188.

27. To Editor, *Ballot Box,* 24 January 1877, *Papers,* 3:284.

28. Susan B. Anthony to William Lloyd Garrison, 1 January 1877, William Lloyd Garrison Papers, Boston Public Library.

29. James M. McPherson, *The Abolitionist Legacy: From Reconstruction to the NAACP* (Princeton, N.J.: Princeton University Press, 1975), 72–73.

30. To Matilda Joslyn Gage and National Woman Suffrage Association, before 24 May 1877, *Papers,* 3:309–10; Keyssar, *Right to Vote,* 141–46.

31. McPherson, *Abolitionist Legacy,* 50–80, 90–94; August Meier, *Negro Thought in America, 1880–1915: Racial Ideologies in the Age of Booker T. Washington* (Ann Arbor, Mich.: University of Michigan Press, 1968), 26–41.

32. See Eric Foner, *Reconstruction: America's Unfinished Revolution, 1863–1877* (New York: Harper and Row, 1988), 581–601.

33. To Isabella Beecher Hooker, 28 November 1877, *Papers,* 3:342.

34. "National Protection for National Citizens," 11 January 1878, *Papers*, 3:345–73.

35. Ellen Carol DuBois, "Outgrowing the Compact of the Father: Equal Rights, Woman Suffrage, and the United States Constitution, 1820–1878," in DuBois, *Woman Suffrage and Women's Rights*, 108.

36. For other evidence of this turn in the use of federal power, see Foner, *Reconstruction*, 582–83.

37. Quotation from extracts reprinted in *New York Tribune*, n.d., Susan B. Anthony scrapbook 8, Rare Books Division, Library of Congress. The symposium appeared in the *North American Review* in March 1879.

38. Speech of 12 September 1879 in Douglass, *Speeches*, 4:522–23.

39. *National Party Platforms, 1840–1968*, ed. Kirk H. Porter and Donald Bruce Johnson (Urbana, Ill.: University of Illinois Press, 1970), 62.

40. Wendell Phillips to Susan B. Anthony, 30 June 1878, *Papers*, 3:390–91.

41. I say "return" cautiously, as it is not clear from the scant sources that African Americans ever left the National Woman Suffrage Association. This problem of sources is treated at length in Rosalyn Terborg-Penn, *African American Women in the Struggle for the Vote, 1850–1920* (Bloomington: Indiana University Press, 1998).

42. McPherson, *Abolitionist Legacy*, 134–38; Keyssar, *Right to Vote*, 108–12.

43. Keyssar, *Right to Vote*, 129–46, 168–71, and Tables A.10, A.11, and A.13.

44. New York Constitutional Convention, 1894, *Revised Record of the Constitutional Convention of the State of New York, May 8, 1894 to September 29, 1894* (Albany, N.Y.: Argus Company, 1900), 2:493–94.

45. Ibid., 2:525.

46. Ibid., 2:508–9.

47 Speech of 21 October 1890 in Douglass, *Speeches*, 5:442.

48. Meier, *Negro Thought in America*, 191–92.

49. Ibid., 39, 78–79, 95; see also Frederick Douglass's critique of Langston in Douglass, *Speeches*, 5:593–96.

50. *Wyoming. The First Free State for Woman. July 4, 1890* (n.p., n.d.).

51. "Educated Suffrage Justified," *Woman's Journal*, 3 November 1894. Her other essays appeared in the issues of 8 and 22 December 1894 and 5 January 1895. The point, as Barbara Andolsen remarked many years ago, was to get woman suffrage to pass, not to bar immigrants from voting; "Daughters of Jefferson," 38.

52. *Woman's Journal*, 5 January 1895.

53. Speech of 21 October 1890 in Douglass, *Speeches*, 5:453.

54. *Crisis*, September 1912, April 1915, quoted in Jean Fagan Yellin, "Du Bois' *Crisis* and Woman's Suffrage," *Massachusetts Review* 14 (Spring 1873): 367–68, 371–72.

Chapter 8

"Lower Orders," Racial Hierarchies, and Rights Rhetoric

Evolutionary Echoes in Elizabeth Cady Stanton's Thought during the Late 1860s

Michele Mitchell

After the Civil War, Elizabeth Cady Stanton harbored a fixation of sorts over "Patrick, Sambo, Hans, and Yung Tung." During the late 1860s, the quartet appeared in her personal correspondence, in articles that she wrote for the *Revolution,* in an address before the American Equal Rights Association. She eventually inserted these fictive, male representations of immigrants and former slaves in the second volume of the *History of Woman Suffrage* as well. The foursome even morphed into "Jonathan, Patrick, . . . Sambo . . . Hans and Yang-Tang" on at least one occasion. Indeed, Stanton's fixation was purposeful:

> Just so . . . woman finds it hard to bear the oppressive laws of a few Saxon fathers, of the best orders of manhood, what may she not be called to endure when all the lower orders . . . legislate for her and her daughters? . . . Think of Patrick and Sambo and Hans and Yung Tung who do not know the difference between a Monarchy and a Republic, who never read the Declaration of Independence or Webster's spelling book, making laws for Lydia Maria Child, Lucretia Mott, or Fanny Kemble.

Each ethnically coded epithet, along with the attendant stereotypes they evoked independently and in concert, enabled Stanton to craft reasons why the Fifteenth Amendment was nefarious legislation that established an "aristocracy of sex." Each appellation allowed Stanton to counterpose disfranchisement of "virtuous, educated . . . women" to enfranchisement of brutish illiterates, aliens, and rabble scarcely able to appreciate the sanctity of the ballot. Stanton trundled out her pantheon of degraded manhood time and again as she archly critiqued the Fifteenth Amendment for denying women the vote; she additionally asked elite white men how they would feel if they were forced to rely upon "Dinah" and "Bridget" to legislate on their behalf. Even on certain occasions when Stanton decided against explicit use of evocative ethnic monikers, the leading women's rights advocate strategically elicited the phantasmagoric possibility of "lower orders of Chinese, Africans, Germans, and Irish" lording political—if not literal—dominion over cultured "American women."[1]

In considering how and why racialized hierarchies could constitute useful weaponry within a suffragist's rhetorical arsenal, the debate of whether Elizabeth Cady Stanton was racist or merely elitist is not as relevant as is the sort of racial knowledge available to her during the volatile, early years of Radical Reconstruction. The context in which Stanton pushed for women's suffrage was one in which citizenship was partially reconfigured through race, in which race, gender, and class were germane to struggles over citizenship. The late 1860s were a time when the term "social equality" elicited anxieties over racial, gendered, and sexual orders gone awry; it was an era during which recalcitrant pro-slavery advocates resuscitated particular theories of human diversity and development as hierarchical notions of difference shifted yet retained currency. The immediate postemancipation period in the United States was, furthermore, a time when an emergent "sexual science" began to rely upon Darwinian concepts in order to assert that all women belonged to a lower evolutionary order than white men. If a variety of antebellum commentators had previously summoned up the image of humans positioned along a "scale of being," such notions of a stratified human continuum were especially politicized and charged during the late 1860s when access to the franchise had tenuous, turbulent potential to expand along both racial and gender lines. Arguably, a feminist abolitionist's politically expedient usage of concepts regarding "lower" and "higher" orders of human beings at a time when "an unprecedented commitment to the idea of national citizenship" existed in the United States is at once intriguing, surprising, regrettable, contradictory, and predictable.[2]

Elizabeth Cady Stanton certainly uttered sentiments during the late 1860s that were directly at odds with the increasingly racialist salvoes she began to lobby against the Fifteenth Amendment's exclusion of women. She was a prodigious writer whose very output makes "[q]uoting selectively from Elizabeth Cady Stanton . . . risky business."[3] Still, Stanton's incantation of "lower orders" was no discursive tick. The very notion of "lower orders" instead constituted a convenient and reliable rhetorical shorthand, one that echoed evolutionist strains when such strains had an especially politicized resonance.[4]

A woman with the insatiable intellectual appetite of Elizabeth Cady Stanton would, prior to the Civil War, likely have been familiar with two distinct bodies of competing ethnological thought: monogenesis and polygenesis. Monogenist thought emerged from biblical creationism and held that all humankind sprang from a single source, while polygenist theory, which percolated through European thought since the seventeenth and eighteenth centuries and ran counter to scriptural narratives regarding creation, argued that human races had different and unequal origins. Whereas "Linnaeus, Buffon, and Blumenbach towered above those who defended a polygenetic position" until the early nineteenth century, monogenetic thought lost some ground in the United States after 1800 due to the coalescence of the polygenetic American school of ethnology.[5]

Polygenesis, specifically its tenet that "Negroes" constituted a less evolved species with smaller cranial capacity, was deployed in defense of slavery even as it undercut biblical creationism and consequently struck some Southerners as heretical.[6] Still, raging debates over slavery actively engaged theories about human origin, diversity, and development. As the proslavery, antisuffragist South Carolina planter Louisa S. McCord observed in 1851, "the question of the 'unity of races'" was an ongoing, "most important [inquiry] in the consideration of . . . slavery."[7] If abolitionists—black and white alike—often felt the urge to proselytize with the biblical refrain that human beings were all "of one blood," slaveholders and their apologists concocted a host of justifications of their own regarding black bondage that allegedly had scriptural bases.[8]

Whether adherent of monogenesis or polygenesis, whether abolitionist or slavery apologist, intellectually inclined antebellum women and men partook of emerging sciences, methods, and theories of the day regarding human variation. Both phrenology and physical anthropology were, along with stratified cultural models that typically placed Anglo-Saxons at the apex of human development, an integral part of a racialist intellectual landscape populated with politically diverse yet intellectually allied notions that humanity was divided into higher and lower orders. Phrenology was indeed distinct from the sort of physical anthropology associated with the American school. Notions that an individual's intellect and characteristics were manifest in the skull nonetheless overlapped with polygenist theories at a time when matters of race and gender animated debates about equality and rights.[9]

Phrenology even made inroads into the very reform circles in which Elizabeth Cady Stanton circulated. In 1853 she sought out her own phreno-logical reading from noted practitioner Lorenzo Fowler.[10] Although con-troversial, phrenology was no insignificant fad when Stanton allowed Fowler to palpate her skull: phrenological science entrenched beliefs that "bodies determined minds" by firmly linking ability to bodily difference, which itself was inscribed with sociopolitical significance regarding the capacity for self-governance, freedom, and citizenship.[11]

Concepts regarding cranial capacity, racial classification, and bodily characteristics that emanated from or complemented the American school of ethnology were in the intellectual mainstream at midcentury. Such con-cepts were sufficiently popular that African American intellectuals, includ-ing abolitionists Frederick Douglass and William Wells Brown, actively countered with their own "vindicationist ethnology" and other works that rebutted claims about African-descended Americans' allegedly innate in-tellectual and physiognomic inferiority.[12] When Douglass advanced his *Claims of the Negro, Ethnologically Considered* in 1854, he attacked the eth-nological corpus of prominent American school polygenists and pointedly mocked "all the scientific moonshine that . . . would have the world believe that humanity . . . is a sort of sliding scale."[13] Unlike Douglass's *Claims*, Brown's *The Black Man, His Antecedents, His Genius, and His Achievements* (1863) did not explicitly engage the American school. His introduction only briefly alluded to ethnological debates regarding the race of Egyp-tians as it pronounced that "blacks on this continent . . . are fast rising in the scale of intellectual development."[14] *The Black Man* responded to con-temporaneous calculations of bodies at some length, however. Brown's de-sire to "vindicat[e] the Negro's character" resulted in many of *The Black Man*'s biographical sketches highlighting prominent individuals' natural endowments, prepossessing physiques, "fertility of imagination," and, quite significantly, their "well-developed head[s]."[15] The former slave-turned-novelist emphasized the head shape of African-descended people, "pure" and "mixed" alike, because he apparently felt that placing such evi-dence in print was useful—if not potent—antiracist strategy.

Whereas phrenology was hardly on the cutting edge in 1863 when Brown published his text, craniology and anthropometry were on the as-cendancy: both attempted to classify and delineate bodies and brain sizes with scientific tools and methods such as calipers, cephalic indices, and carefully calibrated scales; both were firmly associated with the work of physical anthropologists; both contributed mightily to the spread of scientific racialism during the latter half of the nineteenth century.[16] During the Civil War, for example, the U.S. Sanitary Commission undertook a massive anthropometric project in which the bodies of white, "full black," and "mixed rac[e]" Union soldiers were measured in an attempt to "derive a semblance of understanding as to specific racial types."[17] Such scientific endeavor sustained a taxonomic lingua franca regarding human "scales," "orders," and "strata."

The language of gradation—social, cultural, ostensibly natural—was suffused throughout politicized rhetoric about race, gender, class, nativity, and rights that deeply informed interlocked disputes over the "woman question" and the "negro question." That Douglass challenged the tenets of the American School, Brown mustered prevailing classificatory approaches in order to rebut mainstream beliefs regarding Afro-American ability, and both men traveled in the same activist circles as Elizabeth Cady Stanton speaks to the overwhelming likelihood that Stanton was purposeful when she, too, spoke of "scales" and "orders."

Stanton was certainly aware that classificatory rhetoric was politically meaningful and compelling during the 1850s and 1860s. When, for example, she agitated for women's rights in 1854 before the New York legislature, she bemoaned how women were "classed with idiots, lunatics, and negroes" in being denied the vote as she stressed that "rank[s]" of people were positioned either "higher or lower in the civil or political scale." To be sure, Stanton was proffering a specific argument about legal rights and the franchise; she did so, in part, through a class-inflected rhetoric which acknowledged that certain social stations were stigmatized in ways that had dire politico-legal repercussions. Still, with the suffragist's skillful mention of "the scale of being," Stanton likely evoked racialist concepts in the minds of at least some legislators she sought to convince that women of her station should be "on equal terms with . . . proud Saxon m[e]n" when it came to casting ballots.[18] If Stanton's phrasing was suggestive in 1854, the ways in which she invoked developmental concepts would deepen during the 1860s due to momentous changes wrought by the Civil War, her association with a flamboyant politico, and the emergence of Darwinian thought in the United States.

The North American publication of Charles Darwin's *On the Origin of Species* in 1859 and its theory of natural selection began to render the debate between monogenists and polygenists peripheral if not outmoded during the 1860s. Monogenist claims regarding creationism stood at odds with Darwin's theory about humankind's "common anthropoid ancestor"; polygenist thought, along with much of midcentury physical anthropology and ethnology, was incompatible with Darwinian presumptions regarding the "unitary descent for the human species."[19] Given the focus on human origins within both monogenesis and polygenesis as well as polygenist raciology's contention that humans were divided into more and less evolved species, both polygenesis and monogenesis were nonetheless in dialogue with ascendant evolutionary discourses at midcentury. Darwin himself spent relatively little ink theorizing about race. Darwinism did not, however, necessarily overthrow hierarchical assumptions regarding humanity, nor did it assert that no race-based differences existed. Josiah Nott, a Southern physician prominent among American School theorists, would eventually "affirm th[e] potential compatibility between Darwinism and much of the polygenist case for Negro inferiority."[20]

Tellingly, one of Stanton's eventual and more controversial associates acknowledged his familiarity with both the American school and Darwin while debating "slavery and universal emancipation" in London during March 1862. George Francis Train, a charismatic Bostonian who "occupied a space somewhere between brilliance and insanity," argued that it was the "destiny" of black people to be slaves. For Train, humanity was comprised of "stepping-stones"; hence women, men, and children in bondage benefited from their exposure to "a higher order of mankind." While Train implied such contact could "elevat[e]" African Americans, he nevertheless declared that improvement could only go so far:

> Education may develop, but cannot originate mind. Color is not the only thing that marks him. *You must first put inside his thick skull nine cubic inches more of brain!* He may possess the two hundred and forty-eight bones, the four hundred muscles, the fifty-six joints on hands and feet, the twenty miles of arteries that make the white man . . . but the brain, the organ of thought is not there. . . . All men are not born "free and equal." . . . Geology shows us the different strata of the earth; ethnology teaches us the different strata of men—the negro is the *Paleozoic.*

As Train would have it, not only was it impossible for "the African" to go beyond type and equal "the Caucassian [*sic*]," he further maintained that certain contemporaries, Darwin included, "must admit the African is not as intelligent."[21] Race was a matter of innate difference for Train, whose polygenist leanings reflected an expedient strategy undertaken by an important faction within U.S. party politics north of the Mason-Dixon line.

During the 1860s northern Democrats and other Northerners who had either opposed emancipation, supported the Confederacy, or both, reanimated polygenist concepts in concerted attempts to deny African Americans their newly won rights. These Northerners—colloquially known as "Copperheads"—purposefully manipulated discourses about race and evolution in order to forge arguments regarding individual and collective capacities to exercise citizenship rights in an intelligent, judicious manner.[22] Stanton's relationship to the Republican Party was troubled by 1865 but she had been staunchly pro-Union during the war.[23] She was not a Copperhead in terms of her wartime sympathies, then. In December 1865 Stanton even looked forward to the day when "educated women" could "avail [them]selves of the strong arm and blue uniform of the black soldier" as both crossed the threshold of enfranchisement. At that very same moment, however, Stanton rued the painful possibility that women abolitionists who fought ardently for slaves "lowest in the scale of being" might remain disfranchised while constitutional amendments enabled "'Sambo'" to be "secured in all the rights, privileges, and immunities of citizens."[24] Racialist logic in Stanton's thought would become ever more frequent as volatile debates about access to the franchise roiled during the immediate postbellum period. As a matter of fact, the hierarchical rhetoric that Stanton increasingly relied upon would in time strongly ally her with Copperhead sentiments.

So long as universal suffrage (including women as well as men) remained a possibility, however, Stanton was not particularly concerned with the racial politics that so vexed the Copperheads. Matters of class could and did agitate the feminist activist. Stanton crafted a complex, gradated social taxonomy in 1867 when she gave a lecture entitled "Reconstruction" before an audience at the Brooklyn Academy of Music. After asserting that African Americans and women were undeniably "members of the State," Stanton contended "universal suffrage" was necessary, in part, because all Americans were *not* equals:

> I claim to understand the interests of this nation better, the interests of woman better than yonder pauper in your almshouse. . . . Do you think, gentlemen, that it is claiming too much for . . . educated women . . . ? Why we know more and are better fitted to vote on our own interests and the in-

terests of this nation than . . . the lower strata of your white manhood. Now why is it that the rights of every type of white manhood are so sacredly protected, while no safeguards are thrown around those of women?

Not only was it problematic that women could not vote in their own interests, Stanton argued, but it was unconscionable that "loyal mothers," laboring women, and "respectable" matrons were disfranchised while "motley" men fresh from "dens of infamy and vice . . . stagger[ed] up to the polls." Stanton surely associated recent immigrants with the so-called motley, yet here she primarily used the phrase "lower strata" to connote moral rectitude, education, and class. The most biting commentary on race within Stanton's February 1867 speech centered on white manhood. Granted, Stanton contrasted the constitutional rights accorded African American men with those withheld from white "daughters of the State." She significantly refrained from insinuating that black men would eventually join the "cringing, limping, staggering" portion of the U.S. electorate all the same.[25]

Such restraint on Stanton's part soon abated. Her address at the Brooklyn Academy of Music came within two short years of when the Thirteenth Amendment abolished slavery and a mere year after Congress passed the Fourteenth Amendment. Critically, Stanton's Academy of Music address predated contentious debates over whether the Fifteenth Amendment would keep the vote from being denied on the basis of race, color, previous condition of servitude, *or sex*. When she stood before that audience in Brooklyn, universal suffrage still seemed a viable possibility given that Reconstruction had occasioned reinterpretation of the Constitution along with a "belief that the right to vote was a natural right."[26]

Yet, by June 1867, when Stanton reported on the prospects for woman suffrage in the revision of the New York constitution, she extended her attack on universal *manhood* suffrage. On the pages of the *New York Tribune*, Stanton included black men among the problematic "lower orders of . . . washed and unwashed, lettered and unlettered manhood" who she felt were wrongfully prioritized over "the higher orders of womanhood" who possessed the wherewithal to "see the power of the ballot in clearing up this great wilderness of life . . . and use it for the good of the race[.]"[27] After the New York Constitutional Convention left women disfranchised, Stanton's ardor for woman suffrage hardly dampened.

That fall, she, Susan Anthony, and the ever-colorful, "coppery" George Train toured Kansas, where separate state constitutional referenda on woman suffrage and black male suffrage were to be decided in November. Anthony chastised audiences and repudiated "mean, low, sneaking editors" at the helm of newspapers allied with Republicans; for Anthony, too many lecture goers and journalists in Kansas failed to understand the full import of woman suffrage. Train increased support for woman suffrage among Democrats in the state and did so, in part, by urging white male Kansans not to position white women "still lower in the scale of citizenship and humanity" than African American men. Stanton's "pioneer" moment in Kansas witnessed her speaking on behalf of both referenda as she backed away from associating black men with the undeserving and unwashed and instead intoned "the gospel of equality." Privately, she wrote to her husband, Henry, that "[e]verybody says the woman proposition will be carried, but the negro one will not. The Democrats here go for us strong."[28]

Hopeful prediction by Stanton notwithstanding, the trio was unsuccessful in trumping up sufficient support in the state for giving women the vote. Black male Kansans would have to wait for their chance at the ballot box until ratification of the Fifteenth Amendment more than two years later. The outcome in Kansas was disappointing for advocates of universal suffrage, but Republican support for black male suffrage over woman suffrage was an especially bitter dose for Stanton and Anthony. Indeed, the Kansas defeat of woman suffrage—along with the earlier disappointment in New York—would have a noticeable impact on how Stanton used race in her rhetoric.[29]

As men who had been allied with abolitionism stressed the primacy of "manhood suffrage" over universalist claims to the franchise, as the Fifteenth Amendment was debated in Congress and on the state level, as black men voiced expectations to exercise their newfound rights, Stanton's rhetoric regarding black male suffrage became ever more antagonistic. Serendipitously, Stanton had an important new outlet for her evolving views. George Train had provided financial backing for a newspaper devoted to the suffragist cause, the *Revolution*, which Elizabeth Cady Stanton and Susan B. Anthony launched in January 1868. It would not take long for some of Stanton's peers to notice the tenor of her shifting politics. One of the very first issues of the *Revolution* featured William Lloyd Garrison's critique of Stanton and Anthony for making a politically expedient alliance with the " 'anti-nigger' " Train in order to advance the cause of woman suffrage. Six months after the *Revolution* appeared, Theodore Tilton of the *Independent* bemoaned Stanton's "lamentable" editorial choices. "When people who have once been radicals turn aside from the army of progress," opined Tilton, "there is no telling when and where they might finally bring up." As far as the proponent of Radical Reconstruction was concerned, Stanton's mounting opposition to the Fifteenth Amendment transformed her into a veritable "Tammany Hall Democrat."[30]

Stanton's position regarding the Fifteenth Amendment was actually quite complex. She unquestionably recognized that the Fifteenth Amendment would disfranchise black women "as precious in the scale of being as the men"; in time, Stanton even argued that universal manhood suffrage subjected African American women to but a different form of enslavement. The *Revolution,* moreover, still publicized its commitment to "equality of rights" for women and men, black and white, "rich and poor," as late as November 1868.[31] When Stanton turned to vituperative language that underscored the civic worthiness of "Saxon" women, however, she displayed a tendency for inflammatory views that Tilton and other former abolitionists considered "negro-hating Democracy."[32] Additionally, her noticeable penchant for emphasizing that whiteness—and a class-bound, cultured whiteness native to the United States, at that—was the measure of political fitness did more than reflect a deepening commitment to educated suffrage on her part. Stanton's vaunting of "Saxon" womanhood would play into a sexualized logic that at once supported arguments that women's possession of ballot afforded them vital protection and buttressed claims that universal male suffrage would have dire consequences for women's rights *and* bodies.

This complexity is on display in Stanton's response when her cousin, abolitionist Gerrit Smith, refused to sign a petition calling for universal suffrage in December 1868. Stanton upbraided Smith on the pages of the *Revolution* for his "apathy on Woman's enfranchisement" as she forcefully pointed out that advocating universal suffrage was solid strategy for granting African Americans access to the polls. After noting that enfranchising black men alone would not necessarily protect black women, Stanton pressed her claim:

> Mr. Smith . . . would undoubtedly plead the necessity of the ballot for the negro at the south for his protection. . . . Have Saxon women no wrongs to right, and will they be better protected when negroes are their rulers? . . . Society, as organized to-day under . . . man power, is one grand rape of womanhood. . . . Do such men as Gerrit Smith and Wendell Phillips teach this lesson to the lower order of men . . . when they tell the most noble,

virtuous, and educated matrons of this republic, to stand back until all the
sons of Adam are clothed with citizenship?

If likening manhood suffrage to "one grand rape of womanhood" did not
sufficiently dramatize her cause, Stanton also relayed the story of a teen-
aged "Saxon gir[l]" who committed infanticide after being "ruin[ed]" and
impregnated by an African American farmhand. Stanton told this story in
order to suggest that, if brought before a jury containing black men but no
white women, such a "Saxon girl" might be dealt a hard fate for murdering
her child "of negro parentage." In the process, she implied that black jurors
and judges, as men of a "lower order," were perhaps capable of succumb-
ing to the same base sexual impulses as those presumably demonstrated
by said farmhand.[33] White women, according to such logic, not only had
to endure the ignominious sting of submitting to "negro rule," but their
new rulers were less-evolved men who subjected white womanhood to a
"grand rape" of rights—literal as well as figurative, electoral as well as cor-
poreal.

In this instance, Stanton unabashedly played to many white women's
sexual anxieties regarding black men. But as surely as she was wont to argue that black men viewed women as nothing more than objects of carnal
desire, Stanton also classed men of African descent together with immigrants from China, Germany, and Ireland as belonging to a rank of manhood with "low ideas of womankind" and an unfortunate predilection for
"outrag[ing] . . . refined, educated women of all ages."[34] Thus, as much as
the radical suffragist claimed that "low ideas" regarding how men should
interact with women emerged out of ostensible ethnic customs, and
whereas these sundry claims emerged out of her own elitism, racism, and
nativism, Stanton's argument along these lines additionally drew upon
evolutionary schematics that insinuated "lower orders," by fiat of biology,
lacked the rational capacity to control primal sexual urges.

In a June 1869 editorial on the Fifteenth Amendment, Stanton once
again summoned up images of devolution as she argued that women's
disfranchisement did more than humiliate women—it compromised the
nation:

I have seen and felt . . . the far-reaching consequences of this degradation of
one-half the citizens of the republic, on the government, the Saxon race,
and woman herself. . . . As you go down and down in the scale of manhood
the idea strengthens . . . at every step, that woman was created for no higher

purpose than to gratify the lust of man. . . . When a mighty nation, with the scratch of the pen, frames the base ideas of the lower orders into constitutions and statute[s] . . . [it] not only degrade[s] every woman in her own eyes, but in that of every man on the footstool.

The power of what Stanton wrote existed as much in what she baldly stated as in what she skillfully implied. On its surface, the editorial asserted that disfranchisement was tantamount to slavery for women through articulating the horror of women's rights being dismissed by "everything in manhood's form." By speaking of a distinct Saxon people, moreover, Stanton drew upon a now well-established antebellum discourse that not only connected Anglo-Saxons with "good government" but that considered native-born white American "Anglo-Saxons" superior to other Caucasian peoples. Celtic and Teutonic immigrants were not "Saxon" and were thus less evolved in Stanton's eyes. Part of what her editorial insisted, then, was that native-born, educated white women were innately endowed with qualities that made them better voters than foreign-born white males "ignorant of the philosophy of true government." And, as far as Stanton was concerned, one of the primary dangers of the Fifteenth Amendment was that, in addition to placing the ballot in the hands to black men, it would also enfranchise colonized subjects within the expanding U.S. empire, not to mention a host of supposedly less than desirable immigrants—Asian as well as European.[35]

In addition, when Stanton associated universal manhood suffrage with the rape of "hunted girls" in that June editorial, such a line of argumentation likely elicited memories of the tragic girl inseminated by the black farm worker for faithful readers of the *Revolution*. The enfranchisement of "lower orders" was therefore subtly linked with the specter of miscegenation without actual mention of the recently coined term. Taken in tandem with Stanton's *Revolution* articles that discussed immigration in terms of infiltration—if not outright pollution—readers only had to imagine the perils facing white womanhood. Stanton's June 1869 editorial thus insinuated that once "an aristocracy of sex" was entrenched by the Fifteenth Amendment, once the "base ideas" of bestial men made their way into the Constitution and onto state statute books, the consequences could well be catastrophic.[36]

By 1869 Stanton did not have to invoke miscegenation actively, nor did she necessarily have to detail the imagined impact of miscegenation on the "Saxon race" for many of her readers. In terms of former slaves alone, opponents of universal manhood suffrage routinely associated giving black men the vote with giving African Americans license to seek sexual relationships with whites—black men, more specifically, since black women had long been involved in forced, coerced, and consensual relations with white men. It was not uncommon for opponents of universal manhood suffrage to address the question of whether a miscegenated public was capable of sustaining a democratic republic or, for that matter, to appropriate evolutionary concepts. One such pamphlet even couched black suffrage within the question of whether "the highest type of man is but a slow outgrowth from inferior orders of beings." Another incendiary piece of propaganda published after Lincoln's reelection, *What Miscegenation Is!*, featured a vivid illustration that associated miscegenation with heterosexual mating between blacks and whites, specifically between black men and white women.[37] Furthermore, as the Fourteenth and Fifteenth Amendments were introduced in Congress, legislatures in the South swiftly enacted a variety of antimiscegenation laws. In a context where "expressions of white anxiety about sex between black men and white women reached an unprecedented intensity," the mere juxtaposition of universal manhood suffrage with rape played upon a host of fears, including the panicked anxiety that miscegenation would compromise the Anglo-Saxon's position in the scale of being.[38]

Moreover, northern Copperheads such as John Van Evrie resuscitated polygenesis after the war. Van Evrie reissued several of his "anti-abolition tracts," including *The Six Species of Men*, which included the noxious insinuation that since blacks constituted a different species rife with "revolting practices," it was ludicrous to believe whites and blacks could or should "occupy the same position in political and social affairs." Josiah Nott, for his part, "left aside" the origins debate between monogenists and polygenists in *Instincts of Races* (1866). Nott nonetheless remained convinced that different races were "if not distinct species . . . *permanent varieties*" and that African Americans' "intellect permit[ted] no approach to civilization," let alone free labor and productive citizenship. In Nott, Van Evrie and other Copperheads found both common cause and a link to the American school. Polygenist concepts thus served the purposes of opponents of Radical Reconstruction both North and South.[39]

Given her open association with George Francis Train, given that Stanton herself jested that some suffragists and former abolitionists feared that the *Revolution* was at risk of "going over to the copperheads," Stanton's decision to mobilize the language that they so deliberately employed regarding "orders" is highly suggestive. When Elizabeth Cady Stanton consistently editorialized about "lower orders" in the *Revolution* during the late 1860s, then, she did so in a context in which "lower orders" connoted far more than manners, morals, literacy, and culture. Stanton railed against the now ratified Fourteenth Amendment for "seal[ing]" the veritable "doom" of woman; she archly complained that while the Fifteenth Amendment would enfranchise "2,000,000 black men" along with "the foreigners daily landing in our eastern cities, the Chinese crowding our western shores, the inhabitants of Alaska and all those western isles that will soon be ours," women such as herself would remain unjustifiably disfranchised.[40]

Stanton's consistent, strident evocation of "lower orders" occurred when people of color felt pressed to refute this highly political mobilization of racialist claims by manipulating such rhetoric and schemas themselves. In 1868, for example, when the Georgia state legislature's white members excluded duly elected African American legislators, one of those excluded legislators, Henry MacNeal Turner, issued a fiery jeremiad:

The great question . . . is this: Am I a man? If I am such, I claim the rights of a man . . . I want to convince the House, today, that I am entitled to my seat here. A certain gentleman has argued that the negro was a mere development similar to the orangutan or chimpanzee, but it so happens that, when a negro is examined, physiologically, phrenologically and anatomically, and, I may say, physiognomically, he is found to be the same as persons of different color.

That Turner retorted in such a fashion is telling in several regards. A largely self-educated former slave and organic intellectual, Turner was fighting against racialist cant—scientific as well as political—that placed blacks outside of the realm of humanity, not to mention the prerogatives of citizenship. Turner would go on to address ethnology and evolution yet again when he gave his lecture "The Negro in All Ages" five years later in which he expressed his exasperation with "several abominable, anti-scriptural, and pseudo-philosophical theories . . . by a few malevolent vampires of the age," including the long deceased Samuel Morton.[41] As late as 1879, Turner's peer and fellow ex-slave, the prominent writer, thinker, and physician Martin Delany, found it necessary to eschew the claims of the American school prior to asserting, among other things, that African Americans were "worthy to emulate the noble Caucasian and Anglo-Saxon, now at the top of the ladder of moral and intellectual grandeur."[42]

During the 1870s Frances Ellen Watkins Harper, a freeborn black woman suffragist and veteran abolitionist, also referred to contemporary discourses regarding human evolution when analyzing sociopolitical dynamics. Harper appeared at suffrage conventions with Elizabeth Cady Stanton after the war; she helped to establish the American Woman Suffrage Association when the American Equal Rights Association foundered in 1869. In contrast to the sexual specters Stanton evoked, Harper was outraged over the violence that black women, men, and children were withstanding during Reconstruction, and she felt compelled, as abolitionists had done decades before, to assert that African Americans were not "beasts of burden to be bridled and bitted." "Ethnologists may differ about the origin of the human race . . . and Darwin send for the missing links," Harper observed, "but there is one thing of which we may rest assured—that we all come from the living God[.]" War, emancipation, and Reconstruction changed much in the United States by 1875, but Frances Harper still intoned a response to developmental and evolutionary thought that was strikingly similar to the earlier abolitionist rejoinder to polygenism during and after the coalescence of the American school.[43]

Stanton defensively drew upon evolutionary discourses in order to make piqued arguments that universal male suffrage endangered white women and the national body politic. Her politicized usage of race supported and contributed to a wide-ranging brand of antiblack thought that Frances Harper, Henry Turner, and Martin Delany each felt compelled to challenge. Racialist rhetoric of the sort found in the *Revolution* had a life beyond lectures, debates, and the printed page. Arguably, contemporaneous variants of such rhetoric informed—if not justified—ploys to obstruct African Americans' access to full citizenship through chicanery, murder, mob violence, ritualized rape, and forced community expulsions. Successful attempts to disfranchise African American men in the South began virtually upon their gaining the vote and the right to run for political office; thus Stanton's decision during the late 1860s to malign black men's ability to exercise the franchise in a judicious manner was more than an unfortunate rhetorical choice on her part. Stanton might not have capitulated to racism during Reconstruction, but she certainly trafficked in a racialist logic that, in its extreme forms, exacted much from African Americans, some of whom—including Frances Ellen Watkins Harper, Frederick Douglass, Harriet Forten Purvis, Robert Purvis, Sojourner Truth, Mary Ann Shadd Cary, Charles Lenox Remond, and Sarah Parker Remond—were her comrades and peers in activist circles.[44]

Stanton tactically deployed hierarchical racial concepts in her writings and on the pages of the *Revolution* at a significant historical juncture when the stakes were high for African Americans as well as for a feminist who had once been an abolitionist. Although Stanton did not invoke Charles Darwin or Herbert Spencer in her writings and speeches of the late 1860s to the extent that she did positivist philosopher Auguste Comte, she was clearly willing to employ "all the recent revelations of science" in her opposition to a "manhood suffrage" that "ignore[d] the influence of woman in the legislation of the country . . . [yet] blindly insisted upon the recognition of every type of brutalized, degraded manhood[.]" Given that abolitionists routinely rebutted polygenist arguments, that during the 1867 Kansas campaign Stanton alluded to the work of Herbert Spencer, and that the *Revolution* contained at least one squib about Darwinism, the evidence is strong that she possessed enough knowledge of developmental and evolutionary concepts to adroitly maintain that the Fifteenth Amendment's gendered exclusions would result in social, political, and racial devolution.[45]

Elizabeth Cady Stanton's knowledge of evolutionary concepts would only deepen during and after the 1870s as the work of Darwin, Spencer, and other evolutionists became more widely read, debated, and accepted in the United States. For feminists such as Stanton, evolutionism would become freighted with additional significance with the elaboration of social evolutionary thought, which analyzed both gender difference and racial distinctions in light of civilization, culture, education, and progress. As feminists such as Stanton worked ardently to expand women's rights, social evolutionism provided a "framework and language through which changes in woman's sphere were interpreted" as leading evolutionists and social commentators made pointed arguments of their own about lower orders.[46]

Stanton confronted aspects of evolutionary thought that boded ill for women's claims to full citizenship. In *Descent of Man and Selection in Relation to Sex* (1871), Charles Darwin not only detailed the laws of sexual selection among various species, he also contended that both natural and sexual selection resulted in the evolutionary endowment of men with greater "intellectual powers" than women. Herbert Spencer's 1873 article entitled "Psychology of the Sexes" maintained that "bodily specialization" resulted in gendered "mental particularities." Whereas Spencer considered "women of a more evolved race" superior to "men of a less-evolved race," he nonetheless held that women were intellectually inferior to men "of the same society."[47] In the United States, physician and former Harvard professor Edward H. Clarke drew upon both men's arguments in his *Sex in Education; or, A Fair Chance for the Girls* (1873). He came to the "physiological" conclusion that educating young women in the same manner as young men resulted in "female physical degeneracy" that could potentially lead to an enfeebling "hermaphroditic condition." Clarke honed, revised, and elaborated this premise in *The Building of a Brain* (1874); there, he situated the matter of gender, reproduction, intellect capacity, and education within the question of whether the "Anglo-Saxon race" would "maintai[n] a permanent grasp upon this Western world." The physician was loath to argue that women were not equal to men, but he was quite prepared to claim that "ill-regulated cerebration" at once threatened to "unsex" women and inhibit Anglo-Saxons' ability to "ascend in the scale of being" over less-evolved races.[48] Although Clarke, Spencer, and Darwin exalted certain gendered qualities of white women in Western societies, and whereas Spencer and Clarke did not deny that women could exert influence beyond the domestic realm, the work of all three men nevertheless posed challenges to feminist demands for equal access to sociopolitical institutions by insinuating—and even blatantly proclaiming—that women were less evolved than men.

With higher education joining suffrage as a key feminist issue in the United States during the 1870s, feminists hardly remained silent about the implications of such evolutionist arguments. "When . . . Mr. Spencer argues that women are inferior to men because their development must be earlier arrested by reproductive functions, and Mr. Darwin claims that males have evolved muscle and brains much superior to females," replied Antoinette Brown Blackwell, " . . . these conclusions need not be accepted without question." In response to Clarke, Julia Ward Howe acidly but wittily remarked that the physician's "book seems to have found a chance *at* the girls, rather than a chance *for* them."[49] Elizabeth Cady Stanton had her say, too. Whereas in 1874 Stanton viewed Spencer's and Darwin's work as contributing to a "fearless investigation" of "present social evils" that limited women, a year later she argued that when it came to analyzing "[w]oman's true position in the state, the church, and the home," neither Spencer, Darwin, nor Clarke had "satisfactorily explored" the issue.[50] On neither occasion did Stanton vet the allied claims made by Spencer, Darwin, and Clarke that women were, in the main, less evolved than men. She would, however, join other white feminists in referencing evolutionary theory in order "to explain why the expansion of woman's sphere would not endanger the Anglo-Saxon race."[51]

As she continued to employ evolution in her own work even after social evolutionists advanced claims about women's biological and intellectual limitations, Elizabeth Cady Stanton did not, it seems, seize the opportunity to reflect upon how the very rhetoric of "lower orders" simultaneously cut against the citizenship rights of white women, women and men of color, and immigrant women and men alike. Rather, she continued to manipulate social evolutionary theory in order to advance their own arguments about gender, race, equality, and rights after Reconstruction ended. Stanton jotted down references of her own to Darwin and Spencer in a diary that she kept during a trip to England in 1882 but she did so, in part, out of excitement that both men's work undercut biblical orthodoxy.[52] Not surprisingly, Stanton eventually incorporated Darwin into her controversial critique of conservative biblical views regarding women's subordination.[53] Stanton's remarks in *The Woman's Bible* (1895, 1898) concerning the third chapter of Genesis in which Eve is seduced into partaking of the forbidden fruit, and woman was rendered subject to man, indicate that she found Darwinism "more hopeful and encouraging" than biblical creationism. Moreover, in her appendix to *The Woman's Bible,* Stanton concluded that "[i]f . . . we accept the Darwinian theory, that the race has been a gradual growth from a lower to a higher form of life, and that the story of the fall is a myth, we can exonerate the snake, emancipate the woman, and reconstruct a more rational religion[.]"[54]

If, during the late 1860s, Stanton utilized hierarchical arguments about human development and evolution in the name of woman suffrage, she would not recant those arguments three decades later during a period of national reunification that mended critical fissures rent by the Civil War. Stanton might have "frequently lamented the mistreatment of racial, ethnic, and religious groups" as nativism and racism peaked at century's end, but she did not back away from her advocacy of educated suffrage.[55] And, like her earlier opposition to passage of the Fifteenth Amendment, Stanton's push for educated suffrage during the 1890s was firmly situated within the rhetoric of racial hierarchy.[56] Indeed, Stanton's ongoing racialist arguments regarding woman suffrage were, in crucial regards, allied to what may be called a white nationalist vision of U.S. citizenship, which excluded certain European immigrants as much as it did Asian immigrants, Latina/os, Native Americans, and African Americans.[57] Stanton's tactical decision to maintain that some Americans were more worthy of the franchise than others may not have secured the vote for women within her lifetime, but such logic would prove particularly powerful during the late nineteenth century when social Darwinism aided decisively in African Americans' civil rights being steadily, surreptitiously, blatantly, violently wrested from their grasp. Elizabeth Cady Stanton can hardly be blamed for the active, frequently ruthless discrimination faced by black women and men—along with Asian Americans, Latina/os, Native Americans, and immigrants who are now occasionally referred to as "white ethnics"—that had a devastating impact on citizenship rights and continued well into the twentieth century. It is possible, however, to hold Stanton accountable for a strategic choice that she made of her own volition.

NOTES

1. Elizabeth Cady Stanton, "Manhood Suffrage," *Revolution*, December 24, 1868, 392–93, esp. 392. For examples cited above, see Elizabeth Cady Stanton to Gerrit Smith, New York, January 29, 186[9], reprinted in *The Selected Papers of Elizabeth Cady Stanton and Susan B. Anthony*, vol. 2: *Against an Aristocracy of Sex, 1866 to 1873*, ed. Ann D. Gordon (New Brunswick, N.J.: Rutgers University Press, 2000), 212–13; Stanton, "Anniversary of the American Equal Rights Association. Address of Elizabeth Cady Stanton," *Revolution*, May 13, 1869, 289–92; Elizabeth Cady Stanton, Susan B. Anthony, and Matilda J. Gage, eds., *The History of Woman Suffrage*, vol. 2: *1861–1876* (New York: Fowler and Wells, 1882), 348–55; "Correction: Is There an Antagonism between Woman and the Colored Man?" *Revolution*, March 18, 1869, 169; Stanton, "The Sixteenth Amendment," *Revolution*, April 29, 1869, 266. For Stanton's deployment of "Dinah" and "Bridget," see "The Fifteenth Amendment: The Tables Turned," *Revolution*, July 29, 1869, 56. Stanton earlier referenced "Bridget and Dinah" in "Equal Rights to All!" *Revolution*, February 12, 1868, 120–21.

2. George Fredrickson, *The Black Image in the White Mind: The Debate on Afro-American Character and Destiny, 1817–1914* (New York: Harper and Row, 1971), 90–96, 187–93; Cynthia Eagle Russett, *Sexual Science: The Victorian Construction of Womanhood* (Cambridge, Mass.: Harvard University Press, 1989), 1–15; Eric Foner, *Reconstruction: America's Unfinished Revolution, 1863–1877* (New York: Harper and Row, 1988), xxvi; Hannah Rosen, "The Gender of Reconstruction: Rape, Race, & Citizenship in the Postemancipation South," Ph.D. dissertation, University of Chicago, 1999.

3. See Ann D. Gordon, "Stanton and the Right to Vote: On Account of Race or Sex," this volume, chapter 7, p. 117.

4. Louise Michele Newman, *White Women's Rights: The Racial Origins of Feminism in the United States* (New York: Oxford University Press, 1999), 60, 39.

5. Reginald Horsman, *Race and Manifest Destiny: The Origins of American Racial Anglo-Saxonism* (Cambridge, Mass.: Harvard University Press, 1981), 44–52, 99–102, esp. 52.

6. Fredrickson, *The Black Image in the White Mind*, 71–96; Horsman, *Race and Manifest Destiny*, 129–30, 140, 152–53; Thomas F. Gossett, *Race: The History of an Idea in America*, New Edition (New York: Oxford University Press, 1997), 66.

7. L[ouisa] S[usanna] M[cCord], "Diversity of the Races; Its Bearing Upon Negro Slavery," *Southern Quarterly Review*, New Series 3:6 (April 1851): 392–419, esp. 395, 407.

8. Horsman, *Race and Manifest Destiny*, 122–24, 129–33, 140; Mia Bay, *The White Image in the Black Mind: African American Ideas about White People, 1830–1925* (New York: Oxford University Press, 2000), 13–37, 55–58, 69, 72; Frederickson, *Black Image in the White Mind*, 107–9, 126.

9. Fredrickson, *Black Image in the White Mind*, 71–129; John S. Haller, Jr., *Outcasts from Evolution: Scientific Attitudes of Racial Inferiority, 1859–1900* (Urbana: University of Illinois Press, 1969), 3–39; William R. Stanton, *The Leopard's Spots: Scientific Attitudes toward Race in America, 1815–59* (Chicago: University of Chicago Press, 1960); Horsman, *Race and Manifest Destiny*, 53–60, 116–38; Bay, *White Image in the Black Mind*, 38–74; John S. Carson, *The Measure of Merit: Talents, Intelligence, and Inequality in the French and American Republics, 1750–1940* (Princeton, N.J.: Princeton University Press, 2006), chapter 3; Russett, *Sexual Science*, 16–48.

10. For brief discussion of Stanton's attraction to phrenology and for a transcription of Stanton's report, refer to "Phrenological Reports," reprinted in *Elizabeth Cady Stanton–Susan B. Anthony Reader*, 269–74.

11. *Elizabeth Cady Stanton–Susan B. Anthony Reader*, 269; Russett, *Sexual Science*, 19–24, esp. 23, 24.

12. Frederick Douglass, *The Claims of the Negro, Ethnologically Considered. An Address, Before the Literary Societies of Western Reserve College at Commencement, July 12, 1854* (Rochester: Lee, Mann, 1854); William Wells Brown, *The Black Man: His Antecedents, His Genius, and His Achievements* (New York: Thomas Hamilton, 1863); Bay, *The White Image in the Black Mind*, 38–111.

13. Douglass, *Claims of the Negro*, 16, 8.

14. Brown, *The Black Man*, 32–33, 36.

15. Ibid., passim, esp. 57, 92, 103, 131, 192, 207, 237.

16. Russett, *Sexual Science*, 28–39; Stocking, *Race, Culture, and Evolution*, 44–68.

17. Haller, *Outcasts from Evolution*, 17, 19. The U.S. Sanitary Commission's study was published as *Investigations in the Military and Anthropological Statistics of American Soldiers* (New York: Hurd and Houghton, 1869).

18. Stanton's speech referred to here is her "Address to the Legislature of New York on Women's Rights," February 14, 1854, which is reprinted in *Elizabeth Cady Stanton–Susan B. Anthony Reader*, 44–52, esp. 45, 46, 48.

19. George W. Stocking, Jr., "The Persistence of Polygenist Thought in Post-Darwinian Anthropology," in Stocking, *Race, Culture, and Evolution: Essays in the History of Anthropology* (Chicago: University of Chicago Press, 1982), 42–68, esp. 45; Russett, *Sexual Science*, 209 n. 4.

20. Stocking, "The Persistence of Polygenist Thought in Post-Darwinian Anthropology," 45–47; Fredrickson, *Black Image in the White Mind*, 232–35, esp. 233.

21. *Selected Papers of Elizabeth Cady Stanton and Susan B. Anthony*, 2:94–95 n. 11; *Train's Speeches in England, on Slavery and Emancipation. Delivered in London, on March 12th and [17th], 1862 . . .* (Philadelphia: T. B. Peterson and Brothers, [1862]), 20, 21, 22, 26, 27; italics in original.

22. Luc Forest, "De l'abolitionnisme à l'esclavagisme? Les implications des anthropologues dans le débat sur l'esclavage des Noirs aux États-Unis (1840–1879)," *Revue Française d'histoire d'Outre-Mer* 85:3 (septembre 1998): 85–102, esp. 100–101; Stocking, "The Persistence of Polygenist Thought in Post-Darwinian Anthropology," 42–68; Fredrickson, *Black Image in the White Mind*, 232–35.

23. Elisabeth Griffith, *In Her Own Right: The Life of Elizabeth Cady Stanton* (New York: Oxford University Press, 1984), 108–17.

24. Elizabeth Cady Stanton, [Letter to the Editor], *National Anti-Slavery Standard*, December 30, 1865, reprinted in *Selected Papers of Elizabeth Cady Stanton and Susan B. Anthony*, 1:564–66, esp. 564.

25. Stanton, "Reconstruction" [February 19, 1867], reprinted in *Selected Papers of Elizabeth Cady Stanton and Susan B. Anthony*, 2:25–41, esp. 32–33, 35, 30. For a very similar argument by Stanton, see her *Address in Favor of Universal Suffrage, For the Election of Delegates to the Constitutional Convention, Before the Judiciary Committees of the Legislature of New York in the Assembly Chamber, January 23, 1867, in Behalf of the American Equal Rights Association* (Albany, N.Y.: Weed, Parsons, 1867), esp. 11.

26. Ellen Carol DuBois, "Outgrowing the Compact of the Fathers: Equal Rights, Woman Suffrage, and the United States Constitution, 1820–1878," *Journal of American History* 74 (1987): 836–62, esp. 845. The Fourteenth Amendment was passed by Congress in 1866 and ratified two years later; the Fifteenth Amendment was passed in 1869 and ratified in 1870.

27. Stanton, "Female Suffrage Committee," *New York Tribune*, June 19, 1867, reprinted in *Selected Papers of Elizabeth Cady Stanton and Susan B. Anthony*, 2:72–73.

28. "ECS to Theodore Tilton" [September 15, 1867], in *Selected Papers of Elizabeth Cady Stanton and Susan B. Anthony*, 2:89–92, esp. 90; George Francis Train, *The Great Epigram Campaign of Kansas. Championship of Woman. The Revolution* (Leavenworth, Kans.: Prescott and Hume, 1867), 16; Griffith, *In Her Own Right*, 126–29, 133–37; *History of Woman Suffrage*, 2:244; Stanton, "Speech at Lawrence,

Kansas, 1867," in *Elizabeth Cady Stanton–Susan B. Anthony Reader*, 113–18, esp. 115; Stanton, *Eighty Years and More*, 245–58; "ECS to Henry B. Stanton" [October 9, 1867], in *Selected Papers of Elizabeth Cady Stanton and Susan B. Anthony*, 2:96–97, esp. 96; "Speech by SBA in St. Louis, Missouri" [November 25, 1867], in *Selected Papers of Elizabeth Cady Stanton and Susan B. Anthony*, 2:104–13. For usage of the term "coppery," see Parker Pillsbury's response to critics who charged that he and Stanton were too friendly with Democrats in "'The Revolution' Too Democratic," *Revolution*, June 11, 1868, 361–62.

29. *Elizabeth Cady Stanton–Susan B. Anthony Reader*, 88–92.

30. "William Lloyd Garrison," *Revolution*, January 29, 1868, 49–50; [Theodore Tilton], "Editorial Notes," *Independent* (New York, N.Y.), June 18, 1868, 4; *Selected Papers of Elizabeth Cady Stanton and Susan B. Anthony*, 2:161 n. 2.

31. Stanton, "'Sharp Points,'" *Revolution*, April 9, 1868, 212–13, esp. 212; Stanton, "The Fifteenth Amendment," *Revolution*, May 20, 1869, 313; Stanton and Susan B. Anthony [Editorial re: *The Revolution*], *Revolution*, November 26, 1868, 328.

32. [Tilton], "Editorial Notes," *Independent* (New York, N.Y.), June 18, 1868, 4.

33. Stanton, "Gerrit Smith on Petitions," *Revolution*, January 14, 1869, 24–25, in *Elizabeth Cady Stanton-Susan B. Anthony Reader*, 119–24, esp. 121–24. It is not clear from the newspaper account cited in Stanton's article whether the girl was raped or if her relations with the farmhand had been consensual.

34. "Anniversary of the American Equal Rights Association. Address of Elizabeth Cady Stanton," *Revolution*, May 13, 1869, 290, 292. See also Stanton, "The Sixteenth Amendment," *Revolution*, April 29, 1869, 266. For an argument that black men were hostile to (white) women and therefore wished to "'dominate'" them, see Stanton, "Women and Black Men," *Revolution*, February 4, 1869, 88; Stanton, "Correction: Is There an Antagonism between Woman and the Colored Man?" *Revolution*, March 18, 1869.

35. Stanton, "The Fifteenth Amendment," *Revolution*, June 3, 1869, 344; Horsman, *Race and Manifest Destiny*, 1–6. For Stanton's opinion that the Fifteenth Amendment theoretically enfranchised immigrants, Aleuts, and Asian Pacific Islanders, see "Anniversary of the American Equal Rights Association. Address of Elizabeth Cady Stanton," *Revolution*, May 13, 1869, 289.

36. Stanton, "The Fifteenth Amendment," *Revolution*, June 3, 1869. Examples of Stanton's rhetoric regarding immigration may be found in "'Sharp Points,'" *Revolution*, April 9, 1868; "Anniversary of the American Equal Rights Association. Address of Elizabeth Cady Stanton," *Revolution*, May 13, 1869; Stanton, "A Pronunciamento," *Revolution*, July 15, 1869, 24. A rabidly anti-Semitic, anti-Asian, and unsigned item on immigration that was possibly written by George Francis Train appeared on the pages of the *Revolution* in early 1869. See "The Jews and the Chinese—A Warning," *Revolution*, March 18, 1869, 165.

37. [National Union Executive Committee], *Negro Suffrage and Social Equality* (New York?: S.n., 1866?), esp. 3–4; L. Seaman, *What Miscegenation Is! What We Are*

to Expect Now that Mr. Lincoln is Re-elected (New York: Waller and Willets, ca. 1865).

38. David H. Fowler, *Northern Attitudes Towards Interracial Marriage: Legislation and Public Opinion in the Middle Atlantic and the States of the Old Northwest, 1790–1930* (New York and London: Garland, 1987), 222–33; Peter W. Bardaglio, *Reconstructing the Household: Families, Sex, and the Law in the Nineteenth-Century South* (Chapel Hill: University of North Carolina Press, 1995), 179; Martha Hodes, *White Women, Black Men: Illicit Sex in the 19th-Century South* (New Haven and London: Yale University Press, 1997), 147; Newman, *White Women's Rights*, 29–37.

39. John Van Evrie, *The Six Species of Men, With Cuts Representing the Types of The Caucasian, Mongol, Malay, Indian, Esquimaux, and Negro* (New York: Van Evrie, Horton and Company, 1866), 12; John David Smith, ed., *Anti-Abolition Tracts and Anti-Black Stereotypes: General Statements of the "Negro Problem,"* Part One (New York: Garland, 1993), xxv–xxvii; 125–55; Josiah C. Nott, *Instincts of Races* (New Orleans: L. Graham, 1866), reprinted in *Defending Slavery: Proslavery Thought in the Old South; A Brief History with Documents*, ed. Paul Finkelman (Boston: Bedford/St. Martin's, 2003), 201–11, esp. 203, 205.

40. Stanton, "A Pronunciamento," *Revolution*, July 15, 1869, 24; Stanton, "Anniversary of the American Equal Rights Association. Address of Elizabeth Cady Stanton," *Revolution*, May 13, 1869, 289–92, esp. 291.

41. Henry McNeal Turner, "On the Eligibility of Colored Members to Seats in the Georgia Legislature" [September 3, 1868], in *Respect Black: The Writings and Speeches of Henry McNeal Turner*, ed. Edwin S. Redkey (New York: Arno Press, 1971), 14–28, esp. 16; Rev. H. M. Turner, *The Negro in All Ages: A Lecture Delivered in the Second Baptist Church of Savannah, GA., . . . April 8th, 1873* (Savannah: D. G. Patton, 1873), frontispiece, 21; Bay, *White Image in the Black Mind*, 81–82.

42. Martin R. Delany, *Principia of Ethnology: The Origin of Races and Color, with an Archaeological Compendium of Ethiopian and Egyptian Civilization, From Years of Careful Examination and Enquiry* (Philadelphia: Harper and Brother, 1879), 9, 94.

43. Rosalyn Terborg-Penn, *African American Women in the Struggle for the Vote, 1850–1920* (Bloomington: Indiana University Press, 1998), 26, 37; [Editorial Note], "Eleventh National Woman's Rights Convention," in *Selected Papers of Elizabeth Cady Stanton and Susan B. Anthony*, 1:583; *History of Woman Suffrage*, 2:378–98, esp. 391–92; Frances Ellen Watkins Harper, "The Great Problem to be Solved" [April 14, 1875], reprinted in *A Brighter Coming Day: A Frances Ellen Watkins Harper Reader*, ed. Frances Foster Smith (New York: Feminist Press, 1990), 219–22, esp. 220.

44. Rosalyn Terborg-Penn points out that Robert Purvis was "one of the few outspoken Black men to criticize the Fifteenth Amendment for failing to include women." See Terborg-Penn, *African American Women in the Struggle for the Vote*, 34. Indeed, Elizabeth Cady Stanton praised Robert Purvis's "true Roman grandeur" in being vocal about his commitment to woman suffrage during the 1869

National Woman's Suffrage Convention. See "Editorial Correspondence by ECS," *Selected Papers of Elizabeth Cady Stanton and Susan B. Anthony,* 2:204–11, esp. 205.

45. Stanton, "Speech at Lawrence, Kansas, 1867," in *Elizabeth Cady Stanton–Susan B. Anthony Reader,* 113–18, esp. 114; "The Night Side of Darwinism," *Revolution,* April 29, 1869, 261.

46. Newman, *White Women's Rights,* 22.

47. Charles Darwin, *The Descent of Man and Selection in Relation to Sex* (Chicago: Rand, McNally, 1874), 551–79, esp. 558–613, 599; Herbert Spencer, "Psychology of the Sexes," *Popular Science Monthly* 4 (November 1873): 30–38, esp. 35, 32.

48. Edward H. Clarke, M.D., *Sex in Education; or, A Fair Chance for the Girls* (Boston: James R. Osgood, 1873), 14–15, 19, 21–22, 28; Edward H. Clarke, M.D., *The Building of a Brain* (Boston: James R. Osgood, 1874), 13–65, esp. 14–15, 20, 27–29, 64. For incisive commentary on the implications and impact of Clarke's work, consult the following: Rosalind Rosenberg, *Beyond Separate Spheres: Intellectual Roots of Modern Feminism* (New Haven, Conn.: Yale University Press, 1982), 1–27; Russett, *Sexual Science,* 99, 116–20; Newman, *White Women's Rights,* 86–106, 155.

49. Antoinette Brown Blackwell, *The Sexes Throughout Nature* (New York: G. P. Putnam's Sons, 1875), 11–23, esp. 13–14; Julia Ward Howe, "Introduction," in *Sex and Education: A Reply to Dr. E. H. Clarke's "Sex in Education,"* ed. Howe (Boston: Roberts Brothers, 1874), 5–11, esp. 6.

50. "ECS to Alonzo J. Grover" [August 24, 1874], in *The Selected Papers of Elizabeth Cady Stanton and Susan B. Anthony,* vol. 3: *National Protection for National Citizens, 1873 to 1880,* ed. Ann D. Gordon (New Brunswick, N.J.: Rutgers University Press, 2003), 102–10, esp. 103, 107 n. 2; Stanton, "Nothing New" [May 8, 1875], in *Selected Papers of Elizabeth Cady Stanton and Susan B. Anthony,* 3:174–78, esp. 175.

51. Newman, *White Women's Rights,* 39, 155.

52. Kathi Kern, *Mrs. Stanton's Bible* (Ithaca, N.Y., and London: Cornell University Press), 68–69.

53. Elizabeth Munson and Greg Dickinson, "Hearing Women Speak: Antoinette Brown Blackwell and the Dilemma of Authority," *Journal of Women's History* 10:1 (Spring 1998): 108–26.

54. Elizabeth Cady Stanton, *The Woman's Bible* (Boston: Northeastern University Press, 1993), 23–26, 214.

55. Kern, *Mrs. Stanton's Bible,* 251 n. 63, 109.

56. Newman, *White Women's Rights,* 8–14, 22–55; Kern, *Mrs. Stanton's Bible,* 106–16. For earlier, more general discussions along these lines, see Barbara Hilkert Andolsen, *"Daughters of Jefferson, Daughters of Bootblacks": Racism and American Feminism* (Macon, Ga.: Mercer University Press, 1986), 21–44, and Angela Y. Davis, *Women, Race, and Class* (New York: Random House, ca. 1981), 110–26.

57. Newman, *White Women's Rights,* 22–23, 181–82, 188 n. 22; Philip N. Cohen, "Nationalism and Suffrage: Gender Struggle in Nation-Building America," *Signs: Journal of Women in Culture and Society* 21 (1996): 707–27.

Part II

A Selection of Speeches, Articles, and Essays by Elizabeth Cady Stanton, 1854–1901

Chapter 1

"Address to the Legislature of New York, Albany, February 14, 1854"

EDITORS' NOTE: Stanton had helped launch the women's rights movement in the United States by organizing the 1848 Seneca Falls Convention, shortly after the New York legislature began reforming laws that had limited married women's property rights. With a growing brood of children to raise and a household to manage, Stanton could seldom leave her home to attend the continuing conventions that provided the main venues for the development of the movement. Domestic confinement, however, allowed her to read in depth and develop the arguments that made her the intellectual leader of the movement. This speech before the New York state legislature in 1854 was her first major pronouncement on women's wrongs and rights before the law. Her characteristic wit, humor, and flashes of eloquent rage are in fine display here. The rhetoric of this particular speech combines considerable legal erudition and deftly mobilized sentimental pleas on behalf of abandoned mothers, drunkards' widows, and outraged wives.

> "The thinking minds of all nations call for change. There is a deep-lying struggle in the whole fabric of society; a boundless, grinding collision of the New with the Old."

The tyrant, Custom, has been summoned before the bar of Common-Sense. His majesty no longer awes the multitude—his sceptre is broken—his crown is trampled in the dust—the sentence of death is pronounced upon him. All nations, ranks, and classes have, in turn, questioned and repudiated his authority; and now, that the monster is chained and caged, timid woman, on tiptoe, comes to look him in the face, and to demand of her brave sires and sons, who have struck stout blows for liberty, if, in this change of dynasty, she, too, shall find relief. Yes, gentlemen, in republican America, in the nineteenth century, we, the daughters of the revolutionary heroes of '76, demand at your hands the redress of our grievances—a revision of your State Constitution—a new code of laws. Permit us then, as briefly as possible, to call your attention to the legal disabilities under which we labor.

1st. Look at the position of woman as woman. It is not enough for us that by your laws we are permitted to live and breathe, to claim the necessaries of life from our legal protectors—to pay the penalty of our crimes; we demand the full recognition of all our rights as citizens of the Empire State. We are persons; native, free-born citizens; property-holders, taxpayers; yet are we denied the exercise of our right to the elective franchise. We support ourselves, and, in part, your schools, colleges, churches, your poor-houses, jails, prisons, the army, the navy, the whole machinery of government, and yet we have no voice in your councils. We have every qualification required by the Constitution, necessary to the legal voter, but the one of sex. We are moral, virtuous, and intelligent, and in all respects quite equal to the proud white man himself, and yet by your laws we are classed with idiots, lunatics, and negroes; and though we do not feel honored by the place assigned us, yet, in fact, our legal position is lower than that of either; for the negro can be raised to the dignity of a voter if he possess himself of $250; the lunatic can vote in his moments of sanity, and the idiot, too, if he be a male one, and not more than nine-tenths a fool; but we, who have guided great movements of charity, established missions, edited journals, published works on history, economy, and statistics; who have governed nations, led armies, filled the professor's chair, taught philosophy and mathematics to the savants of our age, discovered planets, piloted ships across the sea, are denied the most sacred rights of citizens, because, forsooth, we came not into this republic crowned with the dignity of manhood! Woman is theoretically absolved from all allegiance to the laws of the State. Sec. 1, Bill of Rights, 2 R. S., 301, says that no authority can, on any pretence whatever, be exercised over the citizens of this State but such as is or shall be derived from, and granted by the people of this State.

Now, gentlemen, we would fain know by what authority you have disfranchised one-half the people of this State? You who have so boldly taken possession of the bulwarks of this republic, show us your credentials, and thus prove your exclusive right to govern, not only yourselves, but us. Judge Hurlburt, who has long occupied a high place at the bar in this State, and who recently retired with honor from the bench of the Supreme Court, in his profound work on Human Rights, has pronounced your present position rank usurpation. Can it be that here, where we acknowledge no royal blood, no apostolic descent, that you, who have declared that all men were created equal—that governments derive their just powers from the consent of the governed, would willingly build up an aristocracy that places the ignorant and vulgar above the educated and refined—the alien and the ditch-digger above the authors and poets of the day—an aristocracy that would raise the sons above the mothers that bore them? Would that the men who can sanction a Constitution so opposed to the genius of this government, who can enact and execute laws so degrading to womankind, had sprung, Minerva-like, from the brains of their fathers, that the matrons of this republic need not blush to own their sons!

Woman's position, under our free institutions, is much lower than under the monarchy of England. "In England the idea of woman holding official station is not so strange as in the United States. The Countess of Pembroke, Dorset, and Montgomery held the office of hereditary sheriff of Westmoreland, and exercised it in person. At the assizes at Appleby, she sat with the judges on the bench. In a reported case, it is stated by counsel, and substantially assented to by the court, that a woman is capable of serving in almost all the offices of the kingdom, such as those of queen, marshal, great chamberlain and constable of England, the champion of England, commissioner of sewers, governor of work-house, sexton, keeper of the prison, of the gate-house of the dean and chapter of Westminster, returning officer for members of Parliament, and constable, the latter of which is in some respects judicial. The office of jailor is frequently exercised by a woman.

"In the United States a woman may administer on the effects of her deceased husband, and she has occasionally held a subordinate place in the post-office department. She has therefore a sort of post mortem, postmistress notoriety; but with the exception of handling letters of administration and letters mailed, she is the submissive creature of the old common law." True, the unmarried woman has a right to the property she inherits and the money she earns, but she is taxed without representation, And here again you place the negro, so unjustly degraded by you, in a superior position to your own wives and mothers; for colored males, if possessed of a certain amount of property and certain other qualifications, can vote, but if they do not have these qualifications they are not subject to direct taxation; wherein they have the advantage of woman, she being subject to taxation for whatever amount she may possess. (Constitution of New York, Article 2, Sec. 2.) But, say you, are not all women sufficiently represented by their fathers, husbands and brothers? Let your statute books answer the question.

Again we demand in criminal cases that most sacred of all rights, trial by a jury of our own peers. The establishment of trial by jury is of so early a date that its beginning is lost in antiquity, but the right of trial by a jury of one's own peers is a great progressive step of advanced civilization. No rank of men have ever been satisfied with being tried by jurors higher or lower in the civil or political scale than themselves; for jealousy on the one hand, and contempt on the other, has ever effectually blinded the eyes of justice. Hence, all along the pages of history, we find the king, the noble, the peasant, the cardinal, the priest, the layman, each in turn protesting against the authority of the tribunal before which they were summoned to appear. Charles the First refused to recognize the competency of the tribunal which condemned him: For how, said he, can subjects judge a king? The stern descendants of our Pilgrim Fathers refused to answer for their crimes before an English Parliament. For how, said they, can a king judge rebels? And shall woman here consent to be tried by her liege lord, who has dubbed himself law-maker, judge, juror, and sheriff too?—whose power, though sanctioned by Church and State, has no foundation in justice and equity, and is a bold assumption of our inalienable rights. In England a Parliament-lord could challenge a jury where a knight was not empanneled; an alien could demand a jury composed half of his own countrymen; or, in some special cases, juries were even constituted entirely of women. Having seen that man fails to do justice to woman in her best estate, to the virtuous, the noble, the true of our sex, should we trust to his tender mercies the weak, the ignorant, the morally insane? It is not to be denied that the interests of man and woman in the present undeveloped state of the race, and under the existing social arrangements, are and must be antagonistic. The nobleman cannot make just laws for the peasant; the slaveholder for the slave; neither can man make and execute just laws for woman, because in each case, the one in power fails to apply the immutable principles of right to any grade but his own.

Shall an erring woman be dragged before a bar of grim-visaged judges, lawyers, and jurors, there to be grossly questioned in public on subjects which women scarce breathe in secret to one another? Shall the most sacred relations of life be called up and rudely scanned by men who, by their own admission, are so coarse that women could not meet them even at the polls without contamination? and yet shall she find there no woman's face or voice to pity and defend? Shall the frenzied mother, who, to save herself and child from exposure and disgrace, ended the life that had but just begun, be dragged before such a tribunal to answer for her crime? How can man enter into the feelings of that mother? How can he judge of the agonies of soul that impelled her to such an outrage of maternal instincts? How can he weigh the mountain of sorrow that crushed that mother's heart when she wildly tossed her helpless babe into the cold waters of the midnight sea? Where is he who by false vows thus blasted this trusting woman? Had that helpless child no claims on his protection? Ah, he is freely abroad in the dignity of manhood, in the pulpit, on the bench, in the professor's chair. The imprisonment of his victim and the death of his child detract not a tithe from his standing and complacency. His peers made the law, and shall law-makers lay nets for those of their own rank? Shall laws which come from the logical brain of man take cognizance of violence done to the moral and affectional nature which predominates, as is said, in woman?

Statesmen of New York, whose daughters, guarded by your affection, and lapped amidst luxuries which your indulgence spreads, care more for their nodding plumes and velvet trains than for the statute laws by which their persons and properties are held—who, blinded by custom and prejudice to the degraded position which they and their sisters occupy in the civil scale, haughtily claim that they already have all the rights they want, how, think ye, you would feel to see a daughter summoned for such a crime—and remember these daughters are but human—before such a tribunal? Would it not, in that hour, be some consolation to see that she was surrounded by the wise and virtuous of her own sex; by those who had known the depth of a mother's love and the misery of a lover's falsehood; to know that to these she could make her confession, and from them receive her sentence? If so, then listen to our just demands and make such a change in your laws as will secure to every woman tried in your courts, an impartial jury. At this moment among the hundreds of women who are shut up in prisons in this State, not one has enjoyed that most sacred of all rights—that right which you would die to defend for yourselves—trial by a jury of one's peers.

2d. Look at the position of woman as wife. Your laws relating to marriage—founded as they are on the old common law of England, a compound of barbarous usages, but partially modified by progressive civilization—are in open violation of our enlightened ideas of justice, and of the holiest feelings of our nature. If you take the highest view of marriage, as a Divine relation, which love alone can constitute and sanctify, then of course human legislation can only recognize it. Men can neither bind nor loose its ties, for that prerogative belongs to God alone, who makes man and woman, and the laws of attraction by which they are united. But if you regard marriage as a civil contract, then let it be subject to the same laws which control all other contracts. Do not make it a kind of half-human, half-divine institution, which you may build up, but cannot regulate. Do not, by your special legislation for this one kind of contract, involve yourselves in the grossest absurdities and contradictions.

So long as by your laws no man can make a contract for a horse or piece of land until he is twenty-one years of age, and by which contract he is not bound if any deception has been practiced, or if the party contracting has not fulfilled his part of the agreement—so long as the parties in all mere civil contracts retain their identity and all the power and independence they had before contracting, with the full right to dissolve all partnerships and contracts for any reason, at the will and option of the parties themselves, upon what principle of civil jurisprudence do you permit the boy of fourteen and the girl of twelve, in violation of every natural law, to make a contract more momentous in importance than any other, and then hold them to it, come what may, the whole of their natural lives, in spite of disappointment, deception, and misery? Then, too, the signing of this contract is instant civil death to one of the parties. The woman who but yesterday was sued on bended knee, who stood so high in the scale of being as to make an agreement on equal terms with a proud Saxon man, to-day has no civil existence, no social freedom. The wife who inherits no property holds about the same legal position that does the slave on the Southern plantation. She can own nothing, sell nothing. She has no right even to the wages she earns; her person, her time, her services are the property of another. She cannot testify, in many cases, against her husband. She can get no redress for wrongs in her own name in any court of justice. She can neither sue nor be sued. She is not held morally responsible for any crime committed in the presence of her husband, so completely is her very existence supposed by the law to be merged in that of another. Think of it, your wives may be thieves, libelers, burglars, incendiaries, and for crimes like these they are not held amenable to the laws of the land, if they but commit them in your dread presence. For them, alas!

there is no higher law than the will of man. Herein behold the bloated conceit of these Petruchios of the law, who seem to say:

> "Nay, look not big, nor stamp, nor stare, nor fret,
> I will be master of what is mine own;
> She is my goods, my chattels; she is my house,
> My household stuff, my field, my barn,
> My horse, my ox, my ass, my anything;
> And here she stands, touch her whoever dare;
> I'll bring my action on the proudest he,
> That stops my way, in Padua."

How could man ever look thus on woman? She, at whose feet Socrates learned wisdom—she, who gave to the world a Saviour, and witnessed alike the adoration of the Magi and the agonies of the cross. How could such a being, so blessed and honored, ever become the ignoble, servile, cringing slave, with whom the fear of man could be paramount to the sacred dictates of conscience and the holy love of Heaven? By the common law of England, the spirit of which has been but too faithfully incorporated into our statute law, a husband has a right to whip his wife with a rod not larger than his thumb, to shut her up in a room, and administer whatever moderate chastisement he may deem necessary to insure obedience to his wishes, and for her healthful moral development! He can forbid all persons harboring or trusting her on his account. He can deprive her of all social intercourse with her nearest and dearest friends. If by great economy she accumulates a small sum, which for future need she deposit, little by little, in a savings bank, the husband has a right to draw it out, at his option, to use it as be may see fit.

"Husband is entitled to wife's credit or business talents (whenever their intermarriage may have occurred); and goods purchased by her on her own credit, with his consent, while cohabiting with him, can be seized and sold in execution against him for his own debts, and this, though she carry on business in her own name."—*7 Howard's Practice Reports,* 105, *Lovett agt. Robinson and Whitbeck, sheriff, etc.*

"No letters of administration shall be granted to a person convicted of infamous crime; nor to anyone incapable by law of making a contract; nor to a person not a citizen of the United States, unless such person reside within this State; nor to anyone who is under twenty-one years of age; nor to any person who shall be adjudged incompetent by the surrogate to execute duties of such trust, by reason of drunkenness, improvidence, or want of understanding, nor to any married woman; but where a married woman is entitled to administration, the same may be granted to her husband in her right and behalf."

There is nothing that an unruly wife might do against which the husband has not sufficient protection in the law. But not so with the wife. If she have a worthless husband, a confirmed drunkard, a villain, or a vagrant, he has still all the rights of a man, a husband, and a father. Though the whole support of the family be thrown upon the wife, if the wages she earns be paid to her by her employer, the husband can receive them again. If, by unwearied industry and perseverance, she can earn for herself and children a patch of ground and a shed to cover them, the husband can strip her of all her hard earnings, turn her and her little ones out in the cold northern blast, take the clothes from their backs, the bread from their mouths; all this by your laws may he do, and has he done, oft and again, to satisfy the rapacity of that monster in human form, the rum-seller.

But the wife who is so fortunate as to have inherited property, has, by the new law in this State, been redeemed from her lost condition. She is no longer a legal nonentity. This property law, if fairly construed, will overturn the whole code relating to woman and property. The right to property implies the right to buy and sell, to will and bequeath, and herein is the dawning of a civil existence for woman, for now the "femme covert" must have the right to make contracts. So, get ready, gentlemen; the "little justice" will be coming to you one day, deed in hand, for your acknowledgment. When he asks you "if you sign without fear or compulsion," say yes, boldly, as we do. Then, too, the right to will is ours. Now what becomes of the "tenant for life"? Shall he, the happy husband of a millionaire, who has lived in yonder princely mansion in the midst of plenty and elegance, be cut down in a day to the use of one-third of this estate and a few hundred a year, as long as he remains her widower? And should he, in spite of this bounty on celibacy, impelled by his affections, marry again, choosing for a wife a woman as poor as himself, shall he be thrown penniless on the cold world—this child of fortune, enervated by ease and luxury, henceforth to be dependent wholly on his own resources? Poor man! He would be rich, though, in the sympathies of many women who have passed through just such an ordeal. But what is property without the right to protect that property by law? It is mockery to say a certain estate is mine, if, without my consent, you have the right to tax me when and how you please, while I have no voice in making the tax-gatherer, the legislator, or the law. The right to property will, of necessity, compel us in due time to the exercise of our right to the elective franchise, and then naturally follows the right to hold office.

3d. Look at the position of woman as widow. Whenever we attempt to point out the wrongs of the wife, those who would have us believe that the laws cannot be improved, point us to the privileges, powers, and claims of the widow. Let us look into these a little. Behold in yonder humble house a married pair, who, for long years, have lived together, childless and alone. Those few acres of well-tilled land, with the small, white house that looks so cheerful through its vines and flowers, attest the honest thrift and simple taste of its owners. This man and woman, by their hard days' labor, have made this home their own. Here they live in peace and plenty, happy in the hope that they may dwell together securely under their own vine and fig-tree for the few years that remain to them, and that under the shadow of these trees, planted by their own hands, and in the midst of their household gods, so loved and familiar, they may take their last farewell of earth. But, alas for human hopes! the husband dies, and without a will, and the stricken widow, at one fell blow, loses the companion of her youth, her house and home, and half the little sum she had in bank. For the law, which takes no cognizance of widows left with twelve children and not one cent, instantly spies out this widow, takes account of her effects, and announces to her the startling intelligence that but one-third of the house and lot, and one-half the personal property, are hers. The law has other favorites with whom she must share the hard-earned savings of years. In this dark hour of grief, the coarse minions of the law gather round the widow's hearth-stone, and, in the name of justice, outrage all natural sense of right, mock at the sacredness of human love, and with cold familiarity proceed to place a moneyed value on the old arm-chair, in which, but a few brief hours since, she closed the eyes that had ever beamed on her with kindness and affection; on the solemn clock in the corner, that told the hour he passed away; on every garment with which his form and presence were associated, and on every article of comfort and convenience that the house contained, even down to the knives and forks and spoons—and the widow saw it all—and when the work was done, she gathered up what the law allowed her and went forth to seek another home! This is the much-talked-of widow's dower. Behold the magnanimity of the law in allowing the widow to retain a life interest in one-third the landed estate, and one-half the personal property of her husband, and taking the lion's share to itself! Had she died first, the house and land would all have been the husband's still. No one would have dared to intrude upon the privacy of his home, or to molest him in his sacred retreat of sorrow. How, I ask you, can that be called justice, which makes such a distinction as this between man and woman?

By management, economy, and industry, our widow is able, in a few years, to redeem her house and home. But the law never loses sight of the purse, no matter how low in the scale of being its owner may he. It sends its officers round every year to gather in the harvest for the public crib, and no widow who owns a piece of land two feet square ever escapes this reckoning. Our widow, too, who has now twice earned her home, has her annual tax to pay also—a tribute of gratitude that she is permitted to breathe the free air of this republic, where "taxation without representation" by such worthies as John Hancock and Samuel Adams, has been declared "intolerable tyranny." Having glanced at the magnanimity of the law in its dealings with the widow, let us see how the individual man, under the influence of such laws, doles out justice to his helpmate. The husband has the absolute right to will away his property as he may see fit. If he has children, he can divide his property among them, leaving his wife her third only of the landed estate, thus making her a dependent on the bounty of her own children. A man with thirty thousand dollars in personal property, may leave his wife but a few hundred a year, as long as she remains his widow.

The cases are without number where women, who have lived in ease and elegance, at the death of their husbands have, by will, been reduced to the bare necessaries of life. The man who leaves his wife the sole guardian of his property and children is an exception to the general rule. Man has ever manifested a wish that the world should indeed be a blank to the companion whom he leaves behind him. The Hindoo makes that wish a law and burns the widow on the funeral pyre of her husband, but the civilized man, impressed with a different view of the sacredness of life, takes a less summary mode of drawing his beloved partner after him; he does it by the deprivation and starvation of the flesh, and the humiliation and mortification of the spirit. In bequeathing to the wife just enough to keep soul and body together, man seems to lose sight of the fact that woman, like himself, takes great pleasure in acts of benevolence and charity. It is but just, therefore, that she should have it in her power to give during her life and to will away at her death, as her benevolence or obligations might prompt her to do.

4th. Look at the position of woman as mother. There is no human love so strong and steadfast as that of the mother for her child; yet behold how ruthless are your laws touching this most sacred relation. Nature has clearly made the mother the guardian of the child, but man, in his inordinate love of power, does continually set nature and nature's laws at open defiance. The father may apprentice his child, bind him out to a trade, without the mother's consent—yea, in direct opposition to her most earnest entreaties, prayers and tears. He may apprentice his son to a gamester or rum-seller and thus cancel his debts of honor. By the abuse of this absolute power, he may bind his daughter to the owner of a brothel and, by the degradation of his child, supply his daily wants; and such things, gentlemen, have been done in our very midst. Moreover, the father, about to die, may bind out all his children wherever and to whomsoever he may see fit and, thus, in fact, will away the guardianship of all his children from the mother. The Revised Statutes of New York provide that "every father, whether of full age or a minor, of a child to be born, or of any living child under the age of twenty-one years, and unmarried, may by his deed or last will, duly executed, dispose of the custody and tuition of such child during its minority, or for any less time, to any person or persons, in possession or remainder." 2 R. 8., page 150, sec. 1. Thus, by your laws, the child is the absolute property of the father, wholly at his disposal in life or at death.

In case of separation, the law gives the children to the father, no matter what his character or condition. At this very time we can point you to noble, virtuous, well-educated mothers in this State, who have abandoned their husbands for their profligacy and confirmed drunkenness. All these have been robbed of their children, who are in the custody of the husband, under the care of his relatives, whilst the mothers are permitted to see them but at stated intervals. But, said one of these mothers, with a grandeur of attitude and manner worthy the noble Roman matron in the palmiest days of that republic, I would rather never see my child again, than be the medium to hand down the low animal nature of its father, to stamp degradation on the brow of another innocent being. It is enough that one child of his shall call me mother.

If you are far-sighted statesmen and do wisely judge of the interests of this commonwealth, you will so shape your future laws as to encourage woman to take the high moral ground that the father of her children must be great and good. Instead of your present laws, which make the mother and her children the victims of vice and license, you might rather pass laws prohibiting to all drunkards, libertines, and fools, the rights of husbands and fathers. Do not the hundreds of laughing idiots that are crowding into our asylums, appeal to the wisdom of our statesmen for some new laws on marriage—to the mothers of this day for a higher, purer morality?

Again, as the condition of the child always follows that of the mother, and as by the sanction of your laws the father may beat the mother, so may he the child. What mother cannot bear me witness to untold sufferings which cruel, vindictive fathers have visited upon their helpless children? Who ever saw a human being that would not abuse unlimited power? Base and ignoble must that man be who, let the provocation be what it may, would strike a woman, but he who would lacerate a trembling child is unworthy the name of man. A mother's love can be no protection to a child; she cannot appeal to you to save it from a father's cruelty, for the laws take no cognizance of the mother's most grievous wrongs. Neither at home nor abroad can a mother protect her son. Look at the temptations that surround the paths of our youth at every step; look at the gambling and drinking saloons, the club rooms, the dens of infamy and abomination that infest all our villages and cities—slowly but surely sapping the very foundations of all virtue and strength.

By your laws, all these abominable resorts are permitted. It is folly to talk of a mother moulding the character of her son, when all mankind, backed up by law and public sentiment, conspire to destroy her influence. But when woman's moral power shall speak through the ballot-box, then shall her influence be seen and felt; then, in our legislative debates, such questions as the canal tolls on salt, the improvement of rivers and harbors, and the claims of Mr. Smith for damages against the State, would be secondary to the consideration of the legal existence of all these public resorts, which lure our youth on to excessive indulgence and destruction.

Many times and oft, it has been asked us, with unaffected seriousness, "What do you women want? What are you aiming at?" Many have manifested a laudable curiosity to know what the wives and daughters could complain of in republican America, where their sires and sons have so bravely fought for freedom and gloriously secured their independence, trampling all tyranny, bigotry, and caste in the dust, and declaring to a waiting world the divine truth that all men are created equal. What can woman want under such a government? Admit a radical difference in sex, and you demand different spheres—water for fish, and air for birds.

It is impossible to make the Southern planter believe that his slave feels and reasons just as he does—that injustice and subjection are as galling as to him—that the degradation of living by the will of another, the mere dependent on his caprice, at the mercy of his passions, is as keenly felt by him as his master. If you can force on his unwilling vision a vivid picture of the negro's wrongs and for a moment touch his soul, his logic brings him instant consolation. He says, the slave does not feel this as I would. Here, gentlemen, is our difficulty: When we plead our cause before the law-makers and savants of the republic, they cannot take in the idea that men and women are alike; and so long as the mass rest in this delusion, the public mind will not be so much startled by the revelations made of the injustice and degradation of woman's position as by the fact that she should at length wake up to a sense of it.

If you, too, are thus deluded, what avails it that we show by your statute books that your laws are unjust—that woman is the victim of avarice and power? What avails it that we point out the wrongs of woman in social life, the victim of passion and lust? You scorn the thought that she has any natural love of freedom burning in her breast, any clear perception of justice urging her on to demand her rights.

Would to God you could know the burning indignation that fills woman's soul when she turns over the pages of your statute books, and sees there how like feudal barons you freemen hold your women. Would that you could know the humiliation she feels for sex, when she thinks of all the beardless boys in your law offices, learning these ideas of one-sided justice—taking their first lessons in contempt for all womankind—being indoctrinated into the incapacities of their mothers, and the lordly, absolute rights of man over all women, children, and property, and to know that these are to be our future presidents, judges, husbands, and fathers; in sorrow we exclaim, alas! for that nation whose sons bow not in loyalty to woman. The mother is the first object of the child's veneration and love, and they who root out this holy sentiment, dream not of the blighting effect it has on the boy and the man. The impression left on law students, fresh from your statute books, is most unfavorable to woman's influence; hence you see but few lawyers chivalrous and high-toned in their sentiments toward woman. They cannot escape the legal view which, by constant reading, has become familiarized to their minds: "*femme covert*," "dower," "widow's claims," "protection," "incapacities," "incumbrance," is written on the brow of every woman they meet.

But if, gentlemen, you take the ground that the sexes are alike, and, therefore, you are our faithful representatives—then why all these special laws for woman? Would not one code answer for all of like needs and wants? Christ's golden rule is better than all the special legislation that the ingenuity of man can devise: "Do unto others as you would have others do unto you." This, men and brethren, is all we ask at your hands. We ask no better laws than those you have made for yourselves. We need no other protection than that which your present laws secure to you.

In conclusion, then, let us say, in behalf of the women of this State, we ask for all that you have asked for yourselves in the progress of your development, since the *Mayflower* cast anchor beside Plymouth rock; and simply on the ground that the rights of every human being are the same and identical. You may say that the mass of the women of this State do not make the demand; it comes from a few sour, disappointed old maids and childless women.

You are mistaken; the mass speak through us. A very large majority of the women of this State support themselves and their children, and many their husbands too. Go into any village you please, of three or four thousand inhabitants, and you will find as many as fifty men or more, whose only business is to discuss religion and politics, as they watch the trains come and go at the depot, or the passage of a canal boat through a lock; to laugh at the vagaries of some drunken brother, or the capers of a monkey dancing to the music of his master's organ. All these are supported by their mothers, wives, or sisters.

Now, do you candidly think these wives do not wish to control the wages they earn—to own the land they buy—the houses they build? to have at their disposal their own children, without being subject to the constant interference and tyranny of an idle, worthless profligate? Do you suppose that any woman is such a pattern of devotion and submission that she willingly stitches all day for the small sum of fifty cents, that she may enjoy the unspeakable privilege, in obedience to your laws, of paying for her husband's tobacco and rum? Think you the wife of the confirmed, beastly drunkard would consent to share with him her home and bed, if law and public sentiment would release her from such gross companionship? Verily, no! Think you the wife with whom endurance has ceased to be a virtue, who, through much suffering, has lost all faith in the justice of both heaven and earth, takes the law in her own hand, severs the unholy bond, and turns her back forever upon him whom she once called husband, consents to the law that in such an hour tears her child from her—all that she has left on earth to love and cherish? The drunkards' wives speak through us, and they number 50,000. Think you that the woman who has worked hard all her days in helping her husband to accumulate a large property, consents to the law that places this wholly at his disposal?

Would not the mother whose only child is bound out for a term of years against her expressed wish, deprive the father of this absolute power if she could?

For all these, then, we speak. If to this long list you add the laboring women who are loudly demanding remuneration for their unending toil; those women who teach in our seminaries, academies, and public schools for a miserable pittance; the widows who are taxed without mercy; the unfortunate ones in our work-houses, poor-houses, and prisons; who are they that we do not now represent? But a small class of the fashionable butterflies, who, through the short summer day, seek the sunshine and the flowers; but the cool breezes of autumn and the hoary frosts of winter will soon chase all these away; then they, too, will need and seek protection, and through other lips demand in their turn justice and equity at your hands.

SOURCE: Elizabeth Stanton, "Address to the Legislature of New York, Albany, February 14, 1854," in *History of Woman Suffrage,* edited by Elizabeth Cady Stanton, Susan B. Anthony, and Matilda Joslyn Gage (Rochester, N.Y.: Susan B. Anthony, 1889), vol. 1, 595–605.

"Address to the Legislature on Women's Right of Suffrage, Albany, February 18, 1860"

EDITORS' NOTE: *Stanton again appeared before the state legislature in February 1860 to deliver one of her most powerful arguments for women's emancipation. Susan B. Anthony was coordinating a new campaign to follow up on the modest reforms of 1848 and secure a broader package of economic and property rights for married women in New York. The state assembly had passed a second Married Women's Property Act, and the day after Stanton spoke, so did the state senate. Anticipating victory, Stanton's remarks look past the granting of equal property rights to the broader challenge of securing equal political rights for women. As she spoke, the political crisis over slavery was deepening, and Stanton's words are laced through with references and comparisons to the status of chattel slaves.*

There are certain natural rights as inalienable to civilization as are the rights of air and motion to the savage in the wilderness. The natural rights of the civilized man and woman are government, property, the harmonious development of all their powers, and the gratification of their desires. There are a few people we now and then meet who, like Jeremy Bentham, scout the idea of natural rights in civilization and pronounce them mere metaphors, declaring that there are no rights aside from those the law confers. If the law made man too, that might do, for then he could be made to order to fit the particular niche he was designed to fill. But inasmuch as God made man in His own image, with capacities and powers as boundless as the universe, whose exigencies no mere human law can meet, it is evident that the man must ever stand first; the law but the creature of his wants; the law-giver but the mouthpiece of humanity. If, then, the nature of a being decides its rights, every individual comes into this world with rights that are not transferable. He does not bring them like a pack on his back, that may be stolen from him, but they are a component part of himself, the laws which insure his growth and development. The individual may be put in the stocks, body and soul, he may be dwarfed, crippled, killed, but his rights no man can get; they live and die with him.

Though the atmosphere is forty miles deep all round the globe, no man can do more than fill his own lungs. No man can see, hear, or smell but just so far, and though hundreds are deprived of these senses, his are not the more acute. Though rights have been abundantly supplied by the good Father, no man can appropriate to himself those that belong to another. A citizen can have but one vote, fill but one office, though thousands are not permitted to do either. These axioms prove that woman's poverty does not add to man's wealth, and if, in the plenitude of his power, he should secure to her the exercise of all her God-given rights, her wealth could not bring poverty to him. There is a kind of nervous unrest always manifested by those in power, whenever new claims are started by those out of their own immediate class. The philosophy of this is very plain. They imagine that if the rights of this new class be granted, they must, of necessity, sacrifice something of what they already possess. They cannot divest themselves of the idea that rights are very much like lands, stocks, bonds, and mortgages, and that if every new claimant be satisfied, the supply of human rights must in time run low. You might as well carp at the birth of every child, lest there should not be enough air left to inflate your lungs; at the success of every scholar, for fear that your draughts at the fountain of knowledge could not be so long and deep; at the glory of every hero, lest there be no glory left for you. . . .

If the object of government is to protect the weak against the strong, how unwise to place the power wholly in the hands of the strong. Yet that is the history of all governments, even the model republic of these United States. You who have read the history of nations, from Moses down to our last election, where have you ever seen one class looking after the interests of another? Any of you can readily see the defects in other governments and pronounce sentence against those who have sacrificed the masses to themselves, but when we come to our own case, we are blinded by custom and self-interest. Some of you who have no capital can see the injustice which the laborer suffers; some of you who have no slaves, can see the cruelty of his oppression; but who of you appreciate the galling humiliation, the refinements of degradation, to which women (the mothers, wives, sisters, and daughters of freemen) are subject, in this the last half of the nineteenth century? How many of you have ever read even the laws concerning them that now disgrace your statute-books? In cruelty and tyranny, they are not surpassed by any slaveholding code in the Southern States; in fact they are worse, by just so far as woman, from her social position, refinement, and education, is on a more equal ground with the oppressor.

Allow me just here to call the attention of that party now so much interested in the slave of the Carolinas, to the similarity in his condition and that of the mothers, wives, and daughters of the Empire State. The negro has no name. He is Cuffy Douglas or Cuffy Brooks, just whose Cuffy he may chance to be. The woman has no name. She is Mrs. Richard Roe or Mrs. John Doe, just whose Mrs. she may chance to be. Cuffy has no right to his earnings; he cannot buy or sell, or lay up anything that he can call his own. Mrs. Roe has no right to her earnings; she can neither buy nor sell, make contracts, nor lay up anything that she can call her own. Cuffy has no right to his children; they can be sold from him at any time. Mrs. Roe has no right to her children; they may be bound out to cancel a father's debts of honor. The unborn child, even by the last will of the father, may be placed under the guardianship of a stranger and a foreigner. Cuffy has no legal existence; he is subject to restraint and moderate chastisement. Mrs. Roe has no legal existence; she has not the best right to her own person. The husband has the power to restrain and administer moderate chastisement.

Blackstone declares that the husband and wife are one, and learned commentators have decided that that one is the husband. In all civil codes, you will find them classified as one. Certain rights and immunities, such and such privileges are to be secured to white male citizens. What have women and negroes to do with rights? What know they of government, war, or glory?

The prejudice against color of which we hear so much, is no stronger than that against sex. It is produced by the same cause and manifested very much in the same way. The negro's skin and the woman's sex are both prima facie evidence that they were intended to be in subjection to the white Saxon man. The few social privileges which the man gives the woman, he makes up to the negro in civil rights. The woman may sit at the same table and eat with the white man; the free negro may hold property and vote. The woman may sit in the same pew with the white man in church; the free negro may enter the pulpit and preach. Now, with the black man's right to suffrage, the right unquestioned, even by Paul, to minister at the altar, it is evident that the prejudice against sex is more deeply rooted and more unreasonably maintained than that against color. As citizens of a republic, which should we most highly prize, social privileges or civil rights? The latter, most certainly.

To those who do not feel the injustice and degradation of the condition, there is something inexpressibly comical in man's "citizen woman." It reminds me of those monsters I used to see in the old world, head and shoulders woman, and the rest of the body sometimes fish and sometimes beast. I used to think, What a strange conceit! but now I see how perfectly it represents man's idea! Look over all his laws concerning us, and you will see just enough of woman to tell of her existence; all the rest is submerged, or made to crawl upon the earth. Just imagine an inhabitant of another planet entertaining himself some pleasant evening in searching over our great national compact, our Declaration of Independence, our Constitutions, or some of our statute-books; what would he think of those "women and negroes" that must be so fenced in, so guarded against? Why, he would certainly suppose we were monsters, like those fabulous giants or Brobdignagians of olden times, so dangerous to civilized man, from our size, ferocity, and power. Then let him take up our poets, from Pope down to Dana; let him listen to our Fourth of July toasts and some of the sentimental adulations of social life, and no logic could convince him that this creature of the law, and this angel of the family altar, could be one and the same being. Man is in such a labyrinth of contradictions with his marital and property rights; he is so befogged on the whole question of maidens, wives, and mothers, that from pure benevolence we should relieve him from this troublesome branch of legislation. We should vote and make laws for ourselves. Do not be alarmed, dear ladies! You need spend no time reading Grotius, Coke, Puffendorf, Blackstone, Bentham, Kent, and Story to find out what you need. We may safely trust the shrewd selfishness of the white man and consent to live under the same broad code where he has so comfortably ensconced himself. Any legislation that will do for man, we may abide by most cheerfully. . . .

But, say you, we would not have woman exposed to the grossness and vulgarity of public life, or encounter what she must at the polls. When you talk, gentlemen, of sheltering woman from the rough winds and revolting scenes of real life, you must be either talking for effect, or wholly ignorant of what the facts of life are. The man, whatever he is, is known to the woman. She is the companion, not only of the accomplished statesman, the orator, and the scholar; but the vile, vulgar, brutal man has his mother, his wife, his sister, his daughter. Yes, delicate, refined, educated women are in daily life with the drunkard, the gambler, the licentious man, the rogue, and the villain, and if man shows out what he is anywhere, it is at his own hearthstone. There are over forty thousand drunkards in this State. All these are bound by the ties of family to some woman. Allow but a mother and a wife to each, and you have over eighty thousand women. All these have seen their fathers, brothers, husbands, sons, in the lowest and most debased stages of obscenity and degradation. In your own circle of friends, do you not know refined women, whose whole lives are darkened and saddened by gross and brutal associations? Now, gentlemen, do you talk to woman of a rude jest or jostle at the polls, where noble, virtuous men stand ready to protect her person and her rights, when, alone in the darkness and solitude and gloom of night, she has trembled on her own threshold awaiting the return of a husband from his midnight revels?—when, stepping from her chamber, she has beheld her royal monarch, her lord and master—her legal representative—the protector of her property, her home, her children, and her person, down on his hands and knees slowly crawling up the stairs? Behold him in her chamber—in her bed! The fairy tale of "Beauty and the Beast" is far too often realized in life. Gentlemen, such scenes as woman has witnessed at her own fireside, where no eye save Omnipotence could pity, no strong arm could help, can never be realized at the polls, never equaled elsewhere, this side the bottomless pit. No, woman has not hitherto lived in the clouds, surrounded by an atmosphere of purity and peace—but she has been the companion of man in health, in sickness and in death, in his highest and in his lowest moments. She has worshiped him as a saint and an orator, and pitied him as madman or a fool. In Paradise, man and woman were placed together, and so they must ever be. They must sink or rise together. If man is low and wretched and vile, woman cannot escape the contagion, and any atmosphere that is unfit for woman to breathe is not fit for man. Verily, the sins of the fathers shall be visited upon the children to the third and fourth generation. You, by your unwise legislation, have crippled and dwarfed womanhood, by closing to her all honorable and lucrative means of employment, have driven her into the garrets and dens of our cities, where she now revenges herself on your innocent sons, sapping the very foundations of national virtue and strength. Alas! for the young men just coming on the stage of action, who soon shall fill your vacant places—our future Senators, our Presidents, the expounders of our constitutional law! Terrible are the penalties we are now suffering for the ages of injustice done to woman.

Again, it is said that the majority of women do not ask for any change in the laws; that it is time enough to give them the elective franchise when they, as a class, demand it.

Wise statesmen legislate for the best interests of the nation; the State, for the highest good of its citizens; the Christian, for the conversion of the world. Where would have been our railroads, our telegraphs, our ocean steamers, our canals and harbors, our arts and sciences, if government had withheld the means from the far-seeing minority? This State established our present system of common schools, fully believing that educated men and women would make better citizens than ignorant ones. In making this provision for the education of its children, had they waited for a majority of the urchins of this State to petition for schools, how many, think you, would have asked to be transplanted from the street to the school-house? Does the State wait for the criminal to ask for his prison-house? the insane, the idiot, the deaf and dumb for his asylum? Does the Christian, in his love to all mankind, wait for the majority of the benighted heathen to ask him for the gospel? No; unasked and unwelcomed, he crosses the trackless ocean, rolls off the mountain of superstition that oppresses the human mind, proclaims the immortality of the soul, the dignity of manhood, the right of all to be free and happy.

No, gentlemen, if there is but one woman in this State who feels the injustice of her position, she should not be denied her inalienable rights, because the common household drudge and the silly butterfly of fashion are ignorant of all laws, both human and Divine. Because they know nothing of governments or rights, and therefore ask nothing, shall my petitions be unheard? I stand before you the rightful representative of woman, claiming a share in the halo of glory that has gathered round her in the ages, and by the wisdom of her past words and works, her peerless heroism and self-sacrifice, I challenge your admiration; and, moreover, claiming, as I do, a share in all her outrages and sufferings, in the cruel injustice, contempt, and ridicule now heaped upon her, in her deep degradation, hopeless wretchedness, by all that is helpless in her present condition, that is false in law and public sentiment, I urge your generous consideration; for as my heart swells with pride to behold woman in the highest walks of literature and art, it grows big enough to take in those who are bleeding in the dust.

Now do not think, gentlemen, we wish you to do a great many troublesome things for us. We do not ask our legislators to spend a whole session in fixing up a code of laws to satisfy a class of most unreasonable women.

We ask no more than the poor devils in the Scripture asked, "Let us alone." In mercy, let us take care of ourselves, our property, our children, and our homes. True, we are not so strong, so wise, so crafty as you are, but if any kind friend leaves us a little money, or we can by great industry earn fifty cents a day, we would rather buy bread and clothes for our children than cigars and champagne for our legal protectors. There has been a great deal written and said about protection. We, as a class, are tired of one kind of protection, that which leaves us everything to do, to dare, and to suffer, and strips us of all means for its accomplishment. We would not tax man to take care of us. No, the Great Father has endowed all his creatures with the necessary powers for self-support, self-defense, and protection. We do not ask man to represent us; it is hard enough in times like these for man to carry backbone enough to represent himself. So long as the mass of men spend most of their time on the fence, not knowing which way to jump, they are surely in no condition to tell us where we had better stand. In pity for man, we would no longer hang like a millstone round his neck. Undo what man did for us in the dark ages and strike out all special legislation for us; strike the words "white male" from all your constitutions, and then, with fair sailing, let us sink or swim, live or die, survive or perish together.

At Athens, an ancient apologue tells us, on the completion of the temple of Minerva, a statue of the goddess was wanted to occupy the crowning point of the edifice. Two of the greatest artists produced what each deemed his masterpiece. One of these figures was the size of life, admirably designed, exquisitely finished, softly rounded, and beautifully refined. The other was of Amazonian stature, and so boldly chiselled that it looked more like masonry than sculpture. The eyes of all were attracted by the first and turned away in contempt from the second. That, therefore, was adopted and the other rejected, almost with resentment, as though an insult had been offered to a discerning public. The favored statue was accordingly borne in triumph to the place for which it was designed, in the presence of applauding thousands, but as it receded from their upturned eyes, all, all at once agaze upon it, the thunders of applause unaccountably died away—a general misgiving ran through every bosom—the mob themselves stood like statues, as silent and as petrified, for as it slowly went up and up, the soft expression of those chiselled features, the delicate curves and outlines of the limbs and figure, became gradually fainter and fainter, and when at last it reached the place for which it was intended, it was a shapeless ball, enveloped in mist. Of course, the idol of the hour was now clamored down as rationally as it had been cried up, and its dishonored rival, with no good will and no good looks on the part of the chagrined populace, was reared in its stead. As it ascended, the sharp angles faded away, the rough points became smooth, the features full of expression, the whole figure radiant with majesty and beauty. The rude hewn mass, that before had scarcely appeared to bear even the human form, assumed at once the divinity which it represented, being so perfectly proportioned to the dimensions of the building and to the elevation on which it stood, that it seemed as though Pallas herself had alighted upon the pinnacle of the temple in person, to receive the homage of her worshippers.

The woman of the nineteenth century is the shapeless ball in the lofty position which she was designed fully and nobly to fill. The place is not too high, too large, too sacred for woman, but the type that you have chosen is far too small for it. The woman we declare unto you is the rude, misshapen, unpolished object of the successful artist. From your standpoint, you are absorbed with the defects alone. The true artist sees the harmony between the object and its destination. Man, the sculptor, has carved out his ideal, and applauding, thousands welcome his success. He has made a woman that from his low stand-point looks fair and beautiful, a being without rights, or hopes, or fears but in him—neither noble, virtuous, nor independent. Where do we see, in Church or State, in schoolhouse or at the fireside, the much talked-of moral power of woman? Like those Athenians, we have bowed down and worshiped in woman, beauty, grace, the exquisite proportions, the soft and beautifully rounded outline, her delicacy, refinement, and silent helplessness—all well when she is viewed simply as an object of sight, never to rise one foot above the dust from which she sprung. But if she is to be raised up to adorn a temple, or represent a divinity—if she is to fill the niche of wife and counsellor to true and noble men, if she is to be the mother, the educator of a race of heroes or martyrs, of a Napoleon, or a Jesus—then must the type of womanhood be on a larger scale than that yet carved by man.

In vain would the rejected artist have reasoned with the Athenians as to the superiority of his production; nothing short of the experiment they made could have satisfied them. And what of your experiment, what of your wives, your homes? Alas! for the folly and vacancy that meet you there! But for your club-houses and newspapers, what would social life be to you? Where are your beautiful women? your frail ones, taught to lean lovingly and confidingly on man? Where are the crowds of educated dependents—where the long line of pensioners on man's bounty? Where all the young girls, taught to believe that marriage is the only legitimate object of a woman's pursuit—they who stand listlessly on life's shores, waiting, year after year, like the sick man at the pool of Bethesda, for some one to come and put them in? These are they who by their ignorance and folly curse almost every fireside with some human specimen of deformity or imbecility. These are they who fill the gloomy abodes of poverty and vice in our vast metropolis. These are they who patrol the streets of our cities, to give our sons their first lessons in infamy. These are they who fill our asylums and make night hideous with their cries and groans.

The women who are called masculine, who are brave, courageous, self-reliant and independent, are they who in the face of adverse winds have kept one steady course upward and onward in the paths of virtue and peace—they who have taken their gauge of womanhood from their own native strength and dignity—they who have learned for themselves the will of God concerning them. This is our type of womanhood. Will you help us raise it up, that you too may see its beautiful proportions—that you may behold the outline of the goddess who is yet to adorn your temple of Freedom? We are building a model republic; our edifice will one day need a crowning glory. Let the artists be wisely chosen. Let them begin their work. Here is your temple to Liberty, to human rights, on whose portals behold the glorious declaration, "All men are created equal." The sun has never yet shone upon any of man's creations that can compare with this. The artist who can mold a statue worthy to crown magnificence like this, must be godlike in his conceptions, grand in his comprehensions, sublimely beautiful in his power of execution. The woman—the crowning glory of the model republic among the nations of the earth—what must she not be? (Loud applause).

SOURCE: Elizabeth Stanton, "Address to the Legislature on Women's Right of Suffrage, Albany, February 18, 1860," in *History of Woman Suffrage*, vol. 1, 679–85.

Chapter 3

"Address to the Tenth National Women's Rights Convention on Marriage and Divorce, New York City, May 11, 1860"

EDITORS' NOTE: *Two months after the 1860 passage of a broad Married Women's Property Act for New York State, Stanton called for radical liberalization in state laws governing divorce. At the time, state laws varied greatly, and only Indiana and Connecticut provided relatively liberal terms for securing divorces. Not only did all of the newspaper coverage and most of Stanton's male friends criticize her call that her home state of New York follow in this direction, but many in the women's rights audience disagreed, believing that making marriages easier to dissolve was no way, to use Stanton's phrase, to "protect the sacredness of the family." Stanton began her case on natural rights grounds, citing the Declaration of Independence's guarantee of the right "to pursue happiness" as a basis for reforming the laws of marriage. In addition, she stressed women's greater suffering within bad marriages and thus argued that, if only one sex were to have legislative authority over the laws of marriage, justice demanded that it be women.*

In our common law, in our whole system of jurisprudence, we find man's highest idea of right. The object of law is to secure justice. But inasmuch as fallible man is the maker and administrator of law, we must look for many and gross blunders in the application of its general principles to individual cases.

The science of theology, of civil, political, moral, and social life, all teach the common idea, that man ever has been, and ever must be, sacrificed to the highest good of society; the one to the many—the poor to the rich—the weak to the powerful—and all to the institutions of his own creation. Look, what thunderbolts of power man has forged in the ages for his own destruction!—at the organizations to enslave himself! And through those times of darkness, those generations of superstition, behold all along the relics of his power and skill, that stand like mile-stones, here and there, to show how far back man was great and glorious! Who can stand in those vast cathedrals of the old world, as the deep-toned organ reverberates from arch to arch and not feel the grandeur of humanity? These are the workmanship of him, beneath whose stately dome the architect himself now bows in fear and doubt, knows not himself, and knows not God—a mere slave to symbols—and with holy water signs the Cross; whilst He who died thereon declared man God.

I repudiate the popular idea of man's degradation and total depravity. I place man above all governments, all institutions—ecclesiastical and civil—all constitutions and laws. (Applause). It is a mistaken idea, that the same law that oppresses the individual can promote the highest good of society. The best interests of a community never can require the sacrifice of one innocent being—of one sacred right. In the settlement, then, of any question, we must simply consider the highest good of the individual. It is the inalienable right of all to be happy. It is the highest duty of all to seek those conditions in life, those surroundings, which may develop what is noblest and best, remembering that the lessons of these passing hours are not for time alone, but for the ages of eternity. They tell us, in that future home—the heavenly paradise—that the human family shall be sifted out, and the good and pure shall dwell together in peace. If that be the heavenly order, is it not our duty to render earth as near like heaven as we may?

For years, there has been before the Legislature of this State a variety of bills, asking for divorce in cases of drunkenness, insanity, desertion, cruel and brutal treatment, endangering life. My attention was called to this question very early in life, by the sufferings of a friend of my girlhood, a victim of one of those unfortunate unions called marriage. What my great love for that young girl, and my holy intuitions, then decided to be right, has not been changed by years of experience, observation, and reason. I have pondered well these things in my heart, and ever felt the deepest interest in all that has been written and said upon the subject, and the most profound respect and loving sympathy for those heroic women, who, in the face of law and public sentiment, have dared to sunder the unholy ties of a joyless, loveless union.

If marriage is a human institution about which man may legislate, it seems but just that he should treat this branch of bill legislation with the same common-sense that he applies to all others. If it is a mere legal contract, then should it be subject to the restraints and privileges of all other contracts. A contract, to be valid in law, must be formed between parties of mature age, with an honest intention in said parties to do what they agree. The least concealment, fraud, or deception, if proved, annuls the contract. A man cannot contract for an acre of land, or a horse, until he is twenty-one, but he may contract for a wife at fourteen. If a man sell a horse, and the purchaser find in him great incompatibility of temper—a disposition to stand still when the owner is in haste to go—the sale is null and void, and the man and his horse part company. But in marriage, no matter how much fraud and deception are practiced, nor how cruelly one or both parties have been misled; no matter how young, inexperienced, or thoughtless the parties, nor how unequal their condition and position in life, the contract cannot be annulled. Think of a husband telling a young and trusting girl, but one short month his wife, that he married her for her money; that those letters so precious to her, that she had read and re-read, and kissed and cherished, were written by another; that their splen-did home, of which, on their wedding-day, her father gave him the deed, is already in the hands of his creditors; that she must give up the elegance and luxury that now surround her, unless she can draw fresh supplies of money to meet their wants! When she told the story of her wrongs to me —the abuse to which she was subject, and the dread in which she lived—I impulsively urged her to fly from such a monster and villain, as she would before the hot breath of a ferocious beast of the wilderness. (Applause). And she did fly, and it was well with her. Many times since, as I have felt her throbbing heart against my own, she has said, "Oh, but for your love and sympathy, your encouragement, I should never have escaped from that bondage. Before I could, of myself, have found courage to break those chains my heart would have broken in the effort."

Marriage, as it now exists, must seem to all of you a mere human insti-tution. Look through the universe of matter and mind—all God's ar-rangements are perfect, harmonious, and complete! There is no discord, friction, or failure in His eternal plans. Immutability, perfection, beauty, are stamped on all His laws. Love is the vital essence that pervades and permeates, from the center to the circumference, the graduating circles of all thought and action. Love is the talisman of human weal and woe—the open sesame to every human soul. Where two beings are drawn together, by the natural laws of likeness and affinity, union and happiness are the result. Such marriages might be Divine. But how is it now? You all know our marriage is, in many cases, a mere outward tie, impelled by custom, policy, interest, necessity; founded not even in friendship, to say nothing of love; with every possible inequality of condition and development. In

these heterogeneous unions, we find youth and old age, beauty and deformity, refinement and vulgarity, virtue and vice, the educated and the ignorant, angels of grace and goodness with devils of malice and malignity;
and the sum of all this is human wretchedness and despair; cold fathers,
sad mothers, and hapless children, who shiver at the hearthstone, where
the fires of love have all gone out. The wide world and the stranger's un-
sympathizing gaze are not more to be dreaded for young hearts than
homes like these. Now, who shall say that it is right to take two beings, so
unlike, and anchor them right side by side, fast bound—to stay all time,
until God shall summon one away?

Do wise, Christian legislators need any arguments to convince them
that the sacredness of the family relation should be protected at all haz-
ards? The family, that great conservator of national virtue and strength,
how can you hope to build it up in the midst of violence, debauchery, and
excess? Can there be anything sacred at that family altar, where the chief-
priest who ministers makes sacrifice of human beings, of the weak and the
innocent? where the incense offered up is not to the God of justice and
mercy, but to those heathen divinities, who best may represent the lost
man in all his grossness and deformity? Call that sacred, where woman,
the mother of the race—of a Jesus of Nazareth—unconscious of the true
dignity of her nature, of her high and holy destiny, consents to live in legalized prostitution!–her whole soul revolting at such gross association!—
her flesh shivering at the cold contamination of that embrace, held there
by no tie but the iron chain of the law, and a false and most unnatural
public sentiment? Call that sacred, where innocent children, trembling
with fear, fly to the corners and dark places of the house, to hide themselves from the wrath of drunken, brutal fathers, but, forgetting their past
sufferings, rush out again at their mother's frantic screams, "Help, oh
help"? Behold the agonies of those young hearts, as they see the only being
on earth they love, dragged about the room by the hair of the head, kicked
and pounded, and left half dead and bleeding on the floor! Call that sacred, where fathers like these have the power and legal right to hand down
their natures to other beings, to curse other generations with such moral
deformity and death?

Men and brethren, look into your asylums for the blind, the deaf and
dumb, the idiot, the imbecile, the deformed, the insane; go out into the
by-lanes and dens of this vast metropolis and contemplate that reeking
mass of depravity; pause before the terrible revelations made by statistics
of the rapid increase of all this moral and physical impotency and learn

how fearful a thing it is to violate the immutable laws of the beneficent Ruler of the universe; and there behold the terrible retributions of your violence on woman! Learn how false and cruel are those institutions, which, with a coarse materialism, set aside those holy instincts of the woman to bear no children but those of love! In the best condition of marriage, as we now have it, to woman comes all the penalties and sacrifices. A man, in the full tide of business or pleasure, can marry and not change his life one iota; he can be husband, father, and everything beside; but in marriage, woman gives up all. Home is her sphere, her realm. Well, be it so. If here you will make us all-supreme, take to yourselves the universe beside; explore the North Pole; and, in your airy car, all space; in your Northern homes and cloud-clapt towers, go feast on walrus flesh and air, and lay you down to sleep your six months' night away, and leave us to make these laws that govern the inner sanctuary of our own homes, and faithful satellites we will ever be to the dinner-pot, the cradle, and the old arm-chair. (Applause).

Fathers, do you say, let your daughters pay a life-long penalty for one unfortunate step? How could they, on the threshold of life, full of joy and hope, believing all things to be as they seemed on the surface, judge of the dark windings of the human soul? How could they foresee that the young man, to-day so noble, so generous, would in a few short years be transformed into a cowardly, mean tyrant, or a foul-mouthed, bloated drunkard? What father could rest at his home by night, knowing that his lovely daughter was at the mercy of a strong man drunk with wine and passion, and that, do what he might, he was backed up by law and public sentiment? The best interests of the individual, the family, the State, the nation, cry out against these legalized marriages of force and endurance. There can be no heaven without love, and nothing is sacred in the family and home but just so far as it is built up and anchored in love. Our newspapers teem with startling accounts of husbands and wives having shot or poisoned each other, or committed suicide, choosing death rather than the indissoluble tie; and, still worse, the living death of faithless wives and daughters, from the first families in this State, dragged from the privacy of home into the public prints and courts, with all the painful details of sad, false lives. What say you to facts like these? Now, do you believe, men and women, that all these wretched matches are made in heaven? that all these sad, miserable people are bound together by God? I know Horace Greeley has been most eloquent, for weeks past, on the holy sacrament of ill-assorted marriages, but let us hope that all wisdom does not live and will not die with Horace Greeley. I think, if he had been married to *The New York Herald,* instead of the Republican party, he would have found out some Scriptural arguments against life-long unions, where great incompatibility of temper existed between the parties. (Laughter and applause).

Our law-makers have dug a pit, and the innocent have fallen into it, and now will you coolly cover them over with statute laws, *Tribunes,* and Weeds,* and tell them to stay there and pay the life-long penalty of having fallen in? Nero was thought the chief of tyrants, because he made laws and hung them up so high that his subjects could not read them, and then punished them for every act of disobedience. What better are our Republican legislators? The mass of the women of this nation know nothing about the laws, yet all their specially barbarous legislation is for woman. Where have they made any provision for her to learn the laws? Where is the law school for our daughters? where the law office, the bar, or the bench, now urging them to take part in the jurisprudence of the nation?

But, say you, does not separation cover all these difficulties? No one objects to separation when the parties are so disposed. But, to separation there are two very serious objections. First, so long as you insist on marriage as a divine institution, as an indissoluble tie, so long as you maintain your present laws against divorce, you make separation, even, so odious, that the most noble, virtuous, and sensitive men and women choose a life of concealed misery, rather than a partial, disgraceful release. Secondly, those who, in their impetuosity and despair, do, in spite of public sentiment, separate, find themselves in their new position beset with many temptations to lead a false, unreal life. This isolation bears especially hard on woman. Marriage is not all of life to man. His resources for amusement and occupation are boundless. He has the whole world for his home. His business, his politics, his club, his friendships with either sex, can help to fill up the void made by an unfortunate union or separation. But to woman, marriage is all and everything, her sole object in life—that for which she is educated—the subject of all her sleeping and her waking dreams. Now, if a noble, generous girl of eighteen marries and is unfortunate, because the cruelty of her husband compels separation, in her dreary isolation, would you drive her to a nunnery; and shall she be a nun indeed? Her solitude is nothing less, as, in the present undeveloped condi-

---

* Thurlow Weed, editor of *The Albany Evening Journal,* opposed the passage of the divorce bill before the New York Legislature in 1860.

tion of woman, it is only through our fathers, brothers, husbands, sons, that we feel the pulsations of the great outer world.

One unhappy, discordant man or woman in a neighborhood, may mar the happiness of all the rest. You cannot shut up discord, any more than you can small-pox. There can be no morality where there is a settled discontent. A very wise father once remarked, that in the government of his children, he forbade as few things as possible; a wise legislation would do the same. It is folly to make laws on subjects beyond human prerogative, knowing that in the very nature of things they must be set aside. To make laws that man cannot and will not obey, serves to bring all law into contempt. It is very important in a republic that the people should respect the laws, for if we throw them to the winds, what becomes of civil government? What do our present divorce laws amount to? Those who wish to evade them have only to go into another State to accomplish what they desire. If any of our citizens cannot secure their inalienable rights in New York State, they may in Connecticut and Indiana. Why is it that all agreements, covenants, partnerships, are left wholly at the discretion of the parties, except the contract, which of all others is considered most holy and important, both for the individual and the race? This question of divorce, they tell us, is hedged about with difficulties; that it cannot be approached with the ordinary rules of logic and common-sense. It is too holy, too sacred to be discussed, and few seem disposed to touch it. From man's standpoint, this may be all true, as to him they say belong reason and the power of ratiocination. Fortunately, I belong to that class endowed with mere intuitions, a kind of moral instinct, by which we feel out right and wrong. In presenting to you, therefore, my views of divorce, you will of course give them the weight only of the woman's intuitions. But inasmuch as that is all God saw fit to give us, it is evident we need nothing more. Hence, what we do perceive of truth must be as reliable as what man grinds out by the longer process of reason, authority, and speculation.

Horace Greeley, in his recent discussion with Robert Dale Owen, said, this whole question has been tried, in all its varieties and conditions, from indissoluble monogamic marriage down to free love, that the ground has been all gone over and explored. Let me assure him that but just one-half of the ground has been surveyed, and that half but by one of the parties, and that party certainly not the most interested in the matter. Moreover, there is one kind of marriage that has not been tried, and that is a contract made by equal parties to live an equal life, with equal restraints and privileges on either side. Thus far, we have had the man marriage, and nothing more. From the beginning, man has had the sole and whole regulation of the matter. He has spoken in Scripture, he has spoken in law. As an individual, he has decided the time and cause for putting away a wife, and as a judge and legislator, he still holds the entire control. In all history, sacred and profane, the woman is regarded and spoken of simply as the toy of man—made for his special use—to meet his most gross and sensuous desires. She is taken or put away, given or received, bought or sold, just as the interest of the parties might dictate. But the woman has been no more recognized in all these transactions, through all the different periods and conditions of the race, than if she had had no part nor lot in the whole matter. The right of woman to put away a husband, be he ever so impure, is never hinted at in sacred history. Even Jesus himself failed to recognize the sacred rights of the holy mother of the race. We cannot take our gauge of womanhood from the past, but from the solemn convictions of our own souls in the higher development of the race. No parchments, however venerable with the mould of ages, no human institutions, can bound the immortal wants of the royal sons and daughters of the great I am,—rightful heirs of the joys of time and joint heirs of the glories of eternity.

If in marriage either party claims the right to stand supreme, to woman, the mother of the race, belongs the scepter and the crown. Her life is one long sacrifice for man. You tell us that among all womankind there is no Moses, Christ, or Paul,—no Michael Angelo, Beethoven, or Shakespeare,—no Columbus or Galileo,—no Locke or Bacon. Behold those mighty minds attuned to music and the arts, so great, so grand, so comprehensive,—these are our great works of which we boast! Into you, O sons of earth, go all of us that is immortal. In you center our very life-thoughts, our hopes, our intensest love. For you we gladly pour out our heart's blood and die, knowing that from our suffering comes forth a new and more glorious resurrection of thought and life. (Loud applause).

SOURCE: Elizabeth Stanton, "Address to Tenth National Women's Rights Convention on Marriage and Divorce, New York City, May 11, 1860," in *History of Woman Suffrage*, vol. 1, 716–22.

Chapter 4

"Address to Anniversary of American Equal Rights Association, May 12, 1869, New York City"

EDITORS' NOTE: With the insult of the Fourteenth and Fifteenth Amendments fresh in her mind, Stanton demanded an additional amendment—had it passed it would have been the Sixteenth—to add woman suffrage to the Constitution. This speech, delivered at the meeting in which the Reconstruction-era coalition on behalf of universal (black and woman both) suffrage gave way to a focused woman suffrage movement, is a remarkable mix of Stanton's natural rights convictions with a new set of influences and arguments justifying suffrage for woman as a distinct, even salvational social force. Stanton gave this address at a time of widespread concern over rampant political corruption that would soon reach up to the presidency. Her fear for the viability of political democracy forms the immediate context for the unrestrained contempt for black and immigrant men that so characterizes this piece.

MARCH 16th, 1869, will be memorable in all coming time, as the day when the Honorable George W. Julian submitted a Joint Resolution to Congress to enfranchise the women of the republic, by proposing a Sixteenth Amendment to the Federal Constitution which reads as follows:

> Article XVI. The Right of Suffrage in the United States shall be based on citizenship, and shall be regulated by Congress ; and all citizens of the United States, whether native or naturalized, shall enjoy this right equally without any distinction or discrimination what-ever founded on sex.

Since our famous bill of rights was given to the world, declaring all men equal, there has been no other proposition, in its magnitude, beneficence, and far-reaching consequences, so momentous as this. It is a proposition to secure peace and prosperity in the state; light and liberty in the church; health and happiness in the home; for it is the first step towards the realization of the united thought and action of man and woman in science, religion, and government.

It is the new declaration of equality, proclaiming sex in mind; the marriage of affection and activity, of moral and material forces and the propagation of justice, mercy, truth, and love. This sublime proposition is but the echo of both the old and new dispensations of sacred history; the one proclaiming in Paradise that "it is not good for man to be alone," the other commanding with warning voice, in Palestine, "what God hath joined together let no man put asunder."

A great idea of progress is near its consummation, when statesmen in the councils of the nation propose to frame it into statutes and constitutions; when Reverend Fathers recognize it by a new interpretation of their creeds and canons; when the Bar and Bench at its command set aside the legislation of centuries, and girls of twenty put their heels on the Cokes and Blackstones of the past.

Those who represent what is called "the Woman's Rights Movement" have argued their right to political equality from every standpoint of justice, religion, and logic, for the last twenty years. They have quoted the Constitution, the Declaration of Independence, the Bible, the opinions of great men and women in all ages; they have plead the theory of our government; suffrage as a natural, inalienable right; showing from the lessons of history that one class cannot legislate for another; that disfranchised classes must ever be neglected and degraded; and that all privileges are but mockery to the citizen, until he has a voice in the making and administering of law. Such arguments have been made over and over in Conventions and before the legislatures of several states. Judges, lawyers, priests, and politicians have said again and again that our logic was unanswerable, and although much twaddle has emanated from the male tongue and pen on this subject, no man has yet made a fair, logical argument on the other side. Knowing that we hold the Gibraltar rock of reason on this question, they resort to ridicule and petty objections. Compelled to follow our assailants, wherever they go and fight them with their own weapons, when cornered with wit and sarcasm, some cry out, we have no logic on our platform, forgetting that we have no use for logic until they give us logicians at whom to hurl it, and if, for the pure love of it, we now and then rehearse the logic that is like a, b, c, to all of us, others cry out—the same old speeches we have heard this twenty years. It would be safe to say a hundred years, for they are the same our fathers used when battling old King George and the British Parliament for their right to representation as well as taxation and a voice in the laws by which they were governed. There are no new arguments to be made on human rights, our work to-day is to apply to ourselves those so familiar to all; to teach man that woman is not an anomalous being, outside all laws and constitutions, but one whose rights are to be established by the same process of reason as that by which he demands his own.

When our Fathers made out their famous bill of impeachment against England, they specified eighteen grievances. When the women of this country surveyed the situation in their first convention, they found they had precisely that number, and quite similar in character; and reading over the old revolutionary arguments of Jefferson, Patrick Henry, Otis, and Adams, they found they applied remarkably well to their case. The same arguments made in this country for extending Suffrage from time to time to white men; native born citizens, without property and education, and to foreigners; the same used by John Bright in England, to extend it to a million new voters, and the same used by the great Republican party to enfranchise two million black men in the south, all these arguments we have to-day to offer for woman, and one, in addition, stronger than all beside, and that is the one to which I hinted in opening, the difference in man and woman. Because man and woman are the complement of one another, but divided halves, we need woman's thought in national affairs to make a safe and stable government.

The Republican party to-day congratulates itself on having carried the Fifteenth Amendment of the Constitution, thus securing "manhood suffrage" and establishing an aristocracy of sex on this continent. As several bills to secure Woman's Suffrage in the District and the Territories have been already presented in both Houses of Congress, and as by Mr. Julian's bill, the question of so amending the Constitution as to extend Suffrage to all the women of the country has been presented to the nation for consideration, it is not only the right but the duty of every thoughtful woman to express her opinion on the Sixteenth Amendment. While I hail the late discussions in Congress and the various bills presented as so many signs of progress, I am especially gratified with those of Messrs. Julian and Pomeroy, which forbid any state to deny the right of Suffrage to any of its citizens on account of sex or color.

This fundamental principal of our government—the equality of all the citizens of the republic—should be incorporated in the Federal Constitution, there to remain forever. To leave the question to the states and partial acts of Congress is to defer indefinitely its settlement, for what is done by this Congress may be repealed by the next; and politics in the several states differ so widely that no harmonious action on any question can ever be secured, except as a strict party measure. Hence, we appeal to the party now in power, everywhere, to end this protracted debate on Suffrage, and declare it the inalienable right of every citizen who is amenable to the laws of the land, who pays taxes and the penalty of crime. We have a splendid theory of a genuine republic. Why not realize it and make our government homogeneous, from Maine to California? The Republican party has the power to do this, and now is its only opportunity, for it has been so long in the ascendant and had such large majorities that, in the nature of things, it must soon fall to pieces, especially as it has now no national question for a party issue on which to rouse the enthusiasm of the people. Greenbacks, free trade, land monopoly, Pacific railroads, national banks, swindles, and whiskey frauds equally divide both parties. Woman's Suffrage, in 1873, may be as good a card for the Republicans as Grant was in the last election. It is said that the Republican party made Grant president, not because they thought him the most desirable man in the nation for that office, but they were afraid the Democrats would take him if they did not. We would suggest, there may be the same danger of Democrats taking up Woman's Suffrage if they do not. God, in his providence, may have purified that party in the furnace of affliction. They have had the opportunity safe from the turmoil of political life and the temptations of office to study and apply the divine principles of justice and equality to life; for minorities are always in a position to carry principles to their logical results, while majorities are governed only by votes. You see my faith in Democrats is based on sound philosophy. In the next Congress, the Democratic party will gain thirty-four new members, hence the Republicans have had their last chance to do justice to woman.

It will be no enviable record, for the Fortieth Congress in the darkest days of the republic placed our free institutions in the care and keeping of every type of manhood, in the hands of ignorance and vice, ignoring their own wives and mothers, all the elevating and purifying influences of the most virtuous, humane and educated half of the American people.

In changing the fundamental law of the land, all the people have a right to be heard. The women of this nation have clearly the right to vote on the Fifteenth and Sixteenth Amendments. If our rulers were not blinded, by prejudice and custom, they would see that in common justice woman's consent should be asked when millions of ignorant foreigners are to be introduced into the body politic to legislate for her. It might be a question with an educated American woman whether she would trust her interests in the hands of ignorant Chinamen, with their low ideas of womankind, who might make laws that henceforth we should neither read, write, walk, nor go outside our garden gate. We might not like the legislation of the ignorant German, accustomed to drive his wife and cow side by side before the plough. We might not like the legislation of the ignorant African just from his own land or the southern plantation, in whose eyes woman is simply the being of man's lust. We cannot rest in the assurance that the higher orders of men will protect us, for they are helpless to-day to protect themselves here in the metropolis of the country. The same principles of common justice that apply to states apply to nations, and many able men have expressed the opinion that in the revision of the state constitution the state is for the time being resolved into its original elements and that all the people have a right to vote on the fundamental laws that are to govern them, and this principle was recognized, to a certain extent in both New York and Rhode Island in the revision of their laws. In New York, in 1803 and 1821, when all white men, as well as black, voted on a property qualification, those qualifications were set aside, and all men voted for members to the Constitutional Convention and were eligible to seats there, to frame the fundamental laws by which Governors, Senators and Assemblymen were created, though not permitted to vote in the general elections. I need but state this for all to see its justice and wisdom.

To-day, by the war and the entire revision of our Federal Constitution, this nation is, for the time being, resolved into its original elements, and it is not only the right but the duty of all the people to say on what basis this government shall be reconstructed.

I urge a speedy adoption of the Sixteenth Amendment for many reasons:

1. A government based on the caste and class principle cannot stand. The aristocratic idea, in any form, is opposed to the genius of our free institutions, to our own declaration of rights, and to the civilization of the age. All artificial distinctions, whether of family, blood, wealth, color, or sex, are equally repressive on the degraded classes and equally destructive to national life and prosperity. Governments based on every form of aristocracy, on every degree and variety of inequality, have been tried in despotisms, monarchies, and republics, and all alike have perished. In the

panorama of the past behold the mighty nations that have risen, one by one, but to fall. Behold their temples, thrones, and pyramids, their gorgeous palaces and stately monuments now crumbled all to dust. Behold every crowned head in Europe at this very hour trembling on his throne. Behold the republics on this Western continent convulsed, distracted, divided, the hosts scattered, the leaders fallen, the scouts lost in the wilderness, the once inspired prophets blind and dumb, while on all sides the cry is echoed, "Republicanism is a failure," though that great principle of a government "by the people, of the people, for the people" has never been tried. Thus far, all nations have been built on caste and failed. Why, in this hour of reconstruction, with the experience of generations before us, make another experiment in the same direction? If serfdom, peasantry, and slavery have shattered kingdoms, deluged continents with blood, scattered republics like dust before the wind, and rent our own Union asunder, what kind of a government, think you, American statesmen, you can build, with the mothers of the race crouching at your feet, while iron-heeled peasants, serfs, and slaves, exalted by your hands, tread our inalienable rights into the dust? While all men, everywhere, are rejoicing in new-found liberties, shall woman alone be denied the rights, privileges, and immunities of citizenship?

While in England men are coming up from the coal mines of Cornwall, from the factories of Birmingham and Manchester, demanding the suffrage; while in cold, frigid Russia the 22,000,000 newly-emancipated serfs are already claiming a voice in the government; while here, in our own land slaves, but just rejoicing in the proclamation of emancipation, ignorant alike of its power and significance, have the ballot unasked, unsought, already laid at their feet—think you the daughters of Adams, Jefferson, and Patrick Henry, in whose veins flows the blood of two revolutions, will forever linger round the camp-fires of an old barbarism, with no longings to join this grand army of freedom, in its onward march, to roll back the golden gates to a higher and better civilization?

Of all kinds of aristocracy, that of sex is the most odious and unnatural, invading, as it does, our homes, desecrating our family altars, dividing those whom God has joined together, exalting the son above the mother who bore him, and subjugating, everywhere, moral power to brute force. Such a government would not be worth the blood and treasure so freely poured out in its long struggles for freedom.

Though it has never been tried, we know an experiment on the basis of equality would be safe, for the laws in the world of morals are as immutable as in the world of matter. As the astronomer, Le Verrier, discovered the planet that bears his name [later renamed Neptune] by a process of reason and calculation through the variations of other planets from known laws, so can the true statesman, through the telescope of justice, see the genuine republic of the future, mid the ruins of the mighty nations that have passed away. When we base nations on justice and equality, we lift government out of the mists of speculation into the dignity of a fixed science.

Everything short of this is trick, legerdemain, slight of hand. Magicians may make nations seem to live when they do not. The Newtons of our day who should try to make apples stand in the air and men walk on their heads would be no more puerile than are they who propose to reconstruct this nation outside of law on the basis of inequality.

2. I urge the Sixteenth Amendment, because "manhood suffrage," or a man's government, is civil, religious and social disorganization. The male element is a destructive force, stern, selfish, aggrandizing, loving war, violence, conquest, acquisition, breeding in the material and moral world alike discord, disorder, disease, and death. See what a record of blood and cruelty the pages of history reveal. Through what slavery, slaughter, and sacrifice, through what inquisitions and imprisonments, pains and persecutions, black codes and gloomy creeds, the seed of humanity have struggled for the centuries, while mercy has veiled her face and all hearts have been dead alike to love and hope! The male element has held high carnival thus far, it has fairly run riot from the beginning, overpowering the feminine element everywhere, crushing out all the diviner elements in human nature, until we know but little of true manhood and womanhood, of the latter comparatively nothing, for it has scarce been recognized as an element of power until within the last century. Our creeds, codes, and customs are but the reflections of man himself, untempered by Woman's thought, the hard iron rule we feel alike in the church, the state, and the home. No one need wonder at the disorganization of society, at the fragmentary condition of everything, when we remember that man, who represents but half a complete being with but half an idea on every subject, has undertaken the absolute control of all sublunary matters. People object to the demands of those whom they choose to call the strong-minded, because they say, "the right of suffrage will make the women masculine." That is just the difficulty in which we are involved to-day. Though disfranchised we have few women in the best sense, we have simply so many reflections, varieties, and dilutions of the masculine gender. The strong, natural characteristics of womanhood are repressed and ignored in depen-

dence, for so long as man feeds woman she will try to please the giver and adapt herself to his condition. To keep a foothold in society woman must be as near like man as possible, reflect his ideas, opinions, virtues, motives, prejudices, and vices. She must respect his statutes, though they strip her of every inalienable right and conflict with that higher law written by the finger of God on her own soul. She must believe his theology, though it pave the highways of hell with the skulls of new-born infants and make God a monster of vengeance and hypocrisy. She must look at everything from its dollar and cent point of view, or she is a mere romancer. She must accept things as they are and make the best of them. To mourn over the miseries of others, the poverty of the poor, their hardships in jails, prisons, asylums, the horrors of war, cruelty, and brutality in every form, all this would be mere sentimentalizing. To protest again the intrigue, bribery, and corruption of public life, to desire that her sons might follow some business that did not involve lying, cheating, and a hard, grinding selfishness, would be arrant nonsense. In this way man has been moulding woman to his ideas by direct and positive influences, while she, if not a negation, has used indirect means to control him, and thus in most cases developed the very characteristics both in him and herself that most needed repression. Thus the higher nature of both sexes has been subordinated to the lower, and to-day our journals are filled with murders,— wives killing husbands; husbands, wives; sons, fathers; daughters, mothers. Seduction, rape, elopement, infanticide, poison, arson, garroting, death and destruction meet the eye at every turn. And now man himself stands appalled at the results of his own excesses and mourns in bitterness that falsehood, selfishness, and violence are the law of life. The need of this hour is not territory, gold mines, railroads, or specie payments, but a new evangel of womanhood, to exalt power, virtue, morality, true religion, to lift man up into the higher realms of love, purity, and thought.

We ask woman's enfranchisement, as the first step toward the recognition of that essential element that can only secure the health, strength, and prosperity of the nation. Whatever is done to lift woman to her true position will help to usher in a new day of peace and perfection for the race. In speaking of the masculine element, I do not wish to be understood to say that all men are hard, selfish, and brutal, for many of the most beautiful spirits the world has known have been clothed with manhood, but I refer to those characteristics, though often marked in woman, that distinguish what is called the stronger sex, qualities that are virtues when balanced by feminine virtues, but vices when in excess. For example, the love of acquisition and conquest, the very pioneers of civilization when expended on the earth, the sea, the elements, the riches, and forces of Nature, are powers of destruction when used to subjugate one man to another or to sacrifice nations to ambition. Here that great conservator of woman's love—if permitted to assert itself, as it naturally would in freedom against all oppression, violence, and war, would hold all these destructive forces in check, for woman knows the cost of life better than man does, and not with her consent would one drop of blood ever be shed, one life sacrificed in vain.

With violence and disturbance in the natural world, we see a constant effort to maintain an equilibrium of forces. Nature, like a loving mother, is ever trying to keep land and sea, mountain and valley, each in its place, to hush the angry winds and waves, balance the extremes of heat and cold, of rain and drought, that peace, harmony, and beauty may reign supreme. There is a striking analogy between matter and mind, and the present disorganization of society warns us that in the dethronement of woman we have let loose the elements of violence and ruin that she only has the power to curb.

If the civilization of the age calls for an extension of the suffrage, surely a government of educated men and women would better represent the whole humanitarian idea and protect the interests of all than could the representation of either sex alone. But government gains no new element of strength in admitting all men to the ballot-box for we have too much of the man power there already. We see this in every department of legislation, and it is a common remark than unless some new virtue is infused into our public life, the nation is doomed to destruction. Will the foreign element, the dregs of China, Germany, Ireland, and Africa, supply this needed force, or the nobler types of American womanhood who have taught our president and senators and congressmen the rudiments of all they know? But to ignore the influence of woman in legislation and blindly insist on the recognition of all men, however ignorant, brutalized, or degraded, must prove suicidal to any government on the earth. Hence the highest feelings of patriotism, justice to woman, and wholesale enfranchisement of all types and shades of men, until women are admitted to the polls to outweigh the dangerous excess of the male element.

I urge the Sixteenth Amendment, because when "Manhood Suffrage" is established from Maine to California, woman has reached the lowest depths of political degradation. So long as there is a disfranchised class in this country, and that class is woman, a man's government is worse than a white man's government with suffrage limited by property and educational qualifications, because in proportion as you multiply the rulers, the condition of the politically ostracized is more hopeless and degraded. John Stuart Mill, in his work *On Liberty,* shows that the condition of one disfranchised man in a nation is worse than when the whole nation is under one man, because in the latter case, if the one man is despotic, the nation can easily throw him off, but what can one man do with a nation of tyrants over him? If American women find it hard to bear the oppression of their own Saxon Fathers, the best orders of manhood, what may she not be called to endure when all the lower orders of foreigners now crowding our shores legislate for her and her daughters. Think of Patrick and Sambo and Hans and Yung Tung, who do not know the difference between a monarchy and a republic, who cannot read the Declaration of Independence or Webster's spelling book, making laws for Lucretia Mott, Ernestine L. Rose, Susan B. Anthony, or Anna E. Dickinson. Think of jurors and jailors drawn from these ranks to watch and try young girls for the crime of infanticide, to decide the moral code by which the mothers of this republic shall be governed? This Manhood Suffrage is an appalling question, and it would be well for thinking women, who seem to consider it so magnanimous to hold their own claims in abeyance until all men are crowned with citizenship, to remember that the most ignorant men are ever the most hostile to the equality of women, as they have known her only in slavery and degradation.

"Manhood Suffrage" is national suicide and woman's destruction. Every consideration of patriotism as well as personal safety warns the women of the republic to demand their speedy enfranchisement. Go to our courts of justice, our jails, and prisons; go into the world of work; into the trades and professions; into the temples of science and learning; and see what is meted out everywhere to women; to those who have no advocates in our courts, no representative in the councils of the nation. Hester Vaught, a young English girl, under sentence of death for the alleged crime of infanticide, which could not be proved against her, has dragged out the weary days of a whole year in the solitude and gloom of a Pennsylvania prison, while her destroyer walks this green earth in freedom, enjoying alike the sunshine and the dews of heaven; and this girl sits alone in her cell weeping for friends and native land, while such men as Generals Cole and Sickles, who shot their wives' paramours dead before many witnesses, in broad daylight are not only acquitted but feasted and toasted by the press and the people! Such is "Manhood Suffrage." Shall we prolong and perpetuate injustice, and by increasing this power, risk worse oppressions for ourselves and daughters? It is an open, deliberate insult to American womanhood to be thus cast down under the iron-heeled peasantry of the old world and the slaves of the new, as we shall be in the practical working of the Fifteenth Amendment, and the only atonement the Republican party can make is now to complete its work by enfranchising the women of the nation and thus blot out their dark record on this question. I have not forgotten their action four years ago when Article 14, Sec. 2 was amended by invidiously introducing the word "male" into the Federal Constitution, where it had never been before, thus counting out of the basis of representation all men not permitted to vote, thereby making it the interest of every state to enfranchise its male citizens and virtually declaring it no crime to disfranchise its women. As political sagacity moved our rulers thus to guard the interests of the negro for party purposes, common justice might have compelled them to show like respect for their own mothers, by counting woman too, out of the basis of representation, that she might no longer swell the numbers to legislate adversely to her interests. And this desecration of the last will and testament of the Fathers, this retrogressive legislation for woman, was in the face of the earnest protests of thousands of the best educated, most refined, and cultivated women of the North. Now, when the attention of the whole world is turned to this question of Suffrage, and women themselves are throwing off the lethargy of ages, and in England, France, Germany, Switzerland and Russia are holding their conventions, and their rulers are everywhere giving them a respectful hearing, shall American statesmen, claiming to be liberal, so amend their constitutions as to make their wives and mothers the political inferiors of unlettered and unwashed ditch-diggers, boot-blacks, butchers, and barbers, fresh from the slave plantations of the South and the effete civilizations of the old world? While poets and philosophers, statesmen and men of science are all alike pointing to women as the new hope for the redemption of the race, shall the freest government on the earth be first to establish an aristocracy based on sex alone? To exalt ignorance above education, vice above virtue, brutality and barbarism above refinement and religion? Not since God first called light out of darkness and order of chaos was there ever made so base a proposition as "Manhood Suffrage" in this American Republic after all the discussions we have had on human rights in the last century. On all the blackest pages of history there is no record of an act like this, in any nation, where native born citizens, having the same religion, speaking the same language, equal to their rulers in wealth, family, and education, have been politically ostracized by their own countrymen, outlawed with savages, and subjected to the government of outside barbarians. Remember the Fifteenth Amendment takes in a larger population than the 2,000,000 black men on the southern plantation. It takes in all the foreigners daily landing in our eastern cities, the Chinese crowding our western shores, the inhabitants of Alaska and all those western isles that will soon be ours. American statesmen may flatter themselves that by superior intelligence and political sagacity the higher orders of men will always govern, but when the ignorant foreign vote already holds the balance of power in this country by sheer force of numbers, it is simply a question of impulse or passion, bribery or fraud, how our elections will be carried. When the highest offices of the people are bought and sold in Wall Street, it is a mere chance who will be our rulers. Whither is a nation tending when brains count for less than bullion and clowns make laws for Queens. It is a startling assertion, but nevertheless true, that in none of the nations of modern Europe are the higher classes of women politically so degraded as are the women of this republic to-day. In the old world, where the government is the aristocracy, where it is considered a mark of nobility to share its offices and powers, women of rank have certain hereditary rights which raise them above a majority of the men, certain honors and privileges not granted to serfs and peasants. There women are Queens, hold subordinate offices, and vote on many questions. In our southern states, even before the war, women were not degraded below the working population. They were not humiliated, in seeing their coachmen, gardeners, and waiters go to the polls to legislate for them; but here, in this boasted Northern civilization, women of wealth and education, who pay taxes and obey the laws, who in morals and intellect are the peers of their proudest rulers, are thrust outside the pale of political consideration with minors, paupers, lunatics, traitors, idiots, with those guilty of bribery, larceny, and infamous crimes.

Would those gentlemen who are on all sides telling the women of the nation not to press their claims until the negro is safe beyond a peradventure, be willing themselves to stand aside and trust all their interests to hands like this?

The educated women of this nation feel as much interest in republican institutions, the preservation of the country, the good of the race, their own elevation and success, as any man possibly can, and we have the same distrust in man's power to legislate for us that he has in woman's power to legislate wisely for herself.

4. I would press the Sixteenth Amendment, because the history of

American statesmanship does not inspire me with confidence in man's capacity to govern the nation alone, with justice and mercy. I have come to this conclusion, not only from my own observation, but from what our rulers say of themselves. Honorable Senators have risen in their places again and again and told the people of the wastefulness and corruption of the present Administration. Others have set forth, with equal clearness, the ignorance of our rulers on the question of Finance. Nearly every man in Congress has some different project for stealing the industry of the people, and each one declares that every plan but his own is the ruin of commerce and the destruction of the nation. It is easy to see that all are alike afloat on questions of political economy, jurisprudence, and government, and equally obtuse on political honor and morality. With legislation practically in the hands of a few capitalists who have the power to buy up all the votes they need for a given measure, who regulate the banking system, taxes, rates of interests, gamble in the national debt, send gold and all kinds of stocks up and down at their pleasure, who own the railroads, public lands, government bonds, national banks, ocean and river steamers —the rich will protect their own interests and perpetuate their power, while the laboring classes will be reduced to squalid poverty and utter dependence The most casual observer can trace the same causes at work here that have ever impoverished the masses in the old world. Already we see bloated wealth and gaunt poverty walking side by side in New York as well as in London. That these extremes in society have always existed is no argument for their continuance. Because politicians are ignorant of the laws of political economy and leave everything, as they say, to regulate itself, is no reason why the people should wreck their own interests by following their example. Do not let us longer confound the designs of providence with the legitimate results of human legislation. Priests and politicians from the beginning have hoodwinked the masses with the idea that all the ills of life were divine mercies, for their purification, the good things the result of civil and ecclesiastical organization. It is not Providence who is opening to-day a kind of Pandora's box, destroying the virtue and honor of the people, but our corrupt rulers, who, by their selfish and unjust legislation, have demoralized the political sentiment of the whole country. Everyone who thinks and observes the signs of the times knows that the heart of this nation is rotten to the very core. We have bribery and corruption in all the departments of the government at Washington, in our state legislatures and courts of justice in every branch of commerce and trade.

The recent revelations in the *New York World,* showing the wholesale frauds and adulterations, the short weights, the poisonous substances in all we eat and rink, sacrificing alike the health of man and beast, the petty lying and cheating, the contemptible tricks of trade—all make a fearful picture of human depravity. Verily, like the Israelites of old, we seem to be wholly given over to the worship of the golden calf, and on the altar of mammon we are to-day sacrificing the manhood and womanhood of the nation, our free institutions and glorious country, already twice baptized in the blood of a brave and generous people.

What woman can stand an unmoved spectator while our noblest men in high places are, one after another, drawn down this whirlpool of bribery and corruption? If the strongest and bravest can scarce keep foothold, what can we hope for the young, the weak, the inexperienced? When every morning paper heralds a downfall of some man whom the people have loved, praised, and honored; when Presidents, Senators, Congressmen, Governors, Foreign Ministers, and leading journalists are buried in a common grave, while the living laugh at their misfortunes, dip their pens in gall to blacken their memories like beasts of prey, devour the dead, oh! let the mothers of this nation go watch and pray at the doors of these sepulchres of human hopes and ambition, for unless some power can galvanize the slumbering virtue of this people to new life, the first-born in every household will be sacrificed to mammon:

> "We count the graves of friends now dead
> Within God's acre, holy ground;
> But who the hopes that daily die
> Without a struggle or a sound?"

"We have just finished battle," says Henry Ward Beecher, "for the life of the republic; another one lies right before us. It is the battle of mammon. Capital rightly employed is civilizing and beneficent. As a corrupter it is almost omnipotent. Already our government is assailed by it. If a new administration can find no remedy and things go on as they have, the end is at hand. The purse will outweigh the Constitution. The lobby will control the public policy. If not arrested, mammon will soon be mightier than the President, Senators, and Representatives. Is it for citizens to sit calmly by without a cry or protest, and see one thing after another swept away by this yellow stream that beats against Congress, Legislature, and the Judiciary and threatens to undermine them?"

What thinking mind can look for any improvement in extending Suffrage still farther to the very class that have so terribly demoralized the politics of the nation?

5. I demand the adoption of the Sixteenth Amendment, because the present isolation of the sexes is opposed to the teachings of science, philosophy, and common sense. Comte, the distinguished French writer, in his Positive philosophy, shows clearly that the first step towards social reorganization involves the education and elevation of woman. It is only in giving her sentiments and affections development and an enlightened direction that governments can be made stable, that capital and labor can be reconciled, intellect and activity harmonized.

All late writers on the science of government recognize in woman the great harmonizing element of the new era we are now entering, in which life is to be held sacred, the interests of all guarded, labor dignified, the criminal treated like a moral patient, education made practical and attractive, and brought within the reach of all. Any scientific observer of the sexes, even in the present false condition of society, can see that their mutual influence is ever restraining and elevating. Boys brought up with women are more gentle, pure-minded, and conscientious than those educated wholly by their own sex.

So girls brought up with men are ever more vigorous in thought and action, less vain and frivolous, than when under the care of women alone. Boys and girls in schools together are more healthy and refined in all their associations than either sex alone. When we ask that woman be admitted into the world of politics that it may be purified and elevated, it is not that we consider woman better than man, but that the noblest sentiments of both are called out by such associations. In California and Oregon, when society there was chiefly male and rapidly tending to savagism, women in large numbers went out, and order and decency were soon restored to life. Look, too, at woman's influence in the world of letters. Though she was long forbidden to read and write, and has scarce been recognized in literature until within the last century, yet what a change she has already wrought in popular taste. When she began to read and think and write, such men as Fielding, Rousseau, Swift, and Smollet went out of fashion and became themselves the target for the poisoned arrows they had prepared for her.

No man to-day would be willing to blot out from the literature of the world all the gems of thought that woman has contributed in the last century. The distinguished historian, Henry Thomas Buckle, said, "the turn of thought of women, their habits of mind, insensibly extending over the whole surface of society and frequently penetrating its most intimate structure, have, more than all other things put together, tended to raise us into an ideal world and lift us from the dust into which we are too prone to grovel."

"Manhood Suffrage" is the ignoring of this grand element in government, while the nation is languishing to-day for some new virtue, honor, and truth, some new inspiration to galvanize a slumbering manhood into life.

While such men as John Stuart Mill, Herbert Spencer, Mazzini, Gasparin, Labouiaye, and Jules Favre are all alike pointing to woman as the sun and centre of the higher civilization, shall not American Senators make haste to lay all the rights, privileges, and immunities of citizenship at the feet of their own countrywomen—the noblest type of womankind on which the sun has ever shone? While eloquent tongues in England, France, Germany, and Italy are paying glowing tributes to woman and prophesying for her a nobler future, why is it that the liberal party in this country, whose talk is all of human rights, is so deaf and dumb on woman, when she is the theme the world over? Are the women of this nation less worthy of respect than those of other lands? Nay, nay, America can boast thousands of wives and mothers as remarkable for their domestic virtue as Victoria has been, and many women whose eloquence can far surpass that echoed in the British Parliament by England's Queen.

6. I urge The Sixteenth Amendment on your consideration, because the safety and dignity of woman demand her immediate enfranchisement. "Manhood Suffrage" creates an antagonism everywhere between educated, refined women and the lower orders of men especially at the South, where the slaves of yesterday are the law-makers of to-day. It not only rouses woman's prejudices against the negro but his hostility and contempt for her. Just as the Democratic party cry of a White Man's government created the antagonism between the Irishman and the negro, culminating in the New York riots of 1863, so the Republican cry of "Manhood Suffrage" creates an antagonism between black men and all women and must culminate in tearful outrages on womanhood—especially in the southern states. While I fully appreciate the philosophy that every extension of rights prepares the way to greater freedom to new classes and hastens the day for liberty to all, I at the same time see that the immediate effect of class enfranchisement results in greater tyranny on those who have no

voice in the government. Had Irishmen been disfranchised in this country they would have made common cause with the negro in fighting for their rights, but when exalted above him, they proved his worst enemies. The negro will be the victims, for a generation to come, of the prejudice engendered by the legislation that made this a white man's government. While the enfranchisement of each new class of white men was a step toward his ultimate freedom, it increased his degradation in the transition period, and he touched the depths of human misery when all men but the negro were crowned with citizenship. Just so with woman. While the enfranchisement of all men will haste the day of justice to her, yet her degradation too, in the transition period, will be more complete, and we would fain have woman escape the tyranny, persecutions, insults, and horrors that will surely be hers in the establishment of an aristocracy of sex.

Until the blow is struck in their own home circle, few husbands or fathers appreciate the depths of degradation to which womanhood is daily subjected by the lower orders of ignorant, brutal men, taught by their edicts to believe themselves the rightful owners and masters of all womankind. One cannot take up a daily paper without reading some terrible outrage committed by Germans, Irishmen, or negroes, on refined, educated women of all classes, from the dignified matron on her way to church, to the sweet girl of sixteen, gathering wild flowers in the forest on her way to school. Such are but the outgrowth, of the sentiments and statutes of the higher orders of men of the position of women in the church, the state, and the home. All this talk about woman being too good, too pure, too exalted to vote, is the sheerest hypocrisy, it is a sham and a fraud, for our customs, laws, and opinions all harmonize with the idea of degradation.

It was thought at one time that the Priesthood were too good to vote, and in their case see how well our laws and customs harmonized with that idea. All men pay more respect to the black coat than any other. They are treated like a superior order. The people give the clergy houses to live in, clothes to wear, food to eat. They are a privileged class with all the trades and professions. Lawyers fight their battles for nothing, physicians prescribe for their families without charge. They are the special favorites of the law, too, $1,500 of their property is not taxed. But what one of all these privileges is bestowed upon woman? None whatever. With her the practice is all reversed. She does everything for the rest of the world at half price. She is taxed on all she eats and drinks and wears, and pays full price for all her necessities and luxuries. This is her exaltation. But what, say you, has the ballot to do with all this. Much everyway. The ballot is the symbol of equality, and to recognize woman's equality in every position of life is to teach her self-respect, dignify her in the eyes of man, and throw new safe-guards round her virtue. Let society do as much towards dignifying the woman as the Priest, teach the masses that there is no office so sacred as motherhood, and thus it is a fouler sacrilege to desecrate a young innocent girl than any altar or holy symbol of the church, and we shall soon end the gross assaults on woman so common to-day. We judge of woman's real position by the facts of every-day life, not by the stale platitudes of sickly sentimentalists.

We see something more in the ballot "than a slip of paper, dropped in to a box once a year, to choose a county sheriff." It has a deeper signifi-cance. It is the recognition of the civil, political, and social equality of the citizen. It is throwing aside the badge of degradation for the shield of sov-ereignty, an unknown signature for the seal of the State.

Seeing woman, not only in our own country, but in all the nations of northern Europe, throwing off the lethargy of ages and demanding an ex-tension of rights;—seeing the deep and wide-spread interest among lead-ing minds everywhere in this question;—clearly reading the signs or the times, my pulse beats proudly to-day for enfranchised womanhood, as if my life-long hopes were already fully realized, for as I look through the mists of the dark past and onward to the shining future and mark each milestone of progress on the highway of civilization, I see we are already on the boundaries of that better land where moral power shall govern brute force. Dazzled with the coming glory, it is wearisome to parley with carping minds to-day, answer their absurd objections, listen to their stale platitudes and puny insults to womanhood.

I look not to the old barbarisms of the past, to creeds, or codes, or cus-toms, to learn the rights, the dignity, the destiny of woman, but to the teachings of my own soul, to the inner and the great outer world that lies beyond human legislation.

From yonder hill top, at the setting sun, with Nature in her sweet, con-fiding moods, one may learn all they care to know of human destiny. In hours like this, I have asked the majestic rivers, mighty forests, and eternal hills that in their yearnings seem to touch the heavens; I have asked the sun, the moon, the stars that for ages have looked down on human weal and woe; I have asked my own soul in moments of exaltation and humili-ation, if women, who, in thought, can touch the invisible, explore the planetary world, encompass land and sea, was made by her Creator to be a slave, a subject; a mere reflection of another human will? and in solemn chorus, one and all have answered, no! no!! no!!!

SOURCE: Elizabeth Cady Stanton, "Address to Anniversary of American Equal Rights Association, May 12, 1869, New York City," *The Revolution,* vol. 3, no. 19, 289–91.

Chapter 5

"Subjection of Women" (1875)

EDITORS' NOTE: The title of the speech make it clear that Stanton saw herself in discussion with John Stuart Mill, whose book of the same name appeared eight years earlier in 1867. While Mill wrote from the position of a man, providing calm, reasoned arguments against the subordination of women and a vision of more egalitarian, harmonious marriages, Stanton wrote as a woman who knew full well both the intimate sufferings and the wide capacities of her sex. The other context for this speech is the legal defeat of the efforts of numerous suffragists, including Susan B. Anthony, to take voting into their own hands on the basis of "new departure" arguments. In this speech, in strong contrast with the previous selection, Stanton makes common cause with labor and "subjugated races." "Subjection of Women" goes beyond the demand for political rights to call for a thorough investigation of the deeper roots of women's subjection.

O. B. Frothingham in his late work on the "Religion of Humanity" tells us that "some of the deepest students into the melancholy history of woman's subjection bring back the cheerful report" that her multiplied wrongs and oppressions have their origin not in the tyranny and selfishness of man but in "an unintelligent and well-meaning kindness." In rude time of strife, pillage, and lust, woman's condition was necessarily one of perpetual guardianship in order to preserve her purity and social position. Her family were her protectors. Her Father's authority was her shield, his power her defence, his wealth her provision, insult to her was affront to him, wrong to her brought down his vengeance. She was rooted in the family, could not be detached; in passing from the guardianship of parents, she passed into the guardianship of a second parent. Her husband was in law her Father. It was in his capacity of Father that he acquired rights over her person and property. She was not his slave but daughter, his own blood as it were, part and parcel of himself. The worst injustices, the worst indignities against woman, had this kindly root. True he says, "this root is so deep down under the ground that none but the keenest-sighted naturalists suspect it," but we shall accept the assertion and see how well the facts of our times prove its truthfulness.

It is pleasant for those of us who can trace relationship to some of those sons of Adam to know that men are not as bad as they seem to be. "If in things most evil there is a soul of goodness, our faith in the moral constitution of things is justified." Without however going centuries back to analyze the component elements of man's chivalry, let us glance at his successive acts of goodness in our own day and generation, in the full faith that however bad his deeds may seem on the surface, all injustices and oppressions have been perpetrated against woman, from the highest motives of kindness and protection. If this is true of the Hebrews, Egyptians, Persians, Greeks, and Romans, it must hold true of the German, French, English, and American. When the heroes of 76 made their constitution for the protection of men only, it was not from indifference, or design that they made no mention of woman, but because they knew her natural delicacy would revolt at having her name hawked about in constitutions and declarations, booming at the mouth of the cannon round the globe. When they incorporated the old English laws, by which a wife of to-day is there an actual bond slave, into our codes, they were moved by no feelings of selfishness or tyranny, but a tender sense of her need of guardianship or protection. They legislated her property into their own pockets, that she need not lumber her brain with our complicated systems of finance, with stocks, mortgages, tariffs, and taxes. And they spent her money too, to save her the degradation of bartering on the street corners, in the market place, or exchange; they understood her wants and needs far better than she possibly could herself. True the man on whom this particular woman depended was oftimes ignorant and incompetent himself, or suddenly translated to another sphere, leaving the wife all unprepared to depend on herself, but then that extra sense with which God in his mercy has endowed all women, namely "intuition" came in, enabling her to do things of which she had never dreamt before, changing her in one hour from a helpless dependent to a self, reliant with power.

Thus finding herself ever and anon her own guardian and protector, some women thought it would be wise, by a thorough education, to prepare themselves for the emergencies of life, and begged the privilege of entering the colleges of law, medicine, and divinity. But these excellent men said no, not because they desired to keep woman ignorant and dependent, and feared her competition with themselves, for they all assert that there is nothing in the universe they so much admire as a highly educated woman, and that for the offices of wife and mother woman needs all knowledge; but they feared lest the sciences of physics, jurisprudence, and theology, and contact with the men who fill the temples of learning might demoralize these ideal beings, who are supposed to live in the clouds, to gaze on the stars and the sons of earth from a lofty distance, quite forgetting that the actual woman digs and delves by the side of man all through the hum drum of life. But in the face of all this "unintelligent and self-demeaning kindness" on the part of these good men, women have steadily taken possession of one stronghold after another and are destined to conquer many more. The good men are frightened from their propriety with each new step of aggression, but as the root of all their opposition is based on love, it gracefully yields in time to the inevitable. When women held their first convention the men laughed good naturedly from Maine to California, knowing a rebellion against their best friends must die out in sixty days. But it has gone on twenty-five years. In this quarter of a century of work woman has worked her way into the schools, colleges, hospitals, pulpits, and editorial chairs, into many branches of trade and commerce, and into the telegraph, printing, and post offices. This has been done by argument and assertion, by persistent work, and by taking the positions she claimed. When girls first went into the printing offices, the men laid down their type and walked off. According to Mr. Frothingham, they meant no indignity, but feeling their own unworthiness to stand beside such exalted beings they reverently veiled their faces and retired. When Theodore Cuyler's church was thrown into convulsions by the preaching of Sarah Smiley in their pulpit, it was not because they respected woman less but Paul more. "Good men" are apt to be governed more by authorities and precedents than reason, and those Brooklyn deacons feared that while Miss Smiley's preaching might turn sinners to repentance, it would also turn the Roman Apostle with horror in his grave. For the same reason women are solemnly warned to keep silent in the Fulton Street prayer meeting. It matters not that American women in the 19th century can pray and preach acceptably to God and men, so long as Corinthian women, who could do neither, were forbidden to try 1800 years ago. I wish all deacons would remember, that while each generation makes its own history, it must make its own laws and customs also. And what shall we say of the lawyers, judges, statesmen, and politicians, who deny women the rights of citizenship and compel them to discharge its duties. They must obey the laws; they are forbidden to study in the universities, to practice in the courts, or to discuss and pass in the legislative assemblies. After all these years of discussion, can these gentlemen be "unintelligent" on all the interests involved in this question? The resolution passed at the Massachusetts state convention, pledging the Republican party squarely to woman's suffrage, and the 14th plank in the national platform solemnly promising "respectful consideration of the rights of women["] show plainly that the men of our day thoroughly understand the situation, and that no well-meaning kindness coats the bitter pills of insult and ridicule the women of this republic are daily compelled to swallow. Myra Bradwell is denied the right to practice law in the state of Illinois because she is a married woman. I wonder if she thinks the roots of this decision are based deep down in love. Catherine Stebbins is denied the right to vote in Michigan because she is a married woman, while Annette Gardner at the same time is allowed to vote because she is a widow. Are these men blind that they do not see they are offering bounties or sending husbands off at pack horse speed to heaven? We must think these thrusts at marriage were a premium on celibacy, but lo! Susan B. Anthony, a Republican spinster in Rochester N.Y., having duly registered her name and voted, is arrested by U.S. Republican officers for voting a clean Republican ticket. Carrie Burnham, spinster in Philadelphia, offers her vote and is refused. Whereupon the United States sues the former and the latter sues the United States.

What a labyrinth of difficulties! with these "unintelligent and well meaning kindnesses." Where is all this to end? In the triumph of woman, in her individual sovereignty, in the grand march of progress, her turn has come. Perhaps in the coming centennial celebration of our nation's birth, as women are called to help in the busy preparations, the century may round out with her enfranchisement and the old Liberty bell ring in equality for all. She has already conquered so many difficulties, so many places in the trades and professions, in art, science, and literature, that she has earned the crown of American citizenship. And in all its rights, honors, and dignities, she should be now secured.

As by persistent demand we have gained the heights we hold to-day, so by our own self assertion must we achieve the rights we are still denied. Susan B. Anthony, whom we have long jocosely called the Napoleon of our movement, is leading off in the right direction. Being a citizen of the United States, she is determined to exercise the rights of a citizen. The authorities say she shall not. Thus she found herself at war with the United States and on the 17th of June her rights as a belligerent were tried and decided. On the anniversary of the battle of Bunker Hill, she was denied the sacred right of trial by jury, as Judge Hunt ordered a verdict of guilty and sentenced her as a criminal to pay a fine of one hundred dollars for exercising a citizen's right of suffrage. It must have been a great consolidation to Miss Anthony to know that her sentence was "rooted in love": a ray of sunshine in that dark hour to remember that the arbitrary form of trial was owing to the "unintelligent and well-meaning kindness" of the Judiciary of the United States. Though guilty of the grossest outrage on the Constitutional liberties of a citizen yet the judge behaved like a well-bred gentleman. The polite way in which he robbed Miss Anthony of her most sacred rights reminded me of a remark of Charles O'Conner. Some one asked him what he thought of Judge Hunt. "Judge Hunt," said he, "why I think he is a very lady-like judge."

The case of Carrie S. Burnham decided in the Supreme Court of Pennsylvania about the same time is interesting as showing that "this unintelligent and well-meaning kindness" is apparent in all latitudes. I have just reread the very able argument of Miss Burnham before the court and the opinion of Hon. George Sharswood the presiding judge, and I must say I should rather be the author of the argument than the opinion. In the Pennsylvania Constitution the word "freeman" was at that time substituted for "white male." As the women of that state pay taxes and the penalty of their crimes, Carrie S. Burnham inferred they were "freemen" and had the right to vote, but according to the Judge the word "freemen" had a pickwickian sense, not quite broad enough to include women. Reading the able arguments of Miss Anthony and Miss Burnham in pleading a right for themselves, already secured to every type of degraded manhood in the nation, remembering the youth of the one and the age of the other, and seeing how little effect in both cases, the ablest arguments and highest moral considerations seemed to produce on the opinions of these stolid courts, I felt afresh the mockery of this boasted chivalry of man towards woman. As I read history old and new the subjection of woman may be clearly traced to the same cause that subjugated different races and nations to one another, the law of force, that made might right and the weak the slaves of the strong. Men mistake all the time their reverence for an ideal womanhood for a sense of justice towards the actual being, that shares with them the trials of life. Man's love and tenderness to one particular woman for a time is no criterion for his general feeling for the whole sex for all time. The same man that would die for one woman would make an annual holocaust of others, if his appetites or pecuniary interests required it. Kind husbands and Fathers that would tax every nerve and muscle to the uttermost to give their wives and daughters every luxury, would grind multitudes of women to powder in the world of work for the same purpose.

The subjection of woman to man in the best conditions is rooted in selfishness and sensuality, so insidious in its tyranny that I can liken it only to the subjection of the higher faculties, sentiments, and affections of the individual to the gross animal propensities. Of all kinds of slavery the most hopeless and pitiful is that of an individual of genius, power, ambition, bound to the earth by an appetite. Many of our greatest men have been victims of intemperance, gluttony, or licentiousness. If man will thus abuse himself, subjugate his whole moral and spiritual nature, will he not make woman his victim, impelled by the strongest appetite in his being? Does he not need all the restraint of law and gospel, custom, and constitution to teach him justice to woman, and should not the state and the church throw round her every shield to make her self-reliant and independent instead of making as now, by their creeds and codes, the strong stronger and the weak more helpless? We have arrived at the point in civilization when woman demands a union with man higher and more enduring that that of the chivalry based on sex. The great lesson the reform we press teaches *sex* in mind. A recognition of the masculine and feminine element in art, science, philosophy, and literature will give new force and zest to life and love and lift the race from the animal plane, where woman's degradation holds it to-day. In this higher civilization woman must lead. In demanding political equality we do not begin with the soul of the question. The ballot box is but one of the outposts of progress, a victory that all orders of men can see and understand. Only the few can grasp the metaphysics of this question in all its social, religious, and political bearings, and appreciate the moral effect of according all outward honor and dignity to woman.

We must educate in every way woman's self-respect and show man the momentous responsibilities that rest on her elevation, that all the best interests of the race are at stake in her ignorance and degradation. Let good men in high places remember that their words and sentiments find expression in the acts of the ignorant masses. So long as the press and pulpit of a country teach the subjection of women, so long will our journals be compelled to chronicle the outrages on womanhood so rife to-day. Thieves and robbers seldom enter churches to desecrate the altars or sacramental service, because they are taught from childhood to reverence these temples and emblems of sacred mysteries. They care not for the theologies, the doctrines, the catechisms or the discipline, but they see the great and good pay deference to the externals of religion and they are awed to respect. But who alas! teaches honor and reverence for woman? And yet does not the mother of the race hold a more important place in civilization, than golden goblets, altars, and cathedral walls? Does not the growth of generations, in goodness wisdom and power depend more on the status of womanhood than the Church? We all hesitate to undermine another's religious faith however hedged about with superstitions, knowing the need of every soul for some Gibraltar rock on which to stand. But who fears to undermine the faith of sons and daughters in her who gave them birth? No holy influence held so light! The church tells them, the woman is the weaker vessel, unworthy to enter the presence of God, to preach and pray in the assemblies of the people. The heaven-ordained condition of the wife is in subjection to the husband, drunk or sober, a failure or success.

The laws and the customs of society echo the same ideas. I will not stoop now to quote the insulting laws that degrade ever statute book in the union, but I recommend every woman to read a tract just prepared by Carrie Burnham, a digest of the laws of Pennsylvania for the women of that state. These laws have a twofold influence. They not only cripple and oppress woman in every civil action, but they lower the moral tone of society and woman herself in her own estimation. We cannot estimate the far-reaching demoralization of training the best minds in our country, the expounders of the science of jurisprudence and Constitutional law, in a one-sided justice, that violates the first principles of republican government. No matter how noble the women of their households, what must be the impression in the minds of young men in our law schools, when they first read the codes for women and the opinions of judges as to their status in law and nature.

Charles Sumner in his able speeches made on the passage of the 13th, 14th, and 15th Amendments, clearly traces the evil effects of slavery on the law, religion, and public sentiment of the entire nation. From the standpoint of the slaveholder, constitutions were interpreted and decisions in the supreme courts of the United States given in violation of every principle of natural rights. If the slavery of 4,000,000 Africans on southern plantations could thus make the eternal principles of justice in their administration as uncertain as the sands on the sea shore and poison the fountains of our political, religious, commercial, and social life throughout the union, must not the violation of the same principles in the case of 20,000,000 women in every state of the union cause equal judicial blindness, clerical hypocrisy, and social demoralization? In the case of the slave, statesmen saw that emancipation was a mockery without the power to legislate for himself, and from the highest moral considerations they gave him the ballot for his protection. Politicians saw their party success depended on the votes of the slave, and from humbler motives they said give him the right of suffrage. We ask statesmen to apply the same principles for woman's protection. We ask politicians to use the same policy for their own success in the reorganization of parties.

Do you think the women on this platform have persistently demanded the right of suffrage for twenty-five years, merely to enjoy the pleasure of going to the polls to vote for a Gov. Tilden or Mayor Wickham or to get some picayune office for themselves or some male relation?

I ask to exercise this right first 1st because it is my right and all women need this power for their dignity, protection, and moral influence. With man's chivalry for the one woman he loves, he feels it must be safe to trust the rights of all women to all men, but the experience of life teaches us a different lesson. Brutal men kill wives, daughters, sisters, mothers. Respectable men cheat the women of their households out of their substance. Lawyers can tell of cases on their calendars of Fathers defrauding daughters, brothers, sisters, husbands wives, of their rights of property. Look how women are treated in the world of work crowded into a few employments and half paid there. When a girl is prospective heir to a crown in the old world, every advantage of education is accorded her. She is trained to higher dignity of speech and manner, fitting the station for which she is destined. Our throne is self-government, our crown equality, our sceptre the ballot, and when American girls are heirs to these, the colleges will open wide their doors and vie with each other for the honor of educating these heirs apparent to the rights of American citizens. They will be honored in the world of work, expurgated editions of the creeds and codes will be speedily issued, and party, pulpit, and press will treat woman citizens with as much respect as they now do the new-made southern freeman and the unlettered foreigner, just landed on our shores.

To save the nation from the demoralization openly confessed in every branch of our government, noble woman should be willing to use their influence to elevate the tone of our politics and ensure a wiser policy on many questions. History is full of incidents of woman's wisdom and heroism in hours of distress and danger. What a Florence Nightingale, a Clara Barton, a Grace Darling, an Ida Lewis have done for wounded soldiers and drowning sailors, women who study the political horoscope may soon do for the entire nation's life and save our ship of state now drifting for Lambro light. A page of German history in 1140 tells us of the Duke of Guelph besieged in Weisburgh by Conrad III and being hard pressed he capitulated on the terms that the women should be allowed to depart in safety taking with them all they could carry. Accordingly the Duchess came forth bearing the Duke on her shoulders and all the women of the city with their husbands. The conquerors were so surprised and pleased with this manifestation of woman's strength and devotion that they watched the exodus in silence and inaction. If the hope of family safety could thus nerve faint hearts and make feeble arms so strong, cannot a nation's safety, the triumph of those great principles of republican government so dearly bought and ofttimes redeemed, rouse the women of our day to action.

Great as our country is in her boundless acres, majestic forests, mighty lakes and rivers, and inexhaustible sources of wealth, she has hidden treasures in the undeveloped powers of her women, that if employed would add more to the wealth of the state, than all our other resources together. The white man's "wards" have all alike, Africans, Indians, women and labor, been crippled by his guardianship and protection, and have alike avenged themselves, by art and stratagem outside the rules of war, because denied fair action and debate. His protection has been like that of the eagle to the lamb he carries to his eyrie. I think we should all be willing to forego such protection and stand on our own feet. I often wonder in reading the able articles of the *New York World* on free trade, that it so seldom touches on this most odious form of "protection." We have thrown the African race on its own responsibility and it does not crave the old guardianship again. The best policy we can inaugurate for the Indian is to treat him the same way. Make no discrimination for or against him, hunger and taxation and the just penalty for individual crime would soon settle the problem of work, property, and law. He will stay at home and raise cattle instead of ponies when he provides his own beef and flour. And this is all one asks for woman, the same advantages, opportunities, and code of laws man claims for himself, no discriminations on the ground of sex, no "protection," but justice, liberty, equality, and as these are the cornerstones of national life, peace, prosperity. All partial reforms wait woman's enfranchisement.

The cry of "peace" is mockery, so long as its fundamental principles are scouted as glittering generalities. With 20,000,000 women in chains, with labor ground to powder between the upper and nether millstones of ava-

rice and ignorance, with the church enforcing poverty as a divine ordination, and the state enforcing it by cunning legislation, our jails and prisons
crowded with helpless victims waiting for the tardy justice that seldom
comes, the cry of peace from our leaders is as vain and guilty as it would
have been from the watchtower of the *Atlantic* in that awful hour when
700 souls went down.

Let these who preach temperance, who urge prohibitory law, review the
situation, look deep down for the causes of these overpowering animal appetites. Feeble desponding sons of sickly low-spirited mothers will crave
stimulants for mind and body alike, and no legislation can quench the
thirst, or destroy the means of gratification, so long as our chosen rulers
belong to the whiskey rings. Labor wretchedly housed, fed, and clothed,
when it can purchase Paradise, for a few hours by a dram, will not resist
the temptation. Luxury in its palace home, satiated with the good things
of life, with nothing to hope and nothing to do, if it can lighten its ennui
with a sparkling glass, who can wonder? The radical steps towards peace
and temperance are these: equality before the law; a generation of healthy
happy scientific mothers; educated labor, well housed, fed, clothed, an inviolable homestead; luxury driven to work by a system of graduated taxation. Temperance in the present diseased condition of the race, with the
extremes and antagonisms of its conditions, the risks and strain of competition, the anxieties and disappointments of success and failure, is impossible. Those who are overtaxed with work and those who are enervated for
lack of it will alike seek stimulants.

They who do most to equalize the conditions of society, will do the best
work for all reforms. If we trace all questions of national interest we shall
find that they run in parallel lines together and that each demands a more
radical work than yet done by any government. Let the people now awake
to their duty. That our rulers are lamentably neglecting their duty all admit. In a recent editorial in *The Christian Union*, the question, "is this a
well-governed nation" is thus answered:

What has Congress or any of our Legislatures done toward meeting the
labor difficulty? We readily admit that this class of subjects if full of per-
plexity, and that it is doubtful how far legislative action is called for upon
them. But they are of great and growing importance, and certainly not to
be ignored by any wise government. What have our governments done?
Massachusetts alone has taken action for getting light upon the matter by
official statistics, though this is the least that should be done. In general, our

politicians have confined themselves to buncombe resolutions. Often they have done worse than that. Congress has passed an eight-hour law for the national workmen. The law was a sheer piece of demagogism. It was not based on any intelligent conviction that eight hours was a fair day's work and should receive the old ten hours' wages. It was a sop to voters, and, as far as it went, it said to the laboring class, "Anything you want; only keep us in office!" We do not undertake to say what legislative action is needed in regard to labor; but we do say this: if in any State a hundred intelligent and disinterested men meet daily for three months to consult for the welfare of the community, "labor questions" would come in for a large share of their attention. Why do our governing bodies so entirely ignore this class of subjects? Is it lack of intelligence or of disposition?

Political government is the highest and most difficult of all social arts. The Government is the organ of the entire people in their collective capacity. In the governing power, therefore—which with us is really the legislative assembly—should be found not only pureness of purpose, but the best practical sagacity, the most intelligent consideration of common interests, that the community can afford.

In what degree do our Congress and our average Legislatures display these qualities? We have lately had startling evidence of the want among them of even average honesty. But, waiving for the present any discussion as to the positive corruption in our governing bodies, there is another indictment to be brought against most of them, which is serious enough. We find everywhere the radical trouble that our legislators do not intelligently attend to their proper work. In theory, their business is to take care of the whole community. In practice, to a great extent, their business is to take care for themselves and their party—terms which to a politicians generally mean the same thing. We see, continually, our Congress and our Legislatures slighting the gravest public interests and devoting themselves to squabbles in which the people is the only goose to be plucked. And the plucking is not the worst the goose has to suffer. What we complain of is not chiefly that these gentlemen at Washington and Albany and Harrisburg and elsewhere make us pay so heavily for their services. It is that we get so little in return. The matters most vital to the community—questions of finance, of labor, of social order, of public morals—are left untouched, or bungingly patched up, while it is being settled who shall have the custom-house or the post-office or the next seat in Congress.

Carl Schurz in a late speech in the Senate said

Do we not see and understand what is going on around us? What is it that attracts to the capital of the national that herd of monopolists and speculators and their agents who so assiduously lay siege to the judgment and also to the consciences of those who are to give to the country its laws? What is it that fills the lobbies of these halls with the atmosphere of temptation? What is it that brings forth such melancholy, such deplorable exhibitions as the American people have been beholding this winter, and which we would have been but too glad to hide from the eyes of the world abroad? It is that policy which uses the power of this great Government for the benefit of favored interests; that policy which takes money out of the pockets of the people to put it into the pockets of a few; that policy which in every country where it prevailed has poisoned the very fountain of legislation. Do you think that the consequences can be different here? Are not your great railroad kings and monopolists boasting that they can buy whole State Legislatures to do their bidding? Have we not seen some of them stalking around in this very Capitol like the sovereign lords of creation? Are not some of them vaunting themselves already that they have made and can make profitable investments in Congressmen and United States Senators? Have we not observed the charming catholicity of their operations and the breadth of their cosmopolitanism, as shown before the Credit Mobilier Committee of the House, when Dr. Durant said that he did not care whether the man he supported for election was a Republican or a Democrat, provided he was a good man. And now if you let them know that a man who has purchased his seat here, or for whom it has been purchased, with money, will be secure in the enjoyment of the property so bought, I ask you. Will not their enterprise be limited only by their desires? And will not their rapacious desires, from which the country has already suffered so much pecuniarily and morally, grow with their opportunities? As long as such evils are permitted to exercise their influences, they will spread with the power of contagion, and nothing but the most unflinching resistance can check them. Such is our condition. Everybody sees it and feels it.

It is time that we should face the dangers which threaten this Republic. It has no monarchical traditions, no pretenders of historic right to disturb its repose and to plot its overthrow. It is not likely to succumb to the shock of force. But there have been republics whose original Constitution was as healthy as ours, but which died after all of the slower disease of corruption and demoralization, and that decay of constitutional life and anarchy of power which always go hand in hand with them. It is time for us to keep in mind that it requires more to make and preserve a Republic than the mere absence of a king, and that when a Republic decays its soul is apt to die first, which its outward form may still be lasting.

One good effect of a Presidential campaign is that the rogues all betray each other. And what an unearthing of fraud and corruption we have had enough it seems to me to warn the women of this republic that they cannot trust the interest of 40,000,000 of people and the wealth of a continent to spendthrift and unprincipled legislators. Have the women of property in the state of New York no interest in the heavy taxes enforced by these rings, in bank defalcations, in the public school fund, whether used for good teachers, buildings, and sanitary conditions, or by a dishonest ring. Have women no interest in the accidents by land [or] sea, the result of imperfect rails, sleepers, bridges, boilers, vessels, and incompetent captains and conductors? All this comes from just that want of caution and care that woman with her greater love of life possesses and would sacredly guard if she had a word in the legislation of these matters.

Poets find great beauty in woman's blind faith in man's capacity to do not only his own work but hers also. It may do to turn a stanza but not for the emergencies of life. Had the passengers of the ill-fated *Atlantic* trusted less in their Captain and organized a police of their own to watch at night, how little care and time from each one might have saved that multitude from a watery grave.

Women of America, we are all passengers on the ship [of] state, to share its dangers and delays. We are sailing fast towards an unknown shore, there are breakers ahead, the watchmen in the towers are sleeping. Man's skill in battling with the waves, suspended and ropes and sails will avail us nothing. In the hour of danger without courage and strength in ourselves we must one and all be sacrificed.

SOURCE: Elizabeth Stanton, "Subjection of Women," in *The Papers of Elizabeth Cady Stanton and Susan B. Anthony* (Washington, D.C.: Library of Congress, 1979), reel 17, frames 462–87.

Chapter 6

"National Protection for National Citizens, Address to the Senate Committee on Privileges and Elections, January 11, 1878, Washington, D.C."

EDITORS' NOTE: Even as she pressed for a separate ("sixteenth") amendment for woman suffrage, Stanton continued to advocate universal citizenship and universal suffrage. In "National Protection for National Citizens" Stanton built on the positive lessons of Reconstruction, especially that national government was under obligation to act affirmatively to protect and secure the rights of all those "anomalous classes" of Americans deprived of their natural rights. Stanton reiterated, point by point, the constitutional case for women already having the right to vote without the necessity of any further "enabling" legislation, which the U.S. Supreme Court had heard and dismissed three years before in the Minor v. Happersett *case.*

In appearing before you to ask for a sixteenth amendment to the United States Constitution, permit me to say that with the Hon. Charles Sumner, we believe that our Constitution, fairly interpreted, already secures to the humblest individual all the rights, privileges and immunities of American citizens. But as statesmen differ in their interpretations of constitutional law as widely as they differ in their organizations, the rights of every class of citizens must be clearly defined in concise, unmistakable language. All the great principles of liberty declared by the fathers gave no protection to the black man of the republic for a century, and when, with higher light and knowledge his emancipation and enfranchisement were proclaimed, it was said that the great truths set forth in the prolonged debates of thirty years on the individual rights of the black man, culminating in the fourteenth and fifteenth amendments to the constitution, had no significance for woman. Hence we ask that this anomalous class of beings, not recognized by the supreme powers as either "persons" or "citizens" may be defined and their rights declared in the Constitution.

In the adjustment of the question of suffrage now before the people of this country for settlement, it is of the highest importance that the organic law of the land should be so framed and construed as to work injustice to none, but secure as far as possible perfect political equality among all classes of citizens. In determining your right and power to legislate on this question, consider what has been done already.

As the national constitution declares that "all persons born or naturalized in the United States and subject to the jurisdiction thereof, are citizens of the United States, and of the State wherein they reside," it is evident: *First*—That the immunities and privileges of American citizenship, however defined, are national in character and paramount to all State authority. *Second*—That while the Constitution leaves the qualification of electors to the several States, it nowhere gives them the right to deprive any citizen of the elective franchise; the State may regulate but not abolish the right of suffrage for any class. *Third*—As the Constitution of the United States expressly declares that no State shall make or enforce any law that shall abridge the privileges or immunities of citizens of the United States, those provisions of the several State constitutions that exclude citizens from the franchise on account of sex, alike violate the spirit and letter of the Federal Constitution. *Fourth*—As the question of naturalization is expressly withheld from the States, and as the States would clearly have no right to deprive of the franchise naturalized citizens, among whom women are expressly included, still more clearly have they no right to deprive native-born women-citizens of the right.

Let me give you a few extracts from the national constitution upon which these propositions are based:

> *Preamble*: We, the people of the United States, in order to form a more perfect union, establish justice, insure domestic tranquility provide for the common defense, promote the general welfare, and secure the blessings of liberty to ourselves and our posterity, do ordain and establish this constitution.

This is declared to be a government "of the people." All power, it is said, centers in the people. Our State constitutions also open with the words, "We, the people." Does any one pretend to say that men alone constitute races and peoples? When we say parents, do we not mean mothers as well as fathers? When we say children, do we not mean girls as well as boys? When we say people, do we not mean women as well as men? When the race shall spring, Minerva-like, from the brains of their fathers, it will be time enough thus to ignore the fact that one-half the human family are women. Individual rights, individual conscience and judgment are our great American ideas, the fundamental principles of our political and religious faith. Men may as well attempt to do our repenting, confessing. and believing. as our voting—as well represent us at the throne of grace as at the ballot-box.

> ARTICLE 1, SEC. 9.—No bill of attainder, or *ex post facto* law shall be passed; no title of nobility shall be granted by the United States.
> SEC . 10.—No State shall pass any bill of attainder *ex post facto* law, or law impairing the obligation of contracts, or grant any title of nobility.

Notwithstanding these provisions of the Constitution, bills of attainder have been passed by the introduction of the word "male" into all the State constitutions denying to woman the right of suffrage, and thereby making sex a crime. A citizen disfranchised in a republic is a citizen attainted. When we place in the hands of one class of citizens the right to make, interpret and execute the law for another class wholly unrepresented in the government, we have made an order of nobility.

> ARTICLE 4. SEC. 2.—The citizens of each State shall be entitled to all the privileges and immunities of citizens in the several States.

The elective franchise is one of the privileges secured by this section—approved in *Dunham* vs. *Lamphere* (3 Gray Mass. Rep., 276), and *Bennett* vs. *Boggs* (Baldwin's Rep., p. 72, Circuit Court U.S.).

> ARTICLE 4. SEC. 4.—The United States shall guarantee to every State in the Union a republican form of government.

How can that form of government be called republican in which one-half the people are forever deprived of all participation in its affairs?

> ARTICLE 6.—This Constitution, and the laws of the United States which shall be made in pursuance thereof, . . . shall be the supreme law of the land; and the judges in every State shall be bound thereby, anything in the Constitution or laws of any State to the contrary notwithstanding.

ARTICLE 14. SEC. 1.—All persons born or naturalized in the United States, and subject to the jurisdiction thereof, are citizens of the United States. . . . No State shall make or enforce any law which shall abridge the privileges and immunities of citizens of the United States.

In the discussion of the enfranchisement of woman, suffrage is now claimed by one class of thinkers as a privilege based upon citizenship and secured by the Constitution of the United States. As by lexicographers as well as by the Constitution itself, the definition of citizen includes women as well as men. No State can rightfully deprive a woman-citizen of the United States of any fundamental right which is hers in common with all other citizens. The States have the right to regulate, but not to prohibit the elective franchise to citizens of the United States. Thus the States may determine the qualifications of electors. They may require the elector to be of a certain age—to have had a fixed residence—to be of sane mind and unconvicted of crime, because these are qualifications or conditions that all citizens, sooner or later, may attain. But to go beyond this and say to one-half the citizens of the State, notwithstanding you possess all of these qualifications, you shall never vote, is of the very essence of despotism. It is a bill of attainder of the most odious character.

A further investigation of the subject will show that the constitutions of all the States, with the exception of Virginia and Massachusetts read substantially alike. "White male citizens" shall be entitled to vote, and this is supposed to exclude all other citizens. There is no direct exclusion except in the two States above named. Now the error lies in supposing that an enabling clause is necessary at all. The right of the people of a State to participate in a government of their own creation requires no enabling clause, neither can it be taken from them by implication. To hold otherwise would be to interpolate in the Constitution a prohibition that does not exist.

In framing a constitution, the people are assembled in their sovereign capacity, and being possessed of all rights and powers, what is not surrendered is retained. Nothing short of a direct prohibition can work a deprivation of rights that are fundamental, in the language of John Jay to the people of New York, urging the adoption of the Constitution of the United States: "Silence and blank paper neither give nor take away anything." And Alexander Hamilton says (*Federalist,* No. 83):

Every man of discernment must at once perceive the wide difference between silence and abolition. The mode and manner in which the people shall take part in the government of their creation may be prescribed by the constitution, but the right itself is antecedent to all constitutions. It is inalienable, and can neither be bought. nor sold nor given away.

But even if it should be held that this view is untenable, and that women are disfranchised by the several State constitutions, directly or by implication, then I say that such prohibitions are clearly in conflict with the Constitution of the United States and yield thereto.

Another class of thinkers, equally interested in woman's enfranchisement, maintain that there is, as yet, no power in the United States Constitution to protect the rights of all United States citizens, in all latitudes and longitudes, and in all conditions whatever. When the Constitution was adopted, the fathers thought they had secured national unity. This was the opinion of Southern as well as Northern statesmen. It was supposed that the question of State rights was then forever settled. Hon. Charles Sumner, speaking on this point in the United States Senate, March 7, 1866, said the object of the Constitution was to ordain, under the authority of the people, a national government possessing unity and power. The confederation had been merely an agreement "between the States," styled, "a league of firm friendship." Found to be feeble and inoperative through the pretension of State rights. it gave way to the Constitution which, instead of a "league," created a "union," in the name of the people of the United States. Beginning with these inspiring and enacting words, "We, the people," it was popular and national. Here was no concession to State rights, but a recognition of the power of the people, from whom the Constitution proceeded. The States are acknowledged; but they are all treated as component parts of the Union in which they are absorbed under the Constitution, which is the supreme law. There is but one sovereignty and that is the sovereignty of the United States. On this very account the adoption of the Constitution was opposed by Patrick Henry and George Mason. The first exclaimed, "That this is a consolidated government is demonstrably clear; the question turns on that poor little thing, 'We, the people,' instead of the States." The second exclaimed, "Whether the Constitution is good or bad, it is a national government, and no longer a confederation." But against this powerful opposition the Constitution was adopted in the name of the people of the United States. Throughout the discussions, State rights was treated with little favor. Madison said: "The States are only political societies, and never possessed the right of sovereignty." Gerry said: "The States have only corporate rights." Wilson, the philanthropic member from Pennsylvania, afterward a learned Judge of the Supreme Court of the United States and author of the "Lectures on Law," said: "Will a regard to State rights justify the sacrifice of the rights of men? If we proceed on any other foundation than the last, our building will neither be solid nor lasting."

Those of us who understand the dignity, power and protection of the ballot, have steadily petitioned Congress for the last ten years to secure to the women of the republic the exercise of their right to the elective franchise. We began by asking a sixteenth amendment to the national constitution. March 15, 1869, the Hon. George W. Julian submitted a joint resolution to Congress, to enfranchise the women of the republic, by proposing a sixteenth amendment:

> ARTICLE 16.—The right of suffrage in the United States shall be based on citizenship, and shall be regulated by Congress, and all citizens of the United States, whether native or naturalized, shall enjoy this right equally, without any distinction or discrimination whatever founded on sex.

While the discussion was pending for the emancipation and enfranchisement of the slaves of the South, and popular thought led back to the consideration of the fundamental principles of our government, it was clearly seen that all the arguments for the civil and political rights of the African race applied to women also. Seeing this, some Republicans stood ready to carry these principles to their logical results. Democrats, too, saw the drift of the argument, and though not in favor of extending suffrage to either black men, or women, yet, to embarrass Republican legislation, it was said, they proposed amendments for woman suffrage to all bills brought forward for enfranchising the negroes.

And thus, during the passage of the thirteenth, fourteenth and fifteenth amendments, and the District suffrage bill, the question of woman suffrage was often and ably discussed in the Senate and House, and received both Republican and Democratic votes in its favor. Many able lawyers and judges gave it as their opinion that women as well as Africans were enfranchised by the fourteenth and fifteenth amendments. Accordingly, we abandoned, for the time being, our demand for a sixteenth amendment, and pleaded our right of suffrage, as already secured by the fourteenth amendment—the argument lying in a nut-shell. For if, as therein asserted, all persons born or naturalized in the United States are citizens of the United States, and if a citizen, according to the best authorities, is one possessed of all the rights and privileges of citizenship, namely, the right to make laws and choose lawmakers, women, being persons, must be citizens, and therefore entitled to the rights of citizenship, the chief of which is the right to vote.

Accordingly, women tested their right, registered and voted—the inspectors of election accepting the argument, for which inspectors and women alike were arrested, tried, and punished; the courts deciding that although by the fourteenth amendment they were citizens, still, citizenship did not carry with it the right to vote. But granting the premise of the Supreme Court decision, "that the Constitution does not confer suffrage on anyone," then it inhered with the citizen before the Constitution was framed. Our national life does not date from that instrument. The Constitution is not the original declaration of rights. It was not framed until eleven years after our existence as a nation, nor fully ratified until nearly fourteen years after the inauguration of our national independence.

But however the letter and spirit of the Constitution may be interpreted by the people, the judiciary of the nation has uniformly proved itself the echo of the party in power. When the slave power was dominant the Supreme Court decided that a black man was not a citizen, because he had not the right to vote; and when the Constitution was so amended as to make all persons citizens, the same high tribunal decided that a woman, though a citizen, had not the right to vote. An African, by virtue of his United States citizenship, is declared, under recent amendments, a voter in every State of the Union: but when a woman, by virtue of her United States citizenship, applies to the Supreme Court for protection in the exercise of this same right, she is remanded to the State, by the unanimous decision of the nine judges on the bench, that "the Constitution of the United States does not confer the right of suffrage upon anyone." Such vacillating interpretations of constitutional law must unsettle our faith in judicial authority, and undermine the liberties of the whole people. Seeing by these decisions of the courts that the theory of our government, the Declaration of Independence, and recent constitutional amendments, have no significance for woman that all the grand principles of equality are glittering generalities for her, we must fall back once more to our former demand of a sixteenth amendment to the federal constitution, that, in clear, unmistakable language, shall declare the status of woman in this republic.

The Declaration of Independence struck a blow at every existent form of government by making the individual the source of all power. This is the sun, and the one central truth, around which all genuine republics must keep their course or perish. National supremacy means something more than power to levy war, conclude peace, contract alliances, establish commerce. It means national protection and security in the exercise of the right of self-government which comes alone by and through the use of the ballot. Women are the only class of citizens still wholly unrepresented in the government, and yet we possess every requisite qualification for voters in the United States. Women possess property and education; we take out naturalization-papers and passports and register ships. We preempt lands, pay taxes (women sometimes work out the road-tax with their own hands) and suffer for our own violation of laws. We are neither idiots, lunatics, nor criminals, and according to our State constitutions lack but one qualification for voters, namely, sex, which is an insurmountable qualification, and therefore equivalent to a bill of attainder against one-half the people, a power neither the States nor the United States can legally exercise, being forbidden in article I, sections 9, 10, of the Constitution. Our rulers have the right to regulate the suffrage, but they cannot abolish it for any class of citizens, as has been done in the case of the women of this republic, without a direct violation of the fundamental law of the land. All concessions of privileges or redress of grievances are mockery for any class that have no voice in the laws, and law-makers; hence we demand the ballot, that scepter of power in our own hands, as the only sure protection for our rights of person and property under all conditions. If the few may grant and withhold rights at their pleasure, the many cannot be said to enjoy the blessings of self-government.

William H. Seward said in his great speech on "Freedom and Union," in the United States Senate, February 29, 1860:

> Mankind have a natural right, a natural instinct, and a natural capacity for self-government; and when, as here, they are sufficiently ripened by culture, they will and must have self-government, and no other.

Jefferson said:

> The God who gave us life, gave us liberty at the same time; the hand of freedom may destroy, but cannot disjoin them.

Few people comprehend the length and breadth of the principle we are advocating to-day, and how closely it is allied to everything vital in our system of government. Our personal grievances, such as being robbed of property and children by unjust husbands; denied admission into the colleges, the trades, and professions; compelled to work at starving prices, by no means round out this whole question. In asking for a sixteenth amendment to the United States Constitution, and the protection of Congress against the injustice of State law, we are fighting the same battle as Jefferson and Hamilton fought in 1776, as Calhoun and Clay in 1828, as Abraham Lincoln and Jefferson Davis in 1860, namely, the limit of State rights and federal power. The enfranchisement of woman involves the same vital principle of our government that is dividing and distracting the two great political parties at this hour.

There is nothing a foreigner coming here finds it so difficult to understand as the wheel within a wheel in our national and State governments, and the possibility of carrying them on, without friction; and this is the difficulty and danger we are fast finding out. The recent amendments are steps in the right direction toward national unity, securing equal rights to all citizens, in every latitude and longitude. But our congressional debates, judicial decisions, and the utterances of campaign orators, continually falling back to the old ground, are bundles of contradictions on this vital question. Inasmuch as we are, first, citizens of the United States, and second, of the State wherein we reside, the primal rights of all citizens should be regulated by the national government, and complete equality in civil and political rights everywhere secured. When women are denied the right to enter institutions of learning, and practice in the professions, unjust discriminations made against sex even more degrading and humiliating than were ever made against color, surely woman, too, should be protected by a civil-rights bill and a sixteenth amendment that should make her political status equal with all other citizens of the republic.

The right of suffrage, like the currency or the post-office department, demands national regulation. We can all remember the losses sustained by citizens in traveling from one State to another under the old system of State banks. We can imagine the confusion if each State regulated its post-offices and the transit of the mails across its borders. The benefits we find in uniformity and unity in these great interests would pervade all others where equal conditions were secured. Some citizens are asking for a national bankrupt law, that a person released from his debts in one State may be free in every other. Some are for a religious freedom amendment that shall forever separate church and State, forbidding a religious test as a condition of suffrage or a qualification for office, forbidding the reading of the Bible in the schools and the exempting of church property and sectarian institutions of learning or charity from taxation. Some are demanding a national marriage law, that a man legally married in one State may not be a bigamist in another. Some are asking a national prohibitory law, that a reformed drunkard who is shielded from temptation in one State may not be environed with dangers in another. And thus many individual interests point to a growing feeling among the people in favor of homogeneous legislation. As several of the States are beginning to legislate on the woman suffrage question, it is of vital moment that there should be some national action.

As the laws now are, a woman who can vote, hold office, be tried by a jury of her own peers—yea, and sit on the bench as justice of the peace in the territory of Wyoming, may be reduced to a political pariah in the State of New York. A woman who can vote and hold office on the school board, and act as county superintendent in Kansas and Minnesota, is denied these rights in passing into Pennsylvania. A woman who can be a member of the school board in Maine, Wisconsin, Iowa, and California, loses all these privileges in New Jersey, Maryland, and Delaware. When representatives from the territories are sent to Congress by the votes of women, it is time to have some national recognition of this class of citizens.

This demand of national protection for national citizens is fated to grow stronger every day. The government of the United States, as the Constitution is now interpreted, is powerless to give a just equivalent for the supreme allegiance it claims. One sound democratic principle fully recognized and carried to its logical results in our government, declaring all citizens equal before the law, would soon chase away the metaphysical mists and fogs that cloud our political views in so many directions. When Congress is asked to put the name of God in the Constitution, and thereby pledge the nation to some theological faith in which some United States citizens may not believe and thus subject a certain class to political ostracism and social persecution, it is asked not to protect but to oppress the citizens of the several States in their most sacred rights—to think, reason, and decide all questions of religion and conscience for themselves, without fear or favor from the government. Popular sentiment and church persecution is all that an advanced thinker in science and religion should be called on to combat. The State should rather throw its shield of protection around those uttering liberal, progressive ideas; for the nation has the same interest in every new thought as it has in the invention of new machinery to lighten labor, in the discovery of wells of oil, or mines of coal, copper, iron, silver or gold. As in the laboratory of nature new forms of beauty are forever revealing themselves, so in the world of thought a higher outlook gives a clearer vision of the heights man in freedom shall yet attain. The day is past for persecuting the philosophers of the physical sciences. But what a holocaust of martyrs bigotry is still making of those bearing the richest treasures of thought, in religion and social ethics, in their efforts to roll off the mountains of superstition that have so long darkened the human mind!

The numerous demands by the people for national protection in many rights not specified in the Constitution, prove that the people have outgrown the compact that satisfied the fathers, and the more it is expounded and understood the more clearly its monarchical features can be traced to its English origin. And it is not at all surprising that, with no chart or compass for a republic, our fathers, with all their educational prejudices in favor of the mother country, with her literature and systems of jurisprudence, should have also adopted her ideas of government, and in drawing up their national compact engrafted the new republic on the old constitutional monarchy, a union whose incompatibility has involved their sons in continued discussion as to the true meaning of the instrument. A recent writer says:

> The Constitution of the United States is the result of a fourfold compromise: *First*—Of unity with individual interests; of national sovereignty with the so-called sovereignty of States; *Second*—Of the republic with monarchy; *Third*—Of freedom with slavery; *Fourth*—Of democracy with aristocracy.

It is founded, therefore, on the fourfold combination of principles perfectly incompatible and eternally excluding each other; founded for the purpose of equally preserving these principles in spite of their incompatibility, and of carrying out their practical results—in other words, for the purpose of making an impossible thing possible. And a century of discussion has not yet made the Constitution understood. It has no settled interpretation. Being a series of compromises, it can be expounded in favor of many directly opposite principles.

A distinguished American statesman remarked that the war of the rebellion was waged "to expound the Constitution." It is a pertinent question now, shall all other contradictory principles be retained in the Constitution until they, too are expounded by civil war? On what theory is it less dangerous to defraud twenty million women of their inalienable rights than four million negroes? Is not the same principle involved in both cases? We ask Congress to pass a sixteenth amendment, not only for woman's protection, but for the safety of the nation. Our people are filled with unrest to-day because there is no fair understanding of the basis of individual rights, nor the legitimate power of the national government. The Republican party took the ground during the war that Congress had the right to establish a national currency in every State; that it had the right to emancipate and enfranchise the slaves; to change their political status in one-half the States of the union; to pass a civil rights bill, securing to the freedman a place in the schools, colleges, trades, professions, hotels, and all public conveyances for travel. And they maintained their right to do all these as the best measures for peace, though compelled by war.

And now, when Congress is asked to extend the same protection to the women of the nation, we are told they have not the power and we are remanded to the States. They say the emancipation of the slave was a war measure, a military necessity; that his enfranchisement was a political necessity. We might with propriety ask if the present condition of the nation, with its political outlook, its election frauds daily reported, the corrupt action of men in official position, governors, judges, and boards of canvassers, has not brought us to a moral necessity where some new element is needed in government. But, alas! when women appeal to Congress for the protection of their natural rights of person and property, they send us for redress to the courts, and the courts remand us to the States. You did not trust the Southern freedman to the arbitrary will of courts and States! Why send your mothers, wives and daughters to the unwashed, unlettered, unthinking masses that carry popular elections?

We are told by one class of philosophers that the growing tendency to increase national power and authority is leading to a dangerous centralization; that the safety of the republic rests in local self-government. Says the editor of the *Boston Index:*

What is local self-government? Briefly, that without any interference from without, every citizen should manage his own personal affairs in his own way, according to his own pleasure; that every town should manage its own town affairs in the same manner and under the same restriction; every county its own county affairs, every State its own State affairs. But the independent exercise of this autonomy, by personal and corporate individuals, has one fundamental condition, viz.: the maintenance of all these individualities intact, each in its own sphere of action, with its rights uninfringed and its freedom uncurtailed in that sphere, yet each also preserving its just relation to all the rest in an all comprehensive social organization. Every citizen would thus stand, as it were, in the center of several concentric and enlarging circles of relationship to his kind; he would have duties and rights in each relation, not only as an individual but also as a member of town, county, State and national organization. His local self-government will be at his highest possible point of realization, when in each of these relations his individual duties are discharged and his rights maintained.

On the other hand, what is centralization?

It is such a disorganization of this well-balanced, harmonious and natural system as shall result in the absorption of all substantial power by a central authority, to the destruction of the autonomy of the various individualities above mentioned; such as was produced, for instance, when the *municipia* of the Roman empire lost their corporate independence and melted into the vast imperial despotism which prepared the way for the collapse of society under the blows of Northern barbarism. Such a centralization must inevitably be produced by decay of that stubborn stickling for rights out of which local self-government has always grown. That is, if individual rights in the citizen. the town, the county, the State, shall not be vindicated as beyond all price, and defended with the utmost jealousy, at whatever cost, the spirit of liberty must have already died out. and the dreary process of centralization be already far advanced: It will thus be evident that the preservation of individual rights is the only possible preventative of centralization, and that free society has no interest to be compared for an instant in importance with that of preserving these individual rights. No nation is free in which this is not the paramount concern. Woe to America when her sons and her daughters begin to sneer at rights! Just so long as the citizens are protected individually in their rights, the towns and counties and States cannot be stripped; but if the former lose all love for their own liberties as equal units of society, the latter will become the empty shells of creatures long perished. The nation as such, therefore, if it would be itself free and non-centralized, must find its own supreme interest in the protection of its individual citizens in the fullest possible enjoyment of their equal rights and liberties.

As this question of woman's enfranchisement is one of national safety, we ask you to remember that we are citizens of the United States, and, as such, claim the protection of the national flag in the exercise of our national rights, in every latitude and longitude. on sea, land, at home as well as abroad; against the tyranny of States, as well as against foreign aggressions. Local authorities may regulate the exercise of these rights; they may settle all minor questions of property, but the inalienable personal rights of citizenship should be declared by the Constitution, interpreted by the Supreme Court, protected by Congress and enforced by the arm of the executive. It is nonsense to talk of State rights until the graver question of personal liberties is first understood and adjusted. President Hayes, in reply to an address of welcome at Charlottesville, Va., September 25, 1877, said:

> Equality under the laws for all citizens is the corner-stone of the structure of the restored harmony from which the ancient friendship is to rise. In this pathway I am going, the pathway where your illustrious men led—your Jefferson, your Madison, your Monroe, your Washington.

If, in this statement, President Hayes is thoroughly sincere, then he will not hesitate to approve emphatically the principle of national protection for national citizens. He will see that the protection of all the national citizens in all their rights, civil, political, and religious—not by the muskets of United States troops. but by the peaceable authority of United States courts—is not a principle that applies to a single section of the country, but to all sections alike; he will see that the incorporation of such a principle in the Constitution cannot be regarded as a measure of force imposed upon the vanquished, since it would be law alike to the vanquished and the victor. In short, he will see that there is no other sufficient guarantee of that equality of all citizens which he well declares to be the "corner-stone of the structure of restored harmony." The *Boston Journal* of July 19 said:

> There are cases where it seems as if the Constitution should empower the federal government to step in and protect the citizen in the State, when the local authorities are in league with the assassins; but, as it now reads, no such provision exists.

That the Constitution does not make such provision is not the fault of the president; it must be attributed to the leading Republicans who had it in their power once to change the Constitution so as to give the most ample powers to the general government. When Attorney-General Devens was charged last May with negligence in not prosecuting the parties accused of the Mountain Meadow massacre, his defense was that this horrible crime was not against the United States, but against the territory of Utah. Yet, it was a great company of industrious, honest, unoffending United States citizens who were foully and brutally murdered in cold blood. When Chief Justice Waite gave his charge to the jury in the Ellentown conspiracy cases, at Charleston. S.C., June 1, 1877, he said:

> That a number of citizens of the United States have been killed, there can be no question; but that is not enough to enable the government of the United States to interfere for their protection. Under the Constitution that duty belongs to the State alone. But when an unlawful combination is made to interfere with any of the rights of natural citizenship secured to citizens of the United States by the national constitution, then an offense is committed against the laws of the United States, and it is not only the right but the absolute duty of the national government to interfere and afford the citizens that protection which every good government is bound to give.

General Hawley, in an address before a college last spring, said:

> Why, it is asked, does our government permit outrages in a State which it would exert all its authority to redress, even at the risk of war, it they were perpetrated under a foreign government? Are the rights of American citizens more sacred on the soil of Great Britain or France than on the soil of one of our own States? Not at all. But the government of the United States is clothed with power to act with imperial sovereignty in the one case, while in the other its authority is limited to the degree of utter impotency, in certain circumstances. The State sovereignty excludes the Federal over most matters of dealing between man and man, and if the State laws are properly enforced there is not likely to be any ground of complaint, but if they are not, the federal government, if not specially called on according to the terms of the Constitution, is helpless. Citizen A. B., grievously wronged, beaten, robbed, lynched within a hair's breadth of death, may apply in vain to any and all prosecuting officers of the State. The forms of law that might give him redress are all there; the prosecuting officers, judges, and sheriffs, that might act, are there; but, under an oppressive and tyrannical public sentiment, they refuse to move. In such an exigency the government of the United States can do no more than the government of any neighboring State; that is, unless the State concerned, calls for aid, or unless the offense

rises to the dignity of insurrection or rebellion. The reason is, that the framers of our governmental system left to the several States the sole guardianship of the personal and relative private rights of the people.

SOURCE: "National Protection for National Citizens, Address to the Senate Committee on Privileges and Elections, January 11, 1878, Washington, D.C.," in *History of Woman Suffrage,* vol. 3, 80–90.

Chapter 7

"The Other Side of the Woman Question" (1879)

EDITORS' NOTE: *This essay, published in the influential journal* The North American Review, *highlights Stanton's increasing emphasis on "the difference in sex" as an argument in favor of women's equal political and civil rights. Stanton was responding to the renowned historian Francis Parkman, who wrote a series of articles condemning democratic suffrage in general and woman suffrage in particular. The* Review *invited Stanton and four other noted suffrage advocates to respond. All the pro-suffrage responses defended democratic enfranchisement and challenged Parkman's assertion that the suffrage movement ignored the difference between the sexes in what he regarded as the impossible claim to political rights for women. While Stanton ended her piece with a defense of broad enfranchisement, the core of her response is a rendering of sexual difference in favor of equal rights and capacities. Stanton's case should be read carefully, to assess how she distinguishes "the old idea of different spheres" from the "higher ideal of different responsibilities in the same sphere." To give her argument scientific legitimacy, she cited Darwin in favor of her feminist version of sexual difference. Also note how she shifted Parkman's warnings against the political influence of the "women of the Romish church" to what she regarded as the more general danger of excessive religious influence on women, explicitly identifying Protestant churches as hostile to women's political and social advancement. Finally, Stanton's emphasis on the achievements of educated, cultivated, middle- and upper-class women was a direct response to Parkman's insistence that the disabling difference of sex was so fundamental as to overwhelm all other dimensions of women's lives—education, class, race—an assertion that infuriated Stanton.*

The first half of Mr. Francis Parkman's essay is devoted to a consideration of the difference of sex, in which he asserts—1. That the advocates of woman's rights deny that sex is based on differences rather than resemblances; 2. That these differences set well-defined limitations to woman's activities, and make her inferior to man.

1. The advocates of woman's rights do not deny a difference in sex, but, on the contrary, base their strongest arguments for equal rights on this very principle, because of its mutually protecting, elevating, invigorating power over the sexes. But sex does not necessarily compel so broad a difference in the capacities and employments of men and women as some of Mr. Parkman's positions would indicate, for the resemblances of sex are as great as their differences.

Darwin says that, in every female, all the secondary male characteristics, and, in every male, all the secondary female characteristics, exist in a latent form, ready to be evolved under certain conditions. Galton and Ribot, in their works on heredity, show that daughters more frequently inherit the characteristics of the father, and sons the characteristics of the mother. Since, then, physiological and psychological forces move in continuous circles, men and women cannot be so absolutely different in their feelings and capacities as to require entirely separate spheres of action.

On this point Mr. Parkman himself says: "Whatever qualities of a woman are transmissible by inheritance may descend to all her offspring alike. The male infant would be as apt to receive them as the female. The reciprocity between the two separate halves of human nature extends over a wide field, not only in passions and emotions, but in the regions of moral and intellectual life. Most intelligent men have felt the stimulus and refreshment of the faculties that spring from the companionship of an intelligent and congenial woman, and which is unlike anything resulting from the contact of a male mind. It is a fructifying power, with which neither the world of thought nor the world of action could well dispense. Many men of the higher sort recall as an epoch in their lives that wonderful awakening of energies, ambitions, and aspirations which comes with the first consciousness of the influence of the other sex."

And woman feels the same inspiring, invigorating power in the society of superior men: under such influence she is conscious of a clearer vision of great truths, before but dimly seen; for, as there is just that physical difference in man and woman necessary for the preservation of the race, so there is just that psychical difference necessary to the vitalization of thought.

Why not, then, avail ourselves of these natural forces for the best development of men and women by closer association in the higher departments of thought and action? The old idea of different spheres should now give place to the higher idea of different responsibilities in the same sphere. Wherever duty summons man, woman has a corresponding duty in the same place. If to war, man fights the battles, woman does good service in the hospitals. If to the home, the mother guides the household, the father supplements his home duties with some profitable occupation outside. When he is inefficient, disabled, or dead, the mother fills both offices, as housekeeper and provider, and the facts of life show that this is no uncommon experience. And Mr. Parkman himself admits that, "between the life for which women alone are fit and that for which men alone are fit, there lies a region where both may prosper." As physicians, lawyers, pastors, teachers, laborers in many forms of industry, they now occupy the same positions as men, and as legislators there is no reason why they might not do equally good work for the state.

As women have ably filled all offices in life, "Nature's limitations" are yet to be discovered, unless we accept Mr. Parkman's physical encounters in "lonely places" with the lowest orders of manhood. And even here a right public sentiment would do much to insure woman's safety everywhere. You cannot go so low down in the scale of being as to find a class of men who would desecrate our churches, profane the altars, and toss about the symbols of the sacrament, because they have been taught from their earliest infancy a holy reverence for the priesthood and their temples. But where are taught lessons of respect for woman? And yet, as mother of the race, she is more than churches, altars, symbols, priests, and, in her highest development, will do more to draw man from the hells to heaven than all other powers combined. I hold men in high places responsible for the outrages of the lower orders. The contemptuous phrases and unjust statutes for women learned in our law schools; the allegory of the creation of woman, the curse, the injunctions for her subjection studied in our theological schools and the general tone of literature and the daily press, all tend to degrade woman in the mind of the masses. If all these influences were turned in the direction of justice, equality, and honor for woman, the moral atmosphere would soon be purified. The compass is not a surer guide for the mariner amid darkness and danger than the opinions of leading minds for the multitude. If our best men with pen and word would do for woman now what with their swords brave knights did in the age of chivalry, our daughters would soon be safe everywhere, alike in "lonely places" and the crowded marts of trade. Mrs. Chisholm's narrative shows too well that in the trying emergencies of life, prepared or unprepared, woman must learn to stand alone, and bravely meet danger and death. Chance insults from the lower orders are light indeed compared with those that are coined into laws and constitutions by our husbands, fathers, brothers, sons. No rude jest from an ignorant ruffian could so stir a proud woman's blood as a well-written travesty on her sex from the pen of a man of learning and position.

2. Mr. Parkman clearly makes a difference of sex involve a general inferiority for woman. In the whole range of government, the most exalted of all sciences, he considers her incapable. When we contemplate the wide field thus covered—all our political, religious, educational, commercial, and social interests; the sanitary condition and the discipline of our cities, schools, asylums, jails, prisons, and homes—the question arises, Where is woman capable and where is her sphere of action, if she is to have no voice in the legislation on all these vital subjects? By quoting the opinions of two cultivated women on a given point where right is as clear as the sunlight, from their obtuseness Mr. Parkman argues a general deficiency in woman's moral perceptive faculties.

Again, though Mr. Parkman asserts that "women and not men are of necessity the guardians of the integrity of the family and the truth of succession," yet, even here, he makes "the family unit" man, who is to vote on all questions concerning the home. True, in his analysis of woman, Mr. Parkman refers to some "high and priceless qualities," but seems to take more delight in casting slurs at the ideal enfranchised woman. She is governed by "emotion" rather than by "reason," he informs us; that she is "impetuous," her will is "intractable," she is "impulsive," "excitable," full of "artfulness, effrontery, insensibility"; endowed with "a pushing self-assertion, and a glib tongue"; moved by "motives of love, predilection, jealousy, or schemes of alliance"; she would possess "the cowardly courage of the virago," a "tongue more terrible than the sword," and would give vent to "shrill-tongued discussions," etc.

If this is the idea that the sons of the Pilgrims have of us, no wonder they are afraid to take the word "male" out of the Constitution and admit us to the political arena. But Mr. Parkman tells us that "a man's tongue is strong only as the organ of reason and eloquence." I would his pen were always strong in the same direction! But, had man's tongue through the ages been his only weapon of defense, it might also have come to be "more terrible than the sword." The honest testimony from one hundred families as to the self-control, sound reason, and lofty eloquence with which men use their tongues in domestic life—especially when asked for money—

would afford some interesting statistics by which to estimate the comparative merits of the sexes in their general tone of conversation. It may be confidently asserted, however, that woman has proved herself man's equal in all the great struggles of humanity. Always at a disadvantage on account of artificial burdens and restraints, she has, nevertheless, shown herself possessed of the same courage, intelligence, and moral elevation in all the varied trials she has been called upon to suffer. Brute force should be thrown out of this question, especially as among men our scholars, heroes, statesmen, and orators are so frequently small, delicately organized, and of the same sensitive, nervous temperament as the majority of women. The organism of woman is as complete as that of man. Because a man-of-war could sink one of our magnificent ocean-steamers, does not prove the former superior except for the one purpose of destruction. In the every-day uses of life the steamer has the advantage. The experiment of co-education has proved girls equal to boys in every department of learning.

"This nineteenth century," says Victor Hugo, "belongs to woman." She is stretching forth her hand, as never before, to grasp new power in all directions, and is close in the wake of man in the whole realm of thought and action. With telescopic vision she explores the starry firmament and brings back the history of the planetary world; with chart and compass she pilots ships across the sea; and with skillful fingers sends electric messages around the world. By her the virtues of humanity are immortalized on canvas, and dull blocks of marble are transformed into angels of light. In music she speaks again the language of Mendelssohn and Beethoven, and is a worthy interpreter of their great thoughts; in poetry and romance she holds an equal place; and has touched the key-note of reform in politics, religion, and social life. She fills the editor's and professor's chair, pleads at the bar of justice, and speaks from the pulpit and platform. Such is the type of womanhood the world welcomes to-day.

But a difference in sex has no more to do with the civil and political rights of a citizen than a difference in race; and this brings us to the second part of Mr. Parkman's essay, in which he discusses woman suffrage per se. His objections may be summed up as follows: 1. Women do not want to vote; the best would not, the worst would. 2. Women would debase politics rather than elevate it. 3. Woman suffrage would destroy the unity of the family. 4. If women vote, they must do military duty. 5. Woman suffrage would strengthen the Roman Catholic Church. 6. Woman suffrage based on taxation is opposed to the genius of our Government. 7. Suffrage is not a natural right.

The first three points are answered by the fact, that though women are voting in England and Canada on municipal questions, in Wyoming Territory on the same conditions as men, in some of our States on school affairs, and are filling many offices under Government, the testimony of able and distinguished gentlemen as to the real results are, in all cases, favorable. These facts should outweigh Mr. Parkman's speculations. In Wyoming, where women have voted for nine years, the evidence shows that the best women do go to the polls, the worst do not; that the women are governed by the highest moral considerations in discharging the great responsibilities of citizenship; that family life has not been disturbed; that the women have not become "nervous," "excitable," or "impulsive," but more calm, dignified, and sedate in assuming their new duties. On all these points the printed opinions of three successive Governors of the Territory, a judge who sat on the Wyoming bench four years, the leading editors of the Territory, and prominent citizens of both sexes and of both parties, agree. The Hon. John W. Kingman, late judge of the Wyoming Supreme Court, testified as follows before the Joint Special Committee of the Massachusetts Legislature on woman suffrage in 1876: "At our last election a larger proportion of women voted than of men. We have had no trouble from the presence of bad women at the polls. It has been said that the delicate and cultured women would shrink away, and the bold and indelicate come to the front in public affairs. This we feared; but certainly nothing of the kind has happened. The women manifest a great deal of independence in their preference of candidates, and have frequently defeated bad nominations. They are becoming every year more and more interested in public affairs; they are less under the influence of private interest, friendship, and party feeling, and are less subject to the temptations which bias the political action of men. As jurors women have done excellent service. They are less subject to the distracting influences which sometimes sway the action of men in the jury-box. With a stronger tension on the conscience, they seem more anxious to do right. On petit juries the women held the men up to a higher tone of morality and stricter sense of honesty than they would have exercised if left to themselves."

As regards the number of women who vote in England, the London "Examiner" says: "In sixty-six municipal elections, out of every 1,000 women who enjoy equal rights with men on the register, 516 went to the poll, which is but forty-eight less than the proportionate number of men. And out of 27,949 women registered, where a contest occurred, 14,416 voted. Of men there were 166,781 on the register, and 90,080 at the poll."

3. To say that it would destroy the unity of the family to educate our daughters like our sons with a knowledge of the principles of political economy and constitutional law, and give them an equal right to express their opinions at the ballot-box, is a very serious reflection on the men of our households, and justifies John Stuart Mill's remark that "the generality of the male sex cannot yet tolerate the idea of living with an equal." "The family unit" assumption is opposed to our republican idea of individual rights, to our Protestant tenet of private judgment and conscience. We might as well say that the family is a religious unit, as to assert that it is a political unit, and claim that the head must do the family repenting, praying, and confessing, and represent the family in the courts of heaven as well as at the polling-booth. The doctrine that the head of the family is alone destined for the joys of heaven and the woes of hell would relieve the minds of women and children from many gloomy forebodings. Fortunately for the honor of manhood, the experiment in Wyoming proves that woman suffrage does not destroy the peace of home. The editor of the Laramie (Wyoming) *Sentinel,* in the number for December 16, 1878, says: "While women in this Territory frequently vote contrary to their husbands, we have never heard of a case where the family ties or domestic relations were disturbed by it; and we believe that among the pioneers of the West there is more honor and manhood than to abuse a wife because she does not think as we do about politics or religion."

4. As none of our constitutions make military capacity a qualification for suffrage, this point has no significance. The weakness of this trite objection can be easily shown by a glance at the large class of men who vote but never fight. All the office-holders under Government—and their name is legion—are exempt from military duty. So are the clergy, paupers, the Quakers, the lame, the halt and the blind; but each and all have the right to vote.

5. We are warned against the women of the Romish Church, so absolutely under the power of the priests, as a dangerous element in our free institutions if permitted to vote. The same fear is sometimes expressed in regard to Protestant women: they would destroy the secular nature of our Government if given the ballot. If women were enfranchised, they would not be priest-ridden. Too much of their activity is now confined to the churches. Throw politics open to woman, and you weaken the hold of the Church upon her.

6. If suffrage based on taxation is opposed to the genius of our Government, is not taxation without representation equally opposed to it?

7. Suffrage is a natural right. The right of self-government, of self-protection, the right to defend one's person and property, to secure life, liberty, and happiness, not a natural right? It is the key-stone of the arch on which rests our temple of liberty. In a warm debate on the Fourteenth Amendment in the Senate a member said, "Suffrage is a political right, that the few may give or withhold at their pleasure." "Let that idea," replied Sumner, "crystallize in the minds of our people and we have rung the death-knell of American liberties." To deny this principle takes all significance from the grand debates of the century on human rights that culminated in our civil war! In the most celebrated document which has been put forth on this side of the Atlantic, our ancestors declare that "governments derive their just powers from the consent of the governed." This principle, ofttimes repeated by distinguished statesmen and eminent jurists, in varied forms and language, as far back as Blackstone, should find a ready response in the mind of every American citizen.

SOURCE: Elizabeth Stanton, "The Other Side of the Woman Question," *North American Review,* vol. 129, no. 276 (November 1879), 432–39. For online version, see http://proquest.umi.com/pqdlink?index=9&did=204611561&SrchMode=3&sid =1&Fmt=10&VInst=PROD&VType=PQD&RQT=309&VName=HNP&TS=113216 4533&clientId=48051&aid=3.

Chapter 8

"Has Christianity Benefited
Woman?" (1885)

EDITORS' NOTE: *Stanton wrote this daring, breathtaking overview of women's history before this was a subject in which scholars worked. Imagining women as important actors shaping the destiny of humanity was an act of faith, necessary for her to challenge historians to approach their work with an enlarged understanding of how societies advanced. She had to review books across a variety of fields to cull any references to women's contributions in previous societies. Stanton's methodology suggests her sympathy for new positivist trends in history that were concerned with reconstructing patterns of everyday life rather than narrating the stories of kings, generals, and other famous leaders. Stanton's first reference is to Henry Thomas Buckle (1821–1862), whose most widely read book was his* History of Civilization in England. *Buckle argued that the purpose of history was to uncover the laws of progress, which he measured by the ability of people to work together to control their environment and expand what it could produce. Stanton appreciated Buckle's argument since it allowed her to link women's contribution to the general prosperity and stability of a society. Stanton's essay reveals two contradictory trends. On the one hand, she agreed with Herbert Baxter Adams and other historians that the germ of individual liberty and democratic government in America lay in the ability of Anglo-Americans' "Teutonic" ancestors to maintain their independence from the Roman Empire. On the other hand, the honor accorded to the Virgin Mary and to female saints in general in the Roman Catholic Church deeply impressed Stanton, who saw in Mariolatry evidence that Catholic Christianity had a higher regard for women and had preserved ancient understandings that divinity was both masculine and feminine.*

The assertion that woman owes all the advantages of her present position to the Christian church, has been repeated, so often, that it is accepted, as an established truth by those who would be unwilling to admit that all the injustice and degradation she has suffered might be logically traced to the same source. A consideration of woman's position before Christianity, under Christianity, and at the present time, shows that she is not indebted to any form of religion for one step of progress, or one new liberty; on the contrary, it has been through the perversion of her religious sentiments that she has been so long held in a condition of slavery. All religions thus far have taught the headship and superiority of man, the inferiority and subordination of woman. Whatever new dignity, honor, and self-respect the changing theologies may have brought to man, they have all alike brought to woman but another form of humiliation. History shows that the condition of woman has changed with different forms of civilization, and that she has enjoyed in some periods greater honor and dignity and more personal and property rights than have been accorded her in the Christian era. History shows, too, that the moral degradation of woman is due more to theological superstitions than to all other influences together. It is not to any form of religion that we are to look for woman's advancement, but to material civilization, to commerce, science, art, invention, to the discovery of the art of printing, and the general dissemination of knowledge. Buckle, in his *History of Civilization* calls attention to the fact that when woman became valuable in a commercial sense, in proportion as she secured material elevation and wealth through her property rights, she began to be treated with a deference and respect that the Christian church never accorded. In ancient Egypt, at the most brilliant period of its history, woman sat upon the throne and directed the civilization of the country. In the marriage relation she was supreme in all things—a rule that, according to Wilkinson, was productive of lasting fidelity. As priestess she performed the most holy offices of religion, and to her is traced the foundation of Egyptian literature, the sacred songs of Isis, said by Plato to be ten thousand years old. Colleges for women were founded there twelve hundred years before Christ, and the medical profession was in the hands of women. It is a sad commentary on the Christianity of England and America, to find professors in medical colleges of the nineteenth century less liberal than those in the earliest civilizations. In 1876 four professors in the College of Surgeons in London resigned because three women were licensed for the practice of midwifery, and the whole Royal College of Physicians thanked them for it. In 1869 the professors in the University of Edinburgh refused to teach four highly respectable women that had matriculated, and the students, echoing the contempt of their teachers, mobbed them. Nor did the conduct of American students, when women were admitted to the clinics of the Pennsylvania and New York hospitals, reflect greater credit on American manhood.

All Pagandom recognized a female priesthood, believing that national safety depended on them. Sybils wrote the books of Fate, and oracles where women presided were consulted by many nations. The pages of Roman history are gilded with the honor shown to women, and the civil laws for wives and mothers were more liberal in some respects than those in Christian countries have ever been. The rights of property that were willingly secured to women by ancient Roman law, were wrung out of the English Government by the persistent efforts of women themselves only three years ago. Among the Germanic nations woman was treated with marked respect. Tacitus gives us many striking pictures of the equal privileges of the men and women, of their mutual love and confidence, and their lofty virtue; the dignity of the German bride and the marriage ceremony, and the significance of the wedding presents. Their marriage bond was strict and severe, alike for men and women. Almost alone among barbaric nations, they preserved monogamy. "In all things," says Tacitus, "they consulted their women," who, with strong muscular bodies, possessed clear, vigorous minds; and though, as in all warlike tribes, they performed the agricultural labor, yet they preserved their health and beauty to a great age, because they were respected and honored by their men, who were chaste and temperate in all things; and they enjoyed the inspiration of liberty and love in their daily toil.

The German scholar Curtius says, "The native selfishness of man has been the great power against which moralists, philosophers, and teachers have had to contend." What sooner dissipates this than a deep affection for a noble woman? No love is so all-absorbing, so enduring, or gives such satisfaction to this mortal life; no power can so exalt and quicken civilization. It was this that elevated the Germanic tribes, and infused the poetic sentiment into their earliest literature. It is only in countries where Germanic ideas have taken root, that we see marks of any elevation of woman superior to that of Pagan antiquity; and as the condition of the German woman in her deepest paganism was so striking as to challenge the attention of Tacitus and his contemporaries, it is highly unreasonable to claim it as an achievement of Christianity. In fact, the Christian doctrine of marriage, as propounded by Paul, does not dignify woman as does that which German soundness of heart established at an early day. F.W. Newman, brother of the cardinal, one of the leading authorities on ecclesiastical subjects, says:

With Paul, the sole reason for marriage is, that a man may gratify instinct without sin. He teaches that, but for this object, it would be better not to marry. He wishes that all in this respect were as free as himself, and calls it a special gift from God. He does not encourage a man to desire a mutual soul-union intimately to share his griefs and joys, one in whom the confiding heart can repose, whose smile shall reward and soften toil, whose voice shall beguile sorrow. He does not seem aware that the fascinations of woman refine and chasten society; that virtuous attachment has in it an element of respect which abashes and purifies, and which shields the soul even when marriage is deferred; nor yet, that the union of two persons who have no previous affection can seldom yield the highest fruit of matrimony, but often leads to the severest temptations. How should he know all this? Courtship before marriage did not exist in the society open to him, hence he treats the propriety of giving away a maiden as one in which her conscience, her likes and dislikes, are not concerned. (1 Cor. vii. 37, 38.) As a result of the Apostolic doctrines, in the second, third, and following centuries, very gross views concerning the relations of the sexes prevailed; and they have been everywhere transmitted where men's morality is exclusively formed from the New Testament, viz., in the Armenian, Syrian, and Greek churches, and in the Romish church, in exact proportion as Germanic and poetical influences have been repressed; that is, in proportion as the hereditary Christian doctrine has been kept pure from modern innovations. The marriage service of the Church of England, which incorporates the Pauline doctrine, is felt by English brides and bridegrooms to contain what is so offensive and degrading, that many clergymen mercifully make lawful omissions. The old Roman matron was morally as high as in modern Italy; nor is there any ground for supposing that modern women have advantage over the ancient in Spain and Portugal, where Germanic have been counteracted by Moorish influences. The relative position of the sexes in Homeric Greece exhibits nothing materially different from the present day. In Armenia and Syria perhaps Christianity has done the service of extinguishing polygamy; this is creditable, though nowise remarkable, as Judaism, also, in time unlearned polygamy and made an unbidden improvement on Moses.

Rev. William Ellery Channing, in his essay on Milton's character and writings, says: "There is no prohibition of polygamy in the New Testament. It is an indisputable fact that, although Christianity was first preached in Asia, which had been from the earliest ages the seat of polygamy, the apostles never denounced it as a crime and never required their converts to put away all wives but one."

Hence, we cannot credit Christianity with woman's elevation from the degradation of polygamy, especially as it exists under our own government today, in the Territory of Utah and elsewhere, and concubinage is recognized by statute law in some of the Southern States. The historian Hallam says in his *History of Literature*:

> Love, with the ancient poets, is often tender, sometimes virtuous, but never accompanied by a sense of deference or inferiority. This elevation of the female sex through the voluntary submission of the stronger is a remarkable fact in the philosophical history of Europe. It originated partially in the Teutonic manners. Some have said "the reverence and adoration of the female sex which has descended to our own times, is the offspring of the Christian dispensation." But until it can be shown that Christianity establishes any such principle, we must look a little farther down for its origin. . . . Without rejecting the Teutonic influence, we might ascribe more direct efficacy to the favor shown towards women in succession to lands, through inheritance or dower, by the later Roman law.

Gallantry, in the sense of a general homage to the fair, a respectful deference to woman, independent of personal attachment, first became a perceptible element of European manners in the south of France at the end of the tenth century. This spirit is not found in the ancient poetry of the Franks or Anglo-Saxons, but it is fully developed in the sentiments and usages of northern France. Gallantry toward women was practiced by the Goths before they were acquainted with Christianity. Catholicism has greatly diminished the political and priestly powers of women. It would seem, then, that the authorities are against the proposition that the moral elevation of womankind is due to Christianity and tell us that it is due to altogether different causes, among which we find early Germanic influences and the modern literature of Germany, containing pure and noble views of love; ancient customs, giving woman property rights, and favors shown to woman by later Roman law; French influence; gallantry; the springing up of home life in the dark ages. The brave words and deeds of reformers in every generation, proclaiming the principles of justice and equality for all humanity, must be recognized as one of the essential factors in the civilization in which woman has had a share. With regard to intellectual growth and elevation, we have the same causes alike for man and woman. What either acquired was in opposition to the church, which sedulously tried to keep all learning within itself. Man, seeking after knowledge, was opposed by the church; woman, by both church and man. Educated men in our own day, who have outgrown many of the popular theological superstitions, do not share with the women of their households the freedom they themselves enjoy. Hence, it is not unusual to find the wives of clergymen far more bigoted than their husbands. Among the Greeks there was a class of women that possessed absolute freedom, surrounded by the wisest men of their day. They devoted themselves to study and thought, which enabled them to add to their other charms an intense intellectual fascination, and to make themselves the center of a literary society of matchless splendor. Aspasia was as famous for her genius as for her beauty. She is said to have composed many of Pericles's most famous orations and inspired his loftiest flights of eloquence. Socrates, too, owed his deep obligations to Diotema. In the society of this remarkable type of Grecian womanhood the most brilliant artists, poets, historians, and philosophers found their highest inspiration. True, the position of these women was questionable, but as they were the only class to whom learning and liberty were permitted, they illustrate the civilization of the period. The question is pertinent: Does the same class in Christian civilization enjoy as high culture and equal governmental protection? Since English and American statesmen, by recent legislation, have proved that they consider this phase of social life a necessity, why do not the Church and the State throw some shield of protection over the class of whom Lecky, in his *History of Morals,* speaks so tenderly? What has Christianity done for this type of womanhood? Have eighteen centuries of its influence mitigated the miseries of this phase of life one iota. No, nor ever will, until the mother of the race is recognized as equal in every position in life, honored and dignified at every altar; not until another revision of the Protestant Bible shall strike from its pages all invidious distinctions based on sex. The masculine and feminine elements of humanity, in exact equilibrium, are as necessary to the order and harmony of the world of morals as are the centripetal and centrifugal forces exactly balanced in the world of matter. As long as the religion of a nation teaches the subordination of woman, of the moral and spiritual elements of humanity to physical force, a pure civilization is impossible. Just as slavery in the South, with its lessons of obedience, degraded every black man in the Northern States, so does an accepted system of prostitution, with its lessons of subjection and self-sacrifice, degrade the ideal of womanhood everywhere.

In harmony with the pagan worship of an ideal womanhood of Sybils, oracles, and priestesses, women held prominent positions in the church for several centuries after Christ. We have proof of this in the restrictions that at a later period were placed upon them by canon laws. The Council of Laodicea, three hundred and sixty-five years after Christ, forbade the ordination of women to the ministry and prohibited them from entering the altar. The Council of Orleans, five hundred and eleven years after Christ, consisting of twenty-six bishops and priests, promulgated a canon that, on account of their frailty, women must be excluded from the deaconship. Nearly three hundred, years later we find the Council of Paris complaining that women serve at the altar, and even give to the people the body and blood of Jesus Christ. Through these canons we have the negative proof that for centuries women preached, baptized, administered the sacrament, and filled various offices of the church; and that ecclesiastics, through prohibitory canons, annulled these rights.

In the fifth century the church fully developed the doctrine of original sin, making woman its weak and guilty author. To St. Augustine, whose early life was licentious and degraded, we are indebted for this idea, which was infused into the canon law, and was the basis of all the persecutions woman endured for centuries, in the drift of Christian opinion from the extremes of polygamy to celibacy, from the virtues of chivalry to the cruelties of witchcraft, when the church taught its devotees to shun woman as a temptation and defilement. It was this persecution, this crushing out of the feminine element in humanity, more than all other influences combined, that plunged the world into the dark ages, shadowing the slowly rolling centuries till now with woman's agonies and death, paralyzing literature, science, commerce, education, changing the features of art, the sentiments of poetry, the ethics of philosophy, from the tender, the loving, the beautiful, the grand, to the stern, the dark, the terrible. Even the paintings representing Jesus were gradually changed from the gentle, watchful shepherd to the stern, unrelenting judge. Harrowing representations of the temptation, the crucifixion, the judgment-day, the Inferno, were intensified and elaborated by Dante and Milton. Painter and poet vied with each other in their gloomy portrayals, while crafty bishops coined these crude terrors into canons, and timid, dishonest judges allowed them to throw their dark shadows over the civil law.

The influence of the church on woman's civil position was equally calamitous. A curious old black-letter volume, published in London in 1632, entitled *The Lawes and Resolutions of Woman's Rights,* says, "The reason why women have no controul in Parliament, why they make no laws, consent to none, abrogate none, is their Original Sin." This idea is the chief block in the way of woman's advancement at this hour. It was fully set forth by the canon law, with wearisome repetition, and when, in the fifteenth century, the sacred Scriptures were collected and first printed, the spirit of these canons and all that logically grew out of them were engrafted on its pages, making woman an afterthought in the creation, the author of sin, in collusion with the devil, sex a crime, marriage a condition of slavery for woman and defilement for man, and maternity a curse to be attended with sorrow and suffering that neither time nor knowledge could ever mitigate, a just punishment for having effected the downfall of man. And all these monstrous ideas, emanating from the bewildered brains of men in the dark ages, under an exclusively masculine religion, were declared to be the word of God, penned by writers specially inspired by his Spirit.

Just at the period when the civil code began to recognize the equality and independence of the wife in the marriage relation, the church, to which woman had reason to look for protection, either blindly or perversely gave the whole force of its power against woman's equality in the family, and in fact against her influence altogether. In chapter V of Maine's "Ancient Law" we have a clear statement of the influence of canon law on the liberty of person and property that Roman women then enjoyed. Speaking of their freedom, he says:

> Christianity tended from the very first to narrow this remarkable liberty.
> . . . No society which preserves any tincture of Christian institution is likely
> to restore to married women the personal liberty conferred on them by
> middle Roman law. . . . The expositors of the canon law have deeply injured
> civilization. . . . There are many vestiges of a struggle between the secular
> and ecclesiastical principles, but the canon law nearly everywhere prevailed.
> In some of the French provinces married women of a rank below nobility,
> obtained all the powers of dealing with property which Roman jurispru-
> dence had allowed, and this local law has been largely followed by the code
> Napoleon. The systems, however, which are least indulgent to married
> women are invariably those which have followed the canon law exclusively,
> or those which from the lateness of their contact with European civilization
> have never had their archaisms weeded out.

By the dishonoring of womanhood on the ground of original sin, by the dishonoring of all relations with her as carnal and unclean, the whole sex touched a depth of moral degradation that it had never known before. Rescued in a measure from the miseries of polygamy, woman was plunged into the more degrading and unnatural condition of celibacy. Out of this grew the terrible persecutions of witchcraft, which, raged for centuries, women being its chief victims. They were hunted down by the clergy, tortured, burned, drowned, dragged into the courts, tried, and condemned, for crimes that never existed but in the minds of religious devotees. The clergy sustained witchcraft as Bible doctrine, far into the eighteenth century, until the spirit of rationalism laughed the whole thing to scorn and gave mankind a more cheerful view of life. The reformation brought no new hope to woman. The great head of the movement, while declaring the right of individual conscience and judgment above church authority, as if to warn woman that she had no share in this liberty, was wont to say, "No gown worse becomes a woman than that she should be wise." Here is the key-note to the Protestant pulpit for three centuries, and it grates harshly on our ears to-day. The Catholic Church, in its holy sisterhoods, so honored and revered, and in its worship of the Virgin Mary, Mother of Jesus, has preserved some recognition of the feminine element in its religion; but from Protestantism it is wholly eliminated. Religions like the Jewish and Christian, which make God exclusively male and man supreme, consign woman logically to the subordinate position assigned her in Mohammedism. History has perpetuated this tradition, and her subjection has existed as an invariable element in Christian civilization. It could not be otherwise, with the Godhead represented as a trinity of males. The old masters in the galleries of art have left us their ideals of the Trinity in three bearded male heads. No heavenly Mother is recognized in the Protestant world.

The present position of woman in the spirit of our creeds and codes is far behind the civilization of the age and unworthy the representative women of this day. And now, as ever, the strongest adverse influence to her elevation comes from the church, judging from its Biblical expositions, the attitude of the clergy and the insignificant status that woman holds in the various sectarian organizations. For nearly forty years there has been an organized movement in England and America to liberalize the laws in relation to woman, to secure a more profitable place in the world of work, to open the colleges for higher education, and the schools of medicine, law, and theology, and to give woman an equal voice in the government and religion of the country. These demands, one by one, are slowly being conceded by the secular branch of the government, while the sectarian influence has been uniformly in the opposite direction. Appeals before legislative assemblies, constitutional conventions, and the highest courts have been respectfully heard and decided, while propositions for the consideration even of some honors to women in the church have uniformly been received with sneers and denunciations by leading denominations, who quote Scripture freely to maintain their position. Judges and statesmen have made able arguments in their respective places for woman's civil and political rights; but where shall we look for sectarian leaders that, in their general assemblies, synods, or other ecclesiastical conventions, have advocated a higher position for woman in the church? The attitude of the clergy is the same as in bygone centuries, modified somewhat, on this as on all other questions, by advancing civilization. The Methodists have a lay ministry, but they do not ordain women. Liberal clergymen in other sects have been arraigned and tried by their general assemblies for allowing women to preach in their pulpits. In imitation of the high churches in England, we have some in this country in which boys from twelve to fifteen supply the place of women in the choir, that the sacred altars may not be defiled by the inferior sex—an early Christian idea. The discourses of clergymen, when they enlarge on the condition of woman, read more like canons in the fifth century than sermons in the nineteenth, addressed to those who are their peers in religious thought and scientific attainment. The Rev. Morgan Dix's Lenten lectures last spring, and Bishop Littlejohn's last triennial sermon, are fair specimens. The latter recommends that all the liberal legislation of the past forty years for women should be reversed, while the former is the chief obstacle in the way of woman's admission to Columbia College. And these fairly represent the sentiments of the vast majority, who never refer to the movement for women's enfranchisement but with ridicule and contempt—sentiments that they insidiously infuse into all classes of women under their influence. None of the leading theological seminaries will admit women who are preparing for the ministry, and none of the leading denominations will ordain them when prepared. The Universalists, Unitarians, and Quakers are the only sects that ordain women. And yet women are the chief supporters of the church to-day. They make the surplices and gowns, get up the fairs and donation-parties, and are the untiring beggars for its benefit. They supply its enthusiasm, and are continually making large bequests to its treasury; and their reward is still the echo of the old canon law of woman's subjections, from pulpit to pulpit throughout Christendom. Though England and America are the two nations in which the Christian religion is dominant and can boast the highest type of womanhood, and the greatest number in every department of art, science, and literature, yet even here women have been compelled to clear their own way for every step in progress. Not one wrong has been righted until women themselves made organized resistance against it. In the face of every opposition they are throwing off the disabilities of the old common law, which Lord Brougham said long ago "was in relation to women the opprobrium of the age and Christianity." And not until they make an organized resistance against the withering influence of the canon law, will they rid themselves of the moral disabilities growing out of the theologies of our times. When I was standing near the last resting-place of the Rev. Charles Kingsley not long ago, his warning words for woman, in a letter to John Stuart Mill, seemed like a voice from the clouds, saying with new inspiration and power, "This will never be a good world for woman until the last remnant of the canon law is civilized off the face of the earth."

SOURCE: Elizabeth Stanton, "Has Christianity Benefited Woman," *North American Review*, vol. 140, no. 342 (May 1885), 389–99. For online version, see http://proquest .umi.com/pqdlink?index=3&did=204624661&SrchMode=3&sid=2&Fmt=10&VInst =PROD&VType=PQD&RQT=309&VName=HNP&TS=1132164920&clientId=480 51&aid=5.

Chapter 9

"Divorce versus Domestic Warfare" (1890)

EDITORS' NOTE: This article recalls Stanton's 1860 position on divorce law liberalization, but now Stanton took a much more forceful—and provocative —position. The rise in numbers of divorces which others responded to with a kind of moral panic Stanton saw as wholly encouraging: a sign of the "new woman's" higher aspirations for personal liberty and individual choice. Divorce law reform was once again a live political issue in the 1890s. Christian reformers, members of the Woman's Christian Temperance Union prominent among them, were pushing for a more active role for the federal government in regulating morality. They proposed a constitutional amendment to establish a highly restrictive national law on divorce. Whereas Stanton had called just a decade before for aggressive federal action on behalf of women's citizenship and voting rights, here she argued against national legislation. More was at work here than shifting strategic options: while Stanton believed in an active and democratic polity as part of her deepening sense of the sanctity of personal liberty, she wanted to remove marriage from government purview. She defined marriage as an entirely personal matter, or as she put it, a question of individual happiness rather than of social order. This position on personal life complemented the epistemological approach she took to the self in "Solitude of Self." Interestingly, she did believe that oversight of the quantity and quality of childbirths, as opposed to marriage, was a proper government function, so long as women were fully enfranchised.

The fetich of our time is the legislative enactment. It is considered that men should be more moral, more temperate, immediately a party arises in the State, clamoring for a law to legalize its theories.

But unfortunately, progress cannot be obtained by an Act of Parliament. Development is a plant of slow growth, and the only soil in which it will flourish is that of broad, human culture. Harmonious progress is not to be secured for the individual or society by hasty methods. You can make men hypocrites by prohibitory laws; you cannot make them moral.

There is a demand just now for an amendment to the United States Constitution that shall make the laws of Marriage and Divorce the same in all the States of the Union. As this suggestion comes uniformly from those who consider the present divorce laws too liberal, we may infer that the proposed National Law is to place the whole question on a narrower basis, rendering null and void the laws that have been passed in a broader spirit, according to the needs and experiences in certain sections, of the sovereign people. And here let us bear in mind, that the widest possible law would not make divorce obligatory on anyone, while a restricted law, on the contrary, would compel many living perhaps at one time under more liberal laws, to remain in uncongenial relations.

Moreover, as we are still in the experimental stage on this question, we are not qualified to make a perfect law, that would work satisfactorily over so vast an area as our boundaries now embrace. I see no evidence in what has been published on this question of late by statesmen, ecclesiastics, lawyers, and judges, that any of them have thought sufficiently on the subject, to prepare a well-digested code, or a comprehensive amendment to the national constitution.

Some view it as a civil contract, though not governed by the laws of other contracts; some view it as a religious ordinance, a sacrament; some think it a relation to be regulated by the State, others by the Church, and still other think it should be left wholly the individual. With this wide divergence of opinion among our leading minds, it is quite evident that we are not prepared for a national law.

Moreover, as woman is the most important factor in the marriage relation, her enfranchisement is the primal step in the settlement of the basis of family life. Before public opinion on this question crystalizes into an amendment to the national constitution, the wife and mother must have a voice in the governing power and must be heard on this great social problem in the halls of legislation.

There are many advantages in leaving all these questions, as now, to the States. Local self-government more readily permits of experiments on mooted questions, which are the outcome of the needs and convictions of the community. The smaller the area over which legislation extends, the more pliable are the laws. By leaving the States free to experiment in their local affairs, we can judge of the working of different laws under varying circumstances, and thus learn their comparative merits. The progress education has achieved in America is due to just this fact—that we have left our system of public instruction in the hands of local authorities. How different would be the solution of the great educational question of manual labor in the schools, if the matter had to be settled at Washington! The whole nation might find itself pledged to a scheme that a few years would prove wholly impracticable. Not only is the town meeting, as Emerson says, "the cradle of American liberties," but it is the nursery of Yankee experiment and wisdom. England, with its clumsy national code of education, making one inflexible standard of scholarship for the bright children of manufacturing districts and the dull bairns of the agriculturing counties, should teach us a lesson as to the wisdom of keeping apart state and national government.

Again, before we can decide the just grounds of divorce, we must get a clear idea of what constitutes marriage. In a true relation, the chief object is the loving companionship of man and woman, their capacity for mutual help and happiness, and for the development of all that is noblest in each other. The second object is the building up a home and family, a place of rest, peace, security, in which child-life can bud and blossom like flowers in the sunshine.

The first step towards making the ideal real, is to educate our sons and daughters into the most exalted ideas of the sacredness of married life, and the responsibilities of parenthood. I would have them give at least as much thought to the creation of an immortal being as the artist gives to his landscape or statue. Watch him in his hours of solitude, communing with great nature, for days and weeks in all her changing moods, and when at last his dream of beauty is realized and takes a clearly defined form, behold how patiently he works through long months and years, on sky and lake, on tree and flower, and when complete, it represents to him more love and life, more hope and ambition, than the living child at his side, to whose conception and antenatal development not one soulful thought was ever given. To this impressible period of human life, few parents give any thought, yet here, we must begin to cultivate the virtues that can alone redeem the world.

How oblivious even our greatest philosophers seem to the well-known laws of physiology. Think of a man like Darwin, so close an observer of every form of life, so firm a believer in the laws of heredity, venturing on marriage and fatherhood, while he was the victim of an incurable hereditary disease. That he thought of this while raising a large family is plain from his published letters, in which he deplores his condition, and groans lest his physical afflictions be visited on his children! Alas! who can meas-

ure the miseries of the race resulting from the impure and unholy marriages into which even intelligent men and women so recklessly enter.

The tone of society is indeed low in regard to all these matters. We get a
much fairer idea of the settled opinions of men on any given subject from
their civil and canon laws, their popular literature, their customs in everyday life, the judgments rendered in their courts, the precepts read in their
pulpits, than from their occasional guarded utterances, when called on for
their well-digested theories. Judging their estimate of woman and the
marriage institution by the civil code and the common law of England,
there is very little purity, dignity, or sacredness pertaining thereto.

The contract is wholly an unjust, unequal one; woman is left at a disadvantage at every point. The best writers on law claim that there should
even be a different code of morals for husband and wife, that the violation
of the marriage vow is worse on her part than that of the man.

"Many jurists," says Kent, vol. 2, p. "SB," "are of opinion that the adultery of the husband ought not to be noticed or made subject to the same
animadversions as that of the wife, because it is not evidence of such entire depravity, nor equally injurious in its effects upon the morals, good
order, and happiness of domestic life." Montesquieu, Pothier, and Dr. Taylor all insist that the cases of husband and wife ought to be distinguished,
and that the violation of the marriage vow, on the part of the wife, is the
most mischievous, and the prosecution ought to be confined to the of-
fence on her part,—and remember the administration of justice depends
far more on the opinions of eminent jurists, than on law alone, for law is
powerless when at variance with public sentiment.

Do not the above citations clearly prove inequality? Are not the very
letter and spirit of the marriage contract based on the idea of the supremacy of man as the keeper of woman's virtue—her sole protector and support? Out of marriage, woman asks nothing at this hour but the franchise.
It is only in marriage that she must demand her rights to person, children,
property, wages, life, liberty, and the pursuit of happiness. How can we
discuss all the laws and conditions of marriage, without perceiving its
essential essence, end, and aim? Now, whether the institution of marriage
be human or divine, whether regarded as indissoluble by ecclesiastical
courts, or dissoluble by civil courts, woman, finding herself equally degraded in each and every phase of it, always the victim of the institution, it
is her right and her duty to sift the relation and the compact through and
through, until she finds out the true cause of her false position. How can

we go before the legislatures of our respective States and demand new laws, or no laws, on divorce, until we have some idea of what the true relation is?

We decide the whole question of slavery by settling the sacred rights of the individual. We assert that man cannot hold property in man, and reject the whole code of laws that conflicts with the self-evident truth of that assertion.

So I assert that man cannot hold property in woman, that husband cannot own and hold a wife, except by the power of mutual love and attraction. In this relation they must stand as equals, and all laws that do not recognize this fact should be null and void. The Christian doctrine of marriage, as propounded by Paul in the seventh chapter of Corinthians, degrades alike the woman and the relation. He teaches that the sole reason for marriage is that a man may gratify instinct without sin. But for this object, he says, it would be better not to marry. On this idea, the doctrine of celibacy was made obligatory in the priesthood in the Catholic Church. In fact, Paul's teachings fairly represent the spirit of the Church for centuries. This influence still pervades our laws, corrupts our thoughts, and demoralizes our customs. The marriage service of the Church of England, which incorporates the Pauline doctrine, is felt by English brides and bridegrooms to contain what is so offensive to decency, that many clergymen mercifully make lawful omissions.

The contradictory views in which woman is represented, are as varied as pitiful. While the Magnificat to the Virgin is chanted in all our cathedrals round the globe, on each returning Sabbath day, or her motherhood extolled by her worshippers, maternity for the rest of womankind is referred to as a weakness, a disability, a curse, an evidence of woman's divinely ordained subjection.

Yet surely the real woman should have some points of resemblance in character and position, with the ideal one, whom poets, novelists, and artists portray.

It is folly to talk of the sacredness of marriage, and maternity, while the wife is practically regarded as an inferior, a subject, a slave. Having decided then that companionship and conscientious parenthood are the only true grounds for marriage, if the relation brings out the worst characteristics of each party, or if the home atmosphere is unwholesome for children, is not the very *raison d'être* of the union wanting and the marriage practically annulled? It cannot be called a holy relation,—no, not even a desirable one,—when love and mutual respect are wanting. And let us bear in mind one other important fact: that lack of sympathy and content in the parents indicates radical physical unsuitability, which results in badly organized offspring. As Milton says;—

> Children born in these unhappy and unhallowed connections, are, in the most solemn sense, of unlawful birth—the fruit of lust, but not of love— and so not of God, divinely descended, but from beneath, whence proceed all manner of evil and uncleanliness. Next to the calamity of such a birth to the child, is the misfortune of being trained in the atmosphere of a household where love is not the law, but where discord and bitterness abound; stamping their demoniac features on the moral nature, with all their odious peculiarities—thus continuing, the race in a weakness and depravity that must be a sure precursor of its ruin, as a just penalty of long-violated law.

If then the real object of marriage is defeated, it is for the interest of the State as well as the individual concerned, to see that such pernicious unions be legally dissolved.

Inasmuch, then, as incompatibility of temper defeats the two great objects of marriage, it should be the primal cause for divorce. To quote Milton again, who speaks boldly on this point

> Of all insulting mockeries of heavenly truth and holy law, none can lie greater than that physical impotency is cause sufficient for divorce, while no amount of mental or moral or spiritual imbecility is ever to be pleaded in support, of such a demand. Such a law was worthy those dark periods when marriage was held by the greatest doctors and priests of the Church to be a work of the flesh only, and almost, if not altogether, a defilement—denied wholly to the clergy, and a second time forbidden to all.

We hear from all sides that the indissolubility of marriage is absolutely necessary for the happiness of the family, the purity of society, and the good of the State. But to my mind, so important is unity in marriage, so dependent upon this the usefulness of the home, the good of society, the solidarity of the State; so lamentable the consequences invariably resulting from disunity in marriage, that every encouragement to divorce ought to be given.

Transient lapses from some of the cardinal virtues, might not be as disastrous to the peace of home life as a perpetual domestic warfare, with no truce ever granted and no quarter given.

The true standpoint from which to view this question is individual sovereignty, individual happiness. It is often said that the interests of society are paramount and first to be considered. This was the old Roman idea, the Pagan idea, that the individual was made for the State. The central idea of barbarism has ever been the family, the tribe, the nation, never the individual. But the great doctrine of Christianity is the right of individual conscience and judgment. The reason it took such a hold on the hearts of the people, was because it taught that the individual was primary, the State, the Church, society, the family secondary. However, a comprehensive view of any question of human interest shows that the highest good and happiness of the individual and society lie in the same direction.

The question of Divorce, like Marriage, should be settled as to its most sacred relations, by the parties themselves, neither the State nor the Church having any right to intermeddle therein. As to property or children, it must be viewed and regulated as a civil contract. Then the union should be dissolved with at least as much deliberation and publicity as it was formed.

There might be some ceremony and witnesses to add to the dignity and solemnity of the occasion. Like the Quaker marriage which the parties conduct themselves, so in this case, without any statement of their disagreements, the parties might simply declare, that after living together for several years, they found themselves still unsuited to each other and incapable of making a happy home.

If divorce were made respectable and recognized by society as a duty as well as a right, reasonable men and women could arrange all the preliminaries, often even the division of property and guardianship of children, quite as satisfactorily as it could be done in the courts. Where the mother is capable of training the children, a sensible father would leave them to her care, rather than place them in the hands of a stranger. But where divorce is not respectable, men who have no paternal feeling will often hold the child, not so much for its good, or his own affection, as to punish the wife for disgracing him. The love of children is not strong in most men, and they feel but little responsibility in regard to them. See how readily they turn off young sons to shift for themselves, and unless the law compelled them to support their illegitimate children, they would never give them a second thought. But on the mother-soul rests forever the care and responsibility of human life. Her love for the child born out of wedlock is often intensified by the infinite pity she feels for its disgrace. Even among the lower animals, we find the female ever brooding over the young and helpless.

Limiting the causes of divorce to physical defects or delinquencies; making the proceedings public, prying into all the intimate personal affairs of unhappy men and women; regarding the step as quasi criminal; punishing the guilty party in the suit,—all this will not strengthen frail human nature; will not ensure happy homes; will not banish scandals and purge society of prostitution.

No, no; the enemy of marriage, of the State, of society, is not liberal divorce laws, but the unhealthy atmosphere that exists in the home itself. A legislative atmosphere cannot make a unit of a divided family.

Many writers on divorce dwell on the general corruption and demoralization that has grown out of the liberal laws on that subject. Mr. Gladstone thinks he can see a change for the worse since the English Divorce Act was passed in 1857, and yet it is said that Queen Victoria has kept the purest court known in English history. I think if Mr. Gladstone had taken time, he could have recalled other periods when there was far more social corruption than in his day.

A writer in the *Forum* mourns over the facts brought out in a Report for which Congress made an appropriation in 1887, showing that 25,000 divorces had been granted in a single year in the United States. He says: "This is a disgrace to our country." Our rulers on all sides are sounding the alarm loud and clear. "Our homes, our firesides, our sacred family altars, are all about to be swept away." 25,000 divorces in one year, and the majority demanded by women.

There seems to be almost a panic just now lest the foundations of our social life be swamped in the quicksands of liberal divorce laws. Seeing how difficult a matter it is to trace all the pitfalls in society to their true causes, it is an unwarrantable and wholesale assumption to attribute all our social upheaval to the liberal divorce laws that have been passed within the last fifty years. Whence came all the adverse winds that produced the terrible corruptions and endless changes in the marriage relation, through polyandry, polygamy, the mutterrecht, concubinage, and the morganatic relations so frequent in the royal families in the Old World? Marriage has been a bone of contention in Church and State for centuries, that made the canon and civil law a kind of football for popes and kings, ecclesiastics and statesmen, and now, forsooth, because under free republican institutions, a new type of womanhood has been developed, demanding larger freedom in the marriage relation, justice, liberty, and equality under the law, our conservatives think the whole institution is about to topple on their heads.

I would recommend every rational man and woman thinking and writing on this subject to run through their life-experience, summon up all the divorced people they know, gauge their moral status, and, if possible, the influence of their lives as writers, speakers, artists, and philanthropists, and see if they do not compare favorably with the best men and women of their acquaintance. In my own circle of friends, I can recall at most about two dozen—all as gifted, moral, and refined men and women as I ever knew. But few of the women married again, and those who did, have been exceptionally happy in their new relations.

The rapidly increasing number of divorces, so far from showing a lower state of morals, proves exactly the reverse. Woman is in a transition period from slavery to freedom and she will not accept the conditions in married life that she has heretofore meekly endured.

When the mother, with all her steadfast love of home and children, her natural aversion to change, demands release, we may rest assured her reasons for sundering the tie are all sufficient to herself and should lie to society at large.

The frequent demands for divorce simply mean that we have not yet reached the ideal marriage state. Divorce is a challenge to our present system. Evolution has been the law of life. The relation of the sexes has passed through many phases and is likely to pass through many more.

So long as it is the testimony of missionaries among the abandoned classes that prostitution is largely supported by married men, and so long as it is the verdict of one of the keenest observers of human nature that, after eighteen hundred years, the man is still imperfectly monogamous;—so long as these facts remain, no one need hope for permanent social relations. To quote Milton again:—

> Observation and experience daily show how incompetent are men, as individuals, or as governments, to select partners in business, teachers for their children, ministers of their religion, or makers, adjudicators, or administrators of their laws; and as the same weakness and blindness must attend in the selection of matrimonial partners, the dictates of humanity and common sense alike show that the latter and most important contract should no more be perpetual than either or all of the former.

Thus marriage be in itself divinely founded and is fortified as an institution by innumerable analogies in the whole kingdom of universal nature, still, a true marriage is only known by its results and, like the fountain, if pure, will reveal only pure manifestations. Nor need it ever he said, "What God hath joined together, let no man put asunder," for man could not put it asunder; nor can he any more unite what God and nature have not joined together.

SOURCE: Elizabeth Stanton, "Divorce versus Domestic Warfare," *The Arena*, vol. 1 (April 1890), 560–69.

Chapter 10

"The Matriarchate, or Mother-Age" (1891)

EDITORS' NOTE: Here Stanton provides an explicitly feminist reading of the literature on matriarchy emphasizing the work of anthropological pioneer Lewis Henry Morgan. In his last book, Ancient Society *(1877), Morgan argued that the status of women was the single best indicator of a people's development from "savagery" to "civilization." The level of women's participation was a test for Morgan of a society's movement toward modern civilization and an indication that a militarized aristocracy was being replaced by democratic cooperation. The closing sentences of Morgan's* Ancient Society *reads: "Democracy in government, brotherhood in society, equality in rights and privileges, and universal education, foreshadow the next higher plane of society to which experience, intelligence, and knowledge are steadily tending. It will be a revival, in a higher form, of the liberty, equality, and fraternity of the ancient gentes." Stanton extended Morgan's argument by concluding that the indispensable test of the return of women's influence over society was the right to vote and hold public office and that the test of democracy was the triumph of cooperation between the sexes. Her ultimate message was that women can be powerful in the future because they have been powerful in the past. In other writings on the transition from matriarchy to male rule, Stanton emphasized that men had driven women from public life and degraded them into household servants, a fundamentally political change that was institutionalized in marriage and religion. Stanton was certain that the dark era of male domination and sexual conflict was soon to end, to be replaced by an era of cooperation of the sexes.*

Without going into any of the fine calculations of historians as to the centuries of human growth, I would simply state that some agree on about eighty-five thousand years. They assign sixty thousand to savagery, twenty thousand to barbarism, and five thousand to civilization.

For my present purpose, these facts are only interesting to show for how long a period, in proportion, women reigned supreme, the arbiters of their own destiny, the protectors of their children, the acknowledged builders of all there was of home life, religion, and later, from time to time, of government.

All along from the beginning until the sixteenth century, when Luther eliminated the feminine element wholly from the Protestant religion and brought the full power of the Church to enforce woman's complete subjection, we find traces of the matriarchate. Karl Pearson, in a series of deeply interesting essays, gives us the result of his researches into the works of modern historians and the startling facts they unearth, from what to most of us is the dead, unknown, eternal past, shadowed in mystery. The publication of Wilkeson's *Ancient Egypt* in 1836, of *Das Mutterrecht*, by Bachofen in 1861, of Morgan's *Ancient Society* in 1877, with other lesser lights pursuing the same trend of investigation, all show the leading, independent position women held for ages. What is often said, and repeated from time to time and never contradicted, is accepted as truth. Thus, the assertion that women have always been physically inferior to men, and consequently have always been held in a subject condition, has been universally believed. This view has furnished the opponents to woman's emancipation their chief arguments for holding her in bondage, and logically so, for if at all periods and in all latitudes and longitudes woman had held the same subordinate position, men would naturally infer that what we choose to call Providence, for wise purposes, had made woman the slave of man. The worst feature of these assumptions is that women themselves believe them and feel that to strive for their own emancipation is simply an attempt at the impossible. Fortunately, historical research at last proved the fallacy of these assumptions and all the arguments that grow out of them. Mankind may be traced by a chain of necessary inferences back to a time when, ignorant of fire, without articulate language, without artificial weapons, they depended, like the wild animals, upon the spontaneous fruits of the earth.

Through all this period woman was left to protect herself and forage for her children. Morgan, in his *Ancient Society* gives many remarkable examples of the superior position of women among different tribes in the latter part of the period of barbarism. Among the greater number of the American aborigines the descent of property and children were in the female line. Women sat in the councils of war and peace, and their opinions had equal weight on all questions. Among the Winnebagoes that occupied the territory now known as Wisconsin a woman was at the head of the nation. The same was true among the early tribes or gens in the Eastern

Hemisphere. In the council of the Iroquois gens every adult male or female member had a voice on all questions brought before it. It elected and deposed its sachem and chief, it elected Keepers of the Faith, it condoned or coerced the murder of a *gentilis,* and it adopted persons into the gens.

At the epoch of European discovery, the American Indian males generally were organized into gentes, with descent in the female line. Before paterfamilias was known, the family was nowhere considered a unit around which society centred. Nothing whatever was based on the family in any of its forms, because it was incapable of entering a gens as a whole. The gens was homogeneous and to a great extent permanent in duration and, as such, the natural basis of a social system. A family of the monogamic type might have individualized and become powerful in society at large, but the gens did not and could not recognize the family as an integer of itself.

This is equally true of the modern family and political society. Although individualized by property rights and privileges and recognized as a legal entity by statutory enactments, the family is not the unit of the political system. The State recognizes the counties of which it is composed, the county its townships, but the townships take no note of the family. So in the early periods the nation recognized its tribes, the tribes its phratries, and the phratries its gentes, but the gens took no note of the family.

Thus Morgan flatly contradicts modern historians who assert that the social system of the early Greeks "was the home, the hearth, or family." Like our modern opponents, they cling to the idea of "the family unit," because on that is based the absolute power of the father over the property, children, and the civil and political rights of wives. It is worthy of note that our barbarian ancestors seem to have had a higher idea of justice to woman than American men in the nineteenth century, professing to believe, as they do, in our republican principles of government.

During these early periods the property of woman was in her own line and gens, and man's property was in his own line and gens. The following case at the Pueblo of Oraybe shows that the husband acquires no rights over the property of the wife, or over the children of the marriage. A Zunian married an Oraybe woman and had by her three children. He resided with them at Oraybe until his wife died, when the relatives of the deceased wife took possession of her children and her household property, leaving to him his clothing, horse, and weapons. As was the custom, he returned to his own people at Zuni. A similar case occurred at another of the Moqui Pueblos. A woman died, leaving property, children, and husband. The deceased wife's relatives took the property and children, and all the husband was allowed to take was his own clothing, with the privilege of going whithersoever he desired. From these cases, it appears the children belonged to the mother, not to the father, and that he was not allowed to take them even, after the mother's death. Such, also, was the usage among the Iroquois and other Northern tribes, and among the village Indians of Mexico.

The growth of the idea of property, and the rise of monogamy, which in a measure assured the paternity of children, formed motives sufficiently powerful to bring children into the gens of their father and a participation in the inheritance of his estate. But this invasion of the mother's rights was a slow process and for long periods resisted.

Mr. Morgan shows, too, that the early tribes in Greece, like the American aborigines, were essentially democratic in their government. Historians, accustomed to monarchial governments, would naturally interpret words and actions in harmony with their ideas. Thus, Mr. Grote has a memorable dictum of Ulysses in the *Iliad* to prove that the Greeks had a one-man government: "The rule of many is not a good thing; let us have one ruler only,—one king,—him to whom Zeus hath given the sceptre with the tutelary sanctions." But this saying has no significance as applied to government. Ulysses, from whose address the quotation is taken, was speaking of the command of an army before a besieged city. There was no occasion for Ulysses to discuss or endorse any plan of government; but he had sufficient reason for advocating obedience to a single commander of the army before a besieged city.

As thus we have seen that Grote, in his "History of Greece," writing from his own true inwardness, mistook the spirit of the times of which he wrote, it behooves us women to question all historians, sacred and profane, who teach by examples or precepts any philosophy that lowers the status of the mothers of the race, or favors the masculine power in government.

As far back into the shadowy past as human thought has penetrated, and been able by a process of reason to substantiate the facts of primeval life, we behold woman in all her native dignity, self-poised and self-supporting, her own head and hands her guidance and protection. The instincts of motherhood gave her the first thought of privacy and seclusion, and led her to make a home for herself and children in the caves of the earth, safe from the wild beasts of the forests, and the wily hunter, who lived on uncooked food and slept on the ground, wherever night found him. While his rude activities developed but few of his faculties, the woman, in solitude, was learning the great lessons of life. A new birth! What a mystery for her to ponder! What love and tenderness helpless infancy calls out; what intelligence and activity its necessities compel; what forethought and responsibility in providing for herself and children it involves! Sex relations being transitory and promiscuous, the idea of fatherhood was unknown. As men naturally have no sense of paternal responsibility, no one knew nor cared about the father of a child. To know one's mother was deemed all-sufficient for a legitimate name and an abiding place.

The period of woman's supremacy lasted through many centuries—undisputed, accepted as natural and proper wherever it existed, and was called the matriarchate, or mother-age. It was plainly traceable among the Aryans, the Germans, the Persians, and indications of it are still seen among uncivilized tribes and nations.

Careful historians now show that the greatest civilizing power all along the pathway of natural development has been found in the wisdom and tender sentiments growing out of motherhood. For the protection of herself and her children woman made the first home in the caves of the earth; then huts with trees in the sunshine. She made the first attempts at agriculture; raised grain, fruits, and herbs which she learned to use in sickness. She was her own physician; all that was known of the medical art was in her hands. She domesticated the cow and the goat, and from the necessities of her children learned the use of milk. The women cultivated the arts of peace, and the sentiments of kinship, and all there was of human love and home-life. The necessities of motherhood were the real source of all the earliest attempts at civilization.

Thus, instead of being a "disability," as unthinking writers are pleased to call it, maternity has been the all-inspiring motive or force that impelled the first steps towards a stable home and family life. Clearly the birth of civilization must be sought in the attempt of woman at self-preservation during the period of pregnancy and lactation.

What man achieved at that period was due to the contest for food with his fellows and the wild beasts. He simply invented and improved weapons of warfare; but the woman, handicapped as she appeared to be by child bearing, became on this very account the main factor in human progress. The man's contributions at this early period are nothing as compared to woman's. Her varied responsibilities as mother, bread-winner, protector, defender of a group of helpless children, raised her to intellectual supremacy and made her the teacher and ruler of man.

"Perhaps more interesting for us to-day is the actual existence of the matriarchate in the north of Africa, among the Touaregs. 'The matrix dyes the child' is one of their proverbs. The child belongs to the mother and not to the father; it is the blood of the mother, and not that of the father, which confers on the child the rank he is to take. Formerly, when there was a question of territorial distribution, the lands granted to each family were inscribed in the name of the mother. The Berber law gives to women the administration of their property; at Rhat, they alone dispose of houses, gardens,—in a word, of all the landed property in the country. Among the Touaregs, not only is woman held as the equal of man, but she enjoys a preferable condition. She disposes of her hand, and in the conjugal community she administers her own fortune, without being forced to contribute to the expenses of the household. Thus it happens that, as productions accumulate, the greater part of the wealth is in the hands of the women.

"The Targui (which is the adjective for Touareg) woman is monogamous; she has imposed monogamy on her husband, although the Mussulman law permits him several wives. She is independent in regard to her husband, whom she can repudiate on the slightest pretext; she comes and goes freely. These social customs have produced extraordinary developments in the Targui woman. Her intelligence and her initiative spirit are astonishing in the midst of a Mussulman society. She excels in bodily exercises; on the back of a dromedary she travels a hundred kilometres to attend a soirée; she competes in races with the boldest cavalier of the desert. She is distinguished by intellectual culture; the ladies of the tribe of Ymanan are celebrated for their beauty and their musical talent; when they give concerts the men come eagerly from the most distant parts, adorned like male ostriches. The women of the Berber tribes sing every evening to the accompaniment of their violin; they improvise; in the open desert they revive the *cours d'amour* of Provence. The Touaregs are the descendants of the Lybians spoken of by Herodotus. This historian tells us that 'in the valley of the Nile the women go to market and traffic, whilst the men, shut up in houses, weave the linen. The male children are not compelled by law to maintain their parents; this charge is incumbent by law upon the daughters.' The imposition of such a duty on the daughters sufficed to establish the rule that the wealth of the family should belong to the women, and wherever the woman possesses this economic position she is not under the guardianship of her husband, but is the head of the family."

The Rev. Samuel Gorman, a missionary among the Taguna Pueblo Indians, remarks, in an address before the Historical Society of New Mexico, that "the right of property belongs to the female part of the family, and descends in that line from mother to daughter. Their land is held in common, as the property of the community, but after a person cultivates a lot he has personal claim to it, which he can sell to one of the community. . . . Their women generally have control of the granary, and they are more provident than their Spanish neighbors about the future. Ordinarily they try to have a year's provisions on hand. It is only when two years of scarcity succeed each other that Pueblos, as a community, suffer hunger."

Of the Senecas of North America, the Rev. Arthur Wright wrote in 1873: "As to their family system, when occupying the old long-houses, it is probable that some one clan predominated, the women taking in husbands, however, from other clans. Usually, the females ruled the house. The stores were in common; but woe to the luckless husband or lover who was too shiftless to do his share of the providing. No matter how many children or whatever goods he might have in the house, he might at any time be ordered to pick up his blanket and budge; and after such an order it would not be healthful for him to attempt to disobey. The house would be too hot for him; and, unless saved by the intercession of some aunt or grandmother, he must retreat to his own clan, or go and start a new matrimonial alliance in some other. The women were the great power among the clan, as everywhere else. They did not hesitate, when occasion required, 'to knock off the horns,' as it was technically called, from the head of a chief and send him back to the ranks of the warriors. The original nomination of the chiefs also always rested with the women."

"The account we find given by the Portuguese navigators of the Nairs, a people inhabiting the coast of Malabar in the fifteenth century, is another proof of the superior condition of women under previous family systems. The Nairs were then in a state of actual civilization; they had a marine and well-organized army; their towns were wealthy and the inhabitants courteous in manners. But the previous notions of the European visitors were strangely upset by what they saw of the social position of the women. There were large families, we are told, consisting of several hundred members bearing the same name. The real estate belonged in common to all members of the gens; the most complete equality reigned among them. The husband, instead of living with his wife and his children, lived with his brothers and sisters in the maternal house; when he left it, he was always accompanied by his favorite sister; at his death his personal property did not go to his children, but was distributed between the children of his sisters. The mother, or, in case of her death, her eldest daughter, was the head of family; her eldest brother, named the foster-father, managed the estate; the husband was a guest; he only entered the house on fixed days, and did not sit at table with his wife and children. 'The Nairs,' says Barbosa, 'have an extraordinary respect for their mother; it is from her they receive wealth and honors; they honor equally their eldest sister, who is to succeed the mother and take the management of the family. The children belong to the mother, and she takes their support on herself.' The Nair family system was maintained among the Malabar peoples till the invasion of Hyder Ali in 1766."

Strabo says of the primitive people of Spain, "That they suffered a most foolish governance by women; that the women possessed the property, and it passed from mother to daughter; that the latter gave away their brothers in marriage; that the men took dowry with them into the houses of their wives; that the women performed all the agricultural work, and were as hardy as men."

The women at a later period were not rulers of the home, but they were priestesses; the deities were in a great part goddesses. All there was of learning and tradition was in the hands of the women, and folk custom long recognized their superiority to men.

The woman being the source of traditional religion, the care of the gods was essentially hers. About the hearth arose the first conceptions of the altar and sanctuary and the immortality of the soul. She was essentially the wise, and wrote with her staff in the ashes the will of the gods. Her pots and kettles reappear in every witch trial in the Middle Ages. The safety of mother and child, in the solitudes of the vast primeval forests, was due in no small measure to the superstition that woman was in communion with the gods, who would avenge her wrongs. Her spirit is supposed to linger around the hearth after death, and to-day the solitary student sitting over the fire, or the peasant when his family are out, will tell you they have been alone at the hearth with their mother-soul. As woman forms the religion and tradition of this period, the goddesses, not gods, are the more numerous and most worshipped. The oldest, the wisest, the most mysteriously powerful of the Teutonic deities are female. Jacob Grimm said of the German goddesses years before modern investigations had brought the mother-age to light:

"In the case of the gods, the previous investigation could reach its goal by considering them separately. It seems advisable, however, to consider the goddesses collectively as well as individually, because a common idea lies at the basis of them all and will thus be more clearly marked. They are conceived of peculiarly as divine mother (göttermutter) travelling about and visiting mortals. From them mankind has learned the business and the arts of housekeeping, agriculture, cattle-raising, spinning, weaving, sowing, reaping, as well as watching the hearth, These labors bring peace and rest to the land, and the memory of them remains firmer in pleasing traditions than war and fighting, which, like women, the majority of the goddesses shun." Karl Pearson says, "A truer although unconscious tribute to the civilizing work of women can hardly be imagined. If we add to the arts mentioned by Grimm the art of healing, the elements of religious faith as a tradition, and the runic art of writing, we have a slight picture of what woman accomplished in the centuries which intervened between the promiscuous period and the complete establishment of the father-age."

With such personal independence and superiority, such authority in the national councils, in religious faith, and at the fireside, with the absolute control of her own home, property, and children, how did it come to pass that the mother was at last dethroned and womanhood degraded in every nation on the globe?

The mother's labors had from an early period been re-enforced by those of her sons whose tastes led them to agriculture and the herding of cattle, to domestic life rather than that of the wandering nomad existence of the wily hunter, but this class was proportionally small. However, in process of time,—as the home with its increasing comforts and attractions, fire, cooked food, and woman's tender care in old age, sickness, and death, the innocent prattle of children, the mother's songs and stories, her religious faith and services, all appealed to the better feelings of the wily hunter also,—men began to think, when weary of the battle and the chase, that they would like a permanent foothold in some family group besides the one into which they were born.

As soon as monogamic marriage appeared with property and descent in the male line, and men found themselves comfortably ensconced in a home of their own, they began little by little to make their aggressions, and in time completely dominated woman, leaving her no remnant of authority anywhere, neither in the home, nor at the altar, nor in the councils of the nation.

Having no paternal instinct, no natural love for children, the devices of men to establish the rights of paternity were as varied as ridiculous. It was the custom at one time when the mother gave birth to a child for the acknowledged father to take to his bed to pretend that he had shared in the perils of labor, and thus prove his identity, while the wife waited on him—— for the women, accustomed to agricultural work, were so hardened by it that they did not suffer in childbirth,

On this point Karl Pearson tells us the transition from to the father-age was marked by the appearance of women of gigantic stature. The old legends of contests between men and women for supremacy are not such idle fancies as some would have us believe. Very dark shadows indeed do such figures as those of Ildico, Fredegunde, and Brunhilde cast across the pages of history. Such women were only paralleled by the Clytemnestra and Medea of a like phase in Greek development. Among the Germans, too, the poets represent the contest between men and women for the mastery. Wuodan replaces Hellja; Siegfried conquers Brunhilde; Beowulf, the offspring of Grindel; and Thor, fights with Gialp and Griep, the daughters of Geirrod. One great element of physical and mental vigor is freedom, which women have never enjoyed except under the Matriarchate.

The Amazons, the present body-guard of the King of Dahomey, the astounding powers of endurance exhibited by domestic servants and the peasant girls of Southern Germany and Italy, the fish-women at Boulogne, all point to the great strength when once the physique has been developed.

The victory of man over woman was not easily accomplished. It took long centuries to fully confirm it, and traces of the mother-age remained throughout the Mediaeval times. The permanency of sex relations among the agriculturists and the necessity for organization in matters of defence, which must be intrusted mainly to men, were the beginnings of the father-age.

For though women had been compelled to fight for their own protection and were abundantly able to maintain the contest, yet wars for territory and conquests over other tribes and nations were opposed by all the tenderest sentiments of their nature. Hence they naturally of their own accord would withdraw from the councils of war and the battle-field, but as angels of mercy to minister to the wounded and the dying. Thus man became ruler, tribal organizer, tribal father, before his position of sexual father was recognized. While the mother still ruled the house, "the Alvater" ruled the fight, though ofttimes guided by the woman.

Driven from the commanding position of home mother and deprived of her rights to property and children, the last fortress of the Teutonic woman was her sacerdotal privileges. She remained holy as priestess. She had charge of the tribal sacrifice and the tribal religion.

From this last refuge she was driven by the introduction of the Christian religion, with its narrow Pauline doctrine, which made woman mentally and physically the inferior of man, and lawfully in subjection to him.

The spirit of the Church in its contempt for women, as shown in the Scriptures, in Paul's epistles and the Pentateuch, the hatred of the fathers, manifested in their ecclesiastical canons, and in the doctrines of asceticism, celibacy, and witchcraft, destroyed man's respect for woman and legalized the burning, drowning, and torturing of women by the thousand.

Women and their duties became objects of hatred to the Christian missionaries and of alternate scorn and fear to pious ascetics and monks. The priestess mother became something impure, associated with the devil, and her lore an infernal incantation, her very cooking a brewing of poison, nay, her very existence a source of sin to man. Thus woman, as mother and priestess, became woman as witch. The witch trials of the Middle Ages, wherein thousands of women were condemned to the stake, were the very real traces of the contest between man and woman. Christianity putting the religious weapon into man's hand made his conquest complete. But woman did not yield without prolonged resistance and a courageous final struggle. Driven from the home, an outlaw and a wanderer everywhere, ostracized by the State, condemned by the courts, crucified by the Church, the supreme power of the mother of the race was conquered only by the angel of death, and the Dark Ages tolled her funeral knell.

It was this wholesale, violent suppression of the feminine element, in the effort to establish the Patriarchate, that, more than any other one cause, produced the Dark Ages.

Morgan, in his *Ancient Society,* attributes the premature destruction of ethnic life, in the societies of Greece and Rome, to their failure to develop and utilize the mental and moral conservative forces of the female intellect, which were not less essential than those of men to their progress.

In closing, I would say that every woman present must have a new sense of dignity and self-respect, feeling that our mothers, during some periods in the long past, have been the ruling power, and that they used that power for the best interests of humanity. As history is said to repeat itself, we have every reason to believe that our turn will come again, it may not be for woman's supremacy, but for the as yet untried experiment of complete equality, when the united thought of man and woman will inaugurate a just government, a pure religion, a happy home, a civilization at last in which ignorance, poverty, and crime will exist no more. Those who watch already behold the dawn of the new day.

"Night wanes—the vapor round the mountains curled
Melts into morn, and light awakes the world.
Mighty Nature bounds as from her birth:
The sun is in the heavens, and life on earth;
Flowers in the valley, splendor in the beam,
Health on the gale, and freshness in the stream."

SOURCE: Elizabeth Stanton, "The Matriarchate: Or Mother-Age," address to National Council of Women of the United States, February 22, 1891, Washington, D.C., in *Transactions of the National Council of Women of the United States* (Philadelphia: J. B. Lippincott, 1891), 218–27.

Chapter 11

"Worship of God in Man" (1893)

EDITORS' NOTE: *The same year that Stanton resigned her position as president of the National American Woman Suffrage Association (NAWSA) and delivered "Solitude of Self" to a variety of audiences, she submitted several speeches to be read for her at the Columbian Exposition in Chicago. Stanton prepared addresses to the Women's Congress and to the World's Parliament of Religions. By this time she had begun her work on* The Woman's Bible, *in which she dissected the most sexist portions of the Jewish and Christian scriptures. In the following selection, she highlighted selections from the Bible that promoted respect for human dignity and cautiously evidenced awareness that humans could never know but only guess about the nature of the divine. An important precedent for Stanton's conception of a humanized religion can be found in the work of Unitarian minister Theodore Parker, whose 1843 essay "The Permanent and the Transient in Christianity" Stanton cited in her memoirs as a particularly important influence on her life and thought. Ernest Renan's* The Life of Jesus *(1872) also provided a model for a respectful, humanizing interpretation of the Gospels that stripped away miracles and supernatural events as superstitious tales added as the Church became a powerful social institution.*

As we have not yet reached the ultimatum of religious faith, it may be legitimate to ask: What will the next step be? As we are all alike interested in the trend of religious thought, no one should feel aggrieved in hearing his creed fairly analysed or in listening to speculations as to something better in the near future.

As I read the signs of the times, I think the next form of religion will be the "Religion of Humanity," in which men and women will worship what they see of the divine in each other; the virtues, the beatitudes, the possibilities ascribed to Deity reflected in mortal beings.

To stimulate our reverence for the great Spirit of Life that sets all things in motion and holds them forever in their places, our religious teachers point us to the grandeur of Nature in all her works. We tremble at the earthquake, the hurricane, the rolling thunder and vivid lightning, the raging tempests by sea and land; we are filled with awe and admiration by the splendor of the starry heavens, the boundless oceans and vast continents, the majestic forests, lakes and rivers and snow-capped mountains, that in their yearnings seem to touch the heavens. From all these grand and impressive forces in Nature we turn with relief to the gentle rain and dew, the genial sunshine, the singing birds and fragrant flowers, to the love and tenderness we find in every form of life; we see order and beauty too, in the changing seasons, the planetary world, in the rising sun, moon and stars, in day with its glorious dawn and night with its holy mysteries, which altogether thrill with emotion every chord of the human soul.

By all the wonders and mysteries that surround us, we are led to question the source of what we see and to judge the powers and possibilities of the Creator by the grandeur and beauty of his works.

Measuring man by the same standard, we find that all the forces and qualities the most exalted mind ascribes to his ideal God, are reproduced, in a less degree, in the noble men and women who have glorified the race.

Judging man by his works, what shall we say to the seven wonders of the world? Of the Colossus of Rhodes, Diana's Temple at Ephesus, the Mausoleum at Halicarnassus, the Pyramids of Egypt, the Pharos at Alexandria, the hanging Gardens at Babylon and the Olympian Zeus. Yet, these are all crumbling to dust; but change is the law, too, in all Nature's works.

The manifestation of man's power is more varied and wonderful as the ages roll on. Who can stand in St. Peter's at Rome and listen to the deep-toned organ reverberating from arch to arch, with a chorus of human voices alike pathetic and triumphant in their hymns of praise; without feeling the divine harmony in architecture, poetry, and song? And yet man, so small in stature, conceived and perfected that vast cathedral, with its magnificent dome, strung every key in that grand organ to answer to a master's touch, and trained every voice in that great choir to melody, to perfect time and tune,—a combination in grandeur surpassing far the seven wonders of the world.

And what shall we say of the discoveries and inventions of the last fifty years, by which the labors of the world have been lifted from the shoulders of men, to be done henceforth by tireless machines? Behold the magnitude of the works accomplished by man in his own day and generation. He has leveled mountains and bridged chasms; with his railroads he has linked the Atlantic and the Pacific, the Rocky and Allegheny Mountains together; with steam and the ocean cable he has anchored continents side by side, and melted the nations of the earth in one. With electricity man has opened such vistas of wonder and mystery that scientists and philosophers stand amazed at their own possibilities, and in the wake of these physical triumphs, we are startled with the mysteries revealed to us by psychical researches into what has hitherto been to us the unseen universe.

Man has manifested wisdom, too, as well as power. In fact, what cardinal virtue has he not shown, through all the shifting scenes of the passing centuries? The page of history glows with the great deeds of noble men and women. What courage and heroism, what self-sacrifice and sublime faith in principle have they not shown in persecution and death, 'mid the horrors of war, the sorrows of exile, and the weary years in prison-life? What could sustain mortal men in this awful "solitude of self," but the fact that the great moral forces of the universe are bound up in his organisation? What are danger, death, exile and dungeon walls to the great spirit of life incarnate in him? Our ideas of mankind, as "totally depraved," his morality "but filthy rags," his heart "deceitful above all things and desperately wicked," his aspirations "but idle dreams of luxury and selfishness" are so many reflexions on the Creator, who is said to be perfect and to have made man in his own image.

The new religion will teach the dignity of human nature, and its infinite possibilities for development. Its believers will not remain forever in the valley of humiliation, confessing themselves in the Church service, on each returning Sabbath day, to be "miserable sinners" imploring the "good Lord to deliver them" from the consequences of violated law; but the new religion will inspire its worshippers with self-respect, with noble aspirations to attain diviner heights from day to day than they have yet have reached. It will teach honesty and honor in word and dead, in all the relations of life. It will teach the solidarity of the race, that all must rise or fall as one. Its creed will be Justice, Liberty, Equality for all the children of earth. It will teach our practical duties to man in this life, rather than our sentimental duties to God in fitting ourselves for the next life.

A loving human fellowship is the real divine communion. The spiritual life is not a mystical contemplation of divine attributes, but the associative development of all that is good in the human character. The Old and New Testaments, which Christians accept as their rule of life, are full of these lessons of universal benevolence. "If you love not man whom you have seen, how can you love God whom you have not seen?" Jesus said to his disciples. "Whatsoever you have done unto these my brethren, you have done unto me." "When I was hungry you gave me meat; when naked you clothed me; when in prison, you ministered unto me." . . . When the young man asked what he should do to be saved, Jesus did not tell him he must believe certain dogmas and creeds, but to "to go and sell all that he had and give to the poor."

The prophets and apostles alike taught a religion of deeds rather than of forms and ceremonies—"Away with your new moons, your sabbaths, and your appointed feasts; the worship God asks is that you do justice, love, and mercy." "God is no respecter of persons." "He has made of one blood all the nations of the earth."

When the pulpits in our land preach from these texts and enforce these lessons, the religious conscience of the people will take new forms of expression and those who in very truth accept the teachings of *Jesus* will make it their first duty to look after the lowest stratum of humanity.

To build a substantial house, we begin with the cellar and lay the foundations strong and deep; for on it depends the safely of the whole superstructure. So in race building; for noble specimens of humanity, for peace and prosperity in their conditions, we must begin with the lowest stratum of society and see that the masses are well fed, clothed, sheltered, educated, elevated, and enfranchised. Social morality and clean, pleasant environments must precede a spiritual religion that enables man to understand the mysteries binding him to the seen and unseen Universe.

This radical work cannot be done by what is called charity, but by teaching sound principles of political and domestic economy to our educated classes, showing them that by law, custom, and false theories of natural rights they are responsible for the poverty, ignorance, and vice of the masses. Those who train the religious conscience of the people must teach the lesson that all these artificial distinctions in society must be gradually obliterated by securing equal conditions and opportunities for all. This cannot be done in a day, but this is the goal for which we must strive.

The first step to this end is to educate people into the idea that such a moral revolution is possible.

It is folly to talk of a just government and a pure religion in a nation where the State and the Church alike sustain an aristocracy of wealth and ease, while those who do the hard work of the world have no share in the blessings and riches that their continued labors have made possible for others to enjoy. Is it just that the many should ever suffer, that the few may shine? To reconcile men to things as they are, we have sermons from the texts, "Blessed are the poor in spirit, for theirs is the kingdom of Heaven,"

"The poor ye have always with you," "Servants obey your masters." "Render unto Caesar the things that are Caesar's." As if poverty, servility, and authority were the decrees of Heaven!

Such decrees will not do for our day and generation; the school-master is abroad, Webster's spelling book is a classic. The laboring classes have tasted the tree of knowledge and like the gods they begin to know good and evil. With new liberties and education they demand corresponding improvements in their environments; as they reach new vantage ground from time to time and survey broader fields of usefulness, they learn their rights and duties, their relations to one another, and their true place in the march of civilisation. "Equal rights to all" is the lesson for this hour.

"That cannot be," says some faithless conservative; "if you should distribute all things equally to-day, they would be in the hands of the few to-morrow." Not if the religious conscience of the people was educated to believe that the way to salvation was not in creed and greed but in doing justice to their fellow men. Not if altruism instead of egoism was the law of social morals. Not if cooperation instead of competition was the rule in the world of work. Not if legislation was ever in the interests of the many rather than the few. Educate the rising generation into these broader principles of government, religion, and social life, and then ignorance, poverty, and vice will gradually disappear. The reconciliation of man to his brother is a more practical religion than that of man to his God; and the processes more easily understood. The word religion means to bind again, to unite those who have been separated, to harmonise those who have been in antagonism. Thus far the attitude of man to man has been hostile, ever in competition, trying to overreach and enslave each other.

With hope we behold the dawn of the new day in the general awaking to the needs of the laboring masses. We hail the work of the Salvation Army, the King's Daughters, the Kindergartens and industrial schools for the children of the poor, the University Settlement, etc. All these, added to our innumerable charities, show that the trend of thought is setting in the right direction for the health, happiness, and education of the lowest classes of humanity.

The interests of the race are so essentially one that all must rise or fall together. Our luscious fruits and fragrant flowers on tree and shrub must have rich soil and room for their roots to spread and find abundant nourishment; so the highest development of the best types of humanity must find their enduring soil in the cardinal virtues of the masses. "Blessed is the people which generation after generation has a school of prophets to call men back, with Isaiah-like yearning to the love of the living God in-carnate in man."

SOURCE: Elizabeth Stanton, "Worship of God in Man," address prepared for the World's Parliament of Religions, September 1893, Chicago, in *Open Court,* vol. 7 (October 26, 1893), 3850–52.

Chapter 12

Selections from
The Woman's Bible (1895, 1898)

EDITORS' NOTE: *In 1881, following the publication of the New Revised Bible, Stanton canvassed women historians, classicists, and theologians to determine their interest in a systematic examination of the representation of women in the scriptures. Only a handful of women scholars endorsed her project. In 1888 a first set of commentaries was published in the* Woman's Tribune. *After her 1893 retirement, Stanton took on the project with intense energy. Other suffrage leaders worried that the proposed book would offend the many traditional Christian women who were being drawn into the suffrage movement, and they urged Stanton to terminate the project. Their warnings only served to intensify Stanton's conviction that the Bible needed to be subjected to a fearless women's rights critique.*

Twenty-five members of the Revising Committee who were charged to oversee production of the book are listed in the volume. The author of each contribution is clearly marked, and most of the chapters have several commentaries. As a result, the book has the form of a dialogue between scholars, each exploring her own path toward a feminist theology. Nonetheless, Stanton was entirely responsible for the organization and coordination of the two volumes, published in 1895 and 1898, and she wrote more commentaries than any other contributor. Following a fundamental principle of modernist biblical scholarship, Stanton treated the words of the Bible as human creations shaped by the concerns and conditions of the authors' times. Where scripture condemned women to a secondary status, she called for the offending portion to be excised. She told her readers that "the chief obstacle in the way of woman's elevation today is the degrading position assigned her in the religion of all countries," Protestant Christianity not excluded.

Stanton's assertions in The Woman's Bible *were radical pronouncements in their own time and remain so for many today. She insisted that the Bible needed both to be reinterpreted and radically rewritten. On the one hand, she believed that the original intent of the Bible had been distorted and sup-*

pressed, for instance with respect to the equality of men and women in Creation and the important leadership roles women played in early Christianity. On the other hand, she was convinced that some sections of the Bible truly insulted women and she called for their removal. She warned her readers that religious orthodoxy remained an obstacle to the full emancipation of women and that orthodoxy was contrary to genuine religious faith.

The book consists of selections regarding women printed at the head of each chapter with the authors' commentaries following. She began by observing that there were two versions of the story of Creation in Genesis. In the first account, God creates man and woman in the same instant and equally in the divine image, thus suggesting to her that the Bible taught that the divine incorporated both male and female elements into a higher truth. However, the version most frequently told was the second, of Eve being made from Adam's rib, which allowed male ministers to preach the divinely ordained subordination of women while ignoring the equality of male and female before God.

The Woman's Bible *went through seven printings in six months and was translated into French, German, Italian, Spanish, and several other languages. Religious leaders around the country condemned the book and demanded that the suffrage movement censor Stanton. The National American Woman Suffrage Association (NAWSA) passed a resolution in 1895 condemning the book and its author for heretical beliefs distasteful to most American women. A defiant Stanton appended the censure resolution to the next edition of her book. She continued to chastise her sister suffragists for their embrace of religious orthodoxy until her death in 1902.*

From Part I (1895)

Introduction

From the inauguration of the movement for woman's emancipation the Bible has been used to hold her in the "divinely ordained sphere," prescribed in the Old and New Testaments.

The canon and civil law; church and state; priests and legislators; all political parties and religious denominations have alike taught that woman was made after man, of man, and for man, an inferior being, subject to man. Creeds, codes, Scriptures and statutes, are all based on this idea. The fashions, forms, ceremonies and customs of society, church ordinances and discipline all grow out of this idea.

Of the old English common law, responsible for woman's civil and political status, Lord Brougham said, "it is a disgrace to the civilization and Christianity of the Nineteenth Century." Of the canon law, which is responsible for woman's status in the church, Charles Kingsley said, "this will never be a good world for women until the last remnant of the canon law is swept from the face of the earth."

The Bible teaches that woman brought sin and death into the world, that she precipitated the fall of the race, that she was arraigned before the judgment seat of Heaven, tried, condemned and sentenced. Marriage for her was to be a condition of bondage, maternity a period of suffering and anguish, and in silence and subjection, she was to play the role of a dependent on man's bounty for all her material wants, and for all the information she might desire on the vital questions of the hour, she was commanded to ask her husband at home. Here is the Bible position of woman briefly summed up.

Those who have the divine insight to translate, transpose and transfigure this mournful object of pity into an exalted, dignified personage, worthy our worship as the mother of the race, are to be congratulated as having a share of the occult mystic power of the eastern Mahatmas.

The plain English to the ordinary mind admits of no such liberal interpretation. The unvarnished texts speak for themselves. The canon law, church ordinances and Scriptures, are homogeneous, and all reflect the same spirit and sentiments.

These familiar texts are quoted by clergymen in their pulpits, by statesmen in the halls of legislation, by lawyers in the courts, and are echoed by the press of all civilized nations, and accepted by woman herself as "The Word of God." So perverted is the religious element in her nature, that with faith and works she is the chief support of the church and clergy, the very powers that make her emancipation impossible. When, in the early part of the Nineteenth Century, women began to protest against their civil and political degradation, they were referred to the Bible for an answer. When they protested against their unequal position in the church, they were referred to the Bible for an answer.

This led to a general and critical study of the Scriptures. Some, having made a fetish of these books and believing them to be the veritable "Word of God," with liberal translations, interpretations, allegories and symbols, glossed over the most objectionable features of the various books and clung to them as divinely inspired. Others, seeing the family resemblance between the Mosaic code, the canon law, and the old English common law, came to the conclusion that all alike emanated from the same source; wholly human in their origin and inspired by the natural love of domination in the historians. Others, bewildered with their doubts and fears, came to no conclusion. While their clergymen told them on the one hand, that they owed all the blessings and freedom they enjoyed to the Bible, on the other, they said it clearly marked out their circumscribed sphere of action: that the demands for political and civil rights were irreligious, dangerous to the stability of the home, the state and the church. Clerical appeals were circulated from time to time conjuring members of their churches to take no part in the anti-slavery or woman suffrage movements, as they were infidel in their tendencies, undermining the very foundations of society. No wonder the majority of women stood still, and with bowed heads, accepted the situation.

Listening to the varied opinions of women, I have long thought it would be interesting and profitable to get them clearly stated in book form. To this end six years ago I proposed to a committee of women to issue a Woman's Bible, that we might have women's commentaries on women's position in the Old and New Testaments. It was agreed on by several leading women in England and America and the work was begun, but from various causes it has been delayed, until now the idea is received with renewed enthusiasm, and a large committee has been formed, and we hope to complete the work within a year.

Those who have undertaken the labor are desirous to have some Hebrew and Greek scholars, versed in Biblical criticism, to gild our pages with their learning. Several distinguished women have been urged to do so, but they are afraid that their high reputation and scholarly attainments might be compromised by taking part in an enterprise that for a time may prove very unpopular. Hence we may not be able to get help from that class.

Others fear that they might compromise their evangelical faith by affiliating with those of more liberal views, who do not regard the Bible as the "Word of God," but like any other book, to be judged by its merits. If the Bible teaches the equality of Woman, why does the church refuse to ordain women to preach the gospel, to fill the offices of deacons and elders, and to administer the Sacraments, or to admit them as delegates to the Synods, General Assemblies and Conferences of the different denominations? They have never yet invited a woman to join one of their Revising Committees, nor tried to mitigate the sentence pronounced on her by changing one count in the indictment served on her in Paradise.

The large number of letters received, highly appreciative of the undertaking, is very encouraging to those who have inaugurated the movement, and indicate a growing self-respect and self-assertion in the women of this generation. But we have the usual array of objectors to meet and answer. One correspondent conjures us to suspend the work, as it is "ridiculous" for "women to attempt the revision of the Scriptures." I wonder if any man wrote to the late revising committee of Divines to stop their work on the ground that it was ridiculous for men to revise the Bible. Why is it more ridiculous for women to protest against her present status in the Old and New Testament, in the ordinances and discipline of the church, than in the statutes and constitution of the state? Why is it more ridiculous to arraign ecclesiastics for their false teaching and acts of injustice to women, than members of Congress and the House of Commons? Why is it more audacious to review Moses than Blackstone, the Jewish code of laws than the English system of jurisprudence? Women have compelled their legislators in every state in this Union to so modify their statutes for women that the old common law is now almost a dead letter. Why not compel Bishops and Revising Committees to modify their creeds and dogmas? Forty years ago it seemed as ridiculous to timid, time-serving and retrograde folk for women to demand an expurgated edition of the laws, as it now does to demand an expurgated edition of the Liturgies and the Scriptures. Come, come, my conservative friend, wipe the dew off your spectacles, and see that the world is moving. Whatever your views may be as to the importance of the proposed work, your political and social degradation are but an outgrowth of your status in the Bible. When you express your aversion, based on a blind feeling of reverence in which reason has no control, to the revision of the Scriptures, you do but echo Cowper, who, when asked to read Paine's *Rights of Man,* exclaimed, "No man shall convince me that I am improperly governed while I *feel* the contrary."

Others say it is no *politic* to rouse religious opposition. This much-lauded policy is but another word for *cowardice.* How can woman's position be changed from that of a subordinate to an equal, without opposition, without the broadest discussion of all the questions involved in her present degradation? For so far-reaching and momentous a reform as her complete independence, an entire revolution in all existing institutions is inevitable.

Let us remember that all reforms are interdependent and that whatever is done to establish one principle on a solid basis strengthens all. Reformers who are always compromising have not yet grasped the idea that truth is the only safe ground to stand upon. The object an individual life is not to carry one fragmentary measure in human progress, but to utter the highest truth clearly seen in all directions, and thus to round out and perfect a well balanced character. Was not the sum of influence exerted by John Stuart Mill on political, religious and social questions far greater than that of any statesman or reformer who has sedulously limited his sympathies and activities to carrying one specific measure? We have many women abundantly endowed with capabilities to understand and revise what men have thus far written. But they are all suffering from inherited ideas of their inferiority; they do not perceive it, yet such is the true explanation of their solicitude, lest they should seem to be too self-asserting.

Again there are some who write us that our work is a useless expenditure of force over a book that has lost its hold on the human mind. Most intelligent women, they say, regard it simply as the history of a rude people in a barbarous age and have no more reverence for the Scriptures than any other work. So long as tens of thousands of Bibles are printed every year and circulated over the whole habitable globe, and the masses in all English-speaking nations revere it as the word of God, it is vain to belittle its influence. The sentimental feelings we all have for those things we were educated to believe sacred do not readily yield to pure reason. I distinctly remember the shudder that passed over me on seeing a mother take our family Bible to make a high seat for her child at table. It seemed such a desecration. I was tempted to protest against its use for such a purpose, and this, too, long after my reason had repudiated its divine authority.

To women still believing in the plenary inspiration of the Scriptures, we say give us by all means your exegesis in the light of the higher criticism learned men are now making, and illumine the Woman's Bible, with your inspiration.

Bible historians claim special inspiration for the Old and New Testaments containing most contradictory records of the same events, of miracles opposed to all known laws, of customs that degrade the female sex of all human and animal life, stated in most questionable language that could not be read in a promiscuous assembly, and call all this "The Word of God."

The only points in which I differ from all ecclesiastical teaching is that I do not believe that any man ever saw or talked with God, I do not believe that God inspired the Mosaic code, or told the historians what they say he did about woman, for all the religions on the face of the earth degrade her, and so long as woman accepts the position that they assign her, her emancipation is impossible. Whatever the Bible may be made to do in Hebrew or Greek, in plain English it does not exalt and dignify woman. My standpoint for criticism is the revised edition of 1888. I will so far honor the revising committee of wise men who have given us the best exegesis they can according to their ability, although Disraeli said the last one before he died, contained 150,000 blunders in the Hebrew, and 7,000 in the Greek.

But the verbal criticism in regard the woman's position amounts to little. The spirit is the same in all periods and languages, hostile to her as an equal.

There are some general principles in the holy books of all religions that teach love, charity, liberty, justice and equality for all the human family, there are many grand and beautiful passages, the golden rule has been echoed and re-echoed around the world. There are lofty examples of good and true men and women, all worthy our acceptance and imitation whose luster cannot be dimmed by the false sentiments and vicious characters bound up in the same volume. The Bible cannot be accepted or rejected as a whole, its teachings are varied and its lessons differ widely from each other. In criticizing the peccadilloes of Sarah, Rebecca and Rachel, we would not shadow the virtues of Deborah, Huldah and Vashti. In criticizing the Mosaic code we would not question the wisdom of the golden rule and the fifth Commandment. Again the church claims special consecration for its cathedrals and priesthood, parts of these aristocratic churches are too holy for women to enter, boys were early introduced into the choirs for this reason, woman singing in an obscure corner closely veiled. A few of the more democratic denominations accord women some privileges, but invidious discriminations of sex are found in all religious organizations, and the most bitter outspoken enemies of woman are found among clergymen and bishops of the Protestant religion.

The canon law, the Scriptures, the creeds and codes and church discipline of the leading religions bear the impress of fallible man, and not of our ideal great first cause, "the Spirit of all Good," that set the universe of matter and mind in motion, and by immutable law holds the land, the sea, the planets, revolving round the great centre of light and heat, each in its own elliptic, with millions of stars in harmony all singing together, the glory of creation forever and ever.

Stanton's Commentary on Genesis i: 26, 27, 28

26 And God said, Let us make man in our image, after our likeness: and let them have dominion over the fish of the sea, and over the fowl of the air, and over the cattle, and over all the earth, and over every creeping thing that creepeth upon the earth.

27 So God created man in his own image, in the image of God created he him; male and female created he them.

28 And God blessed them, and God said unto them, Be fruitful, and multiply, and replenish the earth, and subdue it; and have dominion over the fish of the sea, and over the fowl of the air, and over every living thing that moveth upon the earth.

Here is the sacred historian's first account of the advent of woman; a simultaneous creation of both sexes, in the image of God. It is evident from the language that there was consultation in the Godhead, and that the masculine and feminine elements were equally represented. Scott in his commentaries says, "this consultation of the Gods is the origin of the doctrine of the trinity." But instead of three male personages, as generally represented, a Heavenly Father, Mother, and Son would seem more rational.

The first step in the elevation of woman to her true position, as an equal factor in human progress, is the cultivation of the religious sentiment in regard to her dignity and equality, the recognition by the rising generation of an ideal Heavenly Mother, to whom their prayers should be addressed, as well as to a Father.

If language has any meaning, we have in these texts a plain declaration of the existence of the feminine element in the Godhead, equal in power and glory with the masculine. The Heavenly Mother and Father! "God created man in his *own image, male and female.*" Thus Scripture, as well as science and philosophy, declares the eternity and equality of sex—the philosophical fact, without which there could have been no perpetuation of creation, no growth or development in the animal, vegetable, or mineral kingdoms, no awakening nor progressing in the world of thought. The masculine and feminine elements, exactly equal and balancing each other, are as essential to the maintenance of the equilibrium of the universe as positive and negative electricity, the centripetal and centrifugal forces, the laws of attraction which bind together all we know of this planet whereon we dwell and of the system in which we revolve.

In the great work of creation the crowning glory was realized when man and woman were evolved on the sixth day, the masculine and feminine forces in the image of God, that must have existed eternally, in all forms of matter and mind. All the persons in the Godhead are represented in the Elohim the divine plurality taking counsel in regard to this last and highest form of life. Who were the members of this high council, and were they a duality or a trinity? Verse 27 declares the image of God male and female. How then is it possible to make woman an afterthought? We find in verses 5–16 the pronoun "he" used. Should it not in harmony with verse 26 be "they," a dual pronoun? We may attribute this to the same cause as the use of "his" in verse 11 instead of "it." The fruit tree yielding fruit after "his" kind instead of after "its" kind. The paucity of a language may give rise to many misunderstandings.

The above texts plainly show the simultaneous creation of man and woman, and their equal importance in the development of the race. All those theories based on the assumption that man was prior in the creation have no foundation in Scripture.

As to woman's subjection, on which both the canon and the civil law delight to dwell, it is important to note that equal dominion is given to woman over every living thing, but not one word is said giving man dominion over woman.

Here is the first title deed to this green earth giving alike to the sons and daughters of God. No lesson of woman's subjection can be fairly drawn from the first chapter of the Old Testament.

Stanton's Commentary on Genesis ii: 21–25

21 And the Lord God caused a deep sleep to fall upon Adam, and he slept; and he took one of his ribs, and closed up the flesh thereof.

22 And the rib which the Lord God had taken from man, made he a woman, and brought her unto the man.

23 And Adam said, This is now bone of my bone, and flesh of my flesh: she shall be called Woman, because she was taken out of man.

24 Therefore shall a man leave his father and his mother, and shall cleave unto his wife; and they shall be one flesh.

25 And they were both naked, the man and his wife, and were not ashamed.

As the account of the creation in the first chapter is in harmony with science, common sense, and the experience of mankind in natural laws, the inquiry naturally arises, why should there be two contradictory accounts in the same book, of the same event? It is fair to infer that the second version, which is found in some form in the different religions of all nations, is a mere allegory, symbolizing some mysterious conception of a highly imaginative editor.

The first account dignifies woman as an important factor in the creation, equal in power and glory with man. The second makes her a mere afterthought. The world in good running order without her. The only reason for her advent being the solitude of man.

There is something sublime in bringing order out of chaos; light out of darkness; giving each planet its place in the solar system; oceans and lands their limits; wholly inconsistent with a petty surgical operation, to find material for the mother of the race. It is on this allegory that all the enemies of women rest their battering rams, to prove her inferiority. Accepting the view that man was prior in the creation, some Scriptural writers say that as the woman was of the man, therefore, her position should be one of subjection. Grant it, then as the historical fact is reversed in our day, and the man is now of the woman, shall his place be one of subjection?

The equal position declared in the first account must prove more satisfactory to both sexes; created alike in the image of God—The Heavenly Mother and Father.

Thus, the Old Testament, "in the beginning," proclaims the simultaneous creation of man and woman, the eternity and equality of sex; and the New Testament echoes back through the centuries the individual sovereignty of woman growing out of this natural fact. Paul, in speaking of equality as the very soul and essence of Christianity, said, "There is neither Jew nor Greek, there is neither bond nor free, there is neither male nor female; for ye are all one in Christ Jesus." With this recognition of the feminine element in the Godhead in the Old Testament, and this declaration of the equality of the sexes in the New, we may well wonder at the contemptible status woman occupies in the Christian Church of today.

All the commentators and publicists writing on woman's position, go through an immense amount of fine-spun metaphysical speculations to prove her subordination in harmony with the Creator's original design.

It is evident that some wily writer, seeing the perfect equality of man and woman in the first chapter, felt it important for the dignity and dominion of man to effect woman's subordination in some way. To do this a spirit of evil must be introduced, which at once proved itself stronger than the spirit of good, and man's supremacy was based on the downfall of all that had just been pronounced very good. This spirit of evil evidently existed before the supposed fall of man, hence woman was not the origin of sin as so often asserted.

From Part II (1898)

Stanton's Commentary on Matthew xxv

1 Then shall the kingdom of heaven be likened unto ten virgins, which took their lamps, and went forth to meet the bridegroom.

2 And five of them were wise, and five were foolish.

3 They that were foolish took their lamps, and took no oil with them.

4 But the wise took oil in their vessels with their lamps.

5 While the bridegroom tarried, they all slumbered and slept.

6 And at midnight there was a cry made, Behold, the bridegroom cometh; go ye out to meet him.

7 Then all those virgins arose, and trimmed their lamps.

8 And the foolish said unto the wise, Give us of your oil; for our lamps are gone out.

9 But the wise answered, saying, Not so, lest there be not enough for us and you: but go ye rather to them that sell, and buy for yourselves.

10 And while they went to buy, the bridegroom came; and they that were ready went in with him to the marriage, and the door was shut.

11 Afterward came also the other virgins, saying, Lord, Lord, open to us.

12 But he answered and said, Verily, I say unto you, I know you not.

In this chapter we have the duty of self-development impressively and repeatedly urged in the form of parables, addressed alike to man and to woman. The sin of neglecting and of burying one's talents, capacities and powers, and the penalties which such a course involve, are here strikingly portrayed.

This parable is found among the Jewish records substantially the same as in our own Scriptures. Their weddings were generally celebrated at night; yet they usually began at the rising of the evening star; but in this case there was a more than ordinary delay. Adam Clarke in his commentaries explains this parable as referring chiefly to spiritual gifts and the religious life. He makes the Lord of Hosts the bridegroom, the judgment day the wedding feast, the foolish virgins the sinners whose hearts were cold and dead, devoid of all spiritual graces, and unfit to enter the kingdom of heaven. The wise virgins were the saints who were ready for translation, or for the bridal procession. They followed to the wedding feast; and when the chosen had entered "*the door was shut.*"

This strikes us as a strained interpretation of a very simple parable, which, considered in connection with the other parables, seems to apply much more closely to this life than to that which is to come, to the intellectual and the moral nature, and to the whole round of human duties. It fairly describes the two classes which help to make up society in general. The one who, like the foolish virgins, have never learned the first important duty of cultivating their own individual powers, using the talents given to them, and keeping their own lamps trimmed and burning. The idea of being a helpmeet to somebody else has been so sedulously drilled into most women that an individual life, aim, purpose and ambition are never taken into consideration. They oftimes do so much in other directions that they neglect the most vital duties to themselves.

We may find in this simple parable a lesson for the cultivation of courage and of self-reliance. These virgins are summoned to the discharge of an important duty at midnight, alone, in darkness, and in solitude. No chivalrous gentleman is there to run for oil and to trim their lamps. They must depend on themselves, unsupported, and pay the penalty of their own improvidence and unwisdom. Perhaps in that bridal procession might have been seen fathers, brothers, friends, for whose service and amusement the foolish virgins had wasted many precious hours, when they should have been trimming their own lamps and keeping oil in their vessels.

And now, with music, banners, lanterns, torches, guns and rockets fired at intervals, come the bride and groom, with their attendants and friends numbering thousands, brilliant in jewels, gold and silver, magnificently mounted on richly caparisoned horses—for nothing can be more brilliant than were those nuptial solemnities of Eastern nations. As this spectacle, grand beyond description, sweeps by, imagine the foolish virgins pushed aside, in the shadow of some tall edifice, with dark, empty lamps in their hands, unnoticed and unknown. And while the castle walls resound with music and merriment, and the lights from every window stream out far into the darkness, no kind friends gather round them to sympathize in their humiliation, nor to cheer their loneliness. It matters little that women may be ignorant, dependent, unprepared for trial and for temptation. Alone they must meet the terrible emergencies of life, to be sustained and protected amid danger and death by their own courage, skill and self-reliance, or perish.

Woman's devotion to the comfort, the education, the success of men in general, and to their plans and projects, is in great measure due to her self-abnegation and self-sacrifice having been so long and so sweetly lauded by poets, philosophers and priests as the acme of human goodness and glory.

Now, to my mind, there is nothing commendable in the action of young women who go about begging funds to educate young men for the ministry, while they and the majority of their sex are too poor to educate themselves, and if able, are still denied admittance into some of the leading institutions of learning throughout our land. It is not commendable for women to get up fairs and donation parties for churches in which the gifted of their sex may neither pray, preach, share in the offices and honors, nor have a voice in the business affairs, creeds and discipline, and from whose altars come forth Biblical interpretations in favor of woman's subjection.

It is not commendable for the women of this Republic to expend much enthusiasm on political parties as now organized, nor in national celebrations, for they have as yet no lot or part in the great experiment of self-government.

In their ignorance, women sacrifice themselves to educate the men of their households, and to make of themselves ladders by which their husbands, brothers and sons climb up into the kingdom of knowledge, while they themselves are shut out from all intellectual companionship, even with those they love best; such are indeed like the foolish virgins. They have not kept their own lamps trimmed and burning; they have no oil in their vessels, no resources in themselves; they bring no light to their households nor to the circle in which they move; and when the bridegroom cometh, when the philosopher, the scientist, the saint, the scholar, the great and the learned, all come together to celebrate the marriage feast of science and religion, the foolish virgins, though present, are practically shut out; for what know they of the grand themes which inspire each tongue and kindle every thought? Even the brothers and the sons whom they have educated, now rise to heights which they cannot reach, span distances which they cannot comprehend.

The solitude of ignorance, oh, who can measure its misery!

The wise virgins are they who keep their lamps trimmed, who burn oil in their vessels for their own use, who have improved every advantage for their education, secured a healthy, happy, complete development, and entered all the profitable avenues of labor, for self-support, so that when the opportunities and the responsibilities of life come, they may be fitted fully to enjoy the one and ably to discharge the other.

These are the women who to-day are close upon the heels of man in the whole realm of thought, in art, in science, in literature and in government. With telescopic vision they explore the starry firmament, and bring back the history of the planetary world. With chart and compass they pilot ships across the mighty deep, and with skilful fingers send electric messages around the world. In galleries of art, the grandeur of nature and the greatness of humanity are immortalized by them on canvas, and by their inspired touch, dull blocks of marble are transformed into angels of light. In music they speak again the language of Mendelssohn, of Beethoven, of Chopin, of Schumann, and are worthy interpreters of their great souls. The poetry and the novels of the century are theirs; they, too, have touched the keynote of reform in religion, in politics and in social life. They fill the editors' and the professors' chairs, plead at the bar of justice, walk the wards of the hospital, and speak from the pulpit and the platform.

Such is the widespread preparation for the marriage feast of science and religion; such is the type of womanhood which the bridegroom of an enlightened public sentiment welcomes to-day; and such is the triumph of the wise virgins over the folly, the ignorance and the degradation of the past as in grand procession they enter the temple of knowledge, and *the door is no longer shut.*

SOURCE: Selections from *The Woman's Bible:* Introduction and commentaries on the Book of Genesis from *The Woman's Bible,* Part I (New York: European Publishing Co., 1895), 7–16 and 20–21. Commentary on the Book of Matthew from *The Woman's Bible,* Part II (New York: European Publishing Co., 1898), 123–26.

Chapter 13

"Our Proper Attitude toward Immigration" (1895)

EDITORS' NOTE: This brief essay discusses the challenge that a large immigrant population of poorly paid wage earners posed to American conceptions of republican democracy. In the first part of the article, Stanton developed her general position on immigration. She made it clear that she did not support efforts to limit immigration, but she did fear the transfer of European poverty and class distinctions into the United States. She recommended laws that would encourage immigrants to become farmers rather than factory workers. She placed the blame for growing extremes of wealth and poverty on American railroad monopolies, a position she shared with agrarian populists and the Knights of Labor. In the second part, she viewed the question of immigration from the point of view of Anglo-American women, and here the nativist dimension of this perspective is more evident. She called for an educated suffrage that would ensure native-born women full political rights while limiting the rights of immigrants, whether male or female, to those who learn how to read and write in English.

This question has been discussed from every possible standpoint, some conceding the right of every man to make for himself the best possible conditions in any latitude or longitude of the planet he may desire, provided he does not invade the rights of any other man. Others say each country has a right to decide what type and number of immigrants shall be permitted to make homes within their borders. Some say that national safety requires restrictions. Others say there should be none whatever. As the greatest amount of immigration is to the United States—statistics show about 300,000 annually—let us consider the question with reference to this republic.

Thoughtful men in the Old World long ago warned us of coming dangers to our institutions from this source. Lord Macaulay, in his well-known letter to Hon. H. S. Randall in 1857—a letter which Gen. Garfield said startled him "like an alarm bell in the night," said, "Your fate, I believe to be certain, though it is deferred by a physical cause. As long as you have a boundless extent of fertile and unoccupied land, your laboring population will be far more at ease that the laboring population of the Old World. But the time will come when New England will be as thickly populated as Old England. Wages will be as low and will fluctuate as much with you as with us. You will have your Manchesters and Birminghams and in those Manchesters and Birminghams hundreds of thousands of artisans will assuredly be some time out of work. Then your institutions will be fairly brought to the test. Through such seasons the United States will have to pass in the course of the next century, if not of this. I wish you a good deliverance, but my reason and my best wishes are at war and I cannot help forboding the worst."

As the question of Immigration involves that of land monopoly, the first lesson to teach all nations is that there should be no absolute ownership of land, except by the man who occupies and cultivates it, his right ending with his life, the land reverting to the State unless some one of his children desires to occupy still, on the same conditions. The value of the improvement should be fairly estimated and bequeathed to the family.

If a permanent home were secured to every family by wise homestead laws, a sufficient number of acres on the country for the farmer to make a living, a lot in town for the mechanic, a large share of misery and crime would give place to peace and prosperity.

It is the false conditions of the laboring masses in the Old World that complicates immigration here. The immense standing armies in France and Germany, 500,000 soldiers, whom the masses are taxed to support, drive the laboring people from their homes and countries to escape this burden. Great Britain does the same thing with her land monopolies. Traveling there for the first time, I was surprised to see so much unoccupied land, extensive shooting grounds, public parks and many private gardens in the cities. The park in Dublin covers 1,500 acres; the Duke of Argyll owns a belt of land in Scotland running from sea to sea. The Queen has several palaces, with extensive grounds, the Lords their parks for deer, the Bishops their palaces and lands, the Church vast properties, none of which are taxed. The law of primogeniture keeps these estates intact for generations and the House of Lords blocks every step in progress.

Now, if Great Britain would abolish the House of Lords and Disestablish the Church, as she talks of doing, tax church property and stop pensioning the royal family to the third and fourth generation, it would not be necessary to make the United States, Australia and the islands of the sea dumping grounds of the inmates of her jails, prisons, hospitals as she now does. There are immigration societies in England for the express purpose of shipping her criminals, paupers, idiots, maimed, halt and blind, deaf and dumb, here. They go by way of Canada to avoid the inspection they are supposed to pass in New York. Millions of the Queen's subjects who toil and suffer all their days do not own one foot of land, yet, with a fair distribution, there is enough in Great Britain to give every family inviolable shelter. Under proper conditions the Eastern Continent could support its own people and make them feel that they have a country and a home and thus decrease the number of immigrants here and improve the quality of those who came. This would give our young republic time to educate its present population into the broad principles of justice, liberty, equality, and to realize the ideal government proclaimed in our great Declaration of Rights.

It is a terrible strain on our institutions to be called on to digest 300,000 foreigners every year, chiefly men, the majority of whom can neither read nor write, who know nothing of republics and institutions, who have no appreciation of the difference between liberty and license. The Anarchists and Socialists come, too, instead of staying in their own land, to fan the growing discontent of the oppressed millions and to help them fight the battles of liberty on their own soil.

The violent mob element that always appears on the surface when honest labor strikes for better wages is chiefly foreign, so are the criminals in our jails and prisons, the paupers in our charitable institutions, the diseased idiots and lunatics in our hospitals. The majority of our brewers, liquor dealers and saloon keepers are foreigners, and the 20,000 young girls imported annually for the vilest purpose are brought here by foreigners.

Is it possible for this young civilization to carry this rapidly increasing load of ignorance and immorality, crowding into our cities, impoverishing our people, corrupting our youth, a disturbing element everywhere?

It is on this class I would place some well understood restrictions by our foreign consuls and ministers, before they are shipped to this country, and other restrictions on all classes of foreigners before giving them the political rights of American citizens.

I do not wish to be understood as hostile to all immigration, for there is a large class of honest, industrious, intelligent, moral men and women who have borne an honorable and important part in building up this nation, and developing our boundless resources, and there is abundant room and hearty welcome for more of the same character.

For their sake, would that our lands were free for them to occupy and cultivate, and not in the hands of railroad monopolies. Traveling over our vast prairies one can easily realize the immense increase of our national wealth if all these lands were in the hands of thrifty farmers, raising cattle, grains and fruits, instead of lying fallow in the idle hands of speculators. The farmer could then use his capital in necessary improvements, instead of interest on mortgage. With free lands, taxes on incomes and all church property, our country would develop with added rapidity, our national treasury would soon be overflowing, and all these lamentations in Congress about issuing national bonds and shipping gold to Europe would be heard of no more.

While welcoming the best class of foreigners to our shores, it is the right and the duty of the educated women in this republic to protest against the extension of the suffrage to another man until they themselves are first enfranchised. Though "universal suffrage is our national fetish," "manhood suffrage" is all we have attained.

The fact that all foreigners are opposed to the enfranchisement of women compels us in self-defense to oppose the extension of the suffrage to them. And worse still, our rights are not only at their disposal, but the liquor vote, the Irish vote, the German vote intimidate our politicians. It is their policy to keep our question ever in the background. In this way the foreign vote holds the balance of power and in a measure dictates the policy of our government.

Women are awakening to the dangers of "manhood suffrage." As they have equal interest with man in good government, they also have rights and duties in the State, and they now demand a halt to any further extension of the suffrage to men foreign or native, especially to the uneducated masses, until the upper classes of women are first enfranchised.

There can be no question as to the comparative benefit to the State of the votes of intelligent, native-born women or the votes of the ignorant, foreign-born men. Moreover, we need a new element in government, the moral, spiritual forces of humanity supposed to predominate in virtuous, cultured women should have some representation.

To this end we ask Congress for a sixteenth amendment to the national constitution, enfranchising all women who can read and write the English language intelligently, and further providing that no native or foreign men shall be allowed to exercise the suffrage except on the same basis. This would be a wise restriction and not incompatible with our cherished idea of suffrage as a national right. As every person of ordinary ability can learn to read and write, it is a surmountable qualification.

This would prevent immigrants from going directly from the steerage to the polls. Our naturalization laws, as now executed, are a mere travesty. Who can watch the 300,000 people that land annually on our shores and be sure that they have been here five years? We cannot rely on their word for it, especially when politicians bribe them to evade the law, but our educational qualifications would be a barrier to illegal voting; it would dignify the suffrage and purify our elections.

To the women of the nation, it is of vital consequence to limit as far as possible the foreign vote, because it is a unit against their enfranchisement. Amendments to extend the suffrage to women have been submitted in nine different States and defeated every time by a solid foreign vote. This fact further complicates the question of immigration, because it makes the position of native-born educated women so humiliating, placing them practically under a foreign yoke. With the suffrage they become our lawmakers, to decide our political status, our civil and social rights. The ballot in a republic is the crown and sceptre of sovereignty, and they who do not hold it are practically the slaves of those who do.

SOURCE: Elizabeth Stanton, "Our Proper Attitude toward Immigration," *American Woman's Journal,* vol. 11 (April 5, 1895), 90–92. A version of this article appeared under the title "The Perils of Immigration."

Chapter 14

"Significance and History of the Ballot" (1898)

EDITORS' NOTE: *In this address to the Senate Select Committee on Woman Suffrage, Stanton considers the implications of mass immigration for woman suffrage in language that has shifted from mild nativism to outright xenophobia. Her concerns about the growing divide between the educated middle class and urban industrial workers has led her to a rare questioning of the continued relevance of "universal suffrage." She attributed electoral defeats that her cause had suffered in the 1890s, not to native-born men, but to "the immigrant vote." In the context of rapid demographic change, she supported "Americanization" as a requirement for full participation in political life. The too-easy ability of "foreigners" to become U.S. citizens, Stanton claimed with her typical penchant for dramatic, sometimes brutal imagery, transformed the lot of Anglo-American women into that of a "conquered people" in their own country. As she wrote, American military force was spreading across the Caribbean and the Pacific, and the United States was about to acquire its first formal overseas colonies, a development that Stanton supported. Stanton's arguments on both immigration and imperialism contrast starkly with those of Jane Addams, forty-five years her junior. Addams was one of the leaders of the Anti-Imperialist League. In addition, she responded quite differently to the rise in immigration. She moved into immigrant communities to live and work with immigrant families. As in the late 1860s, when Stanton faced the difficult political choices of Reconstruction, here she evidences a striking inability to imagine herself in the position of other sufferers of inequality less privileged than herself. The obverse side of this enduring weakness was Stanton's stubborn foregrounding of the gendered implications of each and every political moment.*

Since our demand for the right of suffrage under the Fourteenth Amendment, which was denied by Congress and the courts, the only discussions in Congress have been our appeals for a sixteenth amendment until the recent bills on immigration by Senator Lodge of Massachusetts and Senator Kyle of South Dakota, indirectly involving this question and affecting the interests of woman. Their proposition to demand a reading and writing qualification on landing, strikes me as arbitrary and equally detrimental to our mutual interests. The danger is not in their landing and living in this country, but in their speedy appearance at the ballot box, there becoming an impoverished and ignorant balance of power in the hands of wily politicians.

While we should not allow our country to be a dumping ground for the refuse population of the Old World, still we should welcome all hardy, common-sense laborers here, as we have plenty of room and work for them. Here they can improve their own condition and our surroundings, developing our immense resources and the commerce of the country. The one demand I would make for this class is that they should not become a part of our ruling power until they ran read and write the English language intelligently and understand the principles of republican government. To make a nation homogeneous, its people should all speak one tongue. The dominion of Francis Joseph in Austria, where fifteen different languages are spoken, illustrates its perils. The officers of the army can be understood by only a small percent of the soldiers. One can readily imagine the confusion and consequent dangers this would cause in time of war.

To prevent the thousands of immigrants daily landing on our shores marching from the steerage to the polls, the National Government should prohibit the States from allowing them to vote in less than five years, and not then until the applicants can read and write the English language. This is the only restrictive legislation we need to protect ourselves against foreign domination. To this end, Congress should pass a bill for "educated suffrage" for our native-born as well as foreign rulers, alike ignorant of our institutions.

With free schools and compulsory education, no one has an excuse for not understanding the language of the country. As women are governed by a "male aristocracy," we are doubly interested in having our rulers able at least to read and write. See with what care in the Old World the prospective heirs to the throne are educated. There as a time when the members of the British Parliament could neither read nor write, but those accomplishments are now required of the Lords and Commons, and even of the king and queen, while we have rulers, native and foreign, voting for laws, who do not understand the letters of the alphabet, and this in a Republic supposed to be based on the virtue and intelligence of the people!

Much as we need these measures for the stability of our Government, we need them still more for the best interests of women. This ignorant vote is solid against woman's emancipation. In States where amendments to their constitutions are proposed for the enfranchisement of women, this vote has been in every case against the measure. We should ask for national protection against this hostile force playing foot-ball with the most sacred rights of one-half of the people. I have long felt that an educational qualification for the exercise of the right of suffrage is a question of such vital consequence that it should be exhaustively discussed by the leaders of thought among our people.

The great political parties fear to propose this measure lest it should insure their defeat. No aspiring politician as an individual would dare express such an opinion lest it should blast his chance for official position. Hence, only those guided by principle rather than policy are in a position to discuss the merits of this question. Such an amendment to our national constitution should go into effect at the dawn of the next century.

As all who prize this right sufficiently to labor to attain it can easily do so, an educational qualification in no way conflicts with our cherished idea of universal suffrage. According to our theory of government, all our citizens are born voters, but they must be of age before they can exercise the right. To say they must also read and write the English language is equally logical and fair. We do not propose to withhold this right from any citizen exercising it but to apply the restriction to all new claimants. Some say that the ignorant classes need the ballot for their protection more than the rich. Well, they have had it and exercised it, and what have they done to protect their own interests? Absolutely nothing, because they did not know in what direction their interests lay, or by what system of legislation they could be lifted out of poverty, vice, and ignorance to enjoy liberty, justice, and equality.

A gun is a good weapon for a man's protection against his enemy, but, if he does not know how to use it, it may prove a danger rather than a defense. There is something lacking in our science of industrial economics when multitudes in this land of plenty are suffering abject poverty. Yet by their ignorant votes they have helped to establish the very conditions from which they suffer. The ballot is of value only in the hands that know how to use it. In establishing free schools, our forefathers said to us in plain words: "The stability of a republic depends on the virtue and intelligence of the people."

"Universal suffrage" with us is a mere pretense, a party cry, as thus far we have had "male suffrage" and nothing more. In most of the States qualifications of property, education, and color have been abolished, but in only four States have our rulers had the courage and conscience to abolish that of sex. A republic based on the theory of universal suffrage, in which a large class of educated women, representing the virtue, intelligence, and wealth of the nation, are disfranchised, is an anomaly in government, especially when all men, foreign and native, black and white, ignorant and educated, vicious and virtuous, by their votes decide the rights and duties of this superior class.

In all national conflicts it is ever deemed the most grievous accident of war for the conquered people to find themselves under a foreign yoke, yet this is the position of the educated women of this Republic today. Foreigners are our judges and jurors, our legislators and municipal officials, and decide all questions of interest to us, as to the discipline in our schools, charitable institutions, jails, and prisons. Woman has no voice as to the education of her children or the environments of the unhappy wards of the State. The love and sympathy of the mother soul have but an evanescent influence in all departments of human interest until coined into law by the hand that holds the ballot. Then only do they become a direct and effective power in the Government. As women have no voice in the laws and lawmakers under which they live, they surely have the right to demand that their rulers, foreign and native, shall be able to read and write the English language. As it would take the ordinary immigrant at least five years to learn our language, we should be sure he had been here the prescribed time before exercising his right to vote. An educational qualification would also stimulate our native population to avail themselves of all the opportunities for learning. In basing suffrage on sex we have defeated the intentions of our ancestors and made their principles of government mere glittering generalities.

The popular objection to woman suffrage is that it would "double the ignorant vote." The patent answer to this is, "Abolish the ignorant vote." Our legislators have this power in their own hands. There have been serious restrictions in the past for men. We are willing to abide by the same for women, provided the insurmountable qualifications of sex be forever removed. In the discussion of this question educated women must now lead the way. Some reformers do not see the wisdom of the measure, so the few who do must take the initiative in arousing public thought and creating a widespread agitation of this important step in woman's emancipation.

During the past month the supreme court of Wyoming has handed down an important and far-reaching decision. The court decided that foreign born citizens of the State of Wyoming must be able to read the constitution of the State in the English language in order to vote, and that the ability to read the constitution in a foreign language is not a compliance with the requirements of the constitution.

Some of the opponents talk as if educated suffrage would be invidious to the best interests of the laboring masses, whereas it would be most beneficial in its ultimate influence. You who can read and write, and enjoy hours in a library, gleaning there the history of the past as well as advancing civilization, you who can visit the galleries of art, and with your knowledge of the classics, poetry, and mythology, appreciate what the pictures say, little realize the starved condition of the uncultured mind. Blot this knowledge from your mind, and you may then understand the solitude of ignorance. Who can measure its misery? Surely, when we compel all classes to learn to read and write, and thus open to themselves the door to knowledge, not by force, lit by the promise of a privilege all intelligent citizens enjoy, we are benefactors and not tyrants. To stimulate them to climb the first rounds of the ladder that they may reach the divine heights where they shall be as gods, knowing good and evil, by withholding the citizen's right to vote for a few years, is a blessing to them as well as to the State.

The condition of the laboring masses to-day, without adequate shelter, food, and clothes, is the result of their own ignorance of the manner in which the broad distinctions in society have been created. I am fully aware that simply reading and writing will not secure the key to the whole situation, but it is the first necessary step without which the laboring-man can never make and control his own environments.

We must inspire our people with a new sense of their sacred duties as citizens of a republic, and place new guards around our ballot box.

Walking in Paris one day I was deeply impressed with an emblematic statue in the square Chateau d'Eau, placed there in 1883 in honor of the Republic. On one side is a magnificent bronze lion with his forepaw on the electoral urn, which answers to our ballot box, as if to guard it from all unholy uses. Having overturned all pretensions to royalty, nobility, and all artificial distinctions in class, and declared the right of the people to a voice in the making of their laws and selection of their rulers, they exalted the idea of republican government and universal suffrage with this magnificent monument—the royal lion guarding the sacred treasures within the electoral urn.

As I turned away I thought of the American Republic and our ballot box with no guardian or sacred reverence for its contents among the people. Ignorance, poverty, and vice crowd its precincts, thousands from every incoming steamer march from the steerage to the polls, while educated women, representing the virtue and intelligence of the nation, are driven away.

I would like to see a monument to "educated suffrage" in front of our National Capitol, guarded by the goddess Minerva, her right hand resting on the ballot box, her left hand on the spelling book, the Declaration of Rights, and the national constitution.

It would be well for us to ponder the Frenchman's idea, but instead of the royal lion, representing force, let us substitute wisdom and virtue in the form of Woman.

SOURCE: Elizabeth Stanton, "Significance and History of the Ballot," in *Report of Hearing before the Committee on Woman Suffrage, February 15, 1898* (Washington, D.C.: Government Printing Office, 1898), 21–24.

Chapter 15

"Progress of the American Woman" (1900)

EDITORS' NOTE: Stanton wrote this piece for the North American Review *as a spirited response to Flora McDonald Thompson's "Retrogression of the American Woman," which had been published by the* Review *the previous month in November 1900. Stanton continued her long debate with conservative religious women about modern progress and its benefits for women. Stanton herself in previous writings had made use of the argument that women were morally superior than men, but in this article, she ridiculed the idea that women's superiority required their confinement to the domestic realm or restricting their access to higher education.*

An article, by Flora McDonald Thompson, entitled "Retrogression of the American Woman," which was published in the November number of the REVIEW, contains many startling assertions, which, if true, would be the despair of philosophers. The title itself contradicts the facts of the last half century.

When machinery entered the home, to relieve woman's hands of the multiplicity of her labors, a new walk in life became inevitable for her. When our grandmothers made butter and cheese, dipped candles, dried and preserved fruits and vegetables, spun yam, knit stockings, wove the family clothing, did all the mending of garments, the laundry work, cooking, patchwork and quilting, planting and weeding of gardens, and all the house-cleaning, they were fully occupied. But when, in course of time, all this was done by machinery, their hands were empty, and they were driven outside the home for occupation. If every woman had been sure of a strong right arm on which to lean until safe "on the other side of Jordan," she might have rested, content to do nothing but bask in the smiles of her husband and recite Mother Goose melodies to her children.

On that theory of woman's position, men gradually took possession of all her employments. They are now the cooks on ocean steamers, on railroads, in all hotels, in fashionable homes and places of resort; they are at the head of laundries, bakeries and mercantile establishments, where tailor-made suits and hats are manufactured for women. Thus, women have been compelled to enter the factories, trades and professions, to provide their own clothes, food and shelter; and, to prepare themselves for the emergencies of life, they have made their way into the schools and colleges, the hospitals, courts, pulpits, editorial chairs, and they are at work throughout the whole field of literature, art, science and government. We should hardly say that the condition of an intelligent human being was retrogressive in teaching mathematics, instead of making marmalade; in instructing others in philosophy, instead of making pumpkin pie; in studying art, instead of drying apples. When hundreds of girls are graduating from our colleges with high honors every year, when they are interested in all the reforms of their day and generation, superintending kindergarten schools, laboring to secure more merciful treatment for criminals in all our jails and prisons, better sanitary conditions for our homes, streets and public buildings, the abolition of the gallows and whipping-post, the settlement of all national disputes by arbitration instead of war, we must admit that woman's moral influence is greater than it has ever been before at any time in the course of human development. Her moral power, in working side by side with man, is greatly to the advantage of both, as the co-education of the sexes has abundantly proved. When the sexes reach a perfect equilibrium we shall have higher conditions in the state, the church, and the home.

Matthew Arnold says: "The first desire of every cultivated mind is to take part in the great work of government." That woman now makes this demand is a crowning evidence of her higher development. For a true civilization, the masculine and feminme elements in humanity must be in exact equilibrium, just as the centripetal and centrifugal forces are in the material world. If it were possible to suspend either of these great forces for five minutes, we should have material chaos,—just what we have in the moral world to-day because of the undue depression of the feminine element.

Tennyson, with prophetic vision, forecasts the true relations between man and woman in all the walks of life. He says:

> "Everywhere
> Two heads in council, two beside the hearth,
> Two in the tangled business of the world.

Two plummets dropped (or one to sound the abyss)
Of science the secrets of the mind."

The first step to be taken in the effort to elevate home life is to make provision for the broadest possible education of woman. Mrs. Thompson attributes the increasing number of divorces to the moral degeneracy of woman; whereas it is the result of higher moral perceptions as to the mother's responsibilities to the race. Woman has not heard in vain the warning voice of the prophets, ringing down through the centuries: "The sins of the fathers shall be visited upon the children unto the third and fourth generations." The more woman appreciates the influences in pre-natal life, her power in moulding the race, and the necessity for a pure, exalted fatherhood, the more divorces we shall have, until girls enter this relation with greater care and wisdom. When Naquet's divorce bill passed the French Chamber of Deputies, there were three thousand divorces asked for the first year, and most of the applicants were women. The majority of divorces in this country are also applied for by women. With higher intelligence woman has learned the causes that produce idiots, lunatics, criminals, degenerates of all kinds and degrees, and she is no longer a willing partner to the perpetuation of disgrace and misery.

The writer of the article on the "Retrogression of the American Woman" makes one very puzzling assertion, that the present superiority of the sex immortalizes woman, but demoralizes man. Does she mean that a liberal education can only be acquired at the expense of one's morals? "The American woman to-day," says the writer, "appears to be the fatal symptom of a mortally sick nation." This is a very pessimistic view to take of our Republic, with its government, religion, and social life, and its people in the full enjoyment of a degree of liberty never known in any nation before! In spite of this alleged wholesale demoralization of man, we have great statesmen, bishops, judges, philosophers, scientists, artists, authors, orators and inventors, who surprise us with new discoveries day by day, giving the mothers of the Republic abundant reason to be proud of their sons.

Virtue and subjection, with this writer, seem to be synonymous terms. Did our grandmother at the spinning wheel occupy a higher position in the scale of being than Maria Mitchell, Professor of Astronomy at Vassar College? Did the farmer's wife at the washtub do a greater work for our country than the Widow Green, who invented the cotton-gin? Could

Margaret Fuller, Harriet Beecher Stowe, Frances E. Willard, Mary Lyon, Clara Barton have done a better work churning butter or weeding their onion beds on their respective farms than the grand work they did in literature, education and reform? Could Fannie Kemble, Ellen Tree, Charlotte Cushman or Ellen Terry (if we may mention English as well as American women) have contributed more to the pleasure of their day and generation had they spent their lives at the spinning-wheel? No! Progress is the law, and the higher development of woman is one of the important steps that have been achieved.

There are great moral laws as fixed and universal as the laws of the material world, and there is a moral as well as material development going on all along the line, bringing the nations of the earth to a higher point of civilization. True, as the nations rise and fall, their great works seem scattered to the winds. For example, Greek art, it is said, has never been equalled, but we would not change our ideas of human liberty, our comforts and conveniences in life, our wonderful inventions and scientific discoveries, the telegraph, telephone, our modes of travel by sea, land and in the air, the general education and demand for better conditions and higher wages by the laboring masses, the abolition of slavery, rapid improvement in woman's condition, the emancipation of large classes from the religious superstitions of the past, for all the wonderful productions of beauty at the very highest period of Greek art. In place of witchcraft, astrology and fortune-telling, we now have phrenology, astronomy and physiology; instead of famine, leprosy and plague, we owe to medical science a knowledge of sanitary laws; instead of an angry God punishing us for our sins, we know that the evils that surround us are the result of our own ignorance of Nature's laws. He who denies that progress is the law, in both the moral and material world, must be blind to the facts of history and to what is passing before his eyes in his own day and generation.

The moral status of woman depends on her personal independence and capacity for self-support. "Give a man a right over my subsistence," says Alexander Hamilton, "and he holds a power over my whole moral being."

De Tocqueville cannot be impressed into the service of the writer, nor fairly quoted, even inferentially, as saying that the moral status of the American woman in 1848, owing to certain causes at work, was higher than it would be in 1900. Progress is the law, and woman, the greatest factor in civilization, must lead the van. Whatever degrades man of necessity degrades woman; whatever elevates woman of necessity elevates man.

SOURCE: Elizabeth Stanton, "Progress of the American Woman," *North American Review,* vol. 171, no. 539 (December 1900), 904–907. For online version, see http://proquest.umi.com/pqdlink?index=76&did=204684261&SrchMode=3&sid=2&Fmt=10&VInst=PROD&VType=PQD&RQT=309&VName=HNP&TS=1132166895&clientId=48051&aid=1.

Chapter 16

"The Degradation of Disfranchisement" (1901)

EDITORS' NOTE: *This late version of the essay was published in the* Boston Investigator *in 1901, but earlier versions appeared in 1891 and as a speech delivered before the Senate Judiciary Committee in 1896 during hearings on woman suffrage. In this piece, Stanton linked discrimination "against color and sex" with her protest against aristocracy, caste systems, and religion that sanctifies hierarchy. The piece concludes with a stirring reminder that "political, religious, industrial and social freedom" are inseparable. It called on those fighting for woman suffrage to remember that equality must be gained in every aspect of women's lives. Constitution, church, family must all be changed for women to develop into full individuals. As published the year before her death, this article underlines the fact that, despite age, anger that her cause had not triumphed, and serious failures of political imagination when it came to sustaining crucial alliances, Stanton never lost her woman-centered, radical, multifaceted vision of America's democratic possibility*

The degradation of disfranchisement begins with the birth into the class or caste to which the individual belongs. In the case of sex there is ever a lower depth for the woman; to whatever class or nationality she may belong, she is not only subject to the powers above her, but to the man at her side.

The bias of sex is apparent at the very hour of birth. If a "fine boy," the fact is announced in a tone of triumph that takes a minor key if "a little girl," unless in a family where boys are already at a discount. This bias of sex runs all through childhood and girlhood, regulating dress, amusements and education. Though equally endowed with two legs and two arms, the same number of vital organs and the same love of liberty in thought and action, the girl's training is one of constant repression, crippled with her dress and endless homilies on morality and propriety, while to the boys is accorded unlimited freedom. It is a pertinent question, "Why are boys always at a premium?" Is it simply because in our present civilization they belong to the ruling class destined to be the active leaders in political, religious and social life, to fill and to hold all the places of responsibility, honor, emolument and power; because, through centuries of injustice, oppression and violence they chanced to be the dominant sex just now, they are supposed to be naturally superior, forgetting the long period when woman reigned supreme, the source and centre of all the first steps in civilization?

·   Some tender hearted gentlemen object to our calling ourselves a distinct class. Well, we object to the fact as much as they do to the name. Nevertheless, as we have a different civil and moral code for men and women, as men make and execute the laws, are absolute rulers in the State, claim to be the inspired writers of scripture and the divinely anointed heads of the Church, and assume the office of high priest at every family altar, and women are mere objects in all their relations, we surely must belong, to different classes of humanity. To say that we do not, and that woman is as free as man is absurd as the plea of the lawyer when talking to his client through the iron door of a prison. After hearing his case, he said:

"You cannot be imprisoned; you have violated no law."
"But," replied the client, "I am in prison."
"You cannot be."
"But I am. If I am not, then open the door."

So, I say, if we belong to the same class, then open the door and give to us the same freedom that you enjoy.

What is disfranchisement in a republic? It is, in effect, passing a bill of attainder in direct violation of Article I, Section 10, of the national constitution, against all American citizens included in its provisions. It is establishing a privileged class, dividing the people into rulers and subjects, one division to make law for the other; not such laws as they make for themselves, for the discrimination is always based on the assumption that the ostracized classes are of an inferior order, that they have not common feelings and interests with themselves, that they need the supervision and protection of the rulers, as children need the care of their parents. Though the strongest of all human affections bind parents to their children, yet we see the best interests of the latter constantly sacrificed to the caprice, the selfishness, the will of parents, just as the ostracized classes are invariably sacrificed to their rulers, because in both cases those in power are guided by their own interests and not by the welfare of the governed. And this governing is always done under the good fatherly name of "protection," such as the common law of England gave to Saxon wives and mothers, such as the United States gave to the African race, such as Great Britain gives to Ireland, such as the Czar of Russia gives to his subjects on the frozen plains of Siberia, and such as the eagle gives to the lamb he carries to his eyrie!

Disfranchisement is the last lingering shadow of the old spirit of caste that has always divided humanity into classes of greater or lesser inferiority, some below even certain animals that were considered special favorites with heaven. One cannot contemplate these revolting distinctions among mankind without amazement and disgust. This spirit of caste that has darkened the lives of millions through the centuries still lives, persecuting the Jews to-day in Russia and Germany, that forbade them not many years ago to walk on the sidewalks of Paris, compelled always to take the centre of the street with the horses and denied them admission to certain hotels in the fashionable watering-places of the American Republic.

The discriminations against color and sex in the United States are both other forms of this same hateful spirit of caste, still sustained by our religion, as in the past. It is the outgrowth of the same idea of favoritism, ascribed to Deity, in regard to race and individuals, but which have their origin in the mind of man. Banish the idea of divine authority for these machinations of the human mind, and the power of the throne and the Church, of a royal family and an apostolic order of succession, of kings and queens, of popes and bishops, and man's headship in the State, the Church and the home will be heard of no more forever. When woman understands the origin of all these assumptions, neither the eloquence of the pulpit nor the arguments of senators in Washington, will reconcile her to the degradation of disfranchisement.

All men of intelligence appreciate the power of holding the ballot in their own hands, of having a voice in the law under which they live, of enjoying the liberty of self-government. Those who have known the satisfaction of wielding political influence would not willingly accept again the degradation of disfranchisement. Yet men cannot understand why women should feel aggrieved in being deprived of this same protection, dignity and power.

This is the Gibraltar of our difficulties to-day. We cannot make men see that woman feel the humiliation of their petty distinctions of sex, precisely as the black man feels those of color. It is no palliation of our wrongs to say that we are not socially ostracized as he is so long as we are politically ostracized as he is not. That all orders of foreigners rank politically above the most intelligent, highly educated women—native born Americans—is indeed the most bitter drop in the cup of our grief that we are compelled to swallow.

All distinctions in society are depressing and aggravating to the classes ostracized. Take a man of superior endowments, once respected and influential, but who, through a series of misfortunes, has lost wealth and position. He now sees men inferior to himself in the places of trust and influence, making palace-homes for themselves and children, driving blue equipages, while his children walk in shabby attire, ostracized by the circle where, by family, intelligence and refinement, they belong, making them feel every day of their lives the impassable gulf between riches and poverty. This man feels for himself, and doubly for his children, the degradation of even such evanescent distinctions between man and man. That glorious Scotch poet, Robert Burns, from the depths of his poverty might say triumphantly in an inspired moment, "A man's a man for a' that," but the sad wail through so many of his poems show that he had tasted the bitterness of want, and hated all distinctions based on wealth.

No one doubts that woman feels all this as well as man—the humiliations of poverty, the bitterness of neglect, the pangs of envy and jealousy of those who enjoy pleasures and luxuries she does not possess; and yet, with the ever turning wheel of fortune, these distinctions are transient—yours today, mine to-morrow; the same sad experiences sooner or later may come to all.

But the hateful spirit of class makes insurmountable distinctions that no turning wheel of fortune can change. Take that noble man, Robert Purvis, with wealth, education and spotless character such as few men possess; with a family of cultivated sons and daughters, and, because a few drops of colored blood were supposed to flow in his veins, he was denied in the city of Philadelphia all social communion with the society in which, by birth and education, he belonged, for he was a Moor and never a slave. Still he was denied equal freedom as a citizen, though a property-owner and taxpayer; denied equal advantages for his wife and children in public amusements, churches, means of travel and opportunities for education. Does anyone doubt that the wife and daughters felt as deeply as the husbands and sons the degradation of distinction on the ground of color and race?

While it is possible that woman may feel precisely as man does all the invidious distinctions in society baaed on wealth, position, classes, races, how can anyone doubt that she feels the deeper degradation of disfranchisement based on sex? This is the most unreasonable ground of all others, because it is insurmountable, antagonizing one vital principle in Nature with another, when both are equally necessary to the very existence to either. To exalt the masculine principle in humanity at the expense of the feminine—two elements that to produce harmony in society must be exactly equal in power to attract and repel—is as futile as to attempt the subjugation of the negative to the positive electricity, the centrifugal to the centripetal forces in Nature which, if it were possible to do, we should be hurled into our original chaos. Can there be any misery more real than proscriptive distinctions between those who, in Nature, are the peers of each other in race, genius, wealth and position, antagonizing brothers and sisters, husbands and wives, making rivals of men and women in art, science and literature, the whole realm of thought, instead of being helpmeets and guides, a constant inspiration to each other?

Here is the secret of the infinite sadness of women of genius, for just in proportion as they occupy an even platform with man, they are surprised and aggravated with his assumptions of superiority and the artificial framework in society that makes him so; an assumption that woman in her inner nature never concedes, an authority she utterly repudiates.

Again, the degradation of woman in this world of work is another result of her disfranchisement. Some deny that and say, "Look at the laboring classes of men; they have the ballot, yet they are still helpless victims of capitalists." They have the power and hold the weapons of defence, but have not yet learned how to use them. The bayonet, the sword, the gun are of no value to the soldier until he knows how to use them; yet without these weapons of defence what could individuals and nation do in time of war for their protection? The first step in learning to use a gun or a ballot is to own one.

In all the struggles of the human race for liberty there has never been one more complicated than the present demand for equality by woman. It is the only reform in which the class to be elevated has fought the prolonged battle for themselves, the only reform in which no appeal to the narrow self-interest of the dominant powers can be made, because it is the selfish interest of all alike to hold woman in subordination. Whenever it has been the interest of the ruling classes to extend new rights to those below them the battles have been fought for them, and victory secured with no effort on their part. The Southern slaves were emancipated and enfranchised because it was the interest of a political party to do so. The extension of the suffrage to English laborers was for the same reason. A sense of justice may have moved some of the actors in these battles, but self-interest carried both measures. The liberal party alike in both countries needed the vote to manipulate at their pleasure, and political rights to the lower orders of men made no essential change in the social and religious condition of the nation.

But political equality for woman compels an entire change in our whole system of government, religion, social customs and industrial life. Our reform is not lifting up an inferior order, but recognizing the rights of equals. It is more like two contending royal families for the crown and sceptre—the right by blood to rule and reign—compelling man at least to share his liberty and powers with his equals in virtue and intelligence and the ability to govern themselves.

But man has the prestige of centuries in his favor, the force to maintain it, and he has possession of the throne, which is nine-tenths of the law. He has statutes and Scriptures, and the universal usages of society, all on his side. And what have we? The settled dissatisfaction of half the race, the unorganized protest of the few, and the open resistance of still fewer. But we have truth and justice on our side, and the natural love of freedom, and, step by step, we shall undermine the present form of civilization and inaugurate the mightiest revolution the world has ever witnessed. But its far-reaching consequences increase the obstacles in the way of success, for the selfish interests of all classes are against us. The rulers in the State are not willing to share their power with a class over whom as equals they could never obtain absolute control, whose votes they could not manipulate to maintain the present conditions of injustice and oppression in every department of life. As in the family the mother desires to see her children equally provided with the good things of life, so, as an equal factor in the State, her influence would be for an equal distribution among all, for a system of political economy that would prevent the extremes of poverty and wealth, secure clothes, food, shelter and education to the whole people. Such, I believe, would be the policy of educated, enlightened women.

The socialistic and the woman's rights movement are but equal throbs of one great impulse—toward liberty for all.

Again, the rulers in the Church are hostile to liberty for a sex supposed for wise purposes to have been subordinated to man by divine decree. The equality of woman as a factor in religious organization would compel an entire change in church canon, discipline and authority, and many doctrines of the Christian faith. As a matter of self-preservation, the Church has no interest in the emancipation of woman, as its very existence depends on her blind faith. What would the tragedy in the Garden of Eden be to a generation of scientific women? Instead of patiently trying to fathom the supposed spiritual significance of the serpent as the representative of Satan, and all the tergiversations involved in his communications with Eve, hers with Adam, and his with the Lord, and the final catastrophe —turned into the great unexplored wilderness; naked and helpless, to meet the terrible emergencies of the situation—instead of pondering on this in sorrow for the down-fall of the race, they would relegate the allegory to the same class of literature as Aesop's fables.

Society at large, based on the principle that might makes right, has in a measure excluded women from the profitable industries of the world, and when she has gained a foothold her labor is at a discount. Man occupies the ground and holds the key to the situation as employer, he plays off the cheap labor of a disfranchised class against the employer, and thus, in a measure, undermines his independence, making wife and sister in the world of work the rivals of husband and father.

The family, too, is based on the idea of woman's subordination, and man has no interest, as far as be sees, in emancipating her from that despotism, by which his narrow, selfish interests are maintained under the law and religion of the country.

Here, then, is a fourfold bondage, so many cords tightly twisted together, strong for one purpose. To attempt to undo one is to loosen all. Conservatives are invariably clear-sighted in maintaining existing conditions, and see farther as to the ultimate effect of one step than radicals themselves; at least, if we can believe what the latter admit is all they do see.

Conservatives on this question have always maintained that political freedom for woman was antagonistic to all existing institutions, and that to sever one strand in her fourfold bondage was to loosen all. Hence, however stoutly the advocates of suffrage have maintained that political equality for woman would not affect religious faith nor family life, whenever the question comes up in the halls of legislative or ecclesiastical assemblies, the argument invariably drifts to the divinely ordained head of the State—the Church and the home—and the Bible is brought into requisition to prove the intention of the Creator as to the sovereignty of man.

Thus, in spite of all the efforts of the most politic adherents to keep the question of suffrage distinct, the opposition would uniformly consider the question of woman's political equality from every standpoint.

To my mind, if we had bravely untwisted all the strands of the fourfold cord that bound us and demanded equality in the whole round of the circle, we should, perhaps, have had a harder battle to fight, but it would have been more effective, and far shorter. Let us henceforth meet conservatives on their own ground and admit that suffrage for woman does mean political, religious, industrial and social freedom—a new and a higher civilization. By making these demands for liberty in all directions, we should quadruple the agitation as well as the antagonism, and meet all our opponents at the same time and answer every argument. Our enemies could not then jump from one point to another, thinking we would not pursue them; for we should sweep the whole board, demanding equality everywhere and the reconstruction of all institutions that do not in their present status admit of it.

Woman's happiness and development are of more importance than all man's institutions. If constitutions and statute laws stand in the way of woman's emancipation, they must be amended to meet her wants and needs, of which she is a better judge than man can possibly be. If church canons and scriptures do not admit of woman's equal recognition in all the sacred offices, then they must be revised in harmony with that idea. If the present family life is necessarily based on man's headship, then we must build a new domestic altar, in which the mother shall have equal dignity, honor and power, and we do not propose to wait another century to secure all this—the time has come. Women understand the situation and are organizing as never before. They have memories of freedom in the past, and dreams of its realization in the future.

There is a deep, unsatisfied longing in the soul of woman for freedom, growing stronger day by day, that sooner or later will burst all bounds and carry every barrier before her. There are instincts alike in man and beast that imperatively demand complete satisfaction.

In the distant northern plains, a hundred miles from the sea, in the midst of a Laplander's village, a young reindeer raises his broad muzzle to the north wind, sniffing for the first time the ocean breezes. He stands still and stares at the limitless distance while a man may count a hundred. He grows restless from that moment, but he is yet alone. The next day a dozen of the herd look up from the cropping of the moss, sniffing the breeze; then the whole herd of young deer stand and gaze northward, breathing hard through their wide nostrils, jostling each other and stamping on the soft ground. They grow unruly; it is hard to harness them in the light sledge; the camp grows daily more unquiet. Then the Laps nod to one another, and they watch the deer more closely, well knowing what will happen sooner or later.

At last in the northern twilight the herd begins to move. The impulse is simultaneous, irresistible. Their heads are all turned in one direction. They move slowly at first, biting still here and there at the bunches of rich moss. Presently, the slow step becomes a trot, they crowd closely together, while the Laps hasten to gather up their cooking utensils, their wooden gods and all their last unpacked possessions. The great herd break together from a trot to a gallop, from a gallop to a breakneck race. The distant thunder of their united tread reaches the camp for a few minutes, and they are gone to drink of the Polar Sea.

Ever swifter and more terrible in their motion the ruthless herd has raced onward, crowding the weaker to death, careless of the slain, careless of food, careless of any drink but the sharp salt water ahead of them. And when at last the Laplanders reach the shore their deer are once more quietly grazing, once more tame and docile, once more ready to draw the sledge wherever they are guided. Once in his life the reindeer must taste of the sea, in one long, satisfying draught, and if he be hindered he perishes. Neither man nor beast dare stand between him and the ocean in the hundred miles of his arrow-like path.

What a picture of human life is this! How like the march and battle of the race in its struggles to satisfy the instincts for freedom; for something of the same longing comes to every human soul, to taste for once the sweet waters of liberty from its fathomless inexhaustible sources.

SOURCE: Elizabeth Stanton, "The Degradation of Disfranchisement," *Boston Investigator*, April 20, 1901, n.p.

About the Contributors

Barbara Caine is Professor and Head of the Department of History at Monash University, Australia. She has published extensively in women's history and the history of feminism. Her sole authored books include *Destined to Be Wives: The Sisters of Beatrice Webb, Victorian Feminists, English Feminism, 1780–1980*. She has edited *Transitions: New Australian Feminisms* with Rosemary Pringle, and is the General Editor of *Australian Feminism: A Companion*. Her most recent book is *Bombay to Bloomsbury: A Biography of the Strachey Family*.

Richard Cándida Smith is Professor of History at the University of California, Berkeley, where he also serves as director of the Regional Oral History Office. He is the author of *Utopia and Dissent: Art, Poetry, and Politics in California* and *Mallarmé's Children: Symbolism and the Renewal of Experience*, as well as of numerous articles and essays on modern and contemporary cultural movements in the United States, Europe, and Latin America. He is completing a book entitled *Improvised Continent: The Question of American Identity, 1898 to the Present*.

Ellen Carol DuBois is Professor of History at the University of California, Los Angeles. She is the author of *Feminism and Suffrage: The Emergence of an Independent Women's Movement in America, 1848–1869; Harriot Stanton Blatch and the Winning of the Woman's Suffrage;* and *Woman Suffrage and Women's Rights*. She is the editor of *The Elizabeth Cady Stanton–Susan B. Anthony Reader: Correspondence, Writings, Speeches* and, with Vicki Ruiz, of *Unequal Sisters: A Multicultural Reader in U.S. Women's History*. She is also the author, with Lynn Dumenil, of *Through Women's Eyes: An American History with Documents*.

Ann D. Gordon is a Research Professor of History at Rutgers University–New Brunswick and Director of the Papers of Elizabeth Cady Stanton and Susan B. Anthony. With Patricia G. Holland, she coedited the comprehensive microfilm edition of *The Papers of Stanton and Anthony*. At work on a six-volume *Selected Papers of Stanton and Anthony*, she has already edited four volumes.

Vivian Gornick is a New York writer: born, bred, and educated. She began her writing career thirty years ago at *The Village Voice* where, for a number of years, she wrote essays, reviews, and articles, concentrating mainly on the burgeoning feminist movement of which she was an early member. In the years since that time her pieces have appeared in the *Nation*, the *New York Times Book Review and Magazine*, the *Washington Post*, the *Los Angeles Times*, the *New Yorker*, and the *Threepenny Review*. She has written eight books, among them an acclaimed memoir, *Fierce Attachments*, and two influential collections of essays, *Approaching Eye Level* and *The End of the Novel of Love*. She has also taught nonfiction writing at a university level for the past fifteen years. Her most recent book is *The Solitude of Self: Thinking about Elizabeth Cady Stanton*.

Kathi Kern is Professor of History at the University of Kentucky. Her research concerns gender, religion, and the women's rights movement in nineteenth-century America. She is the author of several articles as well as a book, *Mrs. Stanton's Bible*. She is actively engaged in research and service outreach to public school teachers. Currently, Kern is working collaboratively with Dr. Linda Levstik (Curriculum and Instruction), Rebecca Hanly (Kentucky Historical Society), and the Harlan Independent School District on "American Legacies," a three-year professional-development program for American-history teachers in Eastern Kentucky.

Michele Mitchell is Professor of History at the University of Michigan. She is the author of *Righteous Propagation: African Americans and the Politics of Racial Destiny after Reconstruction* and the coeditor with Sandra Gunning and Tera W. Hunter of *Dialogues of Dispersal: Gender, Sexuality, and African Diaspora*.

Christine Stansell is Edwards Professor of American History at Princeton University. She is the author of *City of Women: Sex and Class in New York, 1789–1860* and *American Moderns: Bohemian New York and the Creation of a New Century*. She writes frequently on the history of feminism.

Index